Advance Praise

Avinash makes the complex, simple. He makes the futile, useful. He makes the dull, alive. You could make this the best hour a day learning what is and isn't happening in your online business.
> —BRYAN EISENBERG, New York Times Best-Selling Author of
>   *Call to Action* & *Waiting For Your Cat to Bark*

Avinash Kaushik is without a doubt one of the most articulate, bright, and passionate people working in the web analytics industry today. His weblog, Occam's Razor, is a must-read for anyone trying to make heads or tails of their investment in web analytics, search, or Internet marketing and I have no doubt that Web Analytics: An Hour a Day *will be a valuable addition to the existing body of knowledge on the subject of web site measurement. While I was person- ally surprised at the hugely positive response to my first book on the subject,* Web Analytics Demystified, *I have no doubt that* Web Analytics: An Hour a Day *will immediately become another "must read" for anyone concerned about the success of their web site.*
> —ERIC T. PETERSON, author of *Web Analytics Demystified* and *Web Site*
>   *Measurement Hacks*

A great book to cover all you need to know about web analytics: inside out. Beyond the pure technical aspects, the book also covers organization issues around web analytics, from recruiting to scaling up your efforts to meet business require- ments. In a nutshell, a complete guide to the art and science of web analytics, from one of the best experts in the field; both beginners as well as practitioners will for sure learn and expand their thinking. If you know Avinash and his well-known blog, his book is for sure a must read! Enjoy!
> —LAURENT FLORÈS, PhD, FOUNDER & CEO, CRMMETRIX INC.

Avinash's explanation of how web analytics really works is a salutary reminder that the products are just a way to a means, not the ultimate solution. Getting real value for money out of a web analytics project comes from the brain, not the tools used. This book will help your brain map the right connections in order to reap the benefits of web analytics. Avinash's writings are visionary and yet hands on, for both newbies as well as seasoned practitioners. If you are serious about web analytics this is a MUST READ.
> —AURÉLIE POLS, Manager, Web Analytics Team, OX2

Avinash Kaushik writes about web analytics in a clear, absorbing, and insightful way. Web Analytics: An Hour a Day *is an essential source for beginners and advanced users, presenting basic terminology and sophisticated practices. The book is structured as a series of conversations, which makes for a pleasant reading. Avinash's book contains tricks of the trade that teach professionals what to measure and how to do it. Most important, it teaches how to turn data into actionable insights. This is a great guide through the web analytics journey!*

—DANIEL WAISBERG, Web Analyst, esnips.com

Web Analytics

David,

Signals not noise!

Web Analytics

An Hour a Day

Avinash Kaushik

Wiley Publishing, Inc.

Acquisitions Editor: WILLEM KNIBBE
Development Editor: CANDACE ENGLISH
Production Editor: SARAH GROFF-PALERMO
Copy Editor: SHARON WILKEY
Production Manager: TIM TATE
Vice President and Executive Group Publisher: RICHARD SWADLEY
Vice President and Executive Publisher: JOSEPH B. WIKERT
Vice President and Publisher: NEIL EDDE
Media Project Supervisor: LAURA ATKINSON
Media Development Specialist: STEVE KUDIRKA
Media Quality Assurance: ANGIE DENNY
Book Designer: FRANZ BAUMHACKL
Compositor: MAUREEN FORYS, HAPPENSTANCE TYPE-O-RAMA
Proofreader: IAN GOLDER
Indexer: TED LAUX
Anniversary Logo Design: RICHARD PACIFICO
Cover Designer: RYAN SNEED
Cover Image: © SIMON BROWN, DIGITAL VISION, GETTY IMAGES

Dear Reader,

Thank you for choosing *Web Analytics: An Hour a Day*. This book is part of a family of premium quality Sybex books, all written by outstanding authors who combine practical experience with a gift for teaching.

Sybex was founded in 1976. More than thirty years later, we're still committed to producing consistently exceptional books. With each of our titles we're working hard to set a new standard for the industry. From the authors we work with to the paper we print on, our goal is to bring you the best books available.

I hope you see all that reflected in these pages. I'd be very interested to hear your comments and get your feedback on how we're doing. Feel free to let me know what you think about this or any other Sybex book by sending me an email at nedde@wiley.com, or if you think you've found an error in this book, please visit http://wiley.custhelp.com. Customer feedback is critical to our efforts at Sybex.

Best regards,

Neil Edde
Vice President and Publisher
Sybex, an Imprint of Wiley

With love to my Nana and Nani, Ramesh and Madhuri Sharma.

Thanks for teaching me to be irrational and love unconditionally.

I miss you.

Acknowledgments

I would like to expresses my deepest appreciation for my wonderful team at Wiley. Willem Knibbe, Candace English, Sarah Groff-Palermo, Sharon Wilkey, Ian Golder, Nancy Riddiough, and Maureen Forys. I cannot thank them enough for converting me from a person to an ISBN number!

Two important people deserve the credit for the spark that started me down the journey of this book. Andy Beal (author of the blog Marketing Pilgrim) for convincing me that what I need to change my life was to start a blog. I did, and it did change my professional life in a number of ways. Guy Kawasaki (famous author, blogger, VC, and hockey fan) because my blog is modeled on two of his principles: 1) "Eat like a bird, and poop like an elephant" and 2) Think "book" not "diary" (when it comes to writing a blog). I am grateful to Guy for his wisdom and inspiration.

I am also thankful to all my teachers over the years, each of whom had a significant impact on me from their teachings and presence. Mr. and Mrs. Paranjapee and Ms. Lalitha Mishra at Gyan Dham School in Vapi, Professor Narayana and Dr. Ramaniah at MS Bidve Engineering College in Latur, and Professor Rakesh Vohra, Professor Roy Lewicki, and Professor Paul Schultz at Ohio State University in Columbus.

I was lucky to have a wonderful team around me at Intuit; their smarts and hard work brought all of my ideas to life. I want to thank Steven Cox, Michelle Chin, John Baek, Kevin Hutchinson, Owen Adams, and Dave DeCruz. Thanks for putting up with me.

It takes a village, even to write a book. My friends pitched in and helped me review and critique parts of this book and without their input it would not be as good as it is. Three cheers for Beth Comstock, Gradiva Couzin, Blaire Hansen, and Dr. Stephen Turner.

Most of all I want to thank my family, without whom none of this would have been possible. My wife, Jennie, for her love and constant support and wisdom. My daughter, Damini—she is the source of my passion and inspiration. My son, Chirag, at two and half has shown me what it means to be persistent in the quest for anything. This book belongs to them.

About the Author

Avinash Kaushik is the author of the highly rated blog on web research and analytics called Occam's Razor (http://www.kaushik.net/avinash/). His professional career has been focused on decision support systems at Fortune 500 companies such as Silicon Graphics, DirecTV Broadband, Intuit, and DHL in Asia, the Middle East, and the United States.

Currently Avinash is the director of web research and analytics at Intuit, where he is responsible for the business, technical, and strategic elements of the web decision-making platform, supporting more than 60 Intuit websites.

Avinash has given presentations and keynotes at conferences in the United States and Europe, including the Emetrics Summits, Ad:Tech, Frost & Sullivan Internet Marketing Strategies, ATG Insight Live, and E-consultancy Online Marketing Masterclasses. Some of the topics of the presentations were optimal web decision making, testing and experimentation, maximizing campaign ROI and lowering acquisition costs, customer centricity, and evolving from web analytics to web insights.

Avinash has a bachelor's degree in mechanical engineering from Marathwada University and an MBA from Ohio State University. He also holds the title of associate instructor at the University of British Columbia (having contributed teaching modules to the UBC Award of Achievement in web analytics courses).

Contents

Foreword

Dear Friend,

It is my pleasure to introduce you to Avinash Kaushik. I met Avinash at the Emetrics Summit back when they were small and still held in Santa Barbara. It was June 2003 and I had noticed this tall, unassuming figure prowling around the periphery. He seemed intent, but reserved. He was tuned in, but inconspicuous.

I sat with him at lunch to see if I could draw him out. My first impression was that this was a man of exquisite manners and social grace. Graceful in action, in thought, and in his ability to communicate. A refined man. He was so pleased to be there. He was so grateful for the learning opportunity. He was so delighted that I joined him for lunch. After soaking that up for longer than was gentlemanly of me, I asked about him and his work.

He described Intuit in glowing terms. The people, the tools, the opportunity. I started wondering whether anything bothered him or if he was simply just elated to be on planet Earth for the duration. So I asked him my favorite question, "What's the hard part?"

This is a seemingly innocuous question, but it does wonders for allowing people to express themselves. It is so open-ended that you quickly discover whatever is uppermost in your colleague's mind. Avinash's answer caused me to put down my fork and watch him closely.

There wasn't one particular difficulty bothering him. There was a panoply of obstacles that sounded familiar, universal, and persistent but never so eloquently considered, organized, nor communicated. That alone was enough to see that this individual had a thorough grasp of the technology and the business implications, as well as a clear vision of what might be.

But what made me forget about lunch altogether was his passion. Avinash gets wound up. He gets zealous. He borders on the fanatical. But he never strays from reality.

After 30 minutes of conversation, I asked him if he would impart his wisdom, vision, and passion via PowerPoint at the next Emetrics Summit. He appeared shocked. He was nervous. He was doubtful. He suggested that he was too new at this subject and too novice an employee to share the stage with the experienced, knowledgeable speakers he had been learning from for the previous three days. I assured him he was wrong. He has presented at every Emetrics Summit since, and always to rave reviews.

The first time Avinash presented in London, we both spent the final night at the hotel, awaiting our flights the next morning. As he had never visited before, I invited him out to dinner and a walk. It was May. The night was cool. We left the hotel at 7:00 P.M. and after a brief meal, walked until midnight. My feet were sore for a week.

I love London and I hope that Avinash enjoyed what he saw of it. I don't recall seeing a thing. I can't remember where we went. But I treasured our conversation. Literature, photography, family, philosophy and—oh yes—optimizing return on online marketing investment. I was enthralled. Wit, depth, range, scope—I think highly of this man.

And then he started blogging.

I am amused that his bio page shows a posting date of December 31, 1969, but that's my one and only criticism. Avinash's blog is a model of the form. He shares his passion, knowledge, humor, and insights. He links to others who are noteworthy and elicits comments from the entire web analytics community, and we all await his next post.

And what of this book?

I wouldn't have needed to read it to write this introduction. I could have told you without doubt that it was an important book, not just for what Avinash explains about measuring the success of your website, but what he reveals about achieving success in your job, your business, and your life.

Yes, I hope you read my book on the subject and you should have read Eric Peterson's more detailed and technical tomes by now. But this one is a "teach you how to fish" book. It's not pedantic or text-bookish. This is a book that will open your mind and show you how to think, what to consider, and how to approach web marketing optimization issues.

Avinash delves into organizational impact, necessary business and technical skills, corporate culture change management, and process excellence as well as tools and techniques. He covers everything from clicks and visits to search engine optimization and blog and RSS measurement. Then he shows how to make data sing.

And don't for a minute think that this book is only about click-throughs and page views. This is about online marketing optimization. You'll learn about the qualitative side of website measurement as well, from usability testing to surveys. You'll discover what it's really like to get value out of competitive analysis, multivariate testing, and a dozen other measurement techniques.

"Get value" in Avinash's world means eschewing the merely fascinating and focusing entirely on that which allows you to take action. This book will give you the insight to expand your horizons, the knowledge to grasp the consequences, and the means to achieve specific and measurable improvements to your website's value to the company.

All of the above is delivered with a deep understanding of the fundamental necessity of customer centricity—the opposite of scorched-earth marketing. Avinash understands that CRM does not stand for customer relationship manipulation, but is founded on an ideal of serving customers. The goal of your website—of your company—is to service your customers. Avinash's intrinsic belief in service is manifest in his approach to family, friendship, business, web optimization, and the delivery of this book.

The "hour a day" concept proclaims Avinash's knowledge of real life. Nobody has time to sit back and read a book cover to cover anymore. So Avinash wrote this book to be consumed over time—enough time to ingest his wisdom, consider how it applies to your own situation, and then work on each area to become more proficient—before consuming the next section.

If you are in any way responsible for the success of your corporate website, this is the book that will help you understand the gravity of your duty, the pitfalls and triumphs that await you, and the excitement of discovery.

You will be entertained, enthralled, encouraged, and enlightened: a splendid ROI in anybody's book.

Jim Sterne
Santa Barbara, CA

Introduction

With this book I have three simple goals:

- To share with you my deep passion for the Web and web analytics with the utmost evangelistic zeal that I can muster. I love the Web and the complex decision making it demands, and I think you should too.

- To expand your perspective on what web analytics is, what it should be, and how it is the cornerstone of an awesome customer-centric web strategy allowing you to experiment, learn, and measure in ways that were unimaginable with any other customer touch point thus far. Web analytics is more than clickstream, it is more than conversion rate, and it is more than just numbers.

- To provide you a practitioner's perspective of what it takes to be successful at web analytics. This book is the first, certainly not the last, time you will get an insider's view. You will learn practical advice from someone who is not a consultant or a vendor but rather someone who has lived it. You'll be able to relate to the real-world challenges that span people, process, organizational structures, politics, goals, operational rigor, and more.

Web Analytics: An Hour a Day will satiate your appetite to get a very broad and deep view of what it takes to successfully create an effective web analytics program at your company, regardless of the size of your company.

There are words, pictures, audio, and video (on the accompanying CD) that will make this journey a lot of fun.

The Little Book That Could

100 percent of the author's proceeds from this book will be donated to two charities.

The Smile Train does cleft lip and palate surgery in 63 of the world's poorest countries. They help do more than give the smile back to a child. Their efforts eliminate a condition that can have deep physical and emotional implications for a child.

Médecins Sans Frontières (Doctors Without Borders) provides emergency medical assistance to people in danger in more than 70 countries. MSF was awarded the 1999 Nobel Peace Prize for providing medical aid wherever it is needed.

By buying this book, you will elevate your knowledge and expertise about web analytics, but you are also helping me support two causes that are near and dear to my heart. When it comes to helping those in need, every little bit counts. Thank you.

Why Focus on Web Analytics?

Companies in the web space spend millions of dollars on web analytics, chasing optimization of hundreds of millions of dollars being spent on campaigns and their web-sites, which are in turn chasing billions of dollars of online revenue. Yet consistently the number one challenge in surveys, CMO priorities, case studies, and fix-it wish lists is the ability to measure accurately to make optimal decisions for those hundreds of millions of dollars companies spend. The reason this challenge persists is that most people go about solving it wrong.

There is also an amazing confluence of events currently underway, and they are shining a bright spotlight on the world of web analytics:

- For the longest time, companies simply spent money on their websites because it was the thing to do and it was cool. In the last few years, the Web had really "grown up" as a channel for most companies and suddenly there is a deep demand for the web channel to be held accountable just as much as the other channels. The teenager is now being asked to justify expenses. This is an amazingly transforma-tive experience for the teenager, something he/she is not equipped to deal with.

- Even now, people think web analytics = clickstream. This is a million miles from the truth. Yet clickstream forms almost all of the decision-making data pool, and most companies are beginning to express a deep level of frustration with the lack of actionable insights that they can get from just the clickstream data.

- With the entry of Google Analytics (and the upcoming entry of Microsoft), the market has simply exploded because now anyone who wants to have access to data from their website can have it for free, and from a sophisticated tool to boot. But after you get in, it is really hard to figure out what your success metrics are and how to do web analytics right.

- The web is now a major revenue channel for most Fortune 1000 companies. Imag-ine the kind of love and attention that brings, wanting to know what the heck is going on your website.

- With each passing day, more and more companies are coming to realize that the Web is the most effective nonhuman sales drive, the best source of customer learn-ing and feedback, and the most effective purchase channel. But making this dream a reality requires a foundation of a solid measurement, testing, and listening plat-form. Web analytics can provide that.

It seems odd to say that the Web is in its infancy but it is, and web analytics even more so. What we have today will change radically even in the next decade, but if you are to stay relevant during that decade (or at the end of it), you will need to have mastered the challenges that measurement and listening pose on the Web. This book is a step in that journey.

Who Can Use This book?

Everyone. It's that simple.

Through the course of my career, I have come to realize that organizations that are massively successful at decision making practice data democracy. That translates into every cog in the wheel having access to relevant and timely data to make effective decisions as a way of life rather than only on special occasions, when someone will translate data for them.

This does not mean that powerful centers of focused excellence with Numbers Gods who spend their days torturing data for insights are not needed. They are. But if that is all a company relies on, it will be significantly less successful in using data than a company that promotes data democracy.

So if you are *Mr./Ms. Web Interested*, this book is for you because you will learn how you can quickly get started with web analytics. It can help inform decisions you make, no matter how small or big, and can help you be significantly more effective with your web analytics–informed actions.

If you are a *CEO*, you will learn in this book why it is important for you to have an effective web analytics program as a key component of your company strategy—not just to make money from the website but also to create the most amazing and timely experiences for your customers while creating a sustainable competitive advantage.

If you are a *C-level or VP-level or just no-level person* responsible for your web business, you'll learn how to create the optimal web analytics organization, who should own web analytics, the specific roles you need to fill, and what to look for when you fill those roles. You'll learn what it takes—blood, sweat, and tears—to create a data-driven decision-making culture.

If you are a *marketer*, this book will help you understand specific and meaningful ways in which you can use web analytics to identify and execute effective marketing campaigns and measure how your website efforts are performing (everything from search engine marketing to website content creation and consumption).

If you are a *salesperson*, this book will help you identify tools you can use and strategies you can execute to significantly enhance your ability to sell not just more products and services but rather the right thing at the right time to the right person. This will lead to not just a short-term boost in your conversion rate but also a long-term sustainable relationship with a customer.

If you are a *web designer*, this book will share with you how you don't have to compromise on the number of ideas you can put on the website to improve the site. You can have all of your ideas (even the radical ones) go live on the site, and measure which one solves the customers' (or your company's) problems most effectively.

If you are a *user researcher*, this book will help you be exponentially more effective in driving action by identifying your long lost twin: quantitative data analyst. By merging the worlds of quantitative and qualitative data, you can find richer insights and drive ever more effective actions.

If you are an *analyst* or work part-time or full-time with web data, this book will, humbly put, change your life. Okay, so that might be stretching it, but it will come close. This book will provide you a refreshingly different perspective on what web analytics is and how you are perhaps the key to empowering your organization to be outrageously successful on the Web. You will of course learn about the tools and metrics you can use, but even more important the book presents a new and different mindset and approach toward web analytics. The book is chock full of tips, tricks, ideas, and suggestions that you can start implementing immediately, yet they will challenge you for quite some time to come.

What's Inside?

The essence of the book is an eight-month-plus day-by-day program for improving your web analytics efforts from top to bottom, from soup to nuts. The months are divvied into weeks, and those are subsequently divvied into days that focus on tasks that are estimated to take about an hour each. Depending on your circumstances, your familiarity with the subject matter, and the sophistication of your organization and tools, it may take you more or less time to complete certain tasks.

The book is divided into four parts.

Part I: The Foundation of Web Analytics

Part I spans Chapters 1 through 3. It starts with the story of the present and future of web analytics before it steps into laying the foundational groundwork by helping educate you on the strategic mindset and approach to web analytics.

That is followed by spending time to understand the critical importance of the various data collection mechanisms at your disposal (remember, garbage in, garbage out).

Part I concludes with a focus on qualitative data—why it is important, what the available options are, and how you can significantly elevate your ability to listen to your customers.

Part II: The Trinity Approach

Part II starts with Chapter 4, which covers the not-so-fundamentals of web analytics: critical things that we typically don't pay too much attention to, such as creating an optimal organizational structure, applying the 10/90 rule, or knowing what to look for in great web analysts.

Chapter 5 covers some of the fundamentals, such as how to select your optimal web analytics tool, how to deal with data quality on the Web, how to ensure that the implementation of your tool is optimal, and finally, the importance of applying the So What test to all your chosen metrics and key performance indicators (KPIs).

Part III: Implementing your Web Analytics Plan

Part III is the biggest chunk of the book and it includes the day-by-day tasks that you'll perform (just one hour a day). In the first month, Chapter 6, you'll dive deep into the core web analytics concepts such as URLs and cookies, which leads into a process of understanding the basics along with the pros and cons of web analytics reports that are found in every tool out there.

Chapter 7 presents a customized one-month plan for three different types of businesses.

That leads into Chapter 8, which spends month 3 on the world of search analytics (internal search, search engine optimization, and search engine marketing).

Chapter 9, which covers month 4, focuses on measuring the effectiveness of your campaigns and the effectiveness of your multichannel marketing strategies.

Chapter 10, month 5, will be spent on how to take your program to the next level by unleashing the power of experimentation and testing.

In Chapter 11, you'll learn how to overcome the stubbornly hard problem of making your web analytics actionable in month 6. You'll learn the three secrets and leverage them: benchmarking and goals, executive dashboards, and application of Six Sigma and process excellence methodologies.

Chapter 12 closes Part III by spending month 7 internalizing the superhuman powers of competitive intelligence analysis. You'll learn how you can use the outputs of that analysis to set yourself apart from almost everyone out there as you benefit from not only knowing what you know about your site but knowing that in the context of the web ecosystem (including competitors that you know about and those that you had no idea you were competing against).

Part IV: Advanced Web Analytics and "Data in your DNA"

Chapter 13 spends a month illuminating your journey to magnificent success by shattering some of the commonly prevalent myths about web analytics and providing you guidance on how not to be led astray.

Chapter 14 outlines specific advanced analytics concepts that will assist you in turbocharging your web analytics program. You'll learn the power of statistical significance and using segmentation. You'll also learn how to make your reports more connectable to your business users along with best practices in measuring conversion rate. The chapter provides specific tips on measuring complex metrics such as abandonment rates and days and visits to purchase, and what actions you can take from those metrics.

The book concludes with Chapter 15, which provides insights into how you can create a truly data-driven organization that has "data in its DNA." You'll learn practical steps you can take and best practices you can implement.

This Book's Companion Websites

The end of this book is not a destination. You'll be able to leverage two websites as you continue your web analytics journey.

www.webanalyticshour.com is a companion website to this book, where you will find more information related directly to the book, including helpful resources, new and updated links, and options for communicating with the author.

www.kaushik.net/avinash is the blog, Occam's Razor, that hosts a vibrant, evolving, and ongoing discussion on all things web analytics. You'll stay in the loop on the most current topics as well as benefit from the interesting discussion among readers of the blog.

Request for Feedback

I'll stress the importance of customer centricity throughout this book because that is perhaps the only way to ensure the long-term success of any business.

Hence it should not come as a surprise that I would absolutely love to hear from you. Any feedback that you have would be welcome and much appreciated. What was the one thing that you found to be of most value in the book? What was your one big surprise? What could I have done better or stressed more or covered in more detail?

You can reach me via the two websites already noted, or simply email me at feedback@webanalyticshour.com. I would absolutely love to have your feedback; please share your story.

My hope is to learn from all your feedback and also to reply to everyone who writes in, so please do share your perspective, critique, or kudos.

Next Stop: Wonderland

Last but not least, I would like to thank you for buying this book. I started the introduction by professing my passion for web analytics and web research. It is a privilege to share my experience with you.

Although learning web analytics will be loads of hard work, it will be a lot of fun. There is something so pure about wanting to use our skills to make the lives of others better, whether by working for world peace or solving problems that our customers face every day. Let's get going.

Web Analytics

Web Analytics—
Present and Future

1

On March 20, 2007, a search on Google for "web analytics" + definition returns 642,000 results in 0.11 seconds. It is a testament to the complexity and long history of this wonderful topic (and to how fast Google can return results).

The Web Analytics Association (http://www.webanalyticsassociation.org) has recently proposed a standard definition for web analytics:

> Web analytics *is the objective tracking, collection, measurement, reporting, and analysis of quantitative Internet data to optimize websites and web marketing initiatives.*

The dawn of web analytics occurred in the 1990s. However, the preceding definition—the very first standardized definition—was not proposed until 2006, a reflection of how young the field is.

A Brief History of Web Analytics

At the birth of the Internet, things were relatively simple. One would type an address and a Uniform Resource Locator (URL), a file with text and links would be delivered, and that was it. Life was simple.

It was discovered that sometimes errors occurred and the files would not be served or that the links were incorrect, causing a failure. At that point, a clever human discovered server error logs and leveraged them to find information about *hits* made on the web server (quite simply at that time, a hit equaled a request for a file).

These server logs were capturing not only the fact that someone hit the website, but also some additional information such as the filename, time, referrer (website/page making the request), Internet Protocol (IP) address, browser identifier, operating system, and so forth. Things started to get cooler because now you knew something about where the hit came from.

As log files started to get larger, and nontechnical folks started to become interested in data, yet another clever human wrote the first script that would automatically parse the log files and spit out basic metrics (Figure 1.1). Web analytics was officially born.

Daily Summary

(**Go To**: Top: Monthly report: Hourly summary: Directory report: Request report)

Each + represents 200 requests, or part thereof.

```
day: #reqs
---  -----
Sun:  6191: +++++++++++++++++++++++++++++++++
Mon:  9488: +++++++++++++++++++++++++++++++++++++++++++++++++
Tue:  9112: +++++++++++++++++++++++++++++++++++++++++++++++
Wed:  9390: +++++++++++++++++++++++++++++++++++++++++++++++
Thu:  9329: +++++++++++++++++++++++++++++++++++++++++++++++
Fri:  8697: ++++++++++++++++++++++++++++++++++++++++++++
Sat:  6986: +++++++++++++++++++++++++++++++++++++
```

Figure 1.1 A sample report from Analog, version 0.9 beta

Analog, written by Dr. Stephen Turner in 1995, was one of the first log file analysis programs that was widely available on the Web. It is still one of the most widely used web analytics applications and it comes installed on websites from most Internet Service Providers (ISPs). Analog, and tools like it, fueled the adoption of web analytics beyond the Information Technology (IT) team. The reports started to get prettier, and of course marketing folks could now finally understand what was happening.

Around 1995–96, the general users of the Internet started to get exposed to web statistics because of the proliferation of a delightful thing called a *counter*. **25957** Page counters were perhaps the first example of web viral marketing (credited to a company called Web-Counter). Counters were everywhere you went on the Web; they stood for both being cool and showing how popular you were.

Commercial web analytics started several years later, with WebTrends becoming its new poster child. WebTrends took the standard log file parser and added improvements to it, but even more important, added tables and pretty graphs that finally dragged web analytics to the business teams (see Figure 1.2 for sample output).

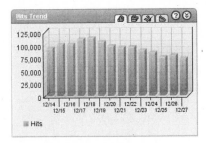

Figure 1.2 WebTrends sample report

By the year 2000, with the popularity of the Web growing exponentially, web analytics was firmly entrenched as a discipline. Companies such as Accrue, WebTrends, WebSideStory, and Coremetrics were all firmly established as key vendors, providing increasingly complex solutions that reported massive amounts of data.

Around the same time, web analytics vendors and customers were discovering that using web server logs as optimal sources of data presented certain challenges.

Challenges with using the logs included the following:

Page Caching by ISP The challenge with caching was that after the ISP had a copy of the page, all subsequent pages would be served from the ISP, and the website log files would not have entries for those requested pages.

Search Robots With the increasing popularity of search engines, *search bots* would frequently crawl sites and leave non-web-user entries in web logs. These entries would be counted in the metrics. Although robot hits could be filtered, it is difficult to keep pace with all the new robots (and they get smarter with time).

Unique Visitors With an increasing number of users being assigned dynamic IP addresses and coming via proxy servers, it became difficult to identify unique visitors, well, uniquely. Vendors resorted to using the IP address plus the user agent ID (user operating system and browser), but that was not quite optimal either. If a site set cookies, those were used, but not all IT departments readily did that.

For these and a few other reasons, *JavaScript tags* (a few lines of JavaScript code) emerged as a new standard for collecting data from websites. It is a much simpler method of collecting data: a few lines of JavaScript are added to each page and are fired off when the page loads and send data to a data collection server. Here is a sample of a complete JavaScript tag that is used by a new web analytics vendor called Crazy Egg:

```
<script type="text/javascript">
//<![CDATA[
  document.write('<scr'+'ipt
  src="http://crazyegg.com/pages/scripts/1111.js?'+
(new Date()).getTime()+'" ~CAtype="text/javascript"></scr'+'ipt>');
//]]>
</script>
```

JavaScript log files were easier to maintain than web server log files. They also shifted the responsibility of collecting and processing data from internal company IT departments to web analytics vendors in most cases. This made implementing web analytics easier. JavaScript tagging also made it simpler to innovate, to capture new pieces of data, and to do things such as set cookies to track visitor activity. Now the vendor could do this rather than having to go through the company IT department.

Note: JavaScript tags have their own set of challenges, which are discussed in great detail in Chapter 2, "Data Collection—Importance and Options."

Perhaps the next evolutionary step in website analytics was the introduction of the *site overlay* (sometimes called *click density*). Now rather than combing through a complex set of data or pouring over tables full of data, decision makers could simply open the web page that they wanted analyzed in a browser—and for the chosen time period, the browser / web analytics application would display exactly where the website visitors clicked.

This democratized to a great extent what had previously been the domain of just the web analysts. It brought about increased usage of analytics solutions because now anyone could, in a very simple view, understand what was happening in the website by looking at the clicks. Optimizing websites based on customer behavior became much easier.

Figure 1.3 shows how easy it was to segment out all the traffic to the site, separating only those who came from Google and how their clicks differed. This gives us a hint of what these two segments were uniquely looking for.

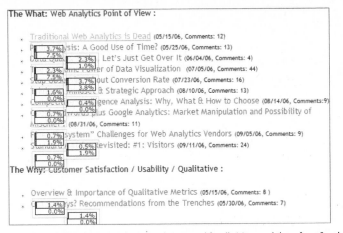

Figure 1.3 ClickTracks site overlay report (segmented for all visitors and those from Google)

Currently there are four big vendors: Coremetrics, Omniture, WebTrends, and WebSideStory. There are also a whole host of mid-market vendors such as Unica, indexTools, and ClickTracks, and many basic solutions such as the open source products AWStats, Webalizer, and StatCounter.

Google had a major effect on the web analytics landscape in 2005 when it purchased Urchin and subsequently, in 2006, released it as a free tool under the Google Analytics moniker. Now anyone who wanted to have access to first-class web analytics could do so for free. The number of customers using Google Analytics is hard to come by, but most estimates peg that number at half a million plus customers in the first six months. It is anticipated that Microsoft will soon follow Google and introduce a free web analytics tool.

The pace of innovation in the web analytics world continues with newer and easier ways to visualize complex sets of data from site interactions. One such recent innovation is *heat maps* from Crazy Egg (Figure 1.4), which is in beta at the time of writing this book. A heat map illustrates the clusters of clicks on a web page and their density by using colors (the brighter the color, the more clicks around that hot spot or link).

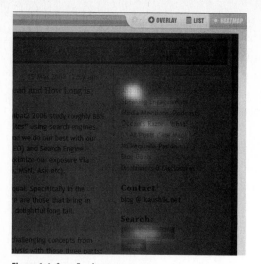

Figure 1.4 Crazy Egg heat map report

Current Landscape and Challenges

Web analytics is, metaphorically speaking, just a toddler. The toddler has grown up a little since birth and can sort of feed itself, yet there is a lot of growth and change in front of it. This proverbial toddler sits at an amazing confluence of events.

For the longest time, companies simply spent money on their websites because it was the thing to do and it was cool. In the past few years, the Web has really "grown up" as a channel for most companies, and suddenly there is a deep demand for the web channel to be held just as accountable as the other channels (phone or retail, for example). Since the boom and bust on the Web, there has been ever-increasing scrutiny, and companies are demanding that the web leadership justify investments being poured into the channel. This is an amazingly transformative experience for the channel as its leadership is looking in all places to prove results.

Even now most people think that web analytics = clickstream. Even though this is a million miles from the truth, for most practitioners clickstream data is very much the source of all web decision making. In reality, because clickstream data is just a portion of web data, most companies are expressing a deep level of frustration with the lack of actionable insights, even after all the investment in expensive web analytics tools over the years. There is lots of data and even more reports, but a profound and pervasive existence of this statement in the minds of decision makers: *"The data is not telling me what I should do."*

At one point during the dot-com boom, there were close to 200 vendors of all shapes and sizes in the market. Since the dot-com bust, there has been a lot of vendor consolidation in the industry. Yet the web analytics ecosystem is dominated by vendors trying to outdo each other by offering more and more features. Vendors dominate the mindset landscape; they set the analysis agenda (in reality, it is a *reporting agenda)*.

The lack of real-world practitioners influencing strategy and direction has had a detrimental effect. Standard techniques such as customer-driven innovation (CDI) have never taken deep roots in the world of web analytics. Most progress has been driven by possibility-driven innovation (PDI)—as in, "What else is possible for us to do with the data we capture? Let's innovate based on that."

There is a deep lack of actual practical knowledge out there. More important, there is a lack of people and approaches that would enable web businesses to glean insights that result in action that enable strategic differentiation vs. their competitors. Universities and colleges are not teaching practical web analytics (there is only one online course, at the University of British Columbia). This—combined with too much data (just in terms of raw size of the data that the Web has the power to throw off)— has created a suboptimal scenario when it comes to providing actionable insights for companies.

Web 2.0 and its associated technologies are increasingly becoming a part of the mainstream customer experience. This change is becoming a major disruptor for most current web analytics approaches and vendors. It is even more important in the world of Web 2.0 that we accelerate the mindset shift and the strategy for implementing successful web analytics. (For example, in the world of Web 2.0, typical clickstream data means very little because the page paradigm dies a little with every new innovation. So how do you measure success?)

With the entry of Google Analytics, the market has simply exploded, because now anyone who wants to have access to data from their website can have it for free, and from a sophisticated tool to boot. Microsoft's anticipated free web analytics tool will only expand the options that practitioners have at their disposal. But access to the tool and data, although empowering, does little to ease the problems related to figuring out what your success metrics are and how to perform web analytics correctly.

There is more data than ever available for a web analytics practitioner to tap into:

- Competitive intelligence lets you know not only what is going on at your site, but also (for a small fee) what is going on at a competitor's website.
- Qualitative data (usability, surveys, direct observation) gives you information about the effect of the web channel on the other channels (think Customer Relationship Management—CRM).

As web analytics has progressed from birth to early infancy (now), an increasingly wide array of complex data has been made available. In almost every web analytics tool, it is now normal to see a couple hundred metrics at the click of a button.

This increasing amount of data provides an opportunity to become better at what we can analyze and act on, yet it is also a trap (think *paralysis by analysis)*.

Companies in the web space spend millions of dollars on web analytics, chasing optimization of hundreds of millions of dollars being spent on campaigns and their websites, which are in turn chasing billions of dollars of online revenue.

Yet consistently the number one challenge in surveys, CMO priorities, case studies, and fix-it wish lists is the ability to measure accurately in order to make optimal decisions for those hundreds of millions of dollars companies spend. The reason this challenge persists is that most people go about solving it wrong.

Traditional Web Analytics Is Dead

In a podcast with *Internet Marketing Voodoo* in March 2006 (included on the CD that comes with this book), I made the proclamation that traditional web analytics was dead. This announcement was probably two years too late.

Web analytics started its life with data sourced from web server logs, which primarily contain technical information and not business information. Because of this unique evolutionary path, the current crop of web analytics tools and the mindsets of customers are rooted in clickstream analysis. Figure 1.5 shows what web analytics has typically looked like.

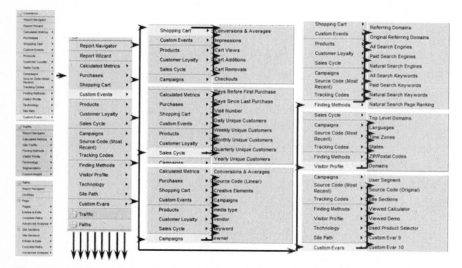

Figure 1.5 Lots and lots of Metrics / Key Performance Indicators at the click of a button

Implementation of a web analytics tool takes just a few minutes, and instantly we have access to massive amounts of data, metrics, key performance indicators, stuff. There are practitioners and vendors and a well-established system of working and thinking in order to report on this data.

So what does this world of traditional web analytics look like? If you measure any of the following sample metrics, it is likely that you live in that traditional world:

Page Views If you run an e-commerce website (or most other types), is it good or bad to have more page views per visitor? If you have frustrating navigation, you'll have lots of page views—but no one will buy. If you have fantastic navigation, you'll have fewer page views—but maybe people decide faster that you don't have competitive prices and they leave anyway. Just from reporting page views, how do you know which is the case? Besides, if you track page views, what kind of behavior is being rewarded?

Hits In the early days, hits tracked the requests that a server received to send data back. Then it was okay to translate a hit as a page or content request. So more hits meant more content consumption, and it sort of meant more visitors in the very early days. Now hits means little, because of all the images and media embedded in a page. A typical page will cause 25 hits on a server. So if you are tracking hits, what are you really tracking? Requests for data to the server? Number of pages viewed? Number of visitors to the website?

Top Exit Pages If you track the pages where more website visitors exit from the site, what does it tell you? That the pages are suboptimal? It could be that they are perfect pages where your customers find exactly what they are looking for and then leave. Consider me researching a Sony digital camera on Amazon.com. I find what I want, customer reviews, and I leave. So do 99 percent of the people representing the traffic to that page. The exit rate doesn't tell you whether your content is good or bad.

Website Engagement Ditto for engagement, often computed as sessions divided by unique visitors. If lots of people come again and again and have lots of sessions with your website, is it because they repeatedly can't find what they are looking for or because you have the most beautiful site in the world with perfect content?

Visitor Screen Resolution Visitor screen resolution is a perfect example of a distracting metric that adds little value in any scenario. Every web analytics tool reports the monitor screen resolution of the website visitor and we have it in our daily reports, yet the metric rarely changes more than once every six months. Yet we keep reporting on it all the time, causing both a distraction and a sub-optimal use of time. Besides, would it not be a better strategy to simply use research from Forrester Research or Gartner on the latest trends in your industry segment and use that to drive what the size of your web pages should be?

The common theme in all these metrics is that they purport to say something, yet they say very little. Worse still, usually they actively lead us down the wrong path. At the end of spending lots of dollars to buy tools and more dollars to get reports, companies have little to show in terms of return on investment (ROI) or improved customer experiences on their websites. Years of being frustrated by an inability to fundamentally understand the data and take action has resulted in the death of the world of traditional web analytics. We have not been able to solve for either the companies or their customers because after all the efforts, we have a fundamental inability to take action.

What Web Analytics Should Be

We are in the midst of a metamorphosis for our industry; web analytics is not what it used to be. This new world of actionable web analytics is about more than simply clickstream data. It also now includes data for all sorts of outcomes that can sometimes be captured by our JavaScript tags and at other times requires us to be creative about measuring. It also now includes qualitative behavior analysis: why do our visitors do the things that they do, and what is their motivation for engaging with our websites?

This expansion of web analytics means that we have a significantly enhanced ability to *listen* to our website customers. We have more-relevant data on tap to analyze so that we can truly understand what action to take and can accelerate the ability of the web channel to be a tour de force in companies where it typically has not been.

The cornerstone of traditional web analytics for the longest time has been prepackaged key performance indicators (KPIs). But because globally defined KPIs often can't accommodate for strategic differences in business operations and execution, they have not been quite as helpful as one might have hoped for. To compete, we have to now use key insights analysis (KIA).

Here are a few metrics that define the new world of actionable web analytics, and in turn examples of KIA:

Click Density Analysis Click density analysis, using the site overlay feature of your web analytics tool, helps you walk in the shoes of your customers. It helps you see your website as your customer does. Are they clicking on what I want them to click on? If not, what do they find interesting vs. what we are imposing on them? What do they find interesting that we were totally clueless about?

If you segment your traffic, you can see what the difference in behavior is for different kinds of traffic to your website (in this case, the clicks by everyone who comes from Google are different from those of other visitors, allowing you to perhaps target content better if someone comes to your website from Google). This analysis is greatly empowering because it enables you to take action. It is not about reports and Microsoft Office Excel spreadsheets; it is about looking, literally, at your actual web pages and seeing what various segments of your customers are doing. You could take this data and begin to create customized (personalized) content for different segments of your website visitors (hence increasing customer engagement and hopefully also moving the dial on your core success metrics).

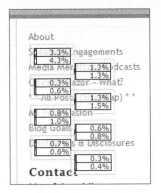

Visitor Primary Purpose Rather than relying on the pages viewed to infer why people come to your website, in our new and improved world we simply ask customers to help us understand *why* they come to our website. The danger in using pages viewed to understand the visitor's primary purpose is that if they are coming for content you don't have, then you have no way of knowing. So why not simply ask? Conduct a survey, do phone interviews. Seek out real customers and ask them why they show up on your website. Be prepared to be absolutely surprised to learn that people come for reasons you never imagined (reasons your business should have been accommodating for during all the years you have existed).

Task Completion Rates We are also migrating away from using clickstream data (presence of a page view) to measure successful task completion. Let's say you have a support website that contains a knowledge base, answers to frequently asked questions (FAQs), and so forth. We measured success in the old world by using our clickstream analysis tool to count anyone who saw a knowledge base article or anyone who viewed a FAQ page. But does the fact that someone saw your long, complex reply really mean success? Success is extremely hard to attribute based on a page view, except in rare cases (for example, on an e-commerce website, where the Thank You page viewed after submitting an order can be counted as a successful completion of a task). In our new world, we expand our web analytics data set to include more-sophisticated qualitative data that enables us to understand whether customers can complete their tasks and whether they found what they were looking for. You can take action because there is no longer a doubt about whether a page view meant success; now you simply ask (by running survey, or doing lab usability, or creating tests on your website) and you find out and take action.

Segmented Visitor Trends Few tools in the market at the moment have a real capability to segment data after it has been captured. In the old world, we embedded attributes in our JavaScript tags. In our new existence, we have tools from vendors such as ClickTracks and Visual Sciences (at very different price points) that allow real segmentation of our data so that we don't have to report Average Time on Site or Top Search Keywords or Popular Content for all visitors to the website in one ugly glob. Tools such as these allow you to segment your customers and their behavior in a meaningful way that allows for a significantly richer understanding of their interaction with your website. This in turn provides insights that fuel action.

Multichannel Impact Analysis The traditional world of web analytics also suffered significantly because it was based on a *silo* (clickstream data from your website). Yet very few companies, big or small, have their web strategy and business execution in a silo. To understand the holistic impact of the web channel, increasingly we are having to view the Web as a part of the larger ecosystem. Obtaining true insights requires measuring the impact of other channels (say your television or newspaper ads) on your website and measuring the impact of your website on other channels (how many people use your website but buy your product via retail or via your phone channel).

This extension of the worldview means that data goes out of the web analytics tool to help facilitate other types of company analysis (think of lifetime value analysis for customers acquired across all channels). It also improves the quality of our analysis by importing key relevant data into the web analytics tool (think of core company metadata that is missing from your clickstream data, survey data, or data about offline conversions).

In a nutshell, you know you live in the world of key insights analysis when you realize that every piece of data you look at drives action—and not just action, but action that adds to whatever bottom-line outcomes that our companies are trying to achieve for our customers. (Note that important difference: not outcomes that your boss wants, not outcomes that his/her boss wants, but outcomes that your customers want.)

The world of web insights takes time to move into but after you get comfortable in it, you will have achieved a long-term strategic advantage (and a fairly substantial bonus or promotion, or both, for yourself).

Measuring Both the What and the Why

Imagine walking into and out of a supermarket. If you did not purchase anything, the supermarket managers probably didn't even know you were there. If you purchased something, the supermarket knows something was sold (they know a bit more if you use a supermarket membership card).

Visiting a website is a radically different proposition if you look from the lens of data collection. During your visit to a website, you leave behind a significant amount of data, whether you buy something or not.

The website knows every "aisle" you walked down, everything you touched, how long you stayed reading each "label," everything you put in your cart and then discarded, and lots and lots more. If you do end up buying, the site manager knows where you live, where you came to the website from, which promotion you are responding to, how many times you have bought before, and so on. If you simply visited and left the website, it still knows everything you did and in the exact order you did it.

Hopefully you'll see how massively advantaged the web is in terms of its ability to collect data and know lots of things about its visitors. All this without ever violating the core customer privacy principles (so, for example, most websites won't know it was Avinash Kaushik visiting; all they know is that it was cookie ID 159ar87te384ae8137). Add to this that now there are more tools than you'll ever realize can that will instantly create reports of all this web data, presenting it in every conceivable slice, graph, table, pivot, or dump, and you can imagine the challenge.

But, no matter what tool you use, the best that all this data will help you understand is *what* happened. It cannot, no matter how much you torture the data, tell you *why* something happened.

We have clicks, we have pages, we have time on site, we have paths, we have promotions, we have abandonment rates, and more. It is important to realize that we are missing a critical facet to all these pieces of data: Why did they click where they clicked? Why did our visitors end up on these pages and not those? Why do 50 percent of them abandon their carts? Why is it that 90 percent of the site traffic reads the top support questions but they still call us on the phone? What's missing is the *why*.

This is the reason qualitative data is so important. It can get us substantially closer to understanding the why. It is the difference between 99 percent of the website analysis that is done yet yields very few insights, and the 1 percent that provides a window into the mind of a customer.

Combining the *what* (quantitative) with the *why* (qualitative) can be exponentially powerful. It is also critical to our ability to take all our clickstream data and truly analyze it, to find the insights that drive meaningful website changes that will improve our customers' experiences.

There are many types of qualitative (Why) data at your disposal, including the following:

- Brand buzz and opinion tracking
- Customer satisfaction

- Net promoter indices
- Open-ended voice-of-customer analysis
- Visitor engagement
- Stickiness
- Blog-pulse

Some of the data elements listed here cover customer interactions at your website, others measure what customers are saying and doing at places other than your website, and yet others measure the soft facets such as brand.

Although there are many options for qualitative analysis, perhaps the most important qualitative data point is how customers/visitors interact with your *web presence*.

In your quest for key insights analysis, your first stop should be understanding all you can about customer interactions at your website. A robust understanding of visitor interactions can lead to actionable insights faster while having a richer impact on your decision making. There is a lot of buzz around "buzzy" metrics such as brand value/impact and blog-pulse, to name a couple. These buzzy metrics can be a second or third stop on our journey because focusing on these metrics can be a suboptimal use of time and resources if we don't first have a hard-core understanding of customer satisfaction and task completion on our websites.

There are many methodologies used to collect customer qualitative (Why) data, including the following:

- Lab usability testing (inviting participants to complete tasks, guided or unguided)
- Site visits, also called follow-me-homes (observing in a customer's native environment)
- Experimentation/testing (the latest new and cool thing to do, A/B or multivariate testing)
- Unstructured remote conversations (engaging with your real customers remotely when they are interacting with your website, by using solutions such as Ethnio)
- Surveying (the granddaddy of them all—see the discussion of Visitor Primary Purpose in the preceding section)

If you are new to this world, the last one is a great way to get your feet wet. Unlike what you might have heard, surveying is easy to implement, can be a continuous methodology, is highly quantitative, and is most often chock full of insights that will lend themselves to be very action oriented.

Combining the *why* (intent, motivation, and so forth) with the *what* (clicks, visitor counts) has to be the cornerstone of any successful actionable web analytics program.

Trinity: A Mindset and a Strategic Approach

A couple of years ago while grappling with all the challenges of web analytics and how to solve them, a need arose for a new paradigm, a different framework about how to think of web analytics. Having lots and lots of KPIs, many reports full of data, and horsepower expended against all that did not yield quite the results that were expected.

Every website had a standard big-three web analytics package installed for a few years, reports were published, and victory was declared upon successful completion of the nightly reports. But if business as normal did not yield any insights to improve the customer experience on the website, then what should the paradigm be?

The answer was *Trinity*, a new way of thinking about decision making on the Web—something that was more than clickstream. Trinity is also a framework that can empower your web strategy. Executing to the Trinity will ensure that you can build a world-class decision-making platform that will create a sustainable competitive advantage for your company.

The central raison d'être of the Trinity strategy is something radical: actionable insights and metrics (see Figure 1.6).

Figure 1.6 Solving for actionable insights and metrics

The goal of this strategy is not to do reporting. The goal is not to figure out how to spam decision makers with reports full of data via email. Actionable insights and metrics are the über-goal simply because they drive strategic differentiation and a sustainable competitive advantage.

Having actionable insights combined with clear goals helps crystalize the efforts of the organization. If you are doing things (reports, data analysis, meetings, reviews, and so forth) that are not singularly geared toward producing actionable insights, then stop. This strategy encourages the right behavior from the organization and is a great way for key stakeholders to make their day-to-day resource allocation decisions.

Behavior Analysis

The first component of the Trinity mindset is *behavior analysis*, what we traditionally consider clickstream data analysis (Figure 1.7).

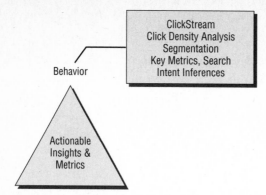

Figure 1.7 Behavior analysis, attempting to infer customer intent

The goal of behavior analysis is to (as best as we can from the data we have) infer the intent of our customers or website visitors based on all that we know about them. We will not follow the rest of the crowd and expect too much of the clickstream data. The best we can do with clickstream data is infer intent, and we have to make peace with that.

After collecting clickstream data, the objective is to analyze it from a higher plane of reference. No more measuring hits or overall time on site or visitor counts or top exit pages. Under the Trinity strategy, we will do click density analysis by using the site overlay report. We will massively segment the data by *n* levels to find core nuggets of valuable insights. We will do search analysis (and not just external keywords, but also internal site searches). The objective is to become really smart about clickstream analysis and to start truly inferring the intent of our site visitors.

There is a downside to inferring intent: two people may look at the same set of data and clicks on the website and form differing sets of interpretation. This is usually because each of us is a collection of our own unique background and experiences. The great thing about acknowledging that we are inferring intents is that we are free to make those inferences, present them to our peer group, validate them, and then draw conclusions and make recommendations.

Outcomes Analysis

The second component of the Trinity mindset is *outcomes analysis* (Figure 1.8). I fondly call it the *so what* element.

This is critical for one simple reason: at the end of the day when all is said and done, you want to know the outcome for the customer and the company. This element also solves one of the critical flaws of traditional web analytics, that of an egregious amount of focus on page, time, and visitors metrics derived from clickstream data. Because web analytics has its roots in log file analysis (which never had outcomes), for the longest time it had lots of data and metrics but not the most important one—an answer to, "*So what happened, what was the outcome?*"

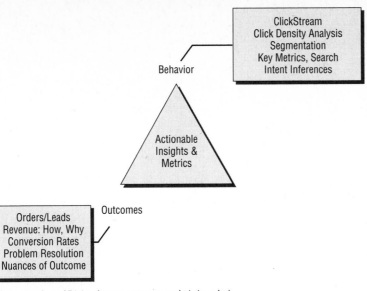

Figure 1.8 Second Trinity element: outcomes analysis (*so what*)

I encourage you to ask a simple question to the site owners: *Why does your website exist?* You might be surprised how many can't answer that question in 15 words or fewer. This element of the Trinity exists to measure how well the website is doing in meeting the goal of its existence.

In the simplest of terms, this measures revenue for e-commerce websites (not just how much, but also why we made as much as we did) and measures conversion rates better. But for support websites, this measures problem resolution and timeliness. For websites that exist for lead generation, this element of the Trinity measures the number of leads and the quality of those leads (and whether the quality improves over time). For your website/business, the outcomes could be different from the ones listed in the illustration, but they will almost always be metrics that affect the bottom line and can be tied to the financials of the company.

Every website should have a clearly articulated outcome. If you don't have the capacity to measure all nuances of outcomes, the recommendation is to give up on measuring behavior (clickstream) altogether. If you don't have the ability to measure outcomes robustly, all the behavior analysis in the world will do you no good because you will have no idea whether all those graphs in the web analytics application you are using that are going up and to the right added any value to your company. Is it a bit extreme to dump clickstream in favor of measuring outcomes first? Yes. Necessary? You bet.

Experience Analysis

The third and last component of the Trinity mindset is *experience* (Figure 1.9). This encompasses our dear elusive best friend, *why*.

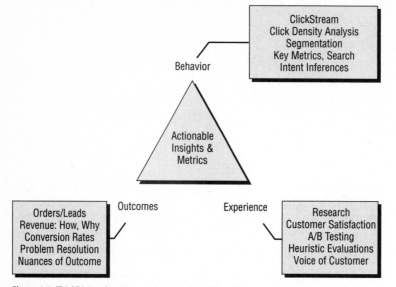

Figure 1.9 Third Trinity element: experience analysis (the *why*)

Although the outcomes element of the Trinity is mandatory, the experience element is perhaps the most critical. For any organization that is stuck in a rut and unable to find any real actionable insights from behavior and outcomes—no matter how hard they try—the recommendation is to invest in experience analysis. This is the *why*. This is the warm hug when you are stymied and tortured by your clickstream data and you want to tear your hair out.

It is hard to choose a favorite among your children, but for me experience is without question the favorite. The reason is quite simple: *experience analysis allows us to get into the heads of our customers and gain insight or an a-ha about why they do the things they do.*

There are many ways to understand the experience of customers on your website. You can leverage surveys and simply ask them, or there are very complex statistical quantitative and qualitative methodologies you can bring to bear. Surveys will allow you to measure customer satisfaction and even predict future behavior (likelihood to buy or to recommend your products or services). As will be clear throughout this book, I am a huge believer of experimentation and testing (let's have the customers tell us what they prefer) by using either the A/B testing methodology or multivariate testing. We also have the traditional user-centric design techniques at our disposal, such as heuristic evaluations. We can also leverage lab usability testing as another great option or do follow-me-homes (site visits), a concept advocated by Scott Cook, the founder of Intuit as the essence of the Customer Driven Innovation (CDI) mindset.

Note: Chapter 3, "Overview of Qualitative Analysis," covers all of these user-centric design methodologies in greater detail.

NOTE

All these experience methodologies are solving for one single purpose: getting companies to listen to the voice of the customer, a voice that in most companies and corporations is lost in the wilderness.

Solving for Companies and Customers: Win-Win

In the end, the Trinity mindset drives the fundamental *understanding of the customer experience* so that you can *influence the optimal customer behavior* that will lead to *win-win outcomes* for your company and your customers (Figure 1.10).

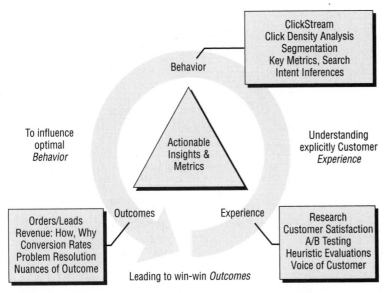

Figure 1.10 Understanding experience to influence behavior for win-win outcomes

That last part is important: Trinity aims for win-win outcomes.

If the right version of the product for a particular website customer is Basic and not the Professional edition, our job as site owners is for us to help customers figure that out and buy Basic. Yes, we can make more money in the short term if the customer buys Professional today. But it is quite likely that the customer will buy Professional, use it, get frustrated because it is too advanced for them, and we'll never see them again (and they will share their suboptimal experience with others). But if we help them buy the right version, Basic, then next year they'll be back for Professional. Trinity aims to solve for the long term.

Understand the needs and wants of your customers and solve for that. By using the Trinity, you can and will win big—and frankly it is a blast solving the problems of your customers when you know what they are.

Each element of the Trinity is supported by a different tool. The Trinity incorporates different methodologies while leveraging repeatable processes. Most important, it requires key people skills. Just having the mindset does not solve the problem (though it will put you on the right path). Executing the Trinity strategic approach means creating the right organizational structure and an evolved culture.

Building an Integrated Trinity Platform

The entire framework will not come into existence overnight. Typically, you'll diagnose what you currently have and will work toward putting the missing pieces of the puzzle together. It is important to ensure that your execution strategy plans for, and postimplementation allows, your analysts to have the ability to tie all the elements of the Trinity together (Figure 1.11). This will be a massive advantage for your company.

As an example, if your visitors place orders or submit leads on your website, some anonymous tracking elements such as the transient session_id and cookie_id can be passed to the orders database. This will allow you to do deep segmented analysis of outcomes and of the behaviors that drive those outcomes.

Another example is passing the (again anonymous) session_ids to your survey tool so that you can segment the most unhappy customers based on survey results. You can then use your web analytics tool to analyze the clickstream data and see what pages happy customers saw as compared to unhappy customers. Or you could see what website experience drives better customer satisfaction, and so forth.

In a world where your analytical world view was severely limited by using only your web analytics tool and clickstream data, the Trinity framework expands the available data, helps you truly understand your customers, and allows you to slice and dice your data to gain holistic insights. Satisfaction of your customers and revenue for your company soon follow. (And your analysts are happy to boot because they finally have the challenge of analyzing qualitative and quantitative pan-session data— what fun!)

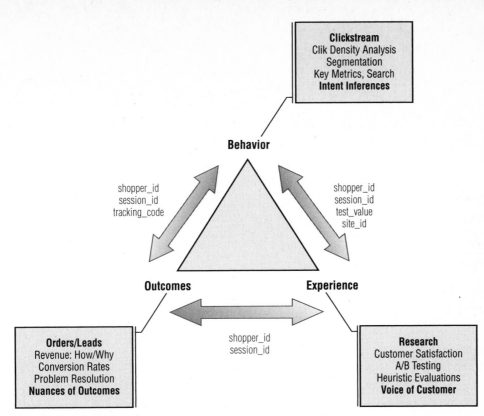

Figure 1.11 Integrated Trinity strategy (primary keys allow key silos to be tied together)

The Trinity framework can be applied to any kind of web business: e-commerce, support, advocacy, nonprofit, small business, and so on. You will find more details and specifically how to apply Trinity to your business in Chapter 6, "Customized Solutions to Jumpstart your Web Data Analysis."

Data Collection—Importance and Options

GIGO (garbage in, garbage out) *was one of the very early acronyms coined in the PC era. The quality of the output was directly related to the quality of the input. Computers have gotten much smarter since the early days and sometimes they can do something smart with garbage going in so that something better than garbage comes out—often something useful.*

But from the perspective of web analytics, we still live very much in the world of GIGO. This is because our field is quite young, our data capture mechanisms are still in a state of flux as they try to keep pace with the changing nature the Web itself, and all the time we have new customer experiences coming online, which forces us to.

In this chapter, you will look at the various data collection choices you will have to make as a web analytics practitioner and the various options to consider. There are four core groups of data I'll talk about: clickstream, outcomes, research (qualitative), and competitive data.

Understanding the Data Landscape

Perhaps as in no other industry, we have to place a very high level of importance on the value of data capture. There are several important elements to consider when it comes to implementing an effective data capture strategy:

- There are a number of ways to collect data as a customer interacts with our websites. There are web log files, web beacons, JavaScript tags, and packet sniffers. Some advanced e-commerce software from companies such as ATG can also leverage built-in data collection mechanisms such as event logging to collect important business events and contextual data.

- A number of data collection mechanisms are in the mold of "you forget it and you are screwed" (miss a JavaScript tag on a page, and you are done for).

- Many industry-leading vendors require you to think through your options up front and make explicit choices on what data you want to capture. If you don't capture the data up front, you don't have the ability to do analysis. So, for example, let's say you launch an analytics tool. After you see the first reports, you realize you want a different slice or you would prefer to see all the page data in a different hierarchy—you are out of luck. A couple of vendors will allow ex post facto analysis (segmentation after the data has been collected, even if you have not necessarily defined and passed all the segmentation variables up front), but most don't have this capability.

- Sometimes you need more than one method of data collection. You might use JavaScript tagging, currently pretty much the standard, to collect website behavior. However, if you want to analyze the behavior of robots on your website, you would need access to your web logs because search engine robots do not execute JavaScript and hence leave no trail in your usual source of data.

- Then there are all other sources of data that you need for making effective decisions: data related to outcomes on your website (to measure true success), or the various types of qualitative data such as from surveys or usability studies that you need to collect to understand customer behavior, or data from other sources in the company such as your CRM or Enterprise Resource Planning (ERP) systems.

- Any great web analytics program also taps into competitive data about the performance of your industry category or your competitors—even data on your performance if you were looking in from the outside rather than simply from within your company.

- Last but not the least is privacy. As you go around putting mechanisms in place to collect data, it is of paramount importance to ensure that you are extremely explicit about the implications of capturing data on the Web. You have to declare in clear legal language to your customers what data you are capturing. You have to be very, very careful that you are not collecting personally identifiable information (PII) data—and if you are, be even more clear to your customers. Validate that your vendor data capture, data storage, and data processing mechanisms comply with your stated standards. It is highly recommended that you conduct periodic security audits of your data capture and storage (at your vendor and in your company). This might seem paranoid, but as a chief marketing officer (CMO) once remarked to me, "*It only takes one privacy slip or story in a newspaper or a tiny data theft for your entire web operation to go down in flames.*" More than ever, customers are concerned about their privacy, as they should be, and we should all do our part in ensuring that we are extremely protective of the trust they place in us.

All of the preceding information should convince you that the single most determining factor in your ability to be successful is to make an informed choice. Yet it is perhaps the single most determining factor in your ability to be successful. Rather than starting your quest for an optimal web analytics implementation with a complex request for proposal (RFP), or from a selection of recommended vendors, my advice is to spend time studying the complexities and nuances of data collection (types, options, methodologies) and let the data collection choices you make drive the choice of vendor, platform, and everything else that goes with it.

With the right data collection choice, you can make a mistake with a vendor and recover. The reverse is almost never true.

Clickstream Data

If you are reading this book, you probably are already using clickstream data, if not outright drowning in it. It is the basis of everything we do in our little niche in the universe. It is delightfully complex, ever changing, and full of mysterious occurrences.

There are four main ways of capturing clickstream data: web logs, web beacons, JavaScript tags, and packet sniffing.

Web Logs

Web logs have been the original source of data collection from the dawn of the Web. They were originally developed to capture errors generated by web servers and over time have been "enhanced" to capture more data as analytical needs shifted from technical to marketing based.

Figure 2.1 shows a simple schematic of how web logs capture data.

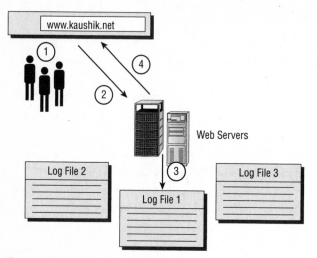

Figure 2.1 How web logs capture data

The data capture process is as follows:

1. A customer types your URL in a browser.

2. The request for the page comes to one of your web servers (a typical business website exists on a cluster of web servers, each of which is capable of serving up pages).

3. The web server accepts the request and creates an entry in the web log for the request (typical pieces of data captured include the page name, IP address and browser of the customer, and date and time stamps).

4. The web server sends the web page to the customer.

In most cases, the web logs are taken from the server on a set schedule (say, nightly). A standard log-parsing tool or a web analytics tool can be pointed in their direction to analyze the web logs and produce standard reports.

Benefits of Using Web Logs as Your Data Collection Mechanism

• Web logs are perhaps the most easily accessible source of data. Every web server simply comes with mechanisms that collect the data and create web logs. You have data even if you don't know that you do.

- There are many log file parsers now easily available for free, so you not only can obtain the data but also can start creating basic reports very quickly.

- Web logs are the only data capture mechanism that will capture and store the visits and behavior of search engine robots on your website. Search engine robots don't execute JavaScript tags, and hence leave no trail in other data capture mechanisms. So if you want to analyze visits by the Google, Microsoft Network (MSN), and Yahoo search engine robots to ensure that your website is being crawled and indexed correctly, you have to use web logs.

- If you use web logs, you always own the data. With most other methodologies, the data will be captured, processed, and stored with your web analytics vendor, who operates under a application service provider (ASP). But you will own and keep all your web logs; if you switch web analytics vendors, it will be easier for you to go back and reprocess history with the new tool.

Concerns about Using Web Logs as Your Data Collection Mechanism

- Web logs are primarily geared toward capturing technical information (404 errors, server usage trends, browser types, and so forth). They are not optimally suited to capture business or marketing information.

- If additional marketing and business information need to be captured, that capture requires a close collaboration with your IT team and a dependency on their release schedules. This is somewhat mitigated with other data capture mechanisms so you can move much faster.

- If the web server is not setting cookies, identifying visitors with any degree of accuracy is very challenging.

- Web logs were created to capture all the hits on the server. Therefore, when using logs, you have to be very careful and deliberate about applying the right filters to remove image requests, page errors, robot traffic, requests for Cascading Style Sheets (CSS) files, and so forth, in order to get accurate traffic trends and behavior.

- Page caching by ISPs and proxy servers could mean that some of your traffic (10 percent or more) is invisible to you. With page caching common, your website pages (say, your home page, product pages, and so forth) are cached at the ISP or proxy servers. So when someone from that ISP's network requests your home page, it is served from the ISP and not your web server. Therefore, you will not have an entry for that request in your log files.

Recommendation

For better or for worse, little innovation is being put into web logs as a source of data for doing true web analysis. Web logs should be used to analyze search engine robot behavior in order to measure success of your search engine optimization efforts. Other data capture mechanisms are better suited for doing almost all other types of web analysis that you'll need. In the best-case scenarios you might use web logs to complement data you capture using other methodologies, but do be wary of the complexity and effort required in those cases.

Web Beacons

Web beacons were developed during a time when banners ruled the Web as the prime way of "capturing eyeballs" and delivering those to "sticky" websites where we were measuring hits. A company would run banner ads across many websites, and often these would be similar banner ads. There was a distinct need to figure out not just how many people who saw the banner ads were clicking through, but also how many of those exposed to the ads were the same individual. Alternatively, if the same person was exposed to different creatives (banner ads, ad text, and so forth), which one worked best?

Web beacons usually are 1×1 pixel transparent images that are placed in web pages, within an `img src` HTML tag. The transparent images are usually hosted on a third-party server—different from the server that is hosting the web page.

Figure 2.2 shows how data is captured by web beacons.

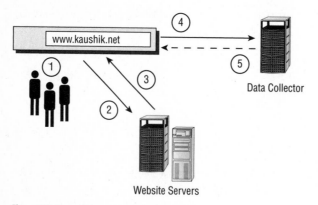

Figure 2.2 How web beacons capture data

The process is as follows:

1. The customer types your URL in a browser.

2. The request comes to one of your web servers.

3. The web server sends back the page along with a get request for a 1×1 pixel image from a third-party server.

4. As the page loads, it executes the call for the 1×1 pixel image, thus sending data about the page view back to the third-party server.

5. The third-party server sends the image back to the browser along with code that can read cookies and capture anonymous visitor data such as the fact that the page was viewed, the IP address, the time the page was viewed, the cookies that were previously set, and more.

Web beacons are also used in emails (such as email newsletters or promotional emails that we all receive). Here, just as in a web page, the transparent image is requested when the email loads in your email reader, and data about the email view is sent back and recorded. Typical data could include the fact that the email was read, by whom (email address), and any other parameters that might be appended at the end of the transparent image request embedded in the email. With the prevalence of JavaScript tagging, the use of web beacons has become less prevalent; they are mostly used to track basics around banner ads and emails.

Benefits of Using Web Beacons as Your Data Collection Mechanism

- Web beacons are easy to implement in most cases because they are just a couple of lines of code wrapped around an `img src` HTML tag request. Most of the "intelligence" in what to capture comes back from the server that received the image request.

- You can optimize exactly what data the beacon collects (for example, just the page viewed, or time, or cookie values, or referrers), and because robots do not execute image requests, you won't collect unwanted data. This can keep your logs to a manageable size and won't require complex filtering.

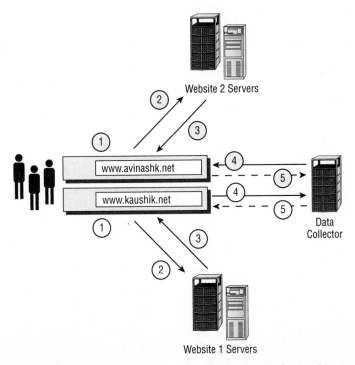

Figure 2.3 Capturing the same data as in Figure 2.2, but from two sites (`avinashk.net` and `kaushik.net`)

- Web beacons shine when it comes to collecting data across multiple websites or domains (see Figure 2.3). If you are a publisher who puts content on many sites, or if you are a company that has many sites in your own network, you can use beacons to easily collect and store data from all these sites on one server (the one sending out all the data collection requests). As a result, you'll know better what happens across different websites and hence target content better to the visitors. The data captured is less deep than with other methodologies, but for targeted narrow purposes (banners, emails, and so forth), it works well.

Concerns about Using Web Beacons as Your Data Collection Mechanism

- Beacons are most closely identified with advertising and advertising networks and therefore have a bit of a bad rap. A lot has been written about the privacy implications of tracking the behavior of one person across many sites. As a result, many visitors apply global opt-outs, or the antispyware programs automatically remove the cookies, which greatly hampers the ability to collect data.

- If image requests are turned off in email programs (as is increasingly the case by default in programs such as Microsoft Office Outlook and Google's Gmail) or some browsers, you can't collect the data.

- Beacons are not as expansive and customizable as JavaScript tags (discussed in the next section) in terms of the data they can capture. They capture less data but can do so across a broad range of websites.

- By their nature, beacons interact with third-party servers and for the most part set third-party cookies. They are also afflicted with the increasingly strict privacy constraints whereby browsers (such as Internet Explorer) either will not accept or will not clear third-party cookies. Antispyware programs will also delete these third-party cookies, making it much harder to track returning visits and in turn track accurate customer behavior.

Recommendation

If you want to track visitor behavior across multiple websites or track email open/view rates, web beacons might be optimal. It is likely that for rich website analytics you might still have to rely on other methods of analyzing data, because the data captured by beacons is typically not as rich as, say, JavaScript tags (in which case please do a careful cost benefit analysis of having more than one methodology on your site).

JavaScript Tags

JavaScript tagging is perhaps the favorite child of the industry at the moment. Most vendors and web analytics solutions are relying on JavaScript tagging to collect data.

After the beaconing season, JavaScript tagging allowed for more data to be collected more accurately and—very important—it ushered in new business models in the industry. Data serving was separated from data capture, hence reducing the reliance on corporate IT departments for various data capture requests. It also meant that data capture moved to third-party web analytics vendors in most cases.

Now web pages could go out from the company servers, with no need to capture data, and be presented to website visitors. In turn, data about the visitor session would be captured on other servers (usually, third-party—for example, your favorite web analytics vendor's servers) and be processed there with reporting available online.

No longer was there a need for companies to host their own infrastructure to collect data, a team to process the data, and systems to support reporting. Of course, nothing in life is perfect, and this rose has its own set of thorns.

But let's first understand how tagging works (see Figure 2.4).

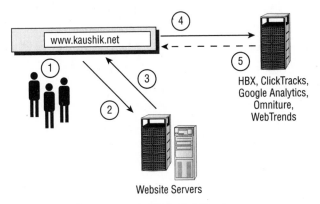

Figure 2.4 How data capture works with JavaScript tagging

The process is as follows:

1. The customer types your URL in a browser.

2. The request comes to one of your web servers.

3. The web server sends back the page along with a snippet of JavaScript code appended to the page.

4. As the page loads, it executes the JavaScript code, which captures the page view, details about the visitor session, and cookies, and sends it back to the data collection server.

5. In some cases, upon receipt of the first set of data, the server sends back additional code to the browser to set additional cookies or collect more data.

Although in Figure 2.4 data is captured on third-party servers, a few companies (ClickTracks and WebTrends among them) sell JavaScript-driven data capture solutions. If you go down this path, you can have the data captured and stored all within your own company and have greater control regarding privacy and setting cookies, while also maintaining ownership of the data. One benefit of having an in-house JavaScript tagging solution is that it becomes exponentially easier to integrate data from other sources of the company into your web analytics solution—you can do it yourself without worrying about having to send sensitive data out of your company.

Benefits of Using JavaScript Tagging as Your Data Collection Mechanism

- Other than web logs, this methodology perhaps has the easiest initial implementation effort. Adding a standard few lines of JavaScript code in a global site element (such as a footer) can instantly tag the entire site, and you can have massive amounts of data and standard reports 30 minutes later.

- If you don't have access to your web servers (technically) and/or your web server logs, JavaScript tagging is your only choice. You can install the tags easily (in your pages) and use an ASP vendor to do your reporting. This is particularly appealing to small- and medium-sized businesses.

- Page caching, either locally on a visitor PC or on cache farms such as those of Akamai Technologies, is not a problem for JavaScript tagging (as it is for web logs). Regardless of where your web page is being served from, the JavaScript tag will execute and your analytics tool will be able to collect the data.

- You have a great deal of control over exactly what data is collected. You also have the ability to implement custom tags on special pages (cart, checkout, order confirmation, knowledge base articles) that allow you to capture additional data for those pages (for example, order value, quantity, product names, and so forth).

- JavaScript enables you to separate data capture from data serving. When you use JavaScript tagging, your site releases will be a little bit faster because your IT department does not have to check anything relating to data capture, other than ensuring that your tag is on the page. (Data capture becomes your vendor's responsibility.) You don't have to trouble your IT department to set cookies to track sessions; your tool can do it now.

- Most vendors' innovation (new features, upgrades to how data is captured, and so forth) is happening in the JavaScript methodology. Most vendors stopped actively improving their web log tool versions. Many don't even offer a web log version of their tool.

- If you use third-party cookies (set by you or, as is usually the case, your vendor), tracking users across multiple domains becomes easier, because your third-party cookie and its identifying elements stay consistent as visitors go across multiple domains where your JavaScript tags exist.

Concerns about Using JavaScript Tagging as Your Primary Data Collection Mechanism

- Not all website visitors have JavaScript turned on, often for privacy or other reasons. For these users, your analytics platform will not collect any data. Benchmarks are hard to come by, but usually 2–6 percent of site visitors have JavaScript turned off. These visitors will be invisible to you.

- Data collected via JavaScript tagging is divorced from other metadata. Hence it is almost imperative that lots of thought and planning be put into creating the tag that will be capturing the site taxonomy and hierarchy, to allow for optimal analysis. This can be a strenuous process and requires regular maintenance as the site evolves.

- JavaScript tags collect data "browser side" and not "server side." Some websites, rather than storing some data in cookies or URL parameters, will store data on the servers during the visitor session. In this case, the tags will not capture essential data. If your IT strategy is to hold key data on the server, rather than on the browser/visitor machine, tags might not work for you (or you will have to go through the pain of changing your IT strategy).

- Capturing data in JavaScript tags about downloads (for example, PDFs or EXEs) and redirects is harder than with web logs, though some vendors are thinking of clever solutions.

- If your website is already JavaScript heavy, with lots of JavaScript on the site trying to do lots of clever things, your web analytics JavaScript tag could cause conflicts. In some cases, using tags to collect data might not even be possible (to allow your website to function).

Recommendation

JavaScript tagging should be seriously considered as a possible option for your data collection strategy. Most web analytics innovation is coming from vendors enhancing their tools to better leverage JavaScript tagging. In addition, JavaScript tagging may be optimal for the amount of control that it gives you, the analytics team, in your ability to capture what you want, when you want it. The only other thing you would have to do is leverage web logs to measure search engine optimization (SEO), or web robot behavior, on your website.

Packet Sniffing

Packet sniffing technically is one of the most sophisticated ways of collecting web data. It has also been around for quite some time, but for a number of reasons it is not quite as popular as the other options outlined in this chapter. Among the vendors who provide packet-sniffing web analytics solutions are Clickstream Technologies. Some interesting ways of leveraging packet sniffers are also emerging—for example, SiteSpect is using the technology for multivariate testing, eliminating the reliance on tagging your website to do testing.

Figure 2.5 illustrates the process of collecting data using packet sniffing.

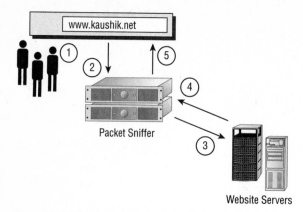

Figure 2.5 How data capture works with packet sniffing

There are a total of five steps to collect data:

1. The customer types your URL in a browser.

2. The request is routed to the web server, but before it gets there, it passes through a software- or hardware-based packet sniffer that collects attributes of the request that can send back more data about the Visitor to the packet sniffer.

3. The packet sniffer sends the request on to the web server.

4. The request is sent back to the customer but is first passed to the packet sniffer. The packet sniffer captures information about the page going back and stores that data. Some vendor packet-sniffing solutions append a JavaScript tag that can send back to the packet sniffer more data about the visitor.

5. The packet sniffer sends the page on to the visitor browser.

A packet sniffer can be a layer of software that is installed on the web servers and runs "on top" of the web server data layer. Alternatively, it can be a physical piece of hardware that is hooked up in your data center, and all traffic is then routed to your web server via the packet sniffer solution.

Benefits of Using Packet Sniffers as Your Data Collection Mechanism

- Because all data passes through the packet sniffer, first it eliminates the need to use JavaScript tags for your website, or in theory, to touch your website at all.

- Your time to market is a bit longer than with JavaScript tagging because of the reliance on IT to approve and install the additional software and hardware in the data center—but it is less than the time required for other methods.

- You can collect lots and lots of data instantly, much more than with standard JavaScript tagging. For example, you can get server errors, bandwidth usage, and all the technical data as well as the page-related business data. It is fair to say that with packet sniffing you will collect the most comprehensive amount of data ever possible (every 0 and 1!).

- Given the nature of the solutions, you do have the ability to always use first party for cookies, and so forth.

Concerns about Using Packet Sniffers as Your Data Collection Mechanism

- For most companies, it is quite a struggle to make a case for and convince the IT department to add an additional layer of software on the web servers or to physically install hardware in their high-profile data centers and route all web traffic via these solutions. Some IT teams have a natural acceptance barrier for things they consider nonstandard. Packet sniffers also place a layer between the customer and the web page, a concept that while mostly benign can raise concerns and create hurdles.

- Remember, you are collecting raw packets of your Internet web server traffic. This poses two important challenges: First, nontrivial amounts of configuration work with your packet-sniffing solution to parse out just the needed data from all the raw data. The second challenge is privacy. In the raw data you will be capturing all the data, including PII data such as passwords, names, addresses, and credit card numbers. This last one, privacy, needs very careful stress testing and legal review. But as you can imagine, using JavaScript tags to complement packet sniffers would expose you to some of the cons discussed earlier for tags.

- When using most packet-sniffing solutions, you would still need JavaScript tags to truly collect all the data that you will need for optimal analysis. For example, without JavaScript tags, the packet sniffer would not get any data for cached pages (because no request comes to the web server). Or consider your inability to collect data from Adobe Flash files or Ajax or rich Internet applications (RIAs): one deeply interactive file goes over to the visitor's browser, and then lots of interaction happens in the visitor browser that would all be invisible to a traditional packet sniffer (again, because the rich media interaction sends no request back to the server). Ditto for the inability to collect some of the core structure and metadata about pages via pure packet sniffer implementation.

- Packet sniffing can get expensive if you have many web servers (which is fairly common) or if you have web servers sitting on many networks. In these cases, you would have to install the software or the hardware on all the networks.

Recommendation

Packet-sniffing methodologies have very specialized implementations and are currently supported by just a few web analytics vendors. For optimal effectiveness, you will have to combine packet-sniffing solutions with JavaScript tagging. The overall recommendation is to consider packet sniffers if JavaScript tagging (or web logs) has particular shortfalls in meeting the data needs of your organization. As with any methodology in your selection process, please review any concerns with your vendor.

Concerns About All Data Capture Mechanisms

There are some common underlying concerns that apply to all data capture mechanisms. Here is an overview of each and what you should be careful about as you attempt to create an optimal data capture mechanism for your company.

First-Party vs. Third-Party Cookies

Most vendors will set their own (third-party) cookies, but you should almost always use your own domain's first-party cookies. This is true for many reasons, the least of which is to overcome security settings and antispyware software.

Data Ownership

Except for web logs, or if you are hosting JavaScript tag solutions in-house, your data is sitting with your vendor. It is possible to get some of that data exported, but only at aggregate levels. If you go deep, it is almost impossible to get at that data. The question is, how much do you need your historical data, and what happens if you switch vendors? This is an often-overlooked valuable consideration in evaluating data collection options.

Time on Last Page

Almost all tools determine the time you have spent on any page by computing the difference between the timestamp of your arrival at a page and the timestamp in the session of your next page view. This works well, except for the last page in your session. There is no way for the data capture mechanism to know how long you spend on that page. The mechanism just terminates your session, usually after 29 minutes of inactivity. Some people have suggested clever "on-load" hacks that would try to figure out whether you are still on the page. This is not a standard approach and hence it is important to be aware of this limitation.

Ditto for the first page, if the first page is the only page that is viewed in a session by a website visitor. In other words, if you have seen only one page during your visit, there is no way for your web analytics tool to know how long you have been on that page (unless there are hacks in place).

Concerns About All Data Capture Mechanisms *(Continued)*

All Data Capture Mechanisms Are Fragile and Imperfect

I will talk a lot about this topic throughout this book, but it is important to simply internalize that there is no good way to capture data that is 100 percent accurate. Every clickstream data capture solution has problems associated with it. Browsers are funky and visitors are funky. Know that you are making decisions based on data that is usually "good enough," and as always your mileage may vary.

Customers First

It is important to remember that ensuring that the customer gets the page is of primary importance, not that the data is collected. Please accommodate for that important fact in your data collection strategy. For example, placing your JavaScript tags at the bottom of your pages will ensure that the page loads even if your web analytics data capture server is dead. Or if you are using a packet sniffer, have failover mechanisms in case there are problems with the sniffer.

Be hypervigilant about customer privacy. We are all customers of one website or another and we should treat our customers better than how we would want our data to be treated. Never collect PII data unless you absolutely have to, and even then first clear it with your legal department and be very explicit in your privacy policies. Audit your vendors or your internal data stores to ensure that customer data, even non-PII, is kept in the most secure and accountable environments.

Cost

When it comes to pricing and cost, there are a few variables that you need to carefully evaluate. There are two primary cost models: recurring payments and one-time payments.

Most vendors in the market are ASP-based at the moment and hence use the recurring payments structure. They will charge you on a per-page-view basis (it is important to define up front what a page view is; it will vary from vendor to vendor). This means that the more popular your website is (or becomes), the more it will cost you. This seems fair because the vendor then has to host the hardware and pay for all costs associated with analyzing larger and larger amounts of data.

Solutions based on web logs and in-house JavaScript tagging solutions (which, for example, Click-Tracks and WebTrends provide) are in the one-time payment structure. You pay them only a one-time fee for the software, along with the standard support price. Then your costs actually go down after the first year. Some companies already have standard web servers that can cover the cost of hardware or you can buy a box to do that.

You can evaluate which model will be cheaper for your company—having an in-house model does mean that you can have as many websites (and hence page views) tagged as you would like, at no extra cost to you.

One final consideration in pricing is to evaluate bang for the buck. Vendors don't have to be selected based on the one that gives you most reports. Most vendors will have an 80 percent commonality in the reports that they provide. The other 20 percent (the differentiated part) can be critically valuable, and expensive. If your business can extract value from the differentiated 20 percent, you should absolutely go with that, or else evaluate all options from the perspective of cost-benefit.

Why Does My Data Not Tie (Reconcile)?

If you switch vendors or data collection methodologies or are simply using more than one (for example, web logs and tags), you will surely run into the brutal fact that none of these tools or methodologies provide metrics or numbers that are consistent. In fact, they might even have a 10–15 percent difference for the same website for the same time period (and you would be lucky if it is just 10 percent).

Here are five key reasons your data might not tie:

- Each tool seems to have its own unique way of creating a session and then identifying when a session is closed. The most common setting for session termination is "29 minutes of inactivity." But some tools will close the session if they detect that a visitor came back from a search engine in fewer than 29 minutes. These tools will start a new session. Check to ensure that your tools for comparing data use the same session parameters.

- If you are comparing data based on log files and JavaScript tags, check how each calculates visits (total visitors) and unique visitors. Often log-file-based solutions don't use cookies and hence rely on IP address plus user agent IDs to track visitors (and in turn uniqueness). JavaScript solutions almost always use a persistent cookie value to do visitor counts. This will ensure that there will almost always be differences in the metrics.

- If you are comparing web log data to anything else, ensure that you are filtering out all the data that other methodologies usually don't even capture. Examples include robot traffic, miscellaneous file requests (CSS files, scripts, and so forth), 404s and other types of errors, redirects, and download requests. Also remember that page caching will render invisible 5–20 percent of the data in the web log files, but other solutions will capture that data (more-precise numbers are hard to come by).

- If you are comparing JavaScript tagging data, one very obvious thing to check is that all your web pages are actually tagged (it is amazing how often this is not true).

- Over the last few years, more and more websites have become dynamic and because of that URLs contain lots of "gibberish." URL stems are longer and contain lots of parameters including intelligence about the page or something about the referrer or some data value that is there for tracking purposes. Some of these URL parameters make pages unique. As you reconcile your data, ensure that both tools are treating the same parameters as "tracking" parameters or "unique page" parameters, or else page counts will be drastically different.

Outcomes Data

Regardless of what methodology you use from those listed earlier in this chapter, and no matter what web analytics tool you use, most of the data that you obtain will be based on customer clicks. You will, in the very short duration of one day, have access to between 80 and 300 reports (depending on the tool you end up using), all illustrating a combination of these facets of your website traffic:

- Visitors (visits, total, unique)
- Page views (individual, aggregates, averages)
- Time (overall, averages, slices)
- Referrers (counts, websites, keywords, trends)

Every report you see will illustrate one of the preceding metrics, or one of them multiplied by or divided by or subtracted from the other.

The important question that is often forgotten in all this deluge of data is, *so what happened?* If all these people came and saw all these pages and spent so much time on the site, what was the outcome for the customer or the company?

This is why it is extremely important to think really hard about your outcomes data strategy—which should begin with the question, *why does your website exist?*

The answer to that is not a 500-page tome, but rather a few words that get to the heart of the site's existence. The answer could sound something like this:

- To make as much money as possible for our company, without causing undue harm to our customers
- To reduce the cost of servicing a support phone call by improving web self-help
- To improve the problem resolution rates for our most in-need customers
- To generate leads for our email database or sales prospecting efforts or future products not yet announced
- To create a customer experience that would reinforce our brand in the hearts and minds of a million people who don't know any better

After you have an answer to the question of why your site exists, it is imperative to investigate how your decision-making platform will capture the data that will help you understand the outcomes and whether your website is successful beyond simply attracting traffic and serving up pages.

In this section, you'll learn a few options for executing an optimal outcomes data capture strategy.

E-commerce

For most e-commerce websites, it is now fairly standard practice to use custom JavaScript tags (or packet sniffers or web beacons) to capture data from the order confirmation page. The data you will capture most frequently via this custom implementation is as follows:

- Order's unique identifier

- Product or service ordered

- Quantity and price of each item

- Discounts and promotions applied

- Metadata about the customer session: A/B or multivariate test (MVT) IDs, cookie values, and so forth

- Metadata about the products or services: product hierarchy, campaign hierarchy, product attributes (all for sophisticated post-data-capture analysis)

This data is then incorporated into your standard clickstream tool, enabling you to report on this e-commerce data.

Lead Generation

For lead generation websites, you might be able to collect data on your website (on the "thank you" page, the one that the customer sees after submitting a successful lead), or you might have to partner with other websites that might be collecting and storing the leads on your behalf. Plan on identifying where the data is being captured and how you can have access to it (for example, via JavaScript tags or beacons or database exports).

Brand/Advocacy and Support

For both brand/advocacy websites and for support websites, the outcomes are less clear. A page view on these sites is nothing more than a viewed page. For the longest time, we have made the leap of faith that if the user sees a certain page, we can call it *mission accomplished*—mostly because we did not know any better. In these cases, we need to know the customer's perception or to ask the customer whether the page view resulted in their problem being solved.

Outcomes in this case are harder to figure out. However, a great way to start is to put a surveying methodology in place on the websites that would continually ask a series of relevant questions to a statistically significant sample of site visitors to get their ratings on success. This can be a great complement to your clickstream data.

An important facet of outcomes analysis is the ability to take key data out of a customer interaction that may or may not be available to a clickstream web analytics tool. We have all come to realize this, and so have the web analytics vendors. Increasingly, a cornerstone of an optimal web analytics strategy is having a data warehouse environment that allows you to have more-complex data in an easy-to-report-from environment. Data warehouses are typically very flexible when it comes to importing data from external sources and hence empowering you to do the required analysis with a view into the end-to-end customer experience.

Vendors such as Omniture and WebTrends have created a V1 version of a true "data warehouse back end" in their tools. Alternatively, many large companies are choosing to build their own data warehouse environments (Figure 2.6) in which click-stream is just one data source. These companies have the ability to use standard software, methodologies, and business intelligence (BI) tools (such as Brio, Business Objects, Cognos, and MicroStrategy) to slice and dice the data.

Having your own environment means that you have immense flexibility in terms of bringing in lots more sources of data (for example, event logs from your Flash or rich Internet applications, Google search data, metadata from other parts of the company, and CRM or phone channel data). This allows you to truly create an end-to-end (e2e) view of customer behavior and outcomes that can scale effectively over time. You can also use standard off-the-shelf tools, which can be a benefit.

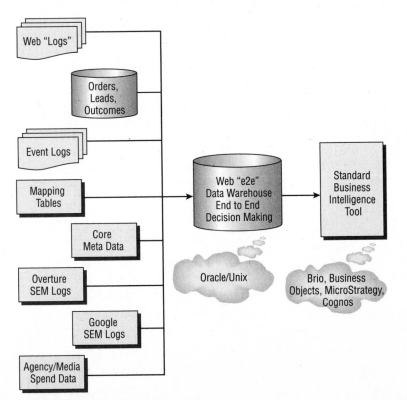

Figure 2.6 How a Web e2e data warehouse looks

Research Data

Chapter 1 discussed the need for understanding the *what* but also how amazingly powerful it can be to understand the *why*. It can make the difference between having lots of data that potentially raises a lot of questions and having access to data, even if small in size, that can act as a catalyst when it comes to enhancing your ability to take action. Capturing data to analyze the what was covered in the "Clickstream Data" and "Outcomes Data" sections of this chapter. Now its time for you to have a cohesive strategy to measure the why.

The core goal of measuring the why, or *qualitative analysis*, is to understand the rationale behind the metrics and trends that we see and to actively incorporate the voice of the customer (VOC) into our decision making. The following user-centric design (UCD) and human-computer interaction (HCI) methodologies are commonly used to understand the customer perspective:

- Surveys
- Heuristic evaluations
- Usability testing (lab and remote)
- Site visits (or follow-me-homes)

Although not a traditional UCD/HCI methodology, experimentation and testing (A/B, multivariate, or experience) increasingly falls into the research data category simply because it can often be the fastest way to answer a hypothesis we might form from quantitative analyses and get the customer perspective to validate or disprove that hypothesis.

Because it is absolutely critical to succeed in this arena, in Chapter 3 we will cover each research methodology and success strategies in great detail.

There are three aspects related to research data that need to be strategically planned when it comes to research data: mindset, organizational structure, and timing.

Mindset

Our industry, traditionally called *web analytics*, is seeped in clickstream and outcomes analysis. We believe that analysis of numbers will provide all the answers. There is a huge mindset challenge to convince all the "quant jocks" (up and down the management chain) to see the value of qualitative data, and perhaps most important, to start to think differently because analysis of research data poses completely different opportunities and challenges.

The recommended approach is to first internalize the value of qualitative data yourself. Then prove the value by actually doing the research and sharing findings—and do that a few times.

Organizational Structure

Most frequently the research team is either in a separate organization (closer to traditional market research or user research), or it is outsourced (typically to an agency or consulting company), or it simply does not exist. The action that needs to be taken in the last scenario is clear: create one. But in the other two it is less clear.

My recommendation is to have a web research team and to have the team members, researchers, sit with and work alongside the web analysis team. The rationale for this is that each of the two pieces separately add up to one and a half, but when they are together, it is a case of one plus one equals four. The qualitative team can benefit from the insights that the quantitative team can provide in order to focus their efforts and have a real-world connection to what is going on (at times researchers can get "disconnected" from the real world). The quantitative team can benefit from getting much closer to the customer and their perspective than was ever possible (no matter how much they use solutions from Omniture or WebTrends or Visual Sciences).

You will have to plan for having such an outcome-maximizing structure, sell it to your decision makers, and staff the team with the right leadership.

Timing

It is always hard for key company decision makers to know when is the best time to engage in research studies in order to maximize the learning potential. Some companies will conduct research on an ad hoc basis, others will do it prior to a big launch, and others when they find something interesting in the quantitative data.

I recommend that you have at least one *continuous listening* program in place. Usually the most effective mechanism for continuous listening, benchmarking, and trending is *surveying*. It is extremely cost-effective to use one of the many industry providers (such as ForeSee Results or iPerceptions) to implement surveying that is geared toward teasing out critical facts—such as why people come to your website, what their task completion rate is, whether they are satisfied, whether they are more or less likely to buy as a result of their website visit, what they would like fixed, and more.

The other methodologies fall into the noncontinuous listening categories (that is, they are deployed on an as-needed or periodic basis). You would use the best-fit methodology based on the following:

- Scope (both size and complexity) of the problem you are trying to solve (entire website, core segments of experience, particular pages, and so forth)
- Timing (whether you need it overnight or over the next few weeks)
- Number of participants (how many customers you would like feedback from)

- Business desire (before and after a site launch, at some random time, or based on external triggers, for example)

Although each methodology is unique, typically costs go up from heuristic evaluation to lab usability to site visits, and the opportunities for learning about your customers also increase in that order.

Competitive Data

The last data collection/analysis methodology is perhaps one of the most effective ways of gaining a strategic advantage.

It is pretty easy to celebrate success (or acknowledge failure) of our websites based on just the metrics from our web analytics tools (Google Analytics, ClickTracks, IndexTools, HBX, or others). But if our visitors are doing better year after year, is that great? Or if your return on investment (ROI) is up for your pay per click (PPC) campaigns, is that fantastic? Or if your revenue has increased 30 percent from last month, is that success? In each of these scenarios, the answer could be a whopping yes. But it is missing the critical *ecosystem context*: what is happening in the landscape that could have caused these outcomes vs. what you are causing?

It could be that visitors on the Web went up 70 percent in your category. Or perhaps your ROI increased because your competitor stopped their campaigns. Or your competitor's revenue increased 80 percent because of all those new visitors, but you could manage only 30 percent.

True delight comes from knowing how you are doing vis-a-vis your competitors or the industry as a whole. This *competitive intelligence* is key to helping you understand your performance in the context of the greater web ecosystem and allows you to better understand whether a certain result is caused by eco-system trends or your actions (or lack thereof). Having a focused competitive intelligence program (which can be all of half a person in reality) can help you exploit market trends, build off the success of your competitors, or help optimize your search engine marketing program—because you know exactly what your competitor is doing.

There are three main methodologies used to collect data that is then analyzed for competitive intelligence on the Web: panel-based measurement, ISP-based measurement, and search engine data.

Panel-Based Measurement

Panel-based measurement is very much inspired by traditional television Nielsen ratings systems, whereby in exchange for an incentive, the participant agrees to have their TV viewing behavior tracked. In that case, the individual tracks the programs, but for the Web this part can be automated.

A company called comScore NetWorks uses panel-based measurement to compile data that is used by many companies for competitive analysis. In exchange for an incentive (server-based virus protection or sweepstakes prizes), the panel member agrees to have all their web surfing activity monitored. comScore accomplishes this by installing monitoring software on the panel member's computer and then funneling 100 percent of the surfing via comScore's proxy servers. All the customer data (HTTP, HTTPS, PII, credit card, social security numbers, and so forth) are captured by comScore.

As of December 2006, comScore's global network is 2 million panelists (though the Media Matrix audience measurement is 120,000 US panelists, and Media Matrix Global services is 500,000 outside the United States).

Benefits of Using comScore (Panel-Based Measurement)

- comScore has in-depth browsing behavior data from their panel and hence the analysis they provide can go really deep in terms of website data.

- comScore can provide metrics such as conversion rates or purchasers. They monitor 100 percent of the traffic for their panel and they apply aggregations and sophisticated computations to approximate these metrics.

- comScore can break down some websites into deep embedded pages; for example, they can measure microsoft.com/office/avinash/information.html, a potential page that could be embedded deep into a directory and can't be tracked effectively by other methodologies.

- comScore can do more-custom work on your behalf because they have every page, HTTP or HTTPS, from their panel members and all the data associated with that panel member and their surfing habits.

Concerns about Using comScore (Panel-Based) Data

- There are approximately 200 million people on the Web in the United States and approximately another 700 million worldwide. Sample size could be a concern with comScore, since you are extrapolating the behavior of 200 million people from that of several hundred thousand.

- comScore offers incentives (virus protection, sweepstakes) that might appeal to a certain type of the Internet population, so sample bias could be an issue.

- Because comScore monitoring software is considered invasive (sometimes spyware) by corporations, it can't be installed in a work environment. This also inserts additional sample bias by not accounting for work surfing, which by many estimates accounts for more web usage (even for personal purposes) than home web usage.

- With most panel-based measurement systems, a small percentage of web users represent the general population. This means that for the most part a website with huge amounts of traffic might have reasonable numbers represented by the panel, whereas websites will smaller traffic (say less than a million visitors a month) would not be represented by accurate numbers.

Recommendation

comScore is most suited for decision making in *advertising*—for example, to determine the number of people on the panel who go to each site each month, and from which site to which site, and deeper site behavior (conversion). It is optimally suited for websites that get more than one million unique visitors per month.

ISP-Based Measurement

The second method of collecting data for competitive analysis uses anonymous data that is captured by various Internet Service Providers (ISPs). While all of us surf, all our data is funneling through the ISPs that we all use to connect to the Internet. Companies such as Hitwise have agreements with ISPs worldwide whereby the ISPs share the anonymous web log data collected on the ISP network with Hitwise. This data is analyzed by Hitwise. The data is further combined with a worldwide opt-in panel to produce demographic and lifestyle information.

According to Hitwise, the company has roughly 10 million US and 25 million worldwide users who provide data (as of December 2006).

Benefits of Using Hitwise (ISP-Based Measurement)

- The sample size is much bigger; this is a huge benefit.
- The basic data capture mechanism means they have a much more diverse pool of people providing data. Participants don't have to agree to have their anonymous data analyzed, and there is higher likelihood that the ISP-based measurement system covers a significantly more diverse set of surfing habits and a more diverse population.
- ISP-based methodologies such as those used by Hitwise also have much deeper and richer search engine traffic data.
- The psychographic (demographic, lifestyle) data Hitwise provides via the Prizm database is significantly better than self-reporting of such data.
- Hitwise has a lot more on-demand reporting available through their web access interface, which is very much amenable to self-service.

Concerns about Using Hitwise (ISP-Based Measurement)

- Hitwise data offers more breadth (websites, participants, search engines, and networks), but it does not go too deep into an individual website (deep pages on the website, insights into HTTPS sessions, and so forth). Hence it can't, yet, provide rich insights into behavior deep into a website.
- Conversion rate–type metrics are best obtained from services that use panel-based methodologies (such as comScore) because they capture every click for the sites the users on their panel use.

- There are certain types of PII data (payment types used or types of credit cards, for example) that can't be obtained from ISP-based methodologies.

Recommendation

Hitwise is most suited as a *marketing* tool: acquiring new customers, benchmarking performance, measuring search campaign effectiveness, and what competitors are doing. It can also be used on large websites as well as those that might have less than a millon unique visitors per month.

Search Engine Data

This is the newest kid on the blog and perhaps the most underutilized source of information about competitive behavior. As you can imagine, search engines collect massive amounts of data related to searches. They also often know information about their users (in the case of MSN, via the account information they have for Hotmail email or Passport / Windows Live ID login systems). Google and MSN have recently opened up lab/beta environments where they enable users to run queries against their databases to glean insights into competitive information.

On Google Trends (www.google.com/trends), you can enter one or more search phrases and Google will indicate the total number of searches done over time for those key phrases, the number of times the phrases have appeared in stories in Google News (it also shows the news story), and the top regions, cities, and languages for the search phrases you typed in. Figure 2.7 shows a Google Trends report.

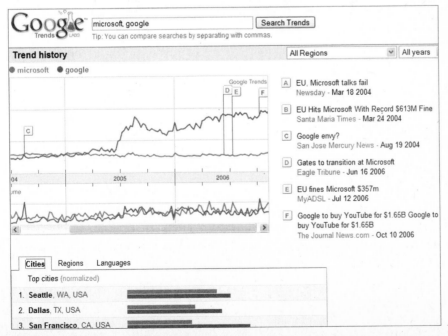

Figure 2.7 Google Trends report for keywords *Microsoft, Google*

On Microsoft adCenter Labs (`adlab.msn.com/demo.aspx`), you are able to do even better. You can predict any website user's age, gender, and other demographic information; do tons of analysis related to search keywords, such as keyword clustering, keyword forecast, search funnels (what people search for before and after they search for your keywords), and keywords expansion; and detect the commercial intent of visitors for any website (for example, are visitors to your website or your competitor's website more likely to buy?). Figure 2.8 shows the Microsoft adCenter Labs.

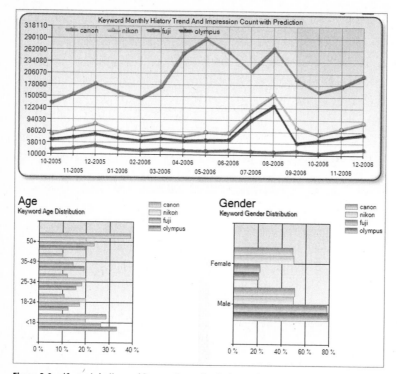

Figure 2.8 adCenter Labs Keyword Forecast Report for the keywords *Canon, Nikon, Fuji, Olympus*

Benefits of Using Search Engine Data

- Access to the data and analysis is completely free.

- Because most web surfers tend to use search engines, this data represents a huge number of web users.

- Search engines are a great source of detailed data related to keyword behavior (adCenter especially has some amazing tools you can leverage).

Concerns about Using Search Engine Data

- The amount of analysis you can do is limited and not close to what Hitwise or comScore can offer.

- The tools are still maturing and in a beta phase.

Recommendation

Search engine data, which is free, is perfectly suited for 1) learning lots and lots and lots about search engine keyword behavior and long-term trends 2) understanding the demographic profiles for your (or your competitor's) website visitors.

Overview of Qualitative Analysis

The prior two chapters have touched on the importance of understanding the why *behind customer behavior in addition to the* what. *You know the* what *from clickstream data that your favorite web analytics tool is reporting. Only by being aware of the* why *can you derive actionable insights around customer behavior on the website and outcomes from that behavior.*

Many of us in the traditional web analytics community do not have an optimal level of awareness of user research methodologies. In this chapter, I will go into great detail about a few of the most common methodologies to help improve your awareness of the options at your disposal and to show how you can best deploy them in your company.

The goal of this chapter is to empower web analysts to become more than passive observers because it is imperative that every successful web analytics program have a strong UCD component to it.

The Essence of Customer Centricity

From the most high-level perspective, *user research* is the science of observing and monitoring how we (and our customers) interact with everyday things such as websites or software or hardware, and to then draw conclusions about how to improve those customer experiences. Sometimes we do this in a lab environment (complete with one-way mirrors and cameras pointed at the participants), other times we do this in people's native environments (offices, homes, and so forth), and still other times we use surveys to monitor key metrics such as customer satisfaction and task completion rates.

The greatest benefit of user research is that it allows all of us to get really close to our customers and get a real-world feel for their needs, wants, and perceptions of interactions with our websites.

UCD methodologies represent the purest sense of customer centricity because they allow you to engage in a dialogue with your customers in a way that you can't when using other methodologies. The UCD methodologies outlined in this chapter empower you to reach a level of Why understanding that is missing from many other methodologies. They move you from talking the talk to being able to walk the walk when it comes to focusing your company/products/websites around customer centricity.

Lab Usability Testing

Lab usability tests measure a user's ability to complete tasks. Usability tests are best for optimizing User Interface (UI) designs and work flows, understanding the customer's voice, and understanding what customers really do. In a typical usability test, a user attempts to complete a task or set of tasks by using a website (or software or a product). Each of these tasks has a specified goal with effectiveness, efficiency, and satisfaction identified in a specified usage context.

A typical study will have eight to twelve participants. Early on during these tests, patterns begin to emerge with as few as five users that highlight which parts of the customer experience or process are working well and which are causing problems.

Lab tests are conducted by a user-centric design or human factors expert, who is typically supported by a note taker. Key stakeholders connected to the website (or product) participate as observers, and their job is to get a close understanding of the customer experience. Stakeholders can be business owners, engineers and developers, web analysts, product managers—anyone who has something to do with the website or customer experience.

Note: Tests can be conducted with a live version of the website, a beta version, an onscreen HTML or Microsoft Office PowerPoint prototype, or even with a paper printout. These paper prototypes, sometimes called wire-frames, approximate what a user might otherwise see on a computer screen, but save the development team from having to produce an onscreen product.

Usability tests are typically held in a specially designed room called a *usability lab*. The lab is split into two rooms that are divided by a one-way mirrored window that allows observers to watch the test without being seen by the test subject. However, you can conduct a usability lab without a lab. All you need is a room with a computer in it and a promise from all test observers that they will remain silent and out of the test subjects' sight (that is, behind them) throughout the test.

As the test subjects work on their tasks, a test moderator observes. The moderator takes notes about the user's actions, and records whether the participant is able to complete the task, in what length of time, and by taking what steps. While the participant is working at the task, the moderator limits their own interactions to providing initial task instructions and occasionally prompting the participant to further explain their comments.

For example, if the participant says, "that was easy," the moderator might say, "tell me more about that." This neutral prompt encourages the participant to explain what they thought happened, and why it worked well for them. Because moderators make nonjudgmental comments and do not assist, the participant is forced to use their own devices—as they would at home or in their office—to complete their task.

All the while the note taker is busy recording comments of the session and making note of the important points. Observers will do the same. Sometimes observers have the option of interacting with the moderator to ask the participant more questions or to clarify something. Often lab usability tests are also recorded on video for later review and to present to a larger audience in a company.

Usability tests are best for optimizing UI designs and work flows, understanding the voice of the customer, and understanding what customers really do.

Conducting a Test

There are four stages to completing a successful lab usability test: preparing, conducting the test, analyzing the data, and following up.

Preparing the Test

The main steps in the preparation phase are as follows:

1. Identify the critical tasks that you are testing for. (For example, for Amazon.com: How easy it is for our customers to return a product or request a replacement?)

2. For each task, create scenarios for the test participant. (For example: You ordered a Sony digital camera from us. When you got the box, it was missing a lens cap. You would like to contact Amazon for help. What do you do next?)

3. For each scenario, identify what success looks like. (For example: The user found the correct page, abc.html, on the support site, followed the link to the Contact Amazon web page, filled out a request, and clicked the Submit button.)

4. Identify who your test participants should be (new users, existing users, people who shop at competitors' sites, and so forth).

5. Identify a compensation structure for the participants.

6. Contact a recruiter, in your company or outside, to recruit the right people for you.

7. Do dry runs of the test with someone internal to the company just to make sure your scripts and other elements work fine. You'll find issues in these pilots that you can clean up before you do the real thing.

Conducting the Test

The rubber hits the road—you get to see real people! The main steps in this phase are as follows:

1. Welcome your participants and orient them to the environment. ("You are here at our company, and there is a mirror, and people are watching you, and we are recording this, and you can do no wrong, so don't worry.")

2. Starting with a "think aloud" exercise is a good idea. You want to "hear" what the participants are thinking, and this exercise will train them to "talk their thoughts." The main goal is to really understand and uncover the problems they will surely have.

3. Have the participants read the tasks aloud to ensure that they read the whole thing and understand the task or scenario.

4. Watch what the participants are doing and carefully observe their verbal and nonverbal clues so you can see where the participants fail in their tasks or if they misunderstand what your web pages say or if they go down the wrong path.

5. The moderator can ask the participants follow-up questions to get more clarity (but be careful not to give out answers and absolutely watch your own verbal and nonverbal clues so as to be as calm and reassuring as you can to the participant).

6. Thank the participants in the end and make sure to pay them right away.

Analyzing the Data

The main steps in this phase are as follows:

1. As soon as possible, hold a debriefing session with all the observers so that everyone can share their thoughts and observations.

2. Take time to note trends and patterns.

3. Do a deep dive analysis with a goal of identifying the root causes of failures based on actual observations. (For example: The FAQ answers on the website were too long. The Contact Us link was not apparent and hidden "below the fold." It was not clear that they could not contact us via phone. Or almost everyone complained that their expectations were not set about when to expect a reply.) The moderator is responsible for tallying successes and failures by each participant for each task.

4. Make recommendations to fix the problems identified. Usually you create a PowerPoint deck that collects all the scores. Then for each critical task identify the points of failure, make concrete recommendations that will improve the customer experience, and categorize the recommendations into Urgent, Important, and Nice to Have (to help business decision makers prioritize).

Following Up

The traditional role of UCD experts and researchers might end at the analysis step, but I feel that their role continues after the test result presentation. These experts and researchers can collaborate with business owners to help fix the problems and can offer their services and expertise to partner with website developers and designers to improve the site experience. This follow-up ensures that all their hard work gets translated into action and positive business outcomes.

> ### Tips on Conducting Lab Usability Tests
>
> Make sure you tell the participants that you are testing the website (or product or software) and not testing them. People tend to blame themselves a lot, so make sure to stress that they are not the problem and that the problem is not their fault.
>
> Don't rely on what people say; focus on their behavior because people often report experiences very different from how they experience them. It is amazing how many times I have observed a completely frustrating (or long) experience from a customer and in the end they rate it as a 4 out of 5. Some people are just nice, and our job is to make up for that by observing (I know that sort of sounds silly).
>
> Try not to answer participants' questions when they ask you how to do something. Try things like "tell me more" or "if this were the case at your home or office, what would you do next?"
>
> This point, which I stated earlier, bears repeating: Watch your body language to ensure that you are not giving participants any subtle clues.

Don't forget to measure success post-implementation. So we spent all the money on testing; what was the outcome? Did we make more money? Are customers satisfied? Do we have lower abandonment rates? The only way to keep funding going is to show a consistent track record of success that affects either the bottom line or customer satisfaction.

Benefits of Lab Usability Tests

- Lab tests are really great at getting close to a customer and really observing them, and even interacting with them. I realize this sounds like going to see an animal in a zoo, but the reality is that 99 percent of us will complete our employment with a company never having seen a real customer (and all the while we are supposed to be solving for them). This is an amazingly eye-opening experience for everyone involved (no matter how much you do it). Be prepared to be surprised.

- For complex experiences, lab tests can be a great way to get customer feedback early in the process to identify big problems early on and save time, money, energy, and sanity.

- For existing experiences, this is a great way to identify what is working and what is not—especially if you are completely stumped by your clickstream data (which happens a lot).

- It can be a great mechanism for generating ideas to solve customer problems. Not solutions—ideas.

Things to Watch For

- Twelve people do not a customer base make. Remember that it is just a representative sample of your customers and that the Hawthorne Effect (which asserts the idea that the mere act of observing or studying something can alter it) can change participant behavior. Don't jump to definitive world-changing opinions as a result of a lab test.

- With availability of complex testing methodologies on the Web, it is increasingly cheaper and faster to put tests in the real world and measure results. So if you want to try five versions of a page now with multivariate testing, you can try fifty versions and measure success very quickly. Before you do a test, see if you can simply throw it up on your real site and ask the million people who come to your site what they think.

- Avoid complex all-encompassing redesigns of websites or customer experience based purely on a lab test. You would be asking too much of the lab test; it is impossible to control for all the factors that are going to occur on your real website.

Besides, there is now a large body of work indicating that on the Web *revolutions* rarely work; *evolution* works when it comes to improving customer experiences.

- One of the best things you can do for your company is to not leave lab usability testing just to your UCD professionals (researchers). Pair them up with your web analysts. The latter will bring their real work data from their tools and what that data is saying, and the former will use that data to construct real tasks and to create good scenarios for each task. Both user researchers and web analysts can benefit tremendously from a close, sustained partnership (the ultimate combination of the qualitative and the quantitative).

Heuristic Evaluations

Here is a UCD/HCI methodology that is not only powerful in terms of how much it can tell you, but impressive in the kinds of amazing results that it can deliver. Without exception, it is my favorite methodology because it is cheap, it is fast, and you probably already have resources in your organization that can do this. Most of all, *heuristic evaluations* are going back to the basics to drive optimal customer experiences. Heuristic evaluations are sometimes also called *expert analysis*.

A *heuristic* is a rule of thumb. In as much, heuristic evaluations follow a set of well-established rules (best practices) in web design and in how website visitors experience websites and interact with them. When conducting a heuristic evaluation, a user researcher (or an HCI expert) acts as a website customer and attempts to complete a set of predetermined tasks (tasks related to the website's reason for existence—for example, trying to place an order, finding out an order's status, determining the price of a product, or finding the solution to error code xyz456 on your support website). In addition to the best practices, the user researcher will draw from their own experience of running usability studies and their general knowledge of standard design principles.

Heuristic evaluations can also be done in groups; people with key skills (such as designers, information architects, web analytics professionals, search experts, and so forth) all attempt to mimic the customer experience under the stewardship of the user researcher. The goal is to attempt to complete tasks on the website as a customer would. The great benefit of using a group heuristic evaluation method is that you can tap into the "wisdom of crowds." On the Web this is especially powerful because the Web is such an intensely personal medium and the group members can offer different points of view. In turn, the company benefits.

The process can be as simple as getting into a conference room and projecting the website on the screen and trying to complete the common customer tasks. Along the way, encourage discussion and pertinent feedback.

Heuristic evaluations are at their best when used to identify what parts of the customer experience are most broken on your website. They can also be very beneficial if you have not yet conducted usability tests (say, on your website) or you would like to have a quick review of prototypes that the designers might be considering. In either case, you can quickly determine the lowest hanging fruit in terms of "broken" parts of the customer experience. With this feedback there can be iterative improvements to the customer experience, potentially leading up to a full-blown usability test, or even a couple of live multivariate or A/B tests on the website to collect feedback from real customers.

Unlike a full usability test, a heuristic evaluation can provide valuable feedback at low cost and in a short amount of time (as little as hours) and can identify obvious usability problems. Heuristic evaluations are best for optimizing work flows, improving user interface design, and understanding the overall level of usability of the website.

However, like all rules of thumb, heuristic evaluations are not guaranteed to lead to correct answers, especially to subtle problems. Researchers leading the tests and the designers and other experts participating in the evaluation are still very close to the website. They are attempting to use best practices and their own wisdom, but they are not the customers. Hence heuristic evaluations are best at identifying the most obvious problems. They can provide critical input into narrowing the field from fifteen solutions to the five that can then undergo full usability or online experimentation and testing.

Conducting a Heuristic Evaluation

Now that you are hopefully all excited about leveraging heuristic evaluations for your website, here are the six steps to conducting a successful evaluation process:

1. Use primary research (surveys) or partner with the website owner to understand the core tasks that the customers are expected to complete on the website. Here are some examples of scenarios:

    - Find information about the top-selling product on the website.
    - Locate a store closest to where the customer lives.
    - Place an order on the website by using PayPal. (If the website doesn't accept PayPal, how easily and quickly can a customer find that out?)
    - Check the delivery status of an order placed on the website.
    - Successfully contact tech support via email.
    - Pick the right product for customer profile x (where x can be a small business owner or a family of four or someone who is allergic to peanuts).
    - Sign up for a company newsletter.

2. Next, establish success benchmarks for each task (for example: success rate for finding information about top selling product = 95 percent, locating a store = 80 percent, and so forth).

3. Walk through each task as a customer would and make note of the key findings in the experience—everything from how long it takes to complete the tasks, to how many steps it takes, to hurdles in accomplishing the tasks.

4. Make note of the specific rule violations against the best-practices checklist.

5. Create a report of your findings. The most common format used is PowerPoint with a screen shot of the web page and clear call-outs for issues found.

6. Categorize the recommendations into Urgent, Important, and Nice to Have, to help business decision makers prioritize. Recommendations should be made regardless of technical feasibility (don't worry about what can be implemented— you are representing the customer, and the IT team can figure out how to implement).

Sample Website Experience Best Practices

Here is a sample best-practices list for conducting heuristic evaluations. It seems simple, but you will be astounded at how even the most supposedly optimal websites break some of these rules.

General

1. Do not obstruct or compete with users' critical tasks.

2. Present elements related to specific tasks based on frequency, importance, or sequence.

3. Use buttons and links consistently. Always use the same label for the same function.

4. Pages should push no unexpected animation or sound at users.

5. Allow users to purchase without registering.

Page Layout

6. Lay out objects hierarchically to match the user's expected task flow: left to right or top to bottom. Most users start by scanning the content area.

7. Ensure manageable page lengths. Don't use scrolling on home pages and make sure interior pages are fewer than 2.5 screens.

8. Ensure that pages can be easily printed and that printing does not cut off critical information. If this is not practical, provide a printable version.

Visual Design

9. Avoid using color as the only source of important data.

10. Don't design critical information so it looks like advertising.

Navigation

11. Use persistent navigation to support frequent movement between tasks.

12. Don't force users to hover over something to see options.

Continues

Sample Website Experience Best Practices *(Continued)*

13. Link names should communicate the content of the page they link to. Avoid generic links such as Click Here and More.

14. Underline all links. Do not underline any other words. Everything clickable should have a roll-over effect.

15. Links should change color to indicate which links the user has visited.

Content

16. Use your users' vocabulary.

17. Write content that is bloat-free (short and simple), correct (spelling, grammar), in the active voice, and interesting.

18. Show price, or lack thereof.

19. Allow users to compare products side by side. Comparison tables should facilitate product differentiation.

Readability

20. Use 10-point font or larger for all text.

21. Maintain high contrast between background and text colors.

22. Use bulleted lists, introductory summaries, clear titles, and stand-alone chunks to facilitate scanning.

23. Use relative rather than fixed fonts.

Search

24. Display a Search box in the upper-right corner of every page.

25. Chunk search results into categories (for example, product information, support, press releases).

Sources: Nielsen/Norman, Human Factors International

Benefits of Heuristic Evaluations

- Heuristic evaluations are extremely fast to perform, with a very quick time to insights.

- They can leverage your existing resources in the company.

- They can identify the most egregious customer issues on your website (often all the low- and medium-hanging fruit).

- They can be used very effectively early in the website development process to find potential hurdles.
- They can reduce the cost of full usability tests by helping fix the obvious problems. Usability tests can then be focused on hidden or tougher challenges.

Things to Watch For

- Usually experts in the company (or from outside) lead heuristic evaluations and they use best practices and their own experience, but they are not our customers.
- When there is disagreement in recommendations from the heuristic evaluations, that can be great input for live web testing or usability tests.
- Heuristic evaluations are best for optimizing work flows, website design, and overall usability of the website.

Site Visits (Follow-Me-Home Studies)

Site visits, also often referred to as *follow-me-home studies*, are perhaps the best way to get as close to the customer's "native" environment as possible. In a site visit, user researchers, and often other key stakeholders, go to the home or office of the customer to observe them completing tasks in a real-world environment. You can observe customers interacting with websites in the midst of all the other distractions of their environment—for example, ringing phones, weird pop-up blockers, or office workers causing interruptions. This experience, as you can imagine, is very different from that of usability testing in a lab because the complicating environmental factors are not present in the lab.

Most often, site visits are conducted by visiting current or prospective customers at their workplaces or homes, as may be appropriate. The customers show us how they interact with our websites. This process is less like an interview and more like a training session, as the customers teach us how they accomplish tasks.

The goal is very much for the company employees to be avid observers of everything that is in front of them: the customer interacting with the website, the layout of the work space, behaviors exhibited by the customer, environmental variables that might affect the customer experience, whether website tasks require the customer to switch applications or look for paperwork.

Site visits can be entirely observational, or interactive—you can simply observe during the entire visit or you can ask questions or for more information or even answer questions that the customer might have. The industry best practice is that the most productive site visits have a mix of observational and interactive elements. However, 80 percent of the time should be spent in observational mode because from a macro-level perspective, we want the customer to teach us how they use the Internet and our websites and not for us to teach them how they should be using the site.

Successful site visits, like lab usability tests, also rely on active observation because customers' perceptions of the experience and the reality of the experience might often differ. Human beings are usually very forgiving, so someone could have a hard time finding what they want on the site but if asked to rate that experience might give it a 6 out of 10 (with 10 being the best), whereas our observation would give that experience a rating of 2.

Conducting a Site Visit

There are three stages to conducting a successful site visit: preparing, conducting the site visit, and analyzing the data. (Site visits usually do not include follow-up site visits, but instead the results are measured online.)

Preparing the Site Visit

The preparation steps for site visits share some steps with lab usability testing, though the protocols are slighter looser because the emphasis is on more open-ended learning. Please refer to the steps for preparing lab usability tests (steps one through six) that cover understanding of the customer experience, identification of critical tasks and test participants, and recruiting. The additional steps in the preparation phase are as follows:

1. Set your customer's expectations clearly. (For example: Indicate when you are going to arrive. Say that they should not change anything about the environment, that is, not to clean up or be concerned with having to look good. Say that you'll just be observing and maybe asking a question here or there.)

2. Assign the proper roles for your company employees up front (moderator—usually as user researcher, note takers, video person, and so forth).

3. Coordinate all facets of the visit with your team and show up on time.

Conducting the Site Visit

The exciting part—you get to see people! Here are the main steps:

1. Remember that 80 percent of your time should be spent observing during the site visit. Practice patience.

2. Ask your customers to show you what they do when you are not there. Watch your customers, listen to them, and look for verbal and nonverbal clues. Let them teach you—let them show you how they are solving their problems.

3. Think of your intents behind how you would solve the customers' problems and think of better ways of helping them as you see in the real world how they experience your website.

4. Don't teach or help the customers or provide them with tips and tricks.

5. The moderator can ask a few clarifying questions, but remember the 80-20 rule (80 percent observation).

6. During the visit, look for small details and be prepared to be surprised. Surprises are a good thing in this case because from them will emerge solutions that will make your company unique in how it solves customer challenges.

7. Thank the customers in the end and make sure to pay them right away.

Analyzing the Data

The following are the main steps of this phase:

1. As soon as possible, usually right after the site visit, hold a debriefing session for all the folks who participated in the site visit. The goal is to collect the freshest observations because even with a brief passage of time some of the subtle observations might be forgotten. Take extensive notes.

2. Use the team to identify the core themes among the observations. Categorize all the insights into similar groups. Be sure to use the examples, and document them, to illustrate the issues (looking at a video snippet of an actual customer struggling to complete a task, simple or complex, can be extremely powerful in its power to communicate).

3. In your analysis, focus on the surprises that you saw and the patterns that were repeated by different customers during your site visit.

4. Do a deep dive on your main themes and identify what the core root causes were for the failures based on actual observations.

5. Develop recommendations and action plans to address each issue. Use the team to prioritize the recommendations into Urgent, Important, and Nice to Have categories to help the decision-making process for actions.

6. Finally, develop a plan to measure success post-implementation. This could be done via follow-up site visits, testing on the website, increased sales or revenues, or customer satisfaction.

Benefits of Site Visits

- Site visits allow us to understand how customers accomplish their goals in the real world, with all the distractions and other environmental variables.

- Site visits are perhaps the only UCD methodology that allows us to have a true dialogue with your customers, glean powerful insights into their experiences (or needs or wants), and get all our Why questions answered in a very direct manner.

- Site visits are especially powerful for gathering information about user requirements, understanding customer problems, and for identifying new and different ways of meeting customer requirements.

- Site visits can be most powerful to the company employees who are usually deep in the trenches: website developers, quality assurance (QA), architects, web analysts—folks who as a part of their day-to-day work obligations rarely have the opportunity to interact with real customers directly.

Things to Watch For

- It is difficult to find and visit with as many customers as would be optimal. One has to always balance for geographic locations and costs.

- It can be a challenge to find the most representative current customers or new prospective customers.

- Site visits, because of the very nature of the methodology, can be time-consuming. They do provide a very rich set of data, but it can take time to go through the entire process with a set of representative customers and pull together the analysis and recommendations.

Surveys (Questionnaires)

Surveys are both the most used of the UCD methods and perhaps the least appreciated in terms of their value. They are the optimal method for collecting feedback from a very large number of customers (participants) relatively inexpensively and quickly. The law of large numbers means that conclusions based on survey data, if done right, will be more accurate and reliable and provide insights and conclusions that help us better understand customer perspectives.

Surveys can be a great complement to other traditional UCD methodologies. They can also be extremely beneficial in filling the "holes" we frequently find in our clickstream analysis. Often clickstream data does not really help us understand the complete picture. For example, for most websites 40 to 50 percent of the referring URLs are blank (have no value). In that case, we presume that those represent visitors who have bookmarked us. But the blank URLs could also be caused by wrong redirects or browser security settings or something weird in the links to your website. You could simply ask your customers in a survey, "How did you find our website today?" This is just a simple example of surveys filling clickstream holes.

There are many types of surveys that you can do and they can be used on the Web for various purposes. There are two prevalent types of surveys: website and post-visit.

Website Surveys

Website surveys are served on the website and are triggered by some rules (on exit, on meeting a certain page-view criteria, or by the customer clicking on a link, and so forth). These surveys pop up or pop under.

Website surveys can be an optimal way to capture the customers' freshest thoughts, usually about the experience of the site, and to get more context about the customer's visit. Website surveys are triggered by automated pop-ups or via clicking a text link (for example, Rate This Page, Give Feedback on This Page, or Comments). Automated pop-ups are considered *site-level surveys*. Surveys requiring the customer to proactively click a link (or an image) to initiate the surveys are called *page-level surveys*.

Site-level surveys are best at helping you understand the holistic customer experience on the website. These surveys cover important facets of the experience, such as product information, website performance, price and transaction costs, internal site search performance, problem resolution rates, and likelihood to buy or recommend. They are very insightful for understanding reasons for visiting and key drivers of customer satisfaction, and for identifying macro-problems with the website experience. They are also particularly good for obtaining open-ended comments (voice of the customer) that are chock full of insights. Site-level surveys will not provide narrow page-level details; rather they allow you to identify macro-factors that influence your customer website experience.

Page-level surveys are best at asking questions about and helping you to understand the performance of individual pages. They are usually much shorter than site-level surveys and aim to collect satisfaction rates or task-completion rates in the narrow context of a page. One scenario where page-level surveys are optimal is on a support website. Most support websites are a collection of knowledge base articles or FAQs. In this case, we really do want to know exactly what our customers think of every single article/FAQ and we want them to tell us if we need to improve the page to solve their problems. Feedback collected on individual pages might not paint a story for the website experience, but it can be used to immediately fix pages with suboptimal ratings. Page-level surveys are initiated by the customer taking an action (clicking a link or a floating image) and due consideration needs to be given to any sample bias that might occur.

Vendors of either type of website survey might say that these surveys can be used interchangeably, or that they can do a page-level survey but provide site-level feedback and vice versa. This claim needs to be taken with a grain of salt. The core mechanisms of how each works usually mean that each type of survey is good at the one it does. Carefully evaluate your business needs and then—equally carefully—choose the website survey methodology that best fits those needs.

Post-Visit Surveys

Post-visit surveys are sent, usually via email, to invite feedback from customers after their experience on the website has been concluded. These surveys are optimal at capturing feedback on follow-up items after a site visit. Examples of these include checking on successful completion of a download version of the product, asking whether a problem was resolved after visiting the support site, or requesting feedback on the order placement process.

Post-visit surveys are usually shorter and much more targeted than website surveys, and are geared toward measuring a slice of the experience. They can't replace website surveys because of the ability of website surveys to capture feedback when it is freshest in the minds of the website visitors, but post-visit surveys can be a great complement to them.

Creating and Running a Survey

There are four stages to creating and implementing a robust survey on your website: preparing the survey, conducting the survey, analyzing the data, and following up.

Preparing the Survey

The main steps in the preparation phase are as follows:

1. You have heard this often, but business objectives are key. Partner with your key decision makers to understand the purpose of the website, the core tasks that the customers are expected to complete on the website, the core elements of the customer experience on the website (product information, internal search, demos, support FAQs, navigation, pricing and promotions, and so forth), and the critical few questions that the company decision makers want answers to.

2. Analyze the clickstream data to understand the main holes in the data that you would like to have answers to. Look at your reports and analysis. What kinds of questions can't you answer from those examples?

3. Ask your vendor to share best practices and tips regarding questions, framing, content, rating scale, survey length, and more.

4. Create the model for the survey that you will be using. Keep in mind these few tips when it comes to constructing questions:

   - The customer should be motivated and be able to answer each question.

   - The customer should be able to easily understand what you are asking.

   - Surveys must be written in the language of your customers (a quick tip is to use language and words that a seventh-grade student can understand and respond to).

   - If a customer has to read a question more than once, the question is too confusing. Avoid long questions with multiple parts or too many examples.

   - Avoid leading questions.

   - As much as possible, use the same response structure for all the questions. The customer should not have to learn a new scale with every question.

Conducting the Survey

The main steps in this phase are as follows:

1. Partner with your vendor and technical team to ensure that the survey is implemented correctly, that your privacy policy is updated on the website if needed, and you have validated that the right metadata (cookie values, and so forth) are being passed through the survey.

2. It is important to have a surveying mechanism that incorporates cookies, or other such technologies, to ensure that you don't spam your customers with too many surveys. Most vendors will now detect that the customer might have already seen the survey, and those customers will not see another survey for 60 to 90 days.

3. If you are doing post-visit surveys, it is important to incorporate clearly visible unsubscribe links so that the customers can opt out easily. Use email subject lines that are least likely to get caught by spam filters.

4. It is important to walk through the customer experience yourself to be aware of exactly how the customers are getting the survey, whether it is showing up in the wrong places, and so forth.

5. Keep a close eye on your daily or weekly (as the case may be) response rates to pick up any problems that might be occurring.

Analyzing the Data

This is the wonderful stage when you get a shot at gleaning key insights:

- It is important to have both an ongoing pulse on the survey responses so they can easily be accessed by the key decision makers and an opportunity to do an in-depth review of all the data that you are collecting (say, twice a month or monthly).

- With most surveys, trends are more important than one-time responses, not only to help gain context around performance but also to isolate anomalies in the data.

- Segmentation is key, as in all analysis. Aggregated numbers will mask issues, so segment the data as much as possible. For example, you can segment by type of respondent, by time, by products purchased, by pages visited, by frequency of visit, or by source arrived from.

- It is important to pair up quantitative and qualitative skills to analyze the data, either in the same person or in two different people. A lot of complex math goes into analyzing the answers, and core UCD skills are required to analyze the open-ended responses.

- Provide a clear set of recommendations for improving the website experience along with all the analysis to increase the likelihood that action will be taken. (In addition, as much as possible tie your recommendation to a metric that affects the bottom line, such as improved customer satisfaction, revenue, or call avoidance).

Following Up

The role of analysts (researchers or web analysts) continues in this stage of the process. Because they are now perhaps the most informed about the data and customer experience, it is imperative that they partner with business owners, website designers, and user experience and information architects (whatever resources you have in your team) to drive action.

Often the follow-up will take the shape of outright changes to the website. Other times it will funnel ideas into the A/B or multivariate tests that you will run. Still other times the recommendations will be put into new versions of the website.

It is important to close the loop from data to action and measuring again to ensure that surveying does not become a mechanism that simply exists for the sake of it.

Tips on Creating and Launching Surveys

It is easy to launch a survey on your website, but in order to maximize your learnings from the survey here are a few important tips / considerations:

Correlations Rule!

One of the biggest reasons surveys fail to drive action, or to drive the right action, is that they are missing a deeply critical facet of measurement. Almost all surveys ask discrete questions and ask customers to provide ratings. But very few attempt to compute correlations between the ratings and an outcome.

So we always ask, "How do you feel about…? "But what we also need to ask (and then compute) is, "How much do you value…?" For example, we can ask these three questions and ask for ratings on a scale of 1 to 10, with 10 being the best:

- Was the product information sufficient and relevant? Answer: 6

- Was the transaction cost of the products appropriate? Answer: 1

- Were you satisfied with the website experience? Answer: 5

With just these answers, you might be tempted to figure out how to give free shipping or coupons on the website. But by computing correlations (by applying statistical multivariate regression), you might find out that that correlation between the first and third question is 4.5 (on a 5-point scale), and the correlation between the second and third question is 1.5. In this case, working on transaction costs would be the wrong action. What the customer values more is product information (yes, price is not always king on the World Wide Web!).

Tips on Creating and Launching Surveys *(Continued)*

Survey Triggers

There are a lot of preconceived notions about when to trigger a survey. Some people believe that you should not interrupt the customer experience, so no pop-ups. Others will say let's interrupt the customer as soon as they get to our website and ask for their feedback. Others will say let's show the survey when the customer exits the website.

There is no golden rule for having the right trigger to show the survey. Depending on what you are solving for, it might make sense to interrupt or not, or do an exit (or even a post-visit) survey. Understand what you are trying to learn, and then experiment with a couple of methodologies to find out what works best for you.

Survey Length

Similar to the trigger issue, there is also the contentious issue of how long the survey should be. The golden rule here is to keep the survey as short as possible. Obviously, you will have to make the trade-off here of what you want to learn vs. the response rate. The interesting fact is that if propositioned correctly and structured optimally, even surveys with as many as 20 questions can get a very good response rate. Humans are social and they want to talk and give you feedback.

It is important that you experiment and come up with the right number of questions for you and your customers (because you are unique). The general response rate for surveys on the Web is about 1 to 2 percent. Optimally you want to shoot for 4 percent or higher and you'll do just great.

Survey-Completion Incentives

There is no beating around the bush on this one. For most website or post-visit surveys, the best practice is not to provide incentives. Customers want to share their experiences on your website and let you know how you can improve it for them. Incentives usually skew the data because the incentive becomes the motivation, and this usually reduces the quality of the data. It is also harder to detect the pollution in the data. If you don't have enough respondents, try to optimize the questions, structure, and triggers. Consider incentives only as a last resort.

Benefits of Surveys

- Surveys are extremely cost-effective and provide insights at a very rapid pace (compared to other UCD methodologies).
- We can benefit more from the voices of a huge number of website visitors as compared to the eight or ten participants we might have in other studies.

- Surveys work very well at filling gaps in our understanding from clickstream analysis by providing reasons for customer behavior. They are also extremely effective at capturing the voice of the customer via open-response questions.

- They are very helpful in shifting the mindset of website owners beyond simply "let's solve for conversion rate" by providing a good understanding of all of the reasons customers come to the website and of the challenges they are having (beyond simply hitting the Add To Cart button).

- Like clickstream data, surveys can be a continuous measurement methodology.

Things to Watch For

- It is critical to ensure that you reduce the sampling bias as much as possible and that you use statistically significant samples of data.

- Remember that customers won't provide solutions. They simply highlight their problems, and it is up to us to review the problems and suggest solutions (hopefully by doing A/B or multivariate testing).

- We all bring our own biases to the table when it comes to the survey (every facet of it). No survey is perfect, and we usually don't represent customers very well. It is important to test and validate customer preferences to ensure optimal survey completion rates.

- Survey analysis might seem very straightforward (as in "lets take the average of the responses and that's the score,") but accurate analysis can be quite challenging, with hidden pitfalls. Ultimately it is only as good as the professionals analyzing the data.

Best Practices for Survey Success

Here are six best practices that will ensure awesome success for your company's surveying efforts:

Partner with an Expert

Surveys are extremely easy to do (just buy a $19.95 per month license—easy to find via any web search) and even easier to get wrong. Surveying is maybe 20 percent art and 80 percent science. If possible, partner with an outside company that can bring a full complement of expertise to the table. This has two great benefits:

- You have to do less work—can't beat that. You don't have to create questions, you don't have to master complex computations (often advanced statistics), you can benefit from best practices, and all you have to bring to the table is your knowledge of your business.

- You can stay focused on value-added analysis rather than in distracting and time-consuming tactical work.

Best Practices for Survey Success *(Continued)*

Benchmark against Industry

Perhaps the single biggest reason that senior decision makers don't take action on survey recommendations is that they don't have context. We run our survey, we measure questions on a scale of 10 or 100, and we provide a rating. Question: Do you like our website? Answer: 7 out of 10. Now is that great? Is that bad?

External benchmarks are great because they give context, and they shame us (when we are below the benchmark) or give us joy and pride (when we beat the benchmark). But most of all they drive action.

The American Customer Satisfaction Index (ACSI) is one such benchmark. The index measures half of the US economy, and its various indices form an awesome global benchmark (available for free at www.theacsi.org). You can visit the website to check the scores for the performance of your industry and some of your competitors. You can compare yourself for aggregate customer satisfaction but also for future predictive behavior (for example, likelihood to recommend the website).

Another company that is developing its own methodology and benchmarks by industry is iPerceptions. They have developed benchmarks for hospitality, auto, media, financial services, retail, and business to business (B2B) industries. iPerceptions also has a great built-in slice-and-dice framework to "play" with data to find insights.

Gain Insights from the Customer Voice

Any good survey consists mostly of questions that respondents rate on a scale, and sometimes a question or two that is open-ended. This leads to a proportional amount of attention being paid during analysis on computing averages and medians and totals. The greatest nuggets of insights are in open-ended questions because it they represent the voice of the customer speaking directly to you. Ask questions such as, "What task were you not able to complete today on our website? If you came to purchase but did not, why not?"

Use quantitative analysis to find pockets of customer discontent, but read the open-ended responses to add color to the numbers. Remember, your directors and vice presidents (VPs) can argue with numbers and brush them aside, but few can ignore the actual words of our customers. Deploy this weapon.

Target Survey Participants Carefully

Randomness is perhaps the most commonly used tactic in inviting customers to take a survey. I believe that is suboptimal in many cases. When trying to understand what people think, I have come to believe that surveying people who have had the chance to engage with the site is best. It shows a commitment on their part, and we will get better-quality answers.

For example, look at your clickstream data, find the average page views per visitor, and then set a trigger for just under that number. The aim is to capture most survey respondents before an average visitor would exit. You'll get some that stay longer—that's a bonus—but you will show the

Continues

Best Practices for Survey Success *(Continued)*

survey to the visitors who have actually had a chance to experience your website. Hence they can give you feedback that will be most relevant.

You also don't have to spam everyone with a survey. Usually 1,100 to 1,400 survey responses are statistically significant (even if you slice and dice it into small pieces). So for most high-traffic websites, if the survey is shown to about 3 to 5 percent of visitors who meet our criteria and if we get a 5 percent response rate, that would easily meet the number we need. The great thing about this is that you will only "bother" a very small percent of your site visitors.

Integrate with Clickstream Data

You can turbocharge your survey analysis if you can figure out how to tie your survey responses to your clickstream data. If your survey technology vendor is a good one, they will accept external variables that you can pass into the survey. Simply pass the 100 percent anonymous `unique_ cookie_id` and a `session_id` (or equivalent values from your website platform). These two values are also being captured in your clickstream data.

When you do find interesting groups of responses (customer segments) in your survey response, you can go back and put those anonymous `unique_cookie_ids` and `session_ids` into your clickstream tool and see the referring URLs of these unhappy people, where they clicked, what pages they saw, where they exited, and so forth.

Use Continual, Not Discrete, Surveys

Most surveys are done as a pulse read: we have a thought in mind, a question we want answered, or a project we are doing, and we conduct a survey. That is great. But surveys can be hugely powerful as a continual and ongoing measurement system.

Having surveys continually deployed on your website means that you will always have your finger on the pulse of your visitors. More important, it means that you can account for seasonality, external influences (such as press releases or company events), marketing campaigns, sudden blog buzz, and more—all factors that can result in a discrete measure in time not being the cleanest read.

Advanced surveying technologies are now quite affordable, especially after you consider how much revenue your website is making or how many customers are being upset by a suboptimal support experience and picking up the phone to call you. Other than clickstream data, surveying is perhaps the cheapest continual method. None of the other usability methodologies can even come close (either in their cost or in the number of customers you can hear from).

Summary

Understanding the "Why" is critical to gleaning actionable insights from your web data. Table 3.1 provides a handy matrix that you can use to choose the right qualitative methodology for the unique needs of your company.

▶ Table 3.1 Web qualitative methodologies: Decision Making Matrix

Methodology	Listening Type	Time Commitment	Cost	Customers Responding	Depth of Insight	Must Have?	Best Application
Lab Usability Testing	Discrete	High	High	8–12	Medium	Depends	Testing new customer experience improvements and new prototypes
Heuristic Evaluations (or Expert Analysis)	Discrete	Low	Low	None	Medium	Yes	Quick identification of low-hanging fruit and obvious barriers to successful completion of customer tasks
Site Visits (or Follow-Me-Home Studies)	Discrete	High	High	5–15	High	Depends	In-depth understanding of customers, their environments, and nonobvious challenges
Surveys (Questionnaires)	Continual	Medium	Low	Hundreds	Medium	Yes	Understanding why customers are there, what they are trying to do, what the barriers are to task completion

Critical Components of a Successful Web Analytics Strategy?

Most people are introduced to web analytics via reports coming out of a web log parser, Google Analytics, or maybe one of the high-end tools. We look at the massive number of reports and try to make sense of them. Web analytics, though, is rather complex, and it is always optimal to step back from the tools and reports and first understand the basics.

This chapter discusses basics that are one abstract level higher than the fundamentals of reports and data (which are discussed in the next chapter). These critical components make up the vision for what the core web analytics approach should be. This requires you to start with the right mindset, use the *business questions* method, and follow the 10/90 rule. You'll need to find the right people to support the 10/90 rule and determine how those people should be organized in your company.

These concepts are indeed critical; most dissections of unsuccessful web analytics programs would identify the root cause for failure to be the topics discussed in this chapter. The first thing to check is that your web analytics approach has the critical components outlined here done right.

Focus on Customer Centricity

After the first euphoria (and it truly is that) of getting metrics and reports out of the website subsides, the natural, if improper, inclination of any web business is to step back a little and ask, "What is the website doing for my company?"

This results in a flurry of new work (identification of key performance indicators, or KPIs, new reports, more horsepower deployed, and so forth). All of this essentially overemphasizes measuring clickstream data and attempts to figure out the effect of the website on the bottom line. Measuring this effect is a nontrivial challenge (and it's the primary reason that most web analysts lose their hair earlier than the rest of the population and, with the responsibility for Web Analysis falling in the marketing function, that CMOs have such a transitional existence in their jobs).

There are two complicating factors that lead to less than stellar success after hacking at clickstream data. First, there is a lot of data beyond clickstream (this was discussed in detail in Chapter 2, "Data Collection—Importance and Options"). Second, the customer is largely missing from that approach.

There are few websites, even if they are hard-core e-commerce sites, where all the visitors come to buy (or to submit their contact information to you in form of a lead or for tech support self-service). Take your own e-commerce website as an example. Measuring its primary purpose (by asking customers, "Why are you here today?") will illustrate that a minority of the website traffic comes to purchase—usually about 15–25 percent of the traffic at best. The rest of the traffic comes to research, look for jobs, check on their order status, email complaints, check prices, learn more about the company, download images or other data, and on and on. The majority does not come to buy.

Our current web analytics tools can help us measure performance of our websites on a limited few of these metrics. If you are currently focused on answering the question of how the website is delivering for the company, then it is extremely likely that you are measuring performance of your site to deliver for a minority (less than 50 percent) of your site traffic. In some cases the drive to somehow measure success with clickstream data can lead to suboptimal leaps of faith, which in turn create an illusion of measuring success when in reality nothing much exists there.

Consider page views as an example. Every tool out there measures page views, and we have come to rely on page views to be the proxy for many different things. For example, page views represent the "health" of the website in the sense that more page views means that the site is performing well technically. Page views have also come to be a proxy for engagement; if we have lots of page views, the website is performing well because customers are *engaging* with the website. Page views have come to represent success as we break the website into discrete chunks (home page, product pages, cart, demos, and so forth) and compute success if enough people make it to product pages (just as an example).

But if you pause and think for a moment, a page view is a page view; it is just a viewed page. Nothing more, nothing less.

The fact that in a session a page was viewed is not an indicator of success (unless the page is a Thank You page that a customer views after placing an order or submitting a lead). There is no way to know whether the customer met their objective after viewing a page simply based on the fact that they clicked and arrived at a page (and that is all you have to go by in clickstream data).

Using metrics such as page views to measure success from clickstream data is one of the reasons that most companies discover after three, six, twelve, or twenty-four months of web analytics that they have not really managed to have a bottom-line impact (and often are frustrated that "reports are not telling them anything"). It bears repeating that a page view is simply a viewed page.

It is critical for near-long-term success and for long-term success that at the heart of your web analytics program you are asking not what the website is doing for your company, but this question: *How is the website doing in terms of delivering for the customer?*

Measuring how your website is delivering for your customers will help focus your web analytics program and cause you to radically rethink the metrics that you needs to measure to rate performance of the website. It means new metrics, approaches, tools, and people. Consider the reasons the website exists (to sell products and services, to support existing customers by providing self-help options, to collect job applications, to create a brand experience, to collect leads for potential future sales, to influence sales via other channels, to provide information to customers, employees, shareholders, and so on).

If you consider these reasons from a customer perspective and not from a business perspective, you can easily see how the metrics measured would be radically different.

A focus on measuring how the website is delivering for your company typically encourages a short-term mindset ("let's force-convert everyone right now"—making money sounds good). Solving for your customer's needs encourages a long-term mindset and in turn long-term success. The latter calls for a lot more caring about (hence measuring) what the customer wants in this instant and solving for that with the assumption (a sane assumption) that it will naturally result in solving for the company in the long term (a sale later, a submitted lead, a support call avoided, and so forth).

It is important not to underestimate the challenge of moving from a company (short-term) focus to a customer (long-term) focus. It is extremely hard for most company employees to pull off (the mindsets are more entrenched the higher up you go in an organization). Most compensation models and reward systems are geared toward rewarding short-term success and getting one more website visitor converted. You will have to work hard to prove the corny, but utterly true, notion that if you solve for your customers, you will solve for your company as well.

The greatest benefit of this mindset shift to you personally is that you will be able to move your measurement options beyond clickstream analysis into deeper outcomes and qualitative analysis, both of which are guaranteed to produce more actionable insights to solve the customer's problems. You will look like a superstar for having provided those insights, and the company will win by creating more-satisfied customers.

The Trinity approach to web analytics (outlined in Chapter 1, "Web Analytics—Present and Future") is rooted in bringing customer centricity to your analytics strategy. The Trinity places a huge emphasis on measuring all facets of customer experience to deeply understand why customers come to your website and how the website is doing in terms of solving their problems.

A business that has implemented the Trinity strategy will have the following metrics to help them understand how they are doing in terms of delivering for customers:

- Primary purpose (Why are you here?)

- Task completion rates (Were you able to complete your task?)

- Content and structural gaps (How can we improve your experience?)

- Customer satisfaction (Did we blow your socks off as a result of your experience today?)

In the Trinity approach, these metrics can be directly correlated to and lead to such obvious behavior and outcome metrics as the following:

- Bounce rates (Can the customers quickly find what they are looking for?)

- Conversion rates (Are those who come to buy able to accomplish that task?)

- Revenue (Is revenue in line with our goals for the websites?)
- Multichannel impact (Are we funneling more customers to our retail partners or our phone channel?)

Customer centricity is not just a buzz phrase; it is a mindset that when executed can create a sustainable competitive advantage for your company.

Solve for Business Questions

Every business is unique, and every website is unique. Even if you completely copy and paste someone else's website or business and start executing, you are probably unique in terms of the individuals you have collected around you and how they work together. Or perhaps while you sell via the retail channel like everyone else, your strategy is different in its focus on driving purchases through the Web or the box store. Or perhaps you have embraced Web 2.0 completely while the others are "stuck on" Web 1.0. Or perhaps you are solving for customer satisfaction, and your competitors are solving for conversion rate.

If you are unique, why should you crack open a standard analytics tool with its standard reports and metrics and get going? Instead, before you start the journey of web analytics (or indeed any decision-making system), stop to ask the business what questions they want answered.

This is of course easier said than done. Typically what you will hear is, I want to know how much traffic is coming to our website, or I want a conversion rate, or I want a path analysis for our visitors, or I want to know what pages are most popular on the website, or I want to know how many leads we have received on our website, or give me a report that shows click-through rates of our home page promotions.

These are all requests for reports; they are not business questions. What we want to do is refocus the discussion and increase the likelihood that you can be something more than a report writer. I recommend that you go back to your key stakeholders (the higher up in the organization, the better) and ask them politely what real business questions they are grappling with that you can help answer.

Business questions have these three characteristics:

- They are usually open-ended and at a much higher level, leaving you room to think and add value.
- They likely require you to go outside your current systems and sources to look for data and guidance in order to measure success.
- They rarely include columns and rows into which you can plunk data you already have.

Here are some examples of solid business questions:

- How can I improve revenue by 15 percent in the next three months from our website?

- What are the most productive inbound traffic streams and which sources are we missing?

- Have we gotten better at allowing our customers to solve their problems via self-help on the website rather than our customers feeling like they have to call us?

- What is the impact of our website on our phone channel?

- How can I increase the number of customer evangelists by leveraging our website?

- What are the most influential buckets of content on our website?

- Are we building brand value on our website?

- Do fully featured trials or Flash demos work better on the website?

- What are the top five problems our customers face on our website?

- What is the cost for us to earn $1.00 on our website?

- What is the effect of our website on our offline sales?

You will run into other business questions that might be more pertinent to your business. But the theme that you are looking for is tough, highest-level business problems that you can help solve by analyzing the data you have (or data you don't have but will figure out how to get).

For the longest time, especially in the web analytics world, we have been content to do one of two things:

- Provide the data we have in our applications in the hope that in the deluge of visitors, page views, referring URLs, time on site, and exit pages, there is something that marketers and business stakeholders will find of interest and take action on.

- Take requests for reports, create them, and figure out how to email them or publish them on the intranet.

Reality is rather messier as a result of this. The business feels frustrated that they are not getting insights that they can act on, and it can't be easy being a senior analyst reduced to running reports. Hence the most important foundational element of any effective web analytics program is to ask real business questions, understand those business questions, and have the freedom to do what it takes to find answers to those questions.

So if you are the business honcho, bare your soul and share the questions that keep you up at night or the factors that you think are required to go out and win against your competitors (again these are not reports you want). If you are the underling, provide the reports that are being asked of you (sadly, you can't avoid that because you are not yet that important), but all the while seek to get a peek into the said soul and understand the strategic questions that the business wants answered. When you learn what the questions are, go get answers, one at a time. All other rules apply (do your best, focus, segment the data, and make leaps of faith in data), but in the end you will be on your way to truly adding value to your company.

Start the process of working with business questions early on—well before you have a web analytics tool, well before you know what the site is or what it does. You'll be on your way to great glory.

Identifying business questions is a journey. As you solve one set, the next will come up. Or you may be in the middle of solving one set, and suddenly that set will become irrelevant and there will be a new set. This evolution and change is a sign that you are actually answering business questions and not just doing reporting, because business is always evolving and changing and you have to simply learn to change with it.

Follow the 10/90 Rule

Numerous studies have pointed out that although almost all Fortune 500 companies have great investments in web analytics, they still struggle to make any meaningful business decisions. Most people complain that there are terabytes of data, gigabytes of reports, and megabytes of Excel and PowerPoint files—yet no actionable insights, no innate awareness of what is really going on through the clutter of site clickstream data. To resolve this problem, I have developed a simple 10/90 rule: 10 percent of the budget should be spent on tools, and 90 percent spent on people (brains) who will be responsible for insights. This speaks to the obvious secret of web analytics success: it's the people, not the tools and cool technology.

The rule works quite simply. If you are paying your web analytics vendor (for example, Omniture, WebTrends, ClickTracks, Coremetrics, or HBX (now owned by WebSideStory) $25,000 for an annual contract, you need to invest $225,000 in people to extract value from that data. If you are paying your vendor $225,000 each year, well, you can do the math.

On the surface, this might sound a bit too simplistic. After all, current web analytics tools have a range of prices, and a really high-end tool can cost up to half a million dollars a year. Here are some of the reasons why I have come to formulate this rule:

- If your website has more than 100 pages and you get more than 10,000 visitors a month, you can imagine the complexity of the interactions that are happening with your website. If you have a drop in marketing campaigns, a dynamic site, search engine marketing (SEM), more pages, more traffic, or promotions and offers, you have a very tough situation to understand by any stretch of the imagination.

- Most web analytics tools will spew out data like there is no tomorrow. We seem to be in a rat race; one vendor says I can provide 100 reports, the next says 250, and the one after that says I can measure the eye color of people who look at your web pages. The bottom line is that it will take a lot of intelligence to figure out what is real in all this data, what is distracting, what is outright fake, and what, if anything, in the canned reports is even remotely meaningful.

- It is a given that most web analytics tools show the exact same metrics. One fact that remains a bit hidden is that almost all of these "standard metrics" are measured and computed differently by each vendor! You are going to have to sort this out.

- The Web changes at a pace that is almost unimaginable. New things pop up each day. You have just gotten the handle on static pages, and here are dynamic pages. You have just gotten on top of measuring dynamic pages, and here are rich interactive applications, and and right around the corner Web 2.0 measurement awaits. Typically, web analytics vendors are slightly behind the curve in providing solutions. In their absence, you are going to have to do it yourself (or stay behind).

- Finally, actionable web insights or key insights analysis (KIA) does not come simply from clickstream data. You will need people who are smart and have business acumen, who can tie clickstream behavior to other sources of information.

All of these reasons are rarely thought of when we put money down on a web analytics application and ask for success in return. Providing a part-time person or your IT Admin access to your favorite expensive analytics tool can't help your management actionable decisions. You need to make a proportional investment in a well-thought-out strategy regarding people (and supporting processes) to truly set your web analytics program up for success.

If you think your company is not following the 10/90 rule, take the following path to get you on your way:

1. Apply for a free Google Analytics account at www.google.com/analytics (or get the free ClickTracks Appetizer tool or the soon-to-be-launched free Microsoft web analytics tool, code name *Gatineau*).

2. You'll get the JavaScript tag at the end of the two-minute sign-up process. Implement Google Analytics on your website in parallel with your favorite expensive analytics tool that you currently have.

3. Get a comfort level for the difference between the two sets of key numbers (typically: visitors, conversions, page views, and so forth) and create a multiplier (for example, your expensive tool shows visitors 10 percent higher and page views 10 percent lower than Google Analytics). You will use this multiplier in the future to compare year-to-year trends if you want to.

82

CHAPTER 4: CRITICAL COMPONENTS OF A SUCCESSFUL WEB ANALYTICS STRATEGY?

4. Cancel the contract with your favorite expensive analytics vendor. Use that $40,000 or $80,000 or $160,000 to hire a smart analyst ($50,000 or higher for a great salary) and put the rest of the money in your pocket. Your smart analyst will be able to extract just as much value from Google Analytics as from your old tool. In fact, it is quite likely that a smart analyst will be able to extract a lot more value from Google Analytics compared to the part-time report writer you had in the past (mostly because the analyst will think at a much more sophisticated level).

5. As the level of savvy in your organization grows, and as the level of sophistication of supporting processes increases, in perhaps a year or two or three you might be ready to plunk down $200,000 on a web analytics tool and then be ready to extract a corresponding amount of value from it. (The following chapter covers the optimal method of selecting a web analytics tool.)

The cool thing about the recommended 10/90 process is that even if you get to step 3, you can walk away—no harm, no fuss, and you would have learned something valuable. But going through the rest of the steps will mean that you can immediately free up funding you need for the people (internal or external) who are key to unlocking the power of the terabytes of data you collect from your website and converting it into bytes of actionable insights (bullet points in an email!).

The 10/90 rule has even been welcomed by most web analytics vendors. After years of trying to earn business by selling the number of reports and sophistication of the tool, they have realized that they don't hold the keys to success anymore—success is determined by the people they hand the tool over to. Vendors have commented publicly (for example on my blog) that they would prefer to have companies invest in good analysts and decision makers who can use the awesome data that is being captured on the Web. It is a realization that stems from the fact that what is good for a client is great for the vendor's business as well.

Addressing Skepticism about the 10/90 Rule

The 10/90 rule raises some concerns; here are three of them and some important considerations.

90 percent of the budget for analysts; that seems like a bit much!

Fair enough. The core thought is that you will invest $90 out of every $100 in analysis and in resources supporting analysis. This translates into web analysts, maybe a senior web analyst (who can help with testing and hence extend web analytics), maybe a senior user researcher (for the much needed qualitative analysis), or maybe a senior manager for analytics who can help champion insights, extend data usage to others, and help drive action. But all of the $90 goes into resources that will obtain data, find insights, and drive action.

Continues

Addressing Skepticism about the 10/90 Rule *(Continued)*

Google Analytics, Microsoft Gatineau, ClickTracks Appetizer! Are you kidding me? These are toys, not tools!!

Having worked in many big companies, I can sympathize with the sentiments: "You get what you pay for" or "Why would a robust tool be free?" Big companies like to pay. But the reality is that on the Web some companies have realized that they can get you to spend more money if they can make you smarter and hence they provide solid tools (such as Google Analytics to measure ROI on your Adwords campaigns or Microsoft Gatineau to measure how well your pay-per-click campaigns are doing). Others such as ClickTracks have realized that if they can make you smarter with Appetizer, you are more likely to pay them for the higher versions. In both scenarios, you win.

It is right to think that the tools will not make you a delicious espresso in the morning along with your reports. But do you need espresso? There absolutely are companies that need highly advanced analytics. If you are one of them, buy a high-end tool when the time comes (after you get to step 5 in the preceding list).

Good analysts are hard to find, rarer than water in the Sahara desert. It is impractical to recommend investing in analysts.

There is certainly more need than there are analysts for hire. But this is still not an excuse to go buy an expensive web analytics tool, because you would not have anyone intelligent to use it (and the expensive tool will only, remember, provide data). If you have a hard time finding analysts, follow the preceding plan and invest the 90 percent in proven consultants on the outside who can fill in for the "big brains" until you can find them and hire them for your company.

One fact cannot be stressed enough: the outcome of your web analytics implementation is 100 percent reliant on the "company brains" you put behind it. A smart brain can extract more value from a simple (or even "mediocre") tool. The reverse is almost never true (not until the world sketched in the movie *Minority Report* exists).

Hire Great Web Analysts

Now that you buy into the 10/90 rule completely (or maybe mostly), it is time to assess the skills that exist in your company or maybe go hire someone now that you have the funding (the 90).

So what should you look for when you hire web analysts? What qualities do good analysts possess? How do you measure whether a resource that already exists in your company is optimal? How do you mentor your more-junior analysts to propel them to become great analysts?

Here are the top signs of an awesomely great web insights analyst (see the end of the list to judge if you are one!):

They have used more than one web analytics tool extensively. Although many of the tools seem similar in our field, each tool is different in some interesting and delightful ways. The way Omniture computes unique visitors is very different from the way ClickTracks or Visual Sciences computes it, or how StatCounter and WebTrends handle sessions. Using different tools gives an analyst a broad perspective on how the same thing can be counted 10 different ways and it also provides a rich understanding of why some tools are great and some suboptimal.

The interesting outcome of a diverse experience is that a great analyst can work with any tool and yet find meaningful insights (which is rarely the case for analysts who have spent all their experience tied to one tool).

They frequent the Yahoo! web analytics group and the top web analytics blogs. The Yahoo! web analytics group (`http://snipurl.com/yahoowagroup`) was founded by Eric Peterson, author of the highly popular book *Web Analytics Demystified* (Celilo Group Media, 2004). The group has the most impressive collection of knowledgeable people in our industry who share their wisdom on every topic that touches our world. Reading the posts provides great insights into challenges others are facing, innovative ways to solve those challenges, general trends in the industry, pointers to the latest and coolest happenings that affect us, and more.

With the advent of blogging, there is so much high-impact information that leaders and practitioners in the industry are sharing freely. Staying up on the blog posts is perhaps one of the best ways for an analyst to stay on the cutting edge of web analytics. A list of good blogs is at `http://snipurl.com/topblogs`.

The core point here is that great analysts stay hungry for new information and are constantly looking to learn and get better. Following the Yahoo! group or the blogs are simply one sign of a desire to learn (or contribute).

Before doing any important analysis, they visit the website and look at the web pages. This might not be quite as obvious, but it is amazing how many times we simply look at tools and numbers and data and have no idea what the website looks like. It is impossible to analyze the data without a solid understanding of the customer experience on the site, what the pages look like, where the buttons are, what new "great" navigation change went live yesterday. A great analyst stays in touch with the website and the changes constantly being made by the designers and marketers.

Great checkout abandonment rate analysis, for example, is powered by going through the site, adding to the cart, starting checkout (using all options available), completing checkout, and getting an order confirmation email. This experience will give the analyst a new and more meaningful perspective on the numbers, and insights will come faster.

Top Web Analytics Blogs

The Web changes all the time, and those changes create pain points on how best to accurately and consistently analyze our websites. One of the most awesome resources at your disposal is the blogs of various industry luminaries and practitioners who unselfishly put out some of the best content you'll find anywhere. A key characteristic of most of these blogs is that they are extremely current and on the cutting edge in their discussions. Get an RSS (really simple syndication) reader and soak up all the information—it's free!

Google Analytics Blog (http://analytics.blogspot.com/): This official blog of the GA team has loads of great GA tips and insights.

Occam's Razor (http://www.kaushik.net/avinash/): My blog focuses on web research and analytics.

Web Analytics Demystified (http://www.webanalyticsdemystified.com/weblog): Eric Peterson is an author, conference speaker, and Visual Sciences VP, and on his blog he shares his wisdom about all things web analytics.

Lies, Damned Lies.... (http://www.liesdamnedlies.com):

Ian Thomas is the Director of Customer Intelligence at Microsoft, and in a prior life helped found WebAbacus, a web analytics company. Ian applies his deep experience and covers complex topics in an easy-to-understand language.

Analytics Talk (http://epikone.com/blog/): Justin Cutroni is one of the smartest web analytics practitioners and consultants around. His focus is on GA, but he has lots of non-GA stuff as well.

Commerce360 Blog (http://blogs.commerce360.com/): Craig Danuloff is the president of Commerce360, a consulting company, and he brings a refreshingly honest perspective on all things web analytics and marketing.

LunaMetrics Blog (http://lunametrics.blogspot.com/): Robbin Steif provides practical tips and tricks on getting the most out of your web analytics tools, specifically with an eye toward improving your conversion rate.

Instant Cognition (http://blog.instantcognition.com/): Clint Ivy calls himself a data visualization journeyman—that says it all! Clint shares his perspective on analytics with a focus on visual report design.

Applied Insights Blog (http://snipurl.com/neilmason/): Neil Mason and John McConnell share their insights from the United Kingdom. I have known Neil for some time now, and he shares absolutely invaluable insights.

OX2 Blog (http://webanalytics.wordpress.com): René Dechamps Otamendi and Aurélie Pols run the pan-European OX2, and their blog always has wonderfully insightful perspectives on web analytics.

Their core approach is customer centric (not company centric). In the morass of data quality and total visitors (TV) and unique visitors (UV) and cookie values and A/B test IDs and sessions and shopper_ids, we look at massive amounts of data and forget that real people are using our websites. Great analysts have a customer-centric view that enables them to think like customers, all 1,000 segments of them. They are aware of customer personas and challenges, which keeps them grounded in reality. This is critically important because following data trends and patterns without using a customer mindset will always complicate thinking.

A great analyst is capable of descending from the "analytical heights" to the customer level and of helping the customer move forward (because customers can't fly).

They understand the technical differences between page tagging, log files, packet sniffing, and beacons. How data is captured is perhaps the most critical part of an analyst's ability to process the data and find insights. Each data capture methodology has its benefits and dangerous negatives. It is critical to understand the technical differences between each data capture methodology and to then appropriately adjust the kind of analysis and the value they extract from it.

They are comfortable in the quantitative and qualitative worlds. Clickstream, on its best day, should be the source of 35 percent of your data (Trinity strategy). The rest comes from site outcomes or qualitative data (the why). Great analysts are just as comfortable in the world of parsing numbers as in the open-ended world of observing customers, reading their words, inferring their unspoken intentions, sitting in a lab usability study to glean insights, and so forth.

They have an inherent ability to hear people and their problems and all the while think of 10 interesting ways in which the site overlay or other clickstream metrics can be sliced to validate ideas. Great analysts follow a presentation slide on core clickstream/outcome KPIs with a slide on segmented VOC Pareto analysis, because nothing else makes sense!

They are avid explorers. Reporting is straightforward. There are inputs, outputs, KPIs, tables, and rows. Analysis is not quite as straightforward. It has no predefined paths to take; it has no preset questions to answer. It requires having an open mind and a high level of inquisitiveness. After hearing ambiguous business questions, it also requires a deep desire to find new and better ways to use data to answer those questions. Great analysts don't worry if and how the analysis will work; they save that for later. They seek out possibilities and the nonobvious.

When faced with incomplete or dirty data, rather than think of all the reasons why they can't analyze it, they make reasonable assumptions and can find a nugget of gold in a coal factory. A vast majority of us fail at this; we face bad or incomplete data and we become paralyzed. Framed another way, great analysts are really, really good at separating the signal from the noise (whether by using data segmentation, using statistics, using common sense, understanding your customer segments, or other methods).

They are effective communicators. In our world, analysts rarely have the power to take action based on their insights or implement recommendations. Great analysts are great communicators; they can present their message in a very compelling, easy-to-understand manner, and be a passionate and persuasive advocate for the company's website users. The 15 hours of complex multivariate statistical regression model analysis is hidden; they put ego aside and tell the decision maker that changing the presentation on product content will have the highest correlated impact on revenue. They are just as comfortable talking to technical folks as presenting to the VP of a company and selling insights that will make a difference (and selling even in the face of opposition).

They are street smart. Business savvy is an incredibly hard quality to find, even harder to judge in a standard interview. Yet it is perhaps the one thing that separates a report writer from an analyst—the ability to see the big picture, the ability to understand and solve for strategic objectives.

Great analysts are not theory-spouting types who make things complicated and much harder than they are in the real world. Think Occam's razor (all things being equal, the simplest solution tends to be the best one). These analysts have oodles of common sense and an inherent ability to reduce a complex situation to its simplest level and look at logical possibilities. This does not mean they can't look at complex situations; on the contrary, they have an impressive ability to absorb complexity but they are also scrappy enough to look through the complexity rather than end up in rat holes. They know how and when to keep things simple.

They play offense and not just defense. Most people in this field play defense: they simply supply data or provide reports or at times provide dashboards—mostly all reactive. Here is what is missing: offense—getting in front of the business and saying this is what you should measure. In response to the question, "Show me what the tool provides," they say, "Tell me your strategic objectives and I'll tell you what insights I can provide with the data I have."

Great analysts spend 30 percent of their time looking at all the available data just to look for trends and insights. They spend time they don't really have, doing things that no one asked them to do. But that 30 percent of the time allows them to play offense, to provide insights that no one thought to ask for, insights that drive truly significant actions. They do it because they realize that they are more knowledgeable about the site and data than anyone else out there and they do it because it is a lot of fun.

Bonus: They are survivors. The reality is that web decision makers mostly just want to measure hits (Jim Sterne, author and the organizer of the Emetrics summit defines *hits* as: how idiots track success). A key skill of a great analyst is the ability to have patience, survive, and stay motivated in a world where people might ask for suboptimal things (such as reports listing the top exit pages or hits or home page conversion etc). Transforming perceptions is a hard job and takes a long time.

Are You a Great Web Analyst?

If you meet six of the preceding criteria, you are a good analyst and you are on your way to greatness.

If you meet nine, you are a great analyst. Congratulations!

If you meet all of the criteria, you are a purple squirrel and you can command any salary at any company in this world!

Suggested Senior Analyst Job Description

As you start to look for a web analyst, here is a suggested job description that you can use to attract the right kinds of candidates. This job description is for a senior analyst. If you are looking for junior-level folks, simply reduce some of the emphasis on years of experience and reduce the breadth of the skills outlined (so the junior analyst wouldn't have to know competitive analysis, for example).

The senior analyst is someone who can come in and provide insights to companies that have massive amounts of clickstream data. These insights can be used to drive actions that have a reasonable chance of success when measured by key site outcome metrics (revenue, conversion rate, problem resolution rate, customer satisfaction, and so forth).

There are four important points this description accomplishes:

Communicates to the candidate: Lots of job descriptions don't do this. They talk about the employer and the jargon of greatness and couch in sometimes ambiguous terms what the job actually is. This job description is explicit about what is expected of the candidate and the typical deliverables.

Emphasizes breadth: The description deliberately tries to emphasize roundness in experience well beyond clickstream and knowledge of a standard web analytics tool. It emphasizes Trinity experience. It also stresses team and leadership skills (the implication being that a senior analyst will not be a report writer or publisher).

Looks beyond loads of clickstream analysis experience: The job calls for much less clickstream analysis experience (to try to attract people with mindsets less entrenched in the old web analytics). The description asks for traditional business intelligence experience (both to look for experience in analysis and also because the future will be less in web analytics tools and more in BI-type environments) and seeks at least basics in SEM, SEO, competitive analysis, testing, and so forth.

Continues

Seeks out business acumen: It is hard to do this in the application, but in the interview you should thoroughly investigate whether the candidate is just a sophisticated "numbers person" or has business acumen. Ideally look for 70 percent of the latter and 30 percent of the former in a senior candidate.

It is important to point out that the following description is pseudo-ideal. Although it describes the ideal candidate, there is really no such thing an ideal candidate. The description can form the basis of what you create for your company, but you will need to customize it by emphasizing the skills and experience that you feel will work best in your company.

Senior Web Analyst

The following text outlines the job description.

Job Content and Scope

- Support the analytic needs of a business unit by using clickstream tools from vendors such as ClickTracks and Omniture to analyze web traffic. Use standard BI tools, from vendors such as Microstrategy or Business Objects, to produce reports relating to outcomes.

- Create holistic dashboards by pulling data from different data sources and websites for presentations to the senior management team.

- Collaborate with external partners such as agencies to assist with data collection and reporting.

- Own the process of driving core insights from available data to suggest, create, and execute multivariate or A/B/C tests that drive fundamental improvements to the site experience.

- Exhibit a high level of expertise in guiding the data strategy across multiple *listening posts* (websites, surveys, testing, CRM systems, market research).

- Senior business analysts will typically focus on reporting and analysis holistically: clickstream analysis, outcomes analysis, search analysis, multivariate testing analysis. They will support analysis that covers campaigns (search and direct marketing), online demand generation, business unit financial performance, product mix, affiliates, and so forth. They will also work closely with the website technology team to identify gaps in the data capture strategy and collaboratively implement enhancements. They will also be expected to partner with other business / functional units and external company partners to ensure that best practices in metrics and decision making are being exposed to the senior management and core website decision makers.

Suggested Senior Analyst Job Description *(Continued)*

Typical Deliverables

- Weekly and monthly reports (Excel, BI tools, clickstream analytics).

- Lead development of senior management dashboards.

- Website behavior and customer experience analysis.

- Data consolidation and validation.

- Coordinating tags, tracking parameter implementations.

- Lead creation and completion of multivariate and A/B testing documents (from hypothesis creation to influencing creatives to identifying success metrics) and post-test analysis.

- Business requirements synthesized from multiple sources including product managers, development teams, and functional group members.

- Documentation relating to existing processes and suggestions for improving those processes.

- Effective and persuasive presentations (verbal and written) for project teams and business leaders.

Knowledge/Background/Experience

- Bachelor's degree (MBA preferred).

- At least three years of working with standard clickstream analysis tools from: Omniture, Click-Tracks, WebTrends, WebSideStory, Coremetrics, or others.

- Three to five years of experience in one or more roles in an online e-commerce or online support environments.

- High level of expertise (three years or more) with business intelligence tools from vendors such as Hyperion, Business Objects, MicroStrategy, and Cognos, and experience writing and tuning SQL queries in an online or offline environment.

- Two to four years of experience in reporting and analyzing performance of online marketing activities such as campaigns, affiliate marketing, online acquisition strategies, and so forth.

- Three to five years of experience in using the Microsoft Office suite, with very strong Excel skills.

- Three to five years of business analysis experience in large companies with multiple functions or business units preferred.

- Two years of experience in advanced web analytics methodologies such as experimentation and testing, competitive analysis, surveys, and market research.

Continues

Suggested Senior Analyst Job Description *(Continued)*

- Mid-level expertise in the search engine marketing (SEM), or pay-per-click (PPC), and search engine optimization (SEO) strategies, and a minimum of one year of experience measuring the success of SEM/PPC and SEO efforts.

- Excellent communication skills and the ability to interact with all levels of end users and technical resources.

Team/Leadership Skills

- Works effectively both independently and as a member of a cross-functional team.

- Uses sound judgment to identify issues and escalates when appropriate.

- Contributes to improvements in processes (technical or business) used by analysts.

- Owns driving focused decisions within specific areas and is a key contributor to decisions beyond the specific scope of the analyst's role.

- Identifies key needs or gaps and provides leadership to close those gaps.

- Resolves disagreements and conflicts constructively, and knows when to involve others.

- Learns from mistakes, takes action to apply that knowledge, and provides peer- and team-wide feedback for those in an immediate area of focus.

- Identifies and communicates specific personal growth goals.

Technical/Functional Skills

- Understands relevant technology applications in their area.

- Uses strong analytical skills, provides insights as well as recommendations for changes, and convinces key company decision makers of business benefits of the proposed solutions.

- Identifies requirements and drives decision making for required trade-offs by proposing solutions to senior leadership.

- Handles multiple tasks, switches priorities, and focuses as needed.

- Exhibits a high degree of proactiveness in analyzing customer behavior by using available data to influence changes on the website.

- Understands the complex web ecosystems and best practices and applies this knowledge to their work.

- Collaborates on the creation of a project plan and tasks for the team.

Note: If you are a web analyst or someone considering a career in the wonderful field of web analytics (which is exciting and cool and awesome in lots of ways), the preceding job description is a suggested guidepost of what you might do to build your skills.

Identify Optimal Organizational Structure and Responsibilities

Thus far you have learned that you should start with a foundation of business questions and that you should follow the 10/90 rule (so that for every $100 of the budget, $10 is spent on tools and $90 on people—the brains—who will actually be responsible for insights). You have learned what makes a great web analyst and have seen a job description so you can look for an analyst for your team. The next step is to think: through where in your company should web analysis be done? Who should "own" the web analytics strategy and execution for maximum impact?

Traditionally, web analytics has been a part of the IT team. It has been one of the functions of the chief information officer (CIO) or chief technical officer (CTO) and usually has been supported by the IT team that works with web servers, databases, web logs, and Apache HTTP Server or/ Microsoft Internet Information Services (IIS). It made a lot of sense initially because, as outlined in Chapter 1, the first folks to get into web analysis were members of the IT team who had access to the web logs and used either custom scripts or a tool such as Analog to analyze the activity of the server.

The advent of early tools from vendors such as WebTrends reinforced the existing mechanisms because the IT folks got tired of their custom scripts (and increasing business complaints about data) and they decided to go out and buy the emerging web analytics tools. The trend was also reinforced because the tools initially provided data that IT needed (server hits, browser types, OS versions, and so forth).

The most common organizational structure was a team of one, or more depending on the overall company size, to sit in IT and be responsible for publishing reports and customizing them after submission of a *ticket* or *case* from the business team. This ticket outlined the data that the business team needed and justified why they needed it. Usually all tickets that came in would have to be prioritized, and IT would commit delivery dates.

In most companies, the IT team still "owns" web analytics and is in the business of selecting vendors and even providing standard reports. However, the world has radically changed. The kinds of metrics and reports needed are different, the vendor/solution models are radically different, and finally the use of web data is different. So what has changed? What's new? Consider the following:

- Web analytics is now very much a business function (marketing, sales and support) and less an IT function. This affects the reports, metrics, analysis, integration, ownership, everything.
- Although many data collection methodologies are available, the one that (for better or for worse) is most prevalent is JavaScript tagging, a methodology that requires perhaps the least amount of work by the IT team as compared to any other methodology.

- It is increasingly apparent that there are distinct IT needs and business needs. IT needs metrics to support their responsibilities (hence *server-level* technical metrics), and the business needs metrics that help them do a better job of marketing and selling. The choice of a web analytics tool is increasingly driven by the business needs, and if the tool does not report on browser types or screen resolutions, that is no big deal because alternatives abound.

- Accountability for the Web has shifted from the CTO/CIO to the CMO.

For all of these reasons, the organizational structure that works optimally for web analytics, and web decision making in general, calls for the holistic ownership of web analytics to rest with the business team and not the IT team. This is a fairly dramatic shift that is fraught with political battles and some fundamental mindset shifts on all sides. But it is a shift that is imperative.

This is not to say that the IT team cannot manage a web analytics program—far from it. But with the macro shifts in the industry, needs, and technologies, it is imperative that web analytics move to the people who are going to be held responsible and accountable for success: business teams. There will be significant benefits from this shift:

- Quite simply, the business teams will have more skin in the game. The days of blaming your IT team for all your troubles will end.

- There is a fundamental difference in the use of data on the IT and business sides, almost as stark as the difference between reporting (the most frequent IT function) to analysis (the most frequent need of the business).

- The IT team, for very good reasons, solves for stability, scalability, repeatability, and process. The mindset required in web analytics is to solve for flexibility, agility, *use and throw* (short life cycle), and fast movement. Having business ownership will increase the chance of these latter goals coming true (of course every company's mileage will vary).

- In cases where ASP-based JavaScript tagging is being used for data collection and reporting, business ownership will shorten the loop to action because the business owners can now directly work with the vendor as they need to.

If the ownership of the web analytics team, platform, and strategy should be with the business teams, then which business team? It depends.

The most optimal solution is to have the holistic web analytics ownership rest with the team that is most responsible for the web channel from the web perspective. In some companies, the sales team is responsible for the web experience and action; in that case, having the analytics team there would make the most sense. If marketing is running the show, they will provide leadership to the web analytics team.

The overall goal is to have the web analytics team, platform, and strategy be tied to the business team that owns the web channel—not in a dotted line or matrixed reporting relationship, but a direct-line reporting relationship.

If you have not at least experimented with this type of organizational structure, it is a very worthwhile Endeavour. You'll observe not only the operational effects (efficiencies of all sorts) but in addition you will also observe a fundamental shift in your team's mindset that is empowered by the recommended change.

In larger companies, the challenge of business ownership becomes a bit more complicated. It is typical in large companies to have centralized (horizontal) functions such as marketing, sales, human resources (HR), and IT and to have many different business units that are focused vertically on a particular line of business. For example Procter & Gamble (P&G) business units include Laundry Detergent, Fragrances, Pet Nutrition, Baby and Child Care, and Small Appliances. In such a case, the Web is a horizontal (that is, everyone uses it for everything to accomplish their differing goals). In cases such as these, who should own web analytics?

There are three ownership models: centralization, decentralization, and centralized decentralization.

Centralization

In the *centralization* model, web analytics is centralized in a corporate function (IT or marketing, for example). The role of the team is to build a common platform for the entire company. Their responsibilities include providing reporting, training, and best practices, and managing the vendor relationships. On the surface, this model makes sense because in a large company it seems suboptimal to have lots of different tools implemented in one company or to have multiple business or functional teams trying to all get better at the same time. Standardization can also yield cost savings and provide numbers and metrics that can be measured the same across many websites.

The challenge with centralization is that far from the actual decision makers and marketers, the team in short order transforms into the IT-driven analytics teams of yore. The central team usually struggles to understand the real needs of their users. They also struggle to take their knowledge and expertise and teach marketers how to make better decisions. It does not take long for the central team to become essentially representatives of vendors who simply create reports and provide custom data dumps to their users. The end result is dissatisfaction across the board, even after implementing state-of-the art tools and spending loads of money.

Decentralization

Decentralization is observed in action either in larger companies that are just getting started or those that have gotten to a tipping point with the centralized model. Under this model, web analytics is completely decentralized, and the various business units are empowered to pursue any strategy that works for them. The result is potentially optimized business units or teams that are each running a different tool and using their own unique set of metrics and strategy.

The challenge with decentralization is that each team is not usually leveraging any economies of scale or building out any strategic advantage that should occur in any large company. Because of the use of multiple potential vendors, this is also often an expensive strategy. Although at a clickstream level things might be okay for the teams, it is nearly impossible to figure out how to integrate data from other sources of the company or to measure customer behavior across the company website ecosystem. There is little in terms of best practices and knowledge and the company becoming more knowledgeable over time.

In summary, neither of these two prevalent models is optimal. The model that is gaining some traction and has already shown a modicum of success is centralized decentralization.

Centralized Decentralization

This is the best of both worlds. Under the *centralized decentralization* model, the company has a central team that is more like a center of excellence for web decision making. The team is typically responsible for implementing a standardized web measurement system across the company in partnership with other business and functional units in the company. The central team is also responsible for establishing various contracts, selecting technology solutions (web analytics or others such as testing and research), creating best practices and, most of all, as the center of excellence, keeping the company on the cutting edge.

But rather than taking on all the reporting and analysis tasks of the business or functional units, under this model a web analyst or a senior web analyst is embedded in each of the business units. The business unit typically funds this analyst, and therefore has some skin in the game. The analyst in turn is very close to the business unit and can understand much better the challenges that the team is facing and can respond accordingly. Although the analyst works as part of the business unit, the analyst still taps into and uses the centralized standard web analytics platform and hence has to worry about only data analysis and not data capture, processing, and storage. That problem is solved centrally for the analyst. Additionally, the centralized team can share best practices and standard dashboards and knowledge and expertise.

By overcoming some of the challenges of each model, centralized or decentralized, this model has benefits of both and enables success at an operational and strategic level. By not having to worry about creating an increasing number of reports all the time, the central team can worry about creating a true center of excellence. This center of excellence will keep the company ahead of the game by investing in newer technological solutions or solving complex problems such as competitive analysis, experimentation and testing, research, and new interesting analysis.

Web Analytics Fundamentals

5

After you have put the right strategy in place for people and the organization, your web analytics program will address data capture, tool selection, data quality (sadly, you can't escape this one), implementation, and metrics selection. Often many of these choices are all rolled into one. You pick a tool, for example, and the rest go with that (how you collect data, where it is stored, how good it is, what metrics you can report on, and so forth).

There is a ton of inherent complexity on the Web. This complexity results in challenges in collecting data and having confidence in its ability to provide insights. *Customer use complexity* relates to what data to use and where and how to use it. *Organizational complexity* translates into reporting data, analyzing it, and putting together a strategy in your company that is geared toward helping you fix structural problems (website, process, people).

This chapter covers the fundamentals of web analytics and strategies at your disposal to handle the challenges you'll face.

Capturing Data: Web Logs or JavaScript tags?

Chapter 2, "Data Collection—Importance and Options," covered all the options we have at our disposal when it comes to collecting web clickstream data. We can use web logs, web beacons, JavaScript tags, and packet sniffers. Each methodology comes with its own set of benefits and challenges.

Most current implementations use either web logs (usually because of history) or JavaScript tags (usually because of the recent evolution of most vendors simply abandoning all other methods except this one).

Practitioners debate which of these two methodologies is better and hence which one they should be using. There are lots of conversations that outline benefits of one methodology or the other (as this book has in Chapter 2). There are even more technically nuanced geeky conversations by one party bashing the other.

What is missing is someone going out on a limb to make a recommendation for choosing web logs or JavaScript tags (assuming that you have ruled out the others). Never one to miss the opportunity to take an unnecessary risk, I'll make a recommendation:

You should use JavaScript tags as your weapon of choice when it comes to collecting data from your website.

The only assumption is that you don't have a website that is so amazingly unique that there is no other website with a web serving platform on the planet like yours. In a nutshell, the only assumption is that you are not uniquely unique.

If you have carefully considered other data collection methodologies and you are stuck between choosing web logs or JavaScript tags, now you have my recommendation. The following sections detail four important reasons for choosing JavaScript tags.

Separating Data Serving and Data Capture

When you use web logs, data serving (web pages with data going out from your web servers upon user requests) is tied completely to data capture (as the web pages go out, the server logs information about that in web log files). Every time you want a new piece of data, you are tied to your IT department and its ability to respond to you. In most companies, this is not a rapid response process.

When you use JavaScript tags, data capture is effectively separated from data serving. Web pages can go out from anywhere (from the company web server, from the visitor's local cache, or from an Akamai-type, or ISP, cache farm) and you will still collect data (the page loads, the JavaScript tag executes, and data goes to the server—ASP or in-house). The beauty of this is that the company IT department and website developers can do what they are supposed to do, serve pages, and the "analytics department" can do what it is supposed to do, capture data. It also means that both parties gain flexibility in their own jobs. Speaking selfishly, this means that the analytics gals and guys can independently enhance code (which does not always have to be updated in tags on the page) to collect more data faster.

The reliance on IT will not go down to 0 percent; it will end up at about 25 percent. However, it is not 100%, and that in itself opens up so many options when it comes to data capture and processing.

Type and Size of Data

Web logs were built for and exist to collect server activity, not business data. Over time we have enhanced them to collect more and more data and store it with some semblance of sanity to meet the needs of business decision makers. Web logs still collect all the technical data as well as the business data (often from multiple web servers that support a single website, each of which has a log file that then needs to be "stitched back" to give the complete view of each user).

JavaScript tags were developed to collect clickstream data for business analysis. Therefore, they are much more focused about what they do and collect only the data that they need (though admittedly not all the JavaScript tags running around are smart, and they do collect unnecessary data).

What this means is that with JavaScript tags you have a much smaller amount of data to capture, store, and process each night (or minute or hour or day), and it can be a much saner existence logically, operationally, and strategically.

Innovation

For better or for worse, most vendors are moving away from supporting versions of their products that use web logs as a source of data. Many offer only JavaScript tag (or packet sniffer) versions of their products. History will decide whether this is a good thing, but the practical implication is that most innovation that is happening in terms of sophistication of data capture, new ways of reporting or analyzing data, and meeting the needs of Web 2.0 experiences, is all happening in JavaScript data capture environments.

This presents us with a stark choice of having to build our own customized solutions of capturing this new data and keeping pace with the necessary innovations, or relying on the expertise that is out there (regardless of which vendor you prefer) and keeping pace with all the necessary innovation by leveraging the investments the vendors are making. Often this is an easy choice to make for any company that considers its core competency to be focusing on its business and not developing web analytics solutions. (Although, admittedly, if you are big enough, you can absolutely do that—for example, Wal-Mart has invented its own database solution because nothing in the world can meet the company's needs for size and scale.)

Integration

Increasingly, we are heading toward doing a lot more measurement and analysis of customer experience beyond just clickstream. Two great examples of this are experimentation and testing (especially multivariate testing) and personalization/behavior targeting. In both cases, add-on solutions are tacked on to the website and the testing or targeting happens. Often these solutions come with their own methods of collecting and analyzing data and measuring success.

But as we head for an integrated end-to-end view of customer behavior, for optimal analysis we have to find ways of integrating data from these add-ons into the standard clickstream data. Otherwise, you are optimizing for each add-on, which is not a great thing. Integrating with these add-on solutions—which often also use JavaScript tags and cookies and URL identifiers—is significantly easier if you use JavaScript tags. It is easy to read cookies in web logs, but you can integrate with the add-on solutions quicker and easier if you are using JavaScript tags.

 Tip: Always consider your choice in the context of your own needs. This is not so much a caveat as a plea that you make an informed choice. Please read Chapter 2 carefully for detailed pros and cons of each data capture methodology (because JavaScript tagging does have some cons that need to be considered, and web logs have a couple of great pros).

If you were waiting for someone else to help you make up your mind, you should have that now! That wasn't hard, was it?

Selecting Your Optimal Web Analytics Tool

As you can imagine, choosing a web analytics tool is a hugely crucial process. Choosing the right or wrong tool can be critical because you will usually be stuck with it for a while. Because we tend to overstate the importance of historical web data, it is quite likely that a quickie divorce will not be in the offing even if you don't get along with your choice.

So in a world where choosing a web analytics tool seems akin to choosing a spouse, how should choose your mate—sorry, web analytics tool—with whom you can live happily ever after?

The Old Way

Currently, the most common process for choosing a web analytics tool is fundamentally flawed. The way tools are chosen at the moment is through an extensive, traditional nine-step process that usually looks like this:

1. Collect all the business requirements (goals, strategy, KPIs, reports, reporting schedule, and so on). Be as inclusive as possible.

2. Collect all the technical requirements (site architecture, servers, scripts, pages, IT needs, and so on), and again be as inclusive as possible.

3. Ensure that anyone who could ever need any kind of access to any kind of web data is contacted (inside and outside the company) and their needs documented.

4. Put all of the preceding information into a request for proposal (RFP). Add vendor financial stability, references, and so forth into the requirements.

5. Send RFPs to many vendors and set an aggressive reply schedule.

6. Receive the RFPs.

7. From those, weed out the "insignificants" based on marketing spin, beauty, and completeness of the RFPs.

8. Through an esteemed committee of cross-functional representatives of your company, select one vendor that meets the requirements.

9. Implement the solution and celebrate.

The search process takes two to four months, implementation one to two, and the guaranteed result is that you will almost always pick the most expansive, and usually one of the most expensive, web analytics solutions. Sometimes you'll make a suboptimal choice and then you will be looking at three, six, twelve months of stress and having to deal with management questions that sound like this: "*How come you are using a web analytics tool that costs a quarter of a million dollars a year and you are not recommending actions?*"

The Achilles' heel of the preceding process is that it involves people who ask for the earth and the moon in terms of the requirements (most of whom will never even log in to the tool) and it is very divorced from the rough and tumble real world of the Web, website, and web analytics. The process is also too long, too time-consuming, and too expensive (just count the people, process, and time commitments required of your company), and you'll always pick the most expensive and expansive tool.

The New Way

As an antidote to the preceding suboptimal outcome, ignore the traditional nine-step process and don't send out an RFP (I assure you that even your vendor will appreciate not having to go through the pain a RFP usually imposes on them). Here is an alternative: a radical six-step process that will set you on a path to finding your right soul mate (I mean web analytics tool), and do so faster and cheaper.

Note: This process will yield excellent results for a company of any size, though the political, structural, and mindset challenges required to pull it off increase with the size of the company. However, large companies probably have the most to benefit from if they follow it.

Follow these steps:

1. Assign optimal ownership (day 1).

   - The project leader should be the highest-level person whose *neck will be on the line* to deliver web insights (not reports). It can be a senior manager or a director, someone whose job is directly related to web insights (which places a stress on taking actions and not just emailing reports out).

   - Provide that leader with a small group of one to two people who will put the tool to hard-core use.

   - Email the entire company (this is only a slight exaggeration) to let them know you are selecting the tool. This is not a request for input, it is an FYI.

2. Implement a web analytics solution (day 2).

   - If you want to use web logging data, obtain ClickTracks Appetizer (www.clicktracks.com/products/appetizer).

   - If you want page tagging data, get Google Analytics (www.google.com/analytics).

   - If you don't trust either, get StatCounter (www.statcounter.com). StatCounter will give you only bare-bones data for free, but that is quite okay.

   It takes one hour to get your hands on any of these tools. It takes five minutes to implement Google Analytics (put the tag in the site footer, click Save, go get a drink, and wait for data). And it takes a couple of hours to implement Click-Tracks, most of which will be spent locating your website log files.

3. Start using simple reports and start the process of creating an intelligent audience in your company (day 3).

   - Email your core users a report that shows traffic (visitors), referring URLs, search key phrases, and top viewed pages. Your core users are those whose job completely depends on the website—so very few people.

- After a week, set up an in-person meeting to get feedback and questions.
- Create a second revision of reports.
- One week later, ask for feedback, in person. Then go to step 4—because in the best case scenario, the feedback will tell you that the reports are not enough, or they show the wrong stuff, or your users want more. In the worst case scenario, you'll learn quickly that no one has looked at the report and you'll make appropriate decisions and follow up with actions.

In just three short days, your company has data for your own website. You can start to use it, argue about it, and see what works and what does not. You are now empowered to make decisions based on your own data, and this greatly accelerates the process of building knowledge and expertise.

4. Teach yourself the limitations of web analytics, tagging, numbers not matching, needing to redo your website information architecture/URLs/ID/parameters/cookies and other data-providing facilities (day 17).

- By now you have found that the reason you can't answer questions is not the fault of your web analytics tool. Make a list of all the problems. You'll need someone with slight technical skills if you don't already have such a person involved. This list will usually include URL structures, missing data (need for new URL parameters or cookie values), maybe updated JavaScript tags, and data "held" by IT at the server level but that you need at the browser level (for tag methodology).
- With the help of your core team, prioritize the problems and quantify their effects on the business. For example, no parameters = no decisions on the acquisition's return on investment (ROI) = $1 million in suboptimal decisions.

5. Cross your fingers and dive in (day 27).

- Partner with your IT or website tech team to roll out the fixes you need to get your website to cough up data.
- This is often a painful process. Cash in any chips you have (borrow some if you have to).
- Don't forget to keep your reporting going, keep the learning process in high gear, and enhance the reports and analysis as new data becomes available.
- Slowly increase your circle of data users.

Step 5 can take a lot of time or a little time depending on the size, organizational structure, and—most important—mindset of your company. I am going to optimistically say this will take a month.

If you have the support of senior leadership, now is the time to tell them the story of business impact and ask for help in driving the necessary change faster across organizational boundaries. If you don't have this support, now is a good time to find leaders who have the most to benefit from awesome web data and wow them with what you have managed to build—for free, I might add—in about a month. Show them the analysis that will mean the most to each of them, and spend a few minutes understanding what type of analysis they will connect with; even at this early stage, you'll find something in your free tool that will "speak" to anyone!

6. Do an honest and deeply critical self-review of your progress (month 2 and later). You have an equal chance of reaching each of the following critical conclusions:

- You find out that reporting does not equal analysis and that you need a major upgrade in terms of the web analytics skills in your company.

- You find that data or tools are not your problem—it really is your company culture, both in terms of using data to drive decisions and getting your site tech teams to make enhancements to give you data.

- You'll find that Google Analytics or ClickTracks completely fill all your company web analytics needs.

- You'll find that ClickTracks or Google Analytics are not the right web analytics tools for your company because your have unique and niche high-end needs.

- You'll realize that web analytics (clickstream data) is not sufficient to find web insights, so you'll take the money you would spend on web analytics vendors and spend it on experience/research analysis (see the Trinity mindset in Chapter 1, "Web Analytics—Present and Future").

If the limitation is anything other than the wrong tool, you have a complex set of actions to take that are unique to each company and take a long time to accomplish. The good news is that you know what needs to be done, and the management team knows what the hurdles are (and it is not that you don't have a tool and it is not the fault of the tool you actually have).

If the limitation is truly the tool, you are ready to make an intelligent choice regarding a different tool. Here are recommendations for executing that selection process successfully:

- Your RFP should now contain the specific problems you are having and the limitations of your current tool (Google Analytics, ClickTracks, StatCounter).

- Your RFP should only be about the tool. No vendor can give you a warm hug and solve your company's problems, such as your inability to capture data or have people to do the analysis or fix your site metadata or missing tags. Those are your problems to solve.

- Select differentiated vendors. Remember, the Big Three offer largely the same set of features and benefits (except perhaps 5 percent of features that niche businesses will value). If your final list of choices has only the Big Three vendors, you might miss out on a real differentiated choice. If you want a real comparison, bring in a vendor that is radically different. So consider Coremetrics, Visual Sciences, IndexTools, Unica, or ClickTracks, each of which has something significantly different to put on the table.

- Do a real proof of concept: implement the final set of vendors' tools on your live site and compare them to the free tool you were using to see whether there is real differentiation. Any vendor that wants your business will allow you to get a free 30-day trial.

Benefits of the New Way

Even with the time spent on step 5, you have moved further faster than in the traditional nine-step process. Under the traditional process, it would take you two to four months just to select the tool and much longer to identify all the non-tool issues and get all the knowledge that you already have.

In just six steps, you have accomplished the seemingly impossible:

- You are not paying through your nose, ears, eyes, and so forth to first fix the problems you had in your company (data capture or basic intelligence up-leveling, for example). If your first step is to pick an expensive and expansive vendor, you are paying them to simply identify that you have problems. You have the option of doing that for free (and because the process of fixing your problems requires months, that can end up being a huge number of dollars saved).

- You have created at least a core group of people who know what web analytics is, and everything that is frustrating and joyous about it:

  IT: They learn that it is trivial to implement a web analytics tool—for the JavaScript tag option: copy, paste, save, done.

  Website developers: They learn all the little things that go into providing data that is critical for the business to take action—parameters to be added to URLs, page names to be updated, duplicated links in pages to be Tid-ed so you can track them, and so forth.

  Report creators: They learn that web analytics is less about report writing and more about analysis, and that this recommended process would have been a convenient exercise for them to evolve to the next level.

  Web analysts: They'll learn that that they can use any tool to find an answer because they are analysts, and of course that they have ultimate job security and we love them so.

Marketers: Magic does not exist. Forethought has to be put into campaigns, and coordination with website developers and analysts is required before launch so that various factors can be tracked after launch. And no, the web analytics tool will not make them coffee each day nor give them a massage.

Business leaders: They learn to do a true assessment of whether their employees have the right skills and whether they have major gaps in their processes. They learn that the true cost of web analytics is not the tools—it is the people (remember the 10/90 rule).

- You will have chosen the best tool for your company, with your eyes open, and you will be upgrading your company's analytics sophistication in the process.

Understanding Clickstream Data Quality

Chapter 2 began by talking about the GIGO principle: garbage in, garbage out. It is important to choose the right data collection methodology for your needs and to ensure that the implementation is done properly. Yet there is perhaps no other activity that is as much a bane of our existence in web analytics as data quality.

The Web is a unique data collection challenge due in part to the following:

- Website experiences are constantly evolving.
- Technology is constantly changing.
- Most clickstream methodologies outlined in Chapter 2 are not foolproof (for example, not all users have JavaScript turned on, web logs don't have data-cached pages served, beacons collect little data and can easily be harmed by the deleted cookies).
- Each vendor has developed their own "optimized" methodologies to capture and process data.
- Users use many different mediums to surf the web (browsers, extensions, add-ons, and so forth).
- Data bounces around the World Wide Web, getting split up and reassembled.
- We rely on "fragile" things such as cookies to track individuals, when cookies track only browsers such as Microsoft's Windows Internet Explorer, Mozilla's Firefox, or Apple's Safari, and not people.
- Individual firewall, security settings, and antispyware software are consistently stymieing our efforts at collecting data accurately.

All of these result in a nonstandard environment that is not conducive to collecting data. Imagine other channels such as phone and retail. There is little variability, data quality controls are much easier to put in place, and companies have coalesced around some standards. Not so on the Web. The effect of all of the challenges on data quality is as follows:

- Nothing seems to tie to anything else.

- Each time you rerun reports, the numbers change, especially for history (even recent history).

- It is difficult, if not darn near impossible, to track people, assuming that your privacy policy legally permits that.

- Every time you change vendors, it is hard to get the old vendor's data to reconcile with the new vendor's data.

- Depending on the methodology, you have to constantly be in a teaching mode and tune your solution to report data correctly (whether by adding new robots, logic, or filters to exclude "bad" data from your logs or by keeping the definitions of what is a page in sync with site URL structure and other changes).

- Often we have to use data sampling to get numbers (not sampling as in putting tags on some high-profile pages on the website, but sampling as in statistically sampling the captured session data to quickly get numbers to report).

- New things keep cropping up that cause measurement problems for our existing tools (think of robots pre-fetching data or Ajax or Adobe Flex or RSS).

All this is enough to make our heads hurt. Even if, like dutiful little hamsters we spin in our wheels round and round and try to make progress, nothing ties to anything else.

Here is a current fact of life that is not going to change for some time to come: *Data quality on the Internet absolutely sucks.*

And there is nothing you can do about it—at least for now.

The sooner we, especially we, internalize this, the sooner we can get over it and the sooner we can move on. Oh, and it really does not matter what your favorite neighborhood vendor, the $0 one or the $1 million one, says. Pretty much all vendors use similar methodologies to collect data. Yes, each vendor has some nice little innovation, but they can't help that the Internet is a weird little animal constantly evolving and changing. In many ways that is its inherent beauty and charm, and why the Web is such a delight.

There are companies that are pouring heavy research and development (R&D) budgets into improving what we have or coming up with new and radically different ways to collect data on the Web. But until something radically different comes along, data quality remains a challenge. We have to expect that data quality will be a problem and we just have to get over it. We can't expect the kind of quality we have come to expect from our ERP and CRM systems (which have been around forever and are created to capture only a fraction of what the Web captures—and even that small fraction is highly structured).

In spite of all of these facts, I'll be the first one to admit that your decision makers are not going to let you get by with my lofty proclamation that data quality sucks. And make no mistake, it will take time to win their trust and convince them that even though data quality is suboptimal, we can still make great decisions from the data we are collecting and analyzing.

To achieve success in defeating the data quality monster, we must take the following steps:

1. Resist the urge to dive deep into the data to find the root cause of any data discrepancy—especially if you are off by less than 10 percent.

   This is a time-consuming and futile exercise. Besides, by the time you do figure out some semblance of an explanation, there are more new reasons why data won't tie (at least at a macro level). If you are off by just 10 percent or less, you are doing fine because that is in the ballpark for deltas you can expect. Less than 10 percent is good. Sad but true.

2. Assume a level of comfort with the data.

   When presented with data, understand clearly how it is collected and then encourage yourself and your decision makers to assume a level of comfort with the data. Say you look at something and can trust it only 80 percent. Your business leader might say 75 percent and perhaps the nice lady on your right might say only 70 percent. That is okay.

   Human beings are complex, and each is a collection of its life experiences, so we will each decide differently. That is okay. Using trial and error, or nimble negotiations, establish a baseline for comfort level with the data. Maybe it ends up being 75 percent confidence in the data. Hurray! The data is now your friend, whereas if you dive into the data, it may get you fired.

3. Make decisions you are comfortable with.

   This step takes the most courage. It requires the biggest leap of faith because humans are innately trained to seek out perfection and look for 100 percent trust (which really does not exist in anything). But after this step, the process is all fun. You can look at your table of data and with just 75 percent comfort level you can make business decisions.

   If with 100 percent confidence in data you would have sent a man to the moon, with 75 percent confidence in that same data at least you'll decide to buy a telescope to study the moon. What's important is that you made a decision and are moving forward.

   For example, say a random important KPI changed by 15 percent. With 100 percent confidence in the data, you might decide to spend $90,000 on the next campaign or completely change the site architecture or build a new checkout process. But with only 75 percent confidence in that 15 percent KPI change, you can still decide that you'll spend only $60,000 or run a multivariate test before you change site architecture to get more confidence in the data or maybe still build a new checkout process because you need only 75 percent confidence in the data because checkout is so important.

This example is a simple illustration that it is possible to make decisions with less than 100 percent confidence in the data. Encourage that behavior. It is okay if you trust the data more than your decision makers trust it; they will come around with time.

It is important that you model this behavior. If in your gut you find it hard to make this leap of faith, it will be monumentally harder for your decision makers or people around you to make the leap of faith that the next step calls for.

4. Drill deeper in specific areas.

    After you get into the groove of making decisions, rather than being paralyzed by data quality not being good, I recommend that you find small narrow niches of data segments to drill into. The goal will be to understand why data for that narrow niche might not be what you expect. If you love data detective work, you are going to like this. It can be so much fun, honestly, to trawl through one terabyte of data looking for answers!

    For example, you could take all the traffic from a particular referring URL, or a particular search key phrase, or all your email marketing traffic in a week, or everyone who saw a particular page, and start digging deeper to understand data issues. By narrowing your focus, you'll reduce the number of distractions, increase the chances of isolating causality, and start to better understand your complex website ecosystem.

5. Get more comfortable with data and its limitations.

    As you understand your data better over time (data collection, storage, manipulation, processing, and analyzing), you'll make the appropriate adjustments in your interpretation and quest for web insights. This in turn will increase your comfort level in data over time, from 75 percent to 78 percent to 85 percent to 90 percent, and so forth. Although you will perhaps never get 100 percent confidence, you'll start making significantly more-confident and more-essential decisions for your business.

    Aim for small increments of improvement in comfort and confidence levels for yourself, and reduce that increment by 50 percent for your decision makers (this is much harder for them).

6. Strive for consistency in calculations.

    On the Web, absolute numbers rarely matter. Trends do, and segmented trends really do. This is important to remember. The quest to get an absolute number right is especially futile because of all the reasons already discussed. Even if you make a mistake, as long as you stay consistent and look at trends *and* important segments for your business in those trends, you will reduce the chances of making suboptimal decisions, even if there is a small difference in data quality.

Do remember that no matter what data collection methodology you use, logs or tags or sniffers, or which vendor tools you use, be it Omniture or WebTrends or Click-Tracks, you can find actionable insights and you can move your business forward. There is no such thing as a *true* number for your websites. When you start segmenting, as you should to get insights, it becomes less important that one method or tool is 10 percent too high or too low.

Two Exceptions That Need Data Quality Attention

Every rule has an exception. In two cases, data quality is dicey but deserves special love and attention to understand what is going on.

Switching from One Analytics Tool to Another

When you switch from one analytics tool to another, there is a lot of data soul-searching because your numbers before and after the switch will be vastly different, sometimes by huge numbers. My recommendation is, rather than reconcile, run the two in parallel for four to eight weeks and simply benchmark the differences in key metrics between the two. Then create a multiplier and use that if you want to compare historical trends.

For example, say you are going to replace Omniture with WebTrends or WebTrends with CoreMetrics or Google Analytics with Omniture or... well you get the idea. Omniture/WebTrends/HBX/Coremetrics with ClickTracks/Google Analytics/WebTrends/Omniture. Run the two in parallel, note that visitors from your old platform are always, for example, 15 percent greater than the new one. Use that multiplier for old data trend comparisons. Do this for your top three or four metrics (page views, unique visitors, time on site) and then forget about reconciliation.

The multiplier will save you lots of dollars, time, and hair on your head.

Performing Cart and Checkout Process Analysis

You want a great degree of precision when analyzing cart and checkout processes because of the amount of money on the line, in the case of e-commerce websites. If you want to spend time reconciling, this is the place to do it. JavaScript tags are a suboptimal way to collect this data. If your platform allows, use something like what ATG uses: event logging. Each time someone is in the checkout process, event logging precisely captures the data from the server (not the pages) along with the business context. This creates a powerful set of data to analyze for key insights.

In summary, the quality of clickstream data can be a huge mindset issue and something that ends up consuming way more energy than necessary. Sadly, it is a quest without a destination or chance of a successful outcome. Maybe someday that will not be the case. Until then, following the six-step process (both as a mindset and approach) will help accelerate your decision making and the time from data to action (and action rules!).

Implementing Best Practices

We have stressed the importance of data collection several times. It is extremely important to ensure that you work with your IT team and your Vendor team to ensure that the web analytics implementation on your website is done correctly. This is especially true for all methodologies except for web logs, where the web servers will capture some information about all the pages that go out. For all others, say JavaScript tags, if implementation is not done right, you won't capture the data and there is no way of going back and getting it.

Often the job of implementation is left to the friendly neighborhood IT person and your web analytics vendor. Yet there are numerous business decisions that need to be made during the course of implementation, many of which have huge data implications. Hence it is imperative that web analysts, website owners, and decision makers are actively involved during the implementation process.

This section covers implementation of best practices from the business perspective. Your goal in using these best practices should be to elevate awareness that will help the folks on the business side ask the right questions and complete a successful implementation. Your individual web analytics vendor will be the best source for unique technical implementation guidelines.

The best practices are as follows:

1. Tag all your pages.
2. Place tags last.
3. Place tags inline.
4. Identify your unique page definition.
5. Use cookies intelligently.
6. Consider link-coding issues.
7. Be aware of redirects.
8. Validate that data is being captured correctly.
9. Correctly encode rich web experiences.

Please note that the best practices are numbered; as you implement them, you may make a numbered list along these lines and check the items off the list as you proceed.

Tag All Your Pages

This step seems fairly straightforward. You should tag all your pages simply because with JavaScript tags, more than with other methodologies, if your page is not tagged you have no data and you have no way of going back and finding it (short of looking in your web log files, which can be a nontrivial challenge).

Simple software such as Web Link Validator from REL Software is useful for checking whether all your pages are tagged correctly. It can do a lot more than check missing tags, and so is a good piece of software to have. See the website for all the features (`http://www.relsoftware.com/wlv/`). Web Link Validator runs between $95–$795—money well spent.

A best practice is to run this nice little program or your own equivalent software once a week. Then send a report to your web development team with a list of pages missing the tags.

Make Sure Tags Go Last (Customers Come First!)

In many web analytics implementations on the Web, you'll see the tag right at the top or in the header or before the <body> tag. This is suboptimal. Your JavaScript tag should be placed as close to the </body> tag as possible. The simple reason for this is that the tag should be the last thing to load on the page. In case your analytics server is slow in responding or has simply died (less likely), or you have a huge tag (lots of lines of code), at least the web page and the content will load quickly.

Our websites are there primarily for customers and secondarily for us to collect data.

Tags Should Be Inline

This one often comes back to bite many implementations. Remember this golden rule: JavaScript tags should be inline. They should not be placed in delightful places such as inside tables or frames and other such things. Your tag placement will greatly affect your ability to collect data accurately.

Identify Your Unique Page Definition

Increasingly, websites are becoming dynamic in how they react to customers or how they personalize content or how they re-leverage the same .html (or .jhtml or .asp or .jsp) page to do different things. What this means is that you can no longer rely on *product-name*.html to define a unique page identity.

JavaScript tags, and perhaps all other methods, collect that entire URL along with all the parameters in the stem. During implementation (and indeed if you change your site often), you will have to make sure that you "teach" your web analytics tool which combination of filename and parameters identifies a page.

As an example, here is a random URL for my blog, which is a static site:

`http://www.kaushik.net/avinash/2006/10/ten-minutes-with-brett-crosby-google-analytics.html`

In this case, the `.html` simply identifies a unique page.

But consider the following, from the Best Buy website:

`http://www.bestbuy.com/site/olspage.jsp?skuId=7686998&type=product&cmp=++&id=1134704163586`

It is `olspage.jsp` *and* the parameter `skuId` that possibly define a unique page. If in this case you plunked down a web analytics tool without teaching it what makes a page unique, you would obviously get wrong numbers.

A Unique Page Definition Challenge

Identifying unique page definitions can be difficult. The following is a real URL from a website (though the actual name of the site has been removed to protect privacy). Can you guess what identifies the unique page?

```
http://removed.4privacy.site.com/cgi-bin/removed.cfg/php/end
 user/std_adp.php?p_faqid=1165&p_created=1137444477&p_sid=k1lMDYoi&p_
 accessibility=&p_lva=&p_sp=cF9zcmNoPTEmcF9zb3JOX2J5PSZwX2dyaWRzb3JOP
 SZwX3Jvd19jbnQ9NjYwJnBfcHJvZHM9JnBfY2F0czOmcF9wdjOxLjUxMiZwX2N2PSZwX
 3NlYXJjaF9OeXBlPWFuc3dlcnMuc2VhcmNoX25sJnBfcGFnZTOxJnBfc2VhcmNoX3Rle
 HQ9ZGVsdXhl&p_li=
```

Use Cookies Intelligently

Use first-party cookies as much as possible and not third-party cookies. There are three types of information you will collect:

Source attributes: These indicate where people come from (websites, campaigns, search engines, and so forth).

Page attributes: These indicate what people see, how often, where, page grouping in all your content, and so forth.

User attributes: These indicate who this "person" is (through persistent anonymous IDs, whether the person has a login, whether the person is part of a test, and more).

Usually source and page attributes are best captured via URLs and parameters. User attributes are best stored in cookies. However, please be careful about capturing only non-PII (personally identifiable information) and disclose in your privacy policies explicitly what you collect. These cookies will stay in the browser and can be easily read by your tags without having to stuff your URLs and make them fat.

Sometimes user attributes—for example, an anonymous cookie value or your login to TimesSelect on the New York Times website—tend to be held on the server after session initiation. Be aware that if this is the case, your JavaScript tags are blind to that data.

Warning: Please be aware that Internet Explorer 6 and 7 limit the number of cookies to 20 per domain. After that, it starts blowing away your first cookie and then the next, and so forth. Not nice. There are ways to get around this—for example, by consolidating cookies or by using subdomains. Please check how many cookies you are setting in total from all solutions on your website that might be setting cookies (web analytics applications, multivariate testing applications, surveys and so forth) and work with your developers to address the issues, if you have any.

Consider Link-Coding Issues

Links are what make the Web tick, and we often have link overload on all our pages. But that fact aside, there are many ways to encode a link compared to the standard <A HREF> HTML tag. The choices we make in encoding our links can affect our critical ability to track the click. Here are a few issues to be aware of and to think about carefully as you implement your web analytics tool.

JavaScript Wrappers

On websites there are often links that are wrapped in JavaScript. Usually these are links to pop-ups, but they could be for other purposes. For example, consider this one:

```
JavaScript:var x=window.open('http://links.ppp.com/pages/prices.asp?)
```

When a visitor clicks on this link, the website pops open a new window where product prices are listed. It is important to be aware that if you are going to be using reports such as site overlay (click density), these links might not show the number of clicks in that report because of the JavaScript *wrapper*. This is not an issue with all vendors, but with enough of them that you should be aware of it.

The recommendation is to use JavaScript wrappers on links only when you absolutely need to. Remember, this is not just a problem for web analytics but also for search engine robots and spiders. They don't follow JavaScript links (or execute

JavaScript), so they will also not reach or index the valuable piece of content you have wrapped in JavaScript (so this is bad for SEO as well).

Anchors

Anchors at the end of links are simply a way for a visitor to jump farther down or up on the same page. For example, consider the following link

```
http://removed.com/finance/basic.jhtml#features
```

By clicking on this link (where #features is part of the anchor), the visitor will stay on the same page but jump to the product features section.

Most website analytics programs won't be able to capture this click as the visitor viewing the features content. They will simply capture this as a reload of the product page. If you want to capture which piece of content on the page is being viewed, you'll have to be aware of that and work with your particular vendor to do special coding.

Multiple Source Links on a Page to the Same Target

It is not uncommon to have multiple links in different locations on a page pointing to the same target page. For example, on Amazon.com's website, a link to the Books section appears in the header and on the left navigation and in the body of the web page, and on the promotional area on the right side of the page. These four links point to the exact same target page.

This can be a problem from a tracking perspective because to your web analytics tool, all of them look like the same link. The tool has no way of telling you which link is being clicked more or that the link on the header is a waste of space.

The solution for most web analytics applications is to simply add a parameter that makes each link unique. To reduce the effort for IT, you can create standardized rules and apply them to global elements of your site. For example, here is how the links can be made unique:

```
http://www.amazon.com/books-used-books-textbooks/?lid=site_header
http://www.amazon.com/books-used-books-textbooks/?lid=left_nav
http://www.amazon.com/books-used-books-textbooks/?lid=right _nav
```

Now, to your web analytics tool each of these is a unique link, and you can measure accurately which link works better. By making the rule global, your web server can automatically add the lid (link ID) parameter to every link in the header, footer, and navigational elements and quickly give you good data across the website.

It is better to be aware of these three issues up front and get the coding done right on the website. That way, you can accurately measure the amount of time required to roll out the tool and the website updates that will be needed. Additionally, you will avoid hassles after launching the tool because these questions will come up and simply make the tool look bad, when in reality it is not the tool's fault that it can't track some of these issues.

Be Aware of Redirects

Redirects are nifty little things that can direct traffic efficiently in case links change or your SEM/ad/creative agency wants to track data. In the good old days of web logs, redirects were used when you wanted to capture clicks that sent data off to other websites (domains). But if not done correctly, redirects can also mess up your web analytics data collection in a big way (and it will also, as noted in the preceding section, possibly mess up your indexing quality by search robots). Let's cover two instances to outline the data collection challenge: internal redirects and external redirects.

Internal Redirects

Having *internal redirects* (redirects that simply lead from one page of your website to another page also on your site) can be suboptimal. For example, let's look at this link from Microsoft's website:

```
http://g.msn.com/mh_mshp/98765?09769308&http://www.microsoft.com/downloads
/search.aspx&&HL=Downloads&CM=Navigation&CE=Resources
```

This link goes from `microsoft.com` to a subdirectory, `microsoft.com/downloads`, on the same site, but it does so via `msn.com`. I'm not sure whether Microsoft is doing this to overcome any challenges with their web analytics tool, but it is quite unnecessary. An extra hop for the data via a second domain can cause problems. You have to make your tool smarter so that from the home page, `www.microsoft.com`, people are not going to `g.msn.com` but instead to `www.microsoft.com/downloads`, and that is the logic that you have to maintain over time (which can get complex as the site changes). Using internal redirects also requires you to capture and store extra data, and this can cause problems when you are deep into segmenting the data.

It is important to stress that it is quite likely that Microsoft is using the internal redirect because they have figured all this out and it works for them. The core point is that you should be aware of the complexity it can pose in measuring and you should go into it with your eyes open (and with support of your website IT folks who might have implemented these things).

The nice thing is that eliminating unnecessary redirects on the website cleans up the code, making it easier for the IT team to maintain. They can do updated website releases a bit faster as well because they don't have to create new redirects all the time or maintain what can become, even with lots of automation, a monster that constantly needs caring and feeding. Most web analytics are smart now; they don't need internal redirects to report data accurately.

External Redirects

Another instance of using redirects occurs while linking to other websites, outside your own. Consider the following dummy URL:

```
http://www.eliminated.com/Navigate.asp?Category=238&AppID=859
&rDirURL=http://www.zsolutions.com/application-for-
payment-solution.htm&UType=6
```

In this example, there are links on `eliminated.com` that are sending traffic to `zsolutions.com`, but this is occurring via a redirect. This was the only option in the past because with web logs the referrer data would go to the destination site. By using a redirect, the web log was able to capture the "click" for reporting purposes.

Now most web analytics tools can do exit tracking, which eliminates the need for this type of redirecting. This, of course, simplifies the website code and makes releases a bit faster thanks to removing this overhead. What is important to know is that if your website is doing these external redirects, you could be hindering your web analytics tool's ability to collect data (unless you are using web logs and you have no other choice).

Another example of using external redirects is as a part of campaigns (banner ads, search marketing, affiliates, and so forth). Here's an example:

A text ad shows up on the Yahoo! network and looks like this:

```
http://ypn-120.overture.com/d/sr/?xargs=sOOOU7A8C4rk9M27-
8w3mbaL1o7n8tRIM1MKG15yaTTYqt1OIMC4KGO52LQGe8M8pF5dUjnqu
XOOoAHgzREB8exjcMUu16vlVNOxyLosI_NEvRbc4c55SJBlZNeL2GUFu
P7dvj7_pkBvrWPmMV7wISkNgJ-y8sy_4OHc-
xsvj1MeEj5UfOBmhfe67YJFqKl1OxNjJrlmQaC1QdUlNazUZM2DUyVaB
mZI28GqX46fE9EEIPPIyYc1GDR_FIOdj59ZPUEh-
v7Djt2yBtkx6TYdilGh1XUyi1hEXX4A2D3q341AacTLynn9-
4f8TLjxABMw
```

If a user clicks on the magical link, the click (and hence the visitor) goes to something like this:

```
http://srch.atdmt.com/search/18957/SRCH56zxfyaj5r/DEFAULT/y
smronpremium/content/.search?ovchn=OVR&ovcpn=ron&ovcrn=y
smronpremium&ovtac=PPC
```

The preceding ad server, probably being used by an agency, ends up at the following:

```
https://www.removed4privacy.com/servlet/LMBServlet?the_acti
on=NavigateHomeLoansAppFirstStep&TAG_ID=D778E3D4BFA722E4
B48F537701A0F06F1165968367230&sourceid=seogtolre121405r1
&moid=4793&q=
```

So one click causes two hops for the customer to end up at your site. At each hop, data is collected by someone else outside your company. Does your web analytics application have any knowledge that the user came from an Overture ad? If this was not proactively thought through, the answer is usually no.

There are two important things to consider to ensure that you can report and analyze data accurately:

- Work with your agency (or internal resource) to ensure that there is at least one parameter that gets passed from one hop to the next hop to you, so that you can accurately track the campaign. This parameter could be the sourceid used in the preceding example.

- Please ensure that everyone is using 301 permanent redirects where possible. Permanent redirects will pass the referrer data because of the special way in which they are coded. They are also understood cleanly by search engines. This will help ensure that the original referrer is passed on to your web analytics website. Otherwise, your referrers report, your search engine and keywords report, and a bunch of other reports will be completely wrong.

Validate That Data Is Being Captured Correctly

Some web analytics tools use one standard tag to collect data. Other vendors have custom tags all over the place—for example, your website could be tagged with 25 different tags on different pages because your vendor needs lots of data to be placed in customized variables up front for post-data-collection analysis or for capturing various pieces of data such as order or lead information.

I won't pontificate on which approach is better, because there is no such thing—both have pros and cons. But it is important that you validate in a quality audit (QA) environment and in production that your 25 customized tags are each capturing exactly what they are supposed to, when they are supposed to.

Omniture, for example, has a nifty utility that you can use to validate and review that data is being collected by Omniture tags as it should be. This is really helpful. Please ask your vendor whether they have something like this (and they probably do).

It is recommended that you check your tags and data collection once a month to validate that normal site releases have not messed something up.

Correctly Encode Your Your Website Rich Media

Standard JavaScript tags, web logs, and most other methodologies were created to function in an environment where it was *pages* that needed to be measured. The concept of a page is critical to the functioning of any web analytics application.

Rich media implementations are obviously not pages. They are *experiences*, and the entire experience could be represented by one page view. If you have lots of rich experiences, you'll need a completely different and deeper (and more painful) strategy to collect data. You will have to use a custom tag or standard tags in custom ways or different data capture mechanisms such as event logs to collect this data.

Tracking rich web experiences requires a lot of deliberate planning and implementation up front, before any rich media gets released on your website. This will ensure that you are able to track some semblance of success via your web analytics tool or via a custom solution.

I am positive that all the technical complexity in this section causes heads to hurt, especially if you are on the business side. It is complicated, it seems really hard, and in your spiffy vendor presentations many of these points were not highlighted. But there is simply no other way of ensuring that you are collecting data accurately other than looking at each of these items in a very deliberate manner and doing so up front. (You may also need to look at other items, say you are using Ajax, that you might be doing that are unique to your website.) It is important for you to personally understand these issues so that you can ask the technical folks (yours and your vendors') the right questions. After you get your first data check, you will also need to make sure that all of these nine recommendations have been done right so that you can have confidence in the data.

Apply the "Three Layers of So What" Test

You have followed the right path and have your business questions. You have also hired the right people and set them up for success. You are ready to drill down to the *nitty gritty* stage of defining metrics. Welcome. There is perhaps no other medium where data and metrics can be accessed quite as fast as on the Web.

Imagine the massive ERP and CRM projects of yore when you would have to spend a year building the system and then more time putting together a data warehouse and a reporting structure, and then finally you would get your hands on some data.

And here is the reality of the Web: You can go to google.com/analytics and sign up for an account in five minutes. You'll be given a snippet of JavaScript code at the end of your sign-up. Take this and put it in the global site footer of your website, click Save, and you are finished. A couple of hours later, you'll have access to roughly 80 reports and more metrics than you would know what to do with.

Notice the difference in the *time to market* in the two situations. A year or more and a lot of cost vs. a couple of hours and no cost. You could decide not to go down the route of Google Analytics and buy another web analytics product. This will slow you down only a little bit, just for the time it will take you to identify another vendor (a couple of months, max).

The danger of getting instant access to so many metrics is that we have no idea which one to use and report on in order to get maximum benefit. This dilemma is compounded by the great amount of hype about many KPIs that makes it easy to head off in the wrong direction. It is difficult in such an environment to figure out where to focus and which metrics to choose to allow for maximum actionable insights.

The answer to your *which metrics should I choose* dilemma is a simple test that I call the Three Layers of So What test: Ask every metric that you report on the question, "So what?" three times. Each question provides an answer that in turn typically raises another question (a "So what?" again). If at the end of the third question you don't get a recommendation for action, you have the wrong metric.

The overall inspiration of the So What test is the central goal of the Trinity strategy: actionable metrics and insights. There are so many metrics available and recommended that often we report on metrics and publish and email hundreds of reports. The So What test is to undo this clutter in your life and allow you to focus on only the metrics that will help you take action, while keeping the distractions at bay, those that fall into the *nice to know* or *I don't know why I am reporting this but it sounds important or looks cool* camp.

Let's illustrate how you would conduct the So What test with a couple of examples.

Key Performance Indicator: Percent of Repeat Visitors

You run a report and notice a trend. Here is how the So What test will work:

- "The trend of repeat visitors for our website is up month to month." *So what?*
- "This is fantastic because it shows that we are a more sticky website now." (At this point, you would inquire how that conclusion was arrived at and ask for a definition of *sticky*, but I digress.) *So what?*
- "We should do more of *xxx* to leverage this trend (or *yyy* or *zzz*, which might have caused the trend to go up, assuming that is a good thing)." *So what?*

If your answer to the last *so what* is, "I don't know...isn't that nice, the trend going up...maybe we can't do anything to exactly leverage this because this metric does not tell us why visitors came back at a higher rate," at this point you should cue the sound of money walking out the door. This might not be the best KPI for you.

There are no universal truths in the world (maybe some religions will dispute that) and hence for you the So What test might yield the right answer at the end of the third question. Consider the preceding walk-through as a just an example that could apply to some websites.

Key Performance Indicator: Top Exit Pages on the Website

You have been reporting the top exit pages of your website each month, and to glean more insights you show trends for the last six months.

- "These are the top exit pages on our website in December 2006." *So what?* They don't seem to have changed in six months.

- "We should focus on these pages because they are major *leakage points* in our website." *So what?* We have looked at this report for six months and tried to make fixes, and even after that the pages listed here have not dropped off the report.

- "If we can stop visitors from leaving the website, we can keep them on our website." *So what?* Doesn't everyone have to exit on some page?

The So What test here highlights that although this metric seems to be a really good one on paper, in reality it provides little insight that you can use to drive action. Because of the macro dynamics of this website, the content consumption pattern of visitors does not seem to change over time (this happens when a website does not have a high content turnover), and we should move on to other actionable metrics.

In this case, the So What test helps you focus your energies on the right metric, but it can also help you logically walk through from measurement to action. As in the prior case, perhaps for your website at the end of the third question there would be an action that could be taken or a business strategy that could be changed.

Key Performance Indicator: Conversion Rate for Top Search Keywords

In working closely with your search agency, or in-house team, you have produced a spreadsheet that shows the conversion rate for the top search keywords for your website.

- "The conversion rate for our top 20 keywords has increased in the last three months by a statistically significant amount." *So what?*

- "Our pay-per-click (PPC) campaign is having a positive outcome, and we should reallocate funds to these nine keywords that show the most promise." *Okay.*

That's it. No more "So what?" With just one question, we have a recommendation for action. This indicates that this is a great KPI and we should continue to use it for tracking. Notice the characteristics of this good KPI:

- Although it uses one of the most standard metrics in the universe, conversion rate, it is applied in a very focused way—just the top search keywords. (You can do the top 10 or top 20 or what makes sense to you—it is the focus that is important.)

- It is pretty clear from the first answer to "So what?" that even for this KPI the analyst has segmented the data between organic and PPC. This is the other little secret: no KPI works at an aggregated level to by itself give us insights. Segmentation does that.

Remember, we don't want to have metrics because they are nice to have, and there are tons of those. We want to have metrics that answer business questions and allow us to take action—do more of something or less of something or at least funnel ideas that we can test and then take action. The So What test is one mechanism for identifying metrics that you should focus on or metrics that you should ditch because although they might work for others, for you they don't pass the So What test.

Month 1: Diving Deep into Core Web Analytics Concepts

Now that you understand the elements that form an effective web analytics strategy, from thought to implementation, you can prepare to blast off into the deep end of the web analytics universe. In this chapter, you will learn about some of the basic terms, methodologies, and metrics that form the bedrock of web analytics.

Metrics such as visits, visitors, page views, time on site, top destinations, and site overlay (click density) are all within easy reach in every web analytics application. Although they look and sound obvious, it is not easy to parse the data to drive action. You are going to spend month 1 in pursuit of a solid understanding of the not-so-basic concepts behind these seemingly basic items.

This chapter covers definitions, why you should care about each concept, metric, and report, and what you should care about in each case. Each section is full of tips and lessons from the real world that will be helpful whether you are a novice in the field or you have already *been there and done that.*

Week 1: Preparing to Understand the Basics

To avoid a common mistake of jumping directly into metrics, the first stop in our journey of understanding metrics starts with developing a robust appreciation of three core pieces of data capture mechanisms: URLs, URL parameters, and cookies.

The core reason to start here, rather than directly on metrics, is that by asking for measurement on your website, you are adding new requirements to your website design and architecture in order to get it to cough up data that you'll need to make effective decisions. So, although this might seem like a mundane discussion of coding conventions, it is fundamental that you spend time absorbing this knowledge. All web analytics tools are fairly "dumb" (GIGO) and suboptimal data quickly turns into pretty but suboptimal reports.

Don't worry too much about your technical background. Start with a simple understanding of why URLs and cookies are important and what they can tell you about your website. Understand the idiosyncrasies and limitations, and you'll come out much better on the flip side.

URLs, URL parameters, and cookies probably have more effect on everything we do in web analytics than any other piece of data. They define the existence of the website, pages, users, acquisition sources, campaigns, logins, lots of anonymous identifiers that make your browsing easier, and many other things. To help you understand these three core items, I will use the New York Times website (www.nytimes.com) as an example. The specific web page tells the story of the Space Shuttle Discovery landing safely (hurray!) at the John F. Kennedy Space Center on December 22, 2006, at 5:32 P.M.(EST).

Monday and Tuesday: URLs

The acronym *URL* stands for *Uniform Resource Locator*. It usually contains the identifier for the website and the address of a web page on the website that the visitor is requesting. For our New York Times example, the URL is as follows:

```
http://www.nytimes.com/2006/12/22/science/space/23shuttlecnd
.html?hp&ex=1166850000&en=9434ee2697934581&ei=5094&partner=homepage
```

The first part of the URL is the domain (www.nytimes.com), the second part usually translates into a directory structure (/2006/12/22/science/space/), and the third part is the filename (23shuttlecnd.html). Everything after that is a parameter (more on this later in this section).

Why Should You Care?

The domain in the URL is important in that when it comes to web analytics applications, the URL identifies a set of data that is usually connected to the domain name in the URL. So www.nytimes.com is different from select.nytimes.com. This can be two different datasets, based on standard implementation. You can also choose how you implement your web analytics solution and you can choose to use a third-party cookie and look at these two domains as one.

What Should You Care About?

There are two very important things that you want to focus on before you establish your web analytics practice.

What is the identity of your website? Is it just www.nytimes.com or it is www.nytimes.com + select.nytimes.com + travel.nytimes.com + others? The URL will determine your data strategy, your customer session, your cookie strategy, and your ability to get views (all for one, or one for all) of your website data. Documentation of your URL structure (except the parameter stem) is really important when it comes to metadata.

What can the URL tell you about your site structure? When you analyze data, maybe you want metrics and numbers for World, Business, Technology, Sports, Science, Health, Opinion, and so forth broken out separately. After documenting what the URL can provide, you'll have to decide whether the URL structure is "intelligent" enough to help you organize your data. If not, you might have to pass custom variables to the web analytics application so that it can understand your website. This will mean more work to be done with your web analytics vendor, with your website developers and with members of your web analytics team to ensure that you are getting the information that you'll need to make effective decisions.

Wednesday: URL Parameters

In our New York Times example, 23shuttlecnd.html?hp&ex=1166850000&en=9434ee2697934581&ei=5094&partner=homepage, everything after the question mark (?) is called a *URL parameter*. We have seen quite a proliferation of URL parameters as websites have become increasingly dynamic (and the URL + filename was insufficient to drive dynamic experiences) and as pressure has increased to track more and more things for reporting and analysis.

URL parameters are used by web platforms to drive dynamic experiences on web pages (so `23shuttlecnd.html` plus a combination of parameters could show 50 different versions of the web page without having 50 separate physical web pages created). They are also used for tracking purposes. For example, in the preceding URL, the parameter "`partner`" is telling the web analytics application that the visitor came to the story from the home page.

Why Should You Care?

Over time we have come to use URL parameters, for a myriad of purposes. This makes them helpful (because they can be quite productive), but also dangerous (because they can mess up the data depending on how they are parsed by the web analytics application). Incorrect definition of parameters can cause your page counts to be wrong and in turn can affect other metrics as well.

What Should You Care About?

Having understood the importance of URL parameters there are four important things to cover that will ensure that your web analytics application understands your website correctly.

Document your parameters. Document all of the parameters that your web platform uses, what each parameter is supposed to do, and what possible values each parameter can have.

Partner with your web IT department to understand which parameters make the page unique and which parameters exist simply for tracking purposes. In our example, it seems that all the parameters (`hp`, `ex`, `en`, `ei`, `partner`) do not define a unique page—only the HTML filename does.

Recall the Best Buy example in Chapter 5, "Web Analytics Fundamentals":

```
http://www.bestbuy.com/site/olspage.jsp?skuId=7686998&type=
product&cmp=++&id=1134704163586
```

In this case, the identifier of the unique page is `olspage.jsp` *and* `skuID`.

Ensure that your web analytics platform is configured correctly in how it treats each parameter. Your web analytics application, usually at a server level, has advanced settings where you can configure, for example, which URL parameters make a page unique and which don't. You will work with your web analytics support person to go through this exercise to ensure fundamental metrics such as number of page views, tracking IDs, etc., are being recorded correctly.

Perform an audit at least once a month. In conjunction with your IT department, conduct an audit of the current parameters and their use and related configuration in your analytics application to ensure that nothing in the latest site release has caused your current web analytics configuration to be incorrect. It is not unusual for developers or your website partners to start passing new URL parameters for a whole host of reasons.

Thursday and Friday: Cookies

Cookies are perhaps more infamous then famous. There is a lot of paranoia associated with cookies, specifically in relation to privacy. The official Web Analytics Association (WAA) definition of a cookie is as follows:

> Cookie: *A message given to a web browser by a web server. The browser stores the message in a text file. The message is then sent back to the server each time the browser requests a page from the server.*

Every time a request comes from a web browser to a web server, the web server will check to see whether cookies from the server already exist. If they do, the server will read them. If they don't, it will send new cookies. At times it will also update the cookies stored in the visitor's web browser.

Typically, but not always, two types of cookies are set by any web server:

Session Cookies These cookies are transient. They exist only as long as the visitor is interacting with the website. Typically they exist to "stitch together" pan-session data that can be used by the web server (for example, to hold items in your shopping cart as long as you are on the site) and by the web analytics application to understand behavior during a visit. These cookies disappear after the visitor session concludes.

Persistent Cookies These are cookies that are set on the visitor browser and are left there even after the session has concluded. They exist until they expire (each cookie has an expiration date, usually far into the future). They contain items such as a persistent, usually anonymous, unique ID that will track the web browser (hoping it is the same person) as it visits the site multiple times.

When I visited www.nytimes.com today, their web server set 10 cookies, including akaushik@nytimes.txt, akaushik@o.nytimes.txt, akaushik@sports.txt, akaushik@wt.o.nytimes.txt, akuashik@tacoda.txt, akaushik@mediaplex.txt, and akaushik@doublick.txt.

Notice that some of these cookies are set by the New York Times and others are set by its partners (Tacoda, DoubleClick, Mediaplex, and so forth) who might be tracking my behavior on the New York Times website separately from the New York Times itself. The partners that are using these cookies can also track my behavior across multiple websites (for example, as I go from nytimes.com to cnn.com).

Here is what is in the akaushik@sports.txt cookie (the nytimes.txt cookie is tracking so much stuff, it would take two pages to print):

```
IXAIInvited528_local
true
```

```
www.nytimes.com/2006/12/22/sports/
1600
56970240
29902060
2334166336
29828634
*
```

Here is what is in the akaushik@doubleclick.txt cookie:

```
id
800000b24beac0d
doubleclick.net/
1024
4059552640
30048910
2279796336
29828634
*
```

All the values you see are translated by each website's web analytics application and used to track visitor behavior on the website. Each cookie contains a unique ID that identifies the browser. As the visitor (me in this case) visits the website, the cookie is read and the unique identifier read and stored (this is used, for example, to compute the metric Repeat Visitor Rate). The cookie also identifies the source that set the cookie (doubleclick.net) and also a set of customized variables that help with additional tracking. For example, the sports.txt cookie tracks when I visited the sports section of the New York Times website, allowing the New York Times to build a profile for my behavior and content consumption on the site (and in turn to use that to target the right ads and promotions to me).

Most cookies contain non-PII and are hence *anonymous*. This is not always the case, but it is highly recommended.

Why Should You Care?

Cookies are important in creating personalized experiences for website visitors ("Welcome back, Avinash" on Amazon.com, for example). They are useful for tracking repeat visits by the same visitors, for isolating test participants if you are using A/B or multivariate testing, and for a number of other purposes. Specifically for web analytics, they can be useful for storing and reporting lots of interesting and useful information (usually some of the most critical).

You should be extra judicious in understanding how your website is using cookies and what data is stored in them. You also need to be sure that your privacy policy is explicit about first-party and third-party cookies that you are using to track visitors.

What Should You Care About?

There are three extremely important things to care about when it comes to use of cookies in the context of your web analytics implementation.

Document exactly what cookies are being set. You should know what cookies are being set by your web server during each customer session and what information is being stored in each cookie. Please do not forget to document all partner cookies that might be set (and what happens to them at the highest-level security setting in a browser, when the browser will reject some cookies).

Your most important cookies should be first-party cookies. They should be first-party cookies and not third-party cookies so that they stand a chance of being accepted by high-security settings or antispyware software. This is especially important because most standard web analytics vendor third-party cookies are blown away by antispyware software. Using third-party cookies can be greatly detrimental in your ability to track repeat visits accurately or to create a personal website experience.

Measure the cookie rejection and deletion rates of your website visitors. This will help you understand how good or bad your web analytics data is when it comes to critical metrics. Figure 6.1 shows cookie deletion rates.

Cookie Support	Visits	%
Enabled	19	86.36%
Disabled	3	13.63%
Total	22	100.00%

Figure 6.1 Cookie deletion rates

Cookie deletion affects other activities as well. For example, cookies specific to A/B and multivariate tests ensure that there is no cross-pollination between test versions, but if the visitor does not accept cookies, they could see different messaging or prices you are testing.

Documenting and validating that the URL, parameters, and cookies are documented and are set up correctly will ensure that your web analytics application is collecting and reporting data accurately and in turn helping you make optimal decisions.

In one short week's worth of work, you have exponentially improved the possibilities of what you can report and the quality of your data. Congratulations.

Week 2: Revisiting Foundational Metrics

Every web analytics journey starts with three foundational questions: How many visitors came to our site? How long did they stay? How many pages did they visit?

These are simple questions, ones that every web analytics application can answer. Yet their measurement is rather complex, and each one has its own set of complexities and limitations that are extremely important to understand and internalize before you use the data. For example, no two tools in the market measure visits the same way. On the exact same website, two web analytics tools will give you different numbers for visits and visitors. Are you curious why?

You'll spend week 2 getting to know each of these foundational metrics much better. In turn, you'll be able to understand and explain them to your bosses and peers.

Monday: Visits and Visitors

The first question on everyone's mind is, How many visitors did we get on our website? It does not matter how long you have had the website, how long you have had analytics tools, or who you are. Your first instinct when thinking of numbers is to wonder about people visiting your website (perhaps it emanates from our primitive desire to be loved).

Almost every report in any web analytics tool either has this metric or is sourced from this metric. It shows up as a raw count or in the form of percentages or in the numerator or denominator or when we torture it by doing global averages. Yet it turns out that there is no standardization, and often this metric (count of visitors) masquerades under different names. The most prevalent names for visitor metrics are visitors, visits, total visitors, unique visitors, sessions, and cookies (!). Depending on the tool you are using, the term *unique visitor* could be measuring completely different things.

```
⊟ Unique Visitor Tracking
   - Daily Visitors
   - Visits & Pageview Tracking
   - Goal Conversion Tracking
   - Absolute Unique Visitors
   - Visitor Loyalty
   - Visitor Recency
⊟ Visitor Segment Performance
   - New vs Returning
   - Referring Source
```

As covered in Chapter 1, "Web Analytics—Present and Future," at the dawn of the Internet, IP addresses were used to identify browsers (a proxy for customers) coming to the website. Very quickly that evolved to using the IP plus the browser ID, and as complexity increased that evolved into setting cookies and using anonymous unique identifiers in cookies to identify visitors.

Visits

This metric is also commonly referred to as *visitors* or *total visitors*. The goal is to measure how many times people visit the website during a given time frame (remember, we can't actually track people and hence we use various proxies such as cookie values). Because most web analytics platforms use cookies and start and end a session when the visitor comes and leaves, here is the simplest definition of the Visits metric:

Visits: A count of all the sessions during a given time period

Sessions are identified by transient cookie values. When a visitor requests the first page, their session starts and typically, though not always, the session continues until one of the following occurs:

1. The visitor exits the website or closes the browser.
2. The web server automatically terminates the session after 29 minutes of inactivity.

For example, in writing this chapter I visited the New York Times website three times between 1 P.M. and 3 P.M. The first time I left the browser open for an hour, and the other two times I just closed it.

In the New York Times analytics session, I have had three Visits today (if you use ClickTracks, that would be recorded as three Visitors).

Unique Visitors

The Unique Visitors metric, as best as it can, attempts to identify unique visitors to the website during a specified time period. It is our attempt at understanding repeat visits by customers and/or how many "people" are coming to our website. This metric is specifically tracked by using the persistent cookie that is set on a visitor's browser application and read by the web server (or analytics JavaScript tag). Here is the simplest definition:

Unique visitors: A count of all the unique cookie_ids during a given time period

If I extend my example of the New York Times website, they would count three visits but one unique visitor in terms of my behavior.

The time period part is important. For visits, we are simply summing up each session. But in the case of unique visitors, we are selecting distinct values of the cookie_id and summing that up.

For example, I read the New York Times website every day. If I visited the website once each day for the past week, the metrics would indicate the following:

- Visits: 7
- Unique visitors: 1

If I do the same thing for a month, the metrics would be as follows:

- Visits: 30
- Unique visitors: 1

When reporting unique visitors, it is extremely important to ensure that your web analytics application is tracking real unique visitors. Some applications have default settings that would cause my weekly report to indicate the following:

• Visits: 7

• Unique visitors: 7

In this case, the application is summing up unique visitors by each day and providing that as the total unique visitors for the week. This is not an optimal methodology for computing unique visitors. On your request, your vendor has the capability to provide you with actual unique visitors. Please ask them for it to report accurate metrics. Figure 6.2 shows a trend of unique visitors over the course of two months (and you'll admit this one is going in the right direction!).

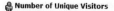
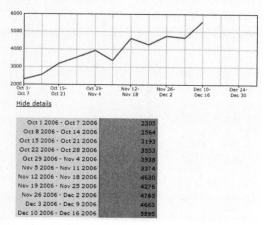

Figure 6.2 Tracking unique visitors

Why Should You Care?

For these two metrics, visits and unique visitors, you don't need a justification for caring! They form the bedrock of all your computations, every single one of them. It is really important that you get them right.

What Should You Care About?

Unique visitor tracking is perhaps the activity that is most under the spotlight when it comes to web metrics. There are three very important facets of tracking that you should care about.

Understand precisely how each of these two critical metrics is being computed. Partner with your web analytics vendor to understand exactly what formula is being used and how is it measured over time. If your vendor's formula differs from what is defined in this text, ask why and ensure that you get an answer that you are satisfied with.

Spend time with your IT team and your web analytics vendor to understand how sessionization is done in the application. *Sessionization* is the process of taking all the requests from a website visitor within a certain time period (usually one visit) and creating a session in the web analytics application. Is your session length set to expire after 29 minutes of inactivity? Does a session end if someone goes to a search engine and comes back in two minutes (with some vendors yes, with others no)? This is especially important if you are trying to reconcile data from two different web analytics applications, because each vendor has their own unique settings.

Tell your web analytics vendor that you are interested in computing real unique visitors. Ask them to compute unique visitors by day, week, and month at the minimum. Most vendors will oblige. Use these numbers in your conversion rate or repeat visitor calculations to get an accurate understanding of site behavior.

Reports	
Dashboards	→
Visitors	→
Last Visitor Details	
Daily Unique Visitors	
Weekly Unique Visitors	
Monthly Unique Visitors	
Visits	

Consider this:

If you use real unique visitors to identify my reading habits, then the repeat visitor rate for me in a week = 7 (7/1).

If you use "fake" unique visitors, your repeat visitor rate in a week = 1 (7/7).

Each provides a totally different picture of customer behavior on your site.

Remember that the unique visitors that you report use cookie values and therefore are dependent on various issues that affect cookies. It is important to not only remember this, but to communicate it to your stakeholders. If you are using third-party cookies and Internet Explorer 7 is rejecting them by default, you will have terrible data because every request or visit will be provided a new cookie by your browser. Alternatively, if you are using third-party cookies and my antispyware program is blowing them away every day, I am a new unique visitor to you every day. If your visitors don't accept cookies at all (first-party or third-party), they are unique visitors with every request to your web server.

Remember this golden rule: Use first-party cookies, measure cookie rejection rates for your website, observe number trends over time, and you'll do fine.

It would really be nice if all the vendors decided that they would standardize how they compute these two metrics. It would be a big step toward making the lives of all web analytics practitioners more sane.

Tuesday and Wednesday: Time on Site

After we ask the question, *How many visitors came?* the next logical question is, *How long did they stay?* The Time on Site metric is also called length of visit or visit length by different vendors. The most frequent use of the Time on Site metric is in the context of engagement, as in, "If my website is engaging and provides relevant content, visitors should be staying on the website for longer than x minutes" (where x will depend on what your website does and why your customers visit the website). With the advent of cookies and better sessionization methodologies, the measurement of this metric has improved over time.

Why Should You Care?

Time on site is such a common metric that it is hard to escape from having it stare at you from every dashboard that you look at. Senior management also seems to love it because it seems like such a simple metric to understand—what's so hard to understand about how long people spend on the website? Yet this lovely metric has many hidden pitfalls that are extremely important to understand if you are to truly unlock the power of insights (or supposed measurement of success) that it is supposed to provide.

What Should You Care About?

Time on Site is such an important metric yet there are a few important nuances that we are frequently not aware of.

It is important to understand how this metric is measured. When the customer makes the first request of a web server, typically a session is started for the visitor. From that point on, as the customer browses the website, each request is logged away with a timestamp on the request (pretty much the same way with each data collection methodology). It is critically important how computation of this metric is done by any web analytics tool and how time on site could be quite meaningless for some customer experiences such as blogs.

To understand how the metric is computed, let's consider an example; let's say that a customer comes to a website, the session is four pages, and the customer leaves the website. Here is how the entries in the log files would look (greatly simplified, of course):

Click 1: `index.html`—0900 hrs

Click 2: `product.html`—0901 hrs

Click 3: `product_detail.html`—0904 hrs

Click 4: `customer_reviews.html`—0905 hrs

Your web analytics tool calculates how long the visitor has spent on a page by computing the difference between the timestamps on one page and the next one. So in the preceding example, time spent on the home page would be one minute (0900 – 0901).

Notice that the last entry has a timestamp but most of us are not aware that if the customer simply walks away from the browser, leaving it open, or exits from the website (by typing a different URL in the browser), the web logs or JavaScript tags have no way of knowing how long the customer spent on that page. In this case, the tool would indicate that the customer spent zero minutes (or seconds) on the last page.

This is important because we have no way of knowing whether a person spent fifteen minutes on that page or zero. The time on site for this customer would be computed as four minutes.

Let's look at a practical example of how this can be a big challenge for you. Figure 6.3 shows the Length of Visit (Time on Site) distribution for a website. It shows that an overwhelming percent of traffic to the website stays on the website for close to zero seconds.

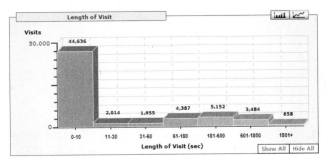

Figure 6.3 Length of visit distribution

The challenge is that the website in question is a blog, and a common feature of most blogs is that most of the content is on the home page (index.html). A majority of the readers would never go deeper into the website, and sadly our web analytics tools have no way of knowing whether visitors spend half an hour consuming all the great content or leave in five seconds. Success is hard to measure.

There are hacks available in JavaScript tags that can indicate that a customer has browsed away from your website by typing a URL or closing the browser. The hack will execute an on-load event that tells the website that the user left. You should check whether you have this nonstandard "feature." However, it still does not solve the problem of someone simply leaving the browser open and walking away.

Many web analytics tools report time on site as an average. The reports will show the average time on site as an aggregate (for the entire site), or as you drill down into various reports. Figures 6.4 and 6.5 provide two examples.

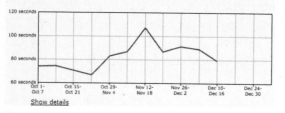

Figure 6.4 Average time on site: overall

Figure 6.5 Average time on site: search engines

The challenge with showing a simple average across all sessions is that it hides the real insights from you. It is always optimal to look at the distribution for this metric (as shown in Figure 6.3). But if you want to average it (which is quite okay), you should attempt to get an intelligent average and not a dumb one.

No matter how hard you try, lots of visits to your website will be single-page visits, for example. We know from the previous example that single-page visits will have a time on site of zero seconds. So if lots of visits are one-page visits and their time on site is zero, your average time on site is a dumb average because it takes into account all these visitors for whom you have no data (and because there are many of these visitors, the effect could be quite large).

In Figure 6.6, the trend shows an overall average time on site of approximately 83 seconds.

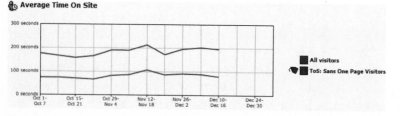

Figure 6.6 Average time on site for overall and sans single-page visits

Now if you simply remove the single-page visits from your data, your graph looks very different (and more intelligent) and shows that the "real" average time on site for visits for which you actually have data is approximately 184 seconds! That extra 100 seconds could be the difference between the website owner getting a salary bonus or not! The difference in the metric is just as stark for your search engine traffic, as you can see in Figure 6.7.

	Total	Google	MSN	Yahoo!	Ask Jeeves	My Web Search	AOL	AltaVista	Netscape
All visitors	57s	53s	68s	98s	33s	64s	239s	98s	185s
ToS: Sans One Page Visitors	164s	157s	164s	272s	141s	205s	547s	328s	278s

Figure 6.7 Average time on site for search engine and sans single-page visits

Figure 6.7 shows the change from 57 seconds for the overall traffic to 164 seconds for those who saw more than one page. It also shows that the traffic from the search engine Ask Jeeves might have looked terrible at 33 seconds average time on site for all visitors, but looking at the Ask Jeeves–referred traffic without the single-page visits shows an average time on site is 141 seconds—not too shabby.

I will talk about bounce rates a bit later in this chapter; it is important to review that. It is also important to point out that there is more to know about single-page visits than that we should not count them. What is critical for you to understand in the context of the Average Time on Site metric is that you don't have data for the last page of the visit. In addition, if the visitor sees only a single page during the visit, you have no awareness of what time on site for their visit is. You should be aware of this and accommodate for it because it can have a large effect on your computation of this critical metric.

It is extremely tricky to have goals for time on site. If you have a website, would you like to have a bigger Time on Site metric or smaller? If you exist to help your customers complete their tasks as fast as possible (buy, get a support question answered, and so forth), should you have a goal of just a few seconds? Or do you want your customers to become engaged with the site and spend a lot of time on the site and hence have a bigger number as your goal? You can have a smaller time on site simply by having fewer pages. You can have a longer time on site by making it harder for your users to find the information they need or having a long checkout process. Although it might seem that these are egregious examples, in our lives goals have a weird way of motivating behavior. Although all metrics should be tied to goals, you should carefully consider what behavior you want the goal of this metric to drive for your company employees (and then make that desired behavior explicit).

Thursday and Friday: Page Views

Page views have been one of our favorite metrics from the dawn of the basic server web log parsers until today. We started by measuring hits to the server, which in the early days literally translated into requests for a simple HTML file. We then moved to measuring pages requested, as pages started to include much more than text. Hits suddenly became a useless metric—each page now typically can send back 5–50 hits to the server, asking for all different kinds of content that will become a single page.

The most commonly used term is *page views* (number or count or average), but the metric is also referred to as depth of visit or pageload activity. They all measure the same thing: the number of pages viewed or requested during a visitor session.

Usually the number of pages viewed on a website is also considered a proxy for customer engagement. The thought is that if website visitors are viewing more pages, our websites have engaging content. This is quite applicable for content websites (cnn.com, sports.yahoo.com, keepmedia.com, and so forth). It is less clear how success can be measured on other types of websites by using the number of pages viewed by a visitor.

Why Should You Care?

As discussed earlier in this chapter, a page can be defined by a unique URL or URL stem or a combination of parameters in the URL. Web analytics applications rely on the URL, or a combination of the URL and the URL parameters, changing to indicate that a different page has been requested. No matter how you look at it at the moment, every single vendor relies on a "page" to exist on a site in order for the analytics to function.

But with the advent of rich media experiences (for example, Ajax, Flash/Flex), the URL never changes and in turn the concept of a page as defined by a URL, or URL and parameters, is dead in the water.

For example, you can work on all your email by using Gmail and your URL will never change. You can go to different folders, reply to email or delete it, and you'll still be on one URL: http://mail.google.com/mail/.

Or consider an experience on Nike at this URL: http://nikeid.nike.com/nikeid/index.jhtml. You can spend hours on this website, and a standard implementation of a typical web analytics application would not tell us much.

Or consider that at my blog, www.kaushik.net/avinash, you could read five different posts but never leave the page. How many page views did you see? What is your engagement score if engagement is number of pages viewed?

It is clear that the concept of a page is dead. It is already dead on many sites, such as the preceding example. This is important because it will mean rewriting software code and logic and a completely different way of approaching web analytics.

This is also important because most of the vendors have not stepped forward to change their fundamental data collection and key metric computation models to move into this new world. Even when new metrics and data capture methods are suggested, vendors still rely on stuffing data or values into the page-centric places in the tools to solve problems. This will be a bigger challenge with every passing day.

What Should You Care About?

You should be aware that page views are topic de jour currently. Everyone is talking about them, mostly in context of evolving web customer experiences. For your web analytics program three things are worth caring about deeply.

Understand what defines a unique page on your website and then ensure that your web analytics application is configured to accurately report on the viewing of a page. This is a quick repetition of a point covered earlier in this chapter. Partner with your IT team and your vendor to accomplish this goal. This is hyperimportant for a dynamic website, because a wrong configuration could give you numbers that are complete garbage.

If you are running a rich media website (your website is purely in Flash), or you have implemented Ajax or rich interactive applications on your website, you are already aware that you are reporting one page view for all of those experiences, no matter how deep they are. This is especially true if you are using web logs as your source of data. You will have to work with your web analytics vendor to figure out how they are supporting capturing data for rich media experiences. A few vendors have taken their existing data collection mechanisms based on JavaScript tags and rigged them to be executed when a certain predefined business event occurs. This data is then stored and reported.

If your vendor does not support tracking of rich media—and a large number of vendors are still in this bucket—you are out of luck and will have to hack something yourself. Seek out the friendliest hacker in your IT department. Fortunately, there are always some there.

Either way, you should be prepared to work closely with the developers of your rich media experiences and to do custom work with your web analytics vendors or your IT department.

Similar to your handling of the time on site, you should rarely report on average page views (per visit, or by source or campaigns or keywords). Page views per visit for most websites will look like Figure 6.8 even though its distribution is for a particular website. The dynamics of visitor behavior is quite similar on vastly different websites. If you have a distribution like the one in Figure 6.8, averaging it out will produce rather suboptimal results. Especially over time, you would have no idea whether you were actually improving or getting worse.

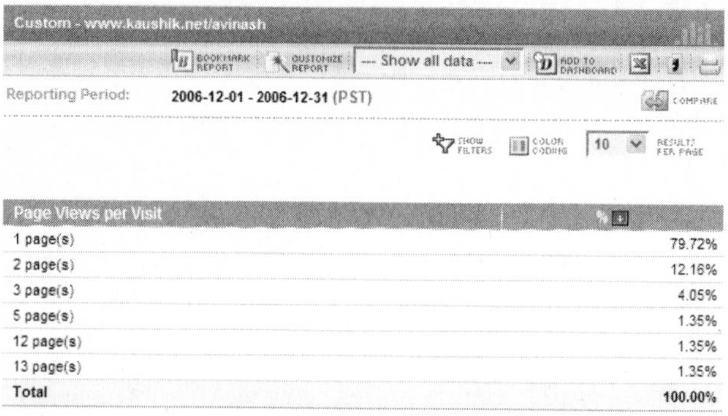

Figure 6.8 Distribution of page views per visit

Week 3: Understanding Standard Reports

Weeks 1 and 2 prepared you for the basic data capture elements and the four foundational metrics. In the third week, you'll focus on better understanding the quality of traffic that you are getting and where the traffic is coming from on your website.

When someone walks into your retail store, you have no idea where that person came from or any context around that visit. But that is not the case on the Web, because the visitors who come to your website bring along with them attributes and context indicating where they came from. What campaigns are they are responding to? What search engine and keywords did they use? What website referred the visitor to you? All this is excellent data that can help you understand your traffic much better and it also gives you context that you can use to react to visitors.

At the same time, not all the sources of your traffic will be of the same quality. How do you know which ones are better? Which are the ones you should chuck?

In week 3, you'll understand how to better answer these questions by using some of the standard reports available in all web analytics tools in the market. You'll also learn what you should be careful of and what actions you can take based on these reports.

Monday and Tuesday: Bounce Rate

I like the Bounce Rate metric very much, and am a bit saddened at its lack of use by web analytics practitioners. It is a metric that has an amazing power to drive insights and actions (and it is all about action, isn't it?).

We all measure visitor trends today. We spend a lot of time and money on customer acquisition efforts (such as search marketing, email marketing, or affiliate marketing). But if you are spending money, are you getting bang for your buck? Are you getting the right traffic that will engage with your sites? Yes, you are measuring conversion rate, but is that metric hiding the real truth about the value of your website?

Bounce rate is simply defined as follows:

Bounce rate: The percent of traffic that stayed on your website for fewer than 10 seconds

There is no hard and fast rule about the time bucket you use. Having tried many versions (for example, visitors who saw only one page or stayed for five seconds or fewer than fifteen seconds), from a best-practice standpoint I have settled on ten seconds. By any stretch of the imagination, in this world of short attention spans, a visitor needs to commit at least ten seconds to a website for the website to have a decent shot at delivering what that visitor wants. If ten seconds is too high a bar for you, you can use five seconds.

It is recommended that you use time and not number of pages to compute bounce rate (because of the reasons I've stated).

Why Should You Care?

Imagine that you run four campaigns (search, email, affiliates, and corporate website). You go back and measure conversion rate. Table 6.1 shows what your report might look like.

▶ **Table 6.1** Report of conversion rate by campaigns

Campaign	Unique Visitors	Converted	Conversion Rate
Search (PPC)	2,165	198	9.1%
Email	634	205	32.3%
Affiliates	401	25	6.2%
Corporate Website	347	90	25.9%

The first three are campaigns on which you spend money to drive traffic. The fourth one is free. Just looking at this report will tell you that email is the most effective medium, followed by your corporate website, and then search.

But did you spend money on driving the highest-quality traffic? Maybe not. See Table 6.2.

Campaign	Unique Visitors	Converted	Conversion Rate	Bounced	Bounce Rate
Search (PPC)	2,165	198	9.1%	1,253	57.9%
Email	634	205	32.3%	395	62.3%
Affiliates	401	25	6.2%	239	59.6%
Corporate Website	347	90	25.9%	151	43.5%

Ah—now this gets interesting. By looking at the Bounce Rate column, you notice that each campaign had a drastically different bounce rate. Email, which had the best conversion rate, also had the worst bounce rate (maybe you need to improve your email list because it's hit or miss at the moment). You might notice that Search is right up there, while our corporate website is doing just fine in terms of sending relevant traffic and converting nicely, thank you very much.

You should care about bounce rate because for your campaigns or for your individual web pages (Figure 6.9) you will get a new and interesting perspective about performance. In other words, you'll see whether they are really doing their jobs. You can use this newfound knowledge to optimize your traffic, your pages, and your site strategy.

	Top Entrances	Entrances	Bounces	Bounce Rate
1.	/avinash/	2,165	1,353	62.49%
2.	/avinash/2006/10/seven-steps-to-creating-a-data-driven-decis	634	497	78.39%
3.	/avinash/2006/11/excellent-analytics-tip-8-measure-the-real-c	401	279	69.58%
4.	/avinash/2006/07/the-awesome-power-of-data-visualization.h	347	151	43.52%
5.	/avinash/2006/09/how-to-choose-a-web-analytics-tool-a-radic	284	179	63.03%
6.	/avinash/2006/11/blogging-how-tos-technical-tips-and-best-w	277	225	81.23%
7.	/avinash/2006/11/web-analysis-inhouse-or-outsourced-or-so	224	167	74.55%
8.	/avinash/2006/11/five-ecosystem-challenges-for-web-analytic	217	135	62.21%
9.	/avinash/2006/06/top-ten-signs-you-are-a-great-analyst.html	212	125	58.96%
10.	/avinash/2006/05/the-10-90-rule-for-magnificient-web-analytic	210	150	71.43%
	Totals:	8,287	5,679	68.53%

Figure 6.9 Website entry pages bounce rate

What Should You Care About?

This is a much-underappreciated metric by most practitioners of web analytics. As you go about measuring this critical metric, there are a few things you should focus on right at the start.

Analyze any existing clickstream and outcomes data about your website to understand what the threshold should be for computing your website's bounce rate. Five and ten seconds are thresholds that are fairly well accepted now in the industry. It is also important to familiarize your decision makers with this metric. Most decision makers do not understand it well enough and hence do not ask for it or use it as often as they use other metrics in making important decisions related to the website.

Ask your web analytics vendor whether they can help you compute bounce rate and whether you can customize it to your needs. Many vendors either don't support customization or consider it a special request (which translates into extra cost).

You can apply bounce rates to any segment of traffic that your company is using. We used campaigns in the preceding example and will use search key phrases in the example in the next section. But you can apply bounce rates to referring URLs, web pages (Figure 6.9), countries (geography), and more. Find the best fit for your company.

Time on site and bounce rate can be great friends. As you create reports and do your own unique analysis, combining these two metrics on the report can often have revealing consequences related to performance. Try it. You'll discover valuable sources of traffic to your site and you'll discover areas of pain in your website. For example, you might find that certain entry pages or landing pages to your site have high bounce rates and those who don't bounce tend to spend an extraordinarily long time on your website indicating problems with calls to action, relevant content, or navigation structures.

Remember, bounced traffic is not to be thrown away. It is valuable traffic, and you should put resources into understanding where this traffic is coming from, why the visitors are coming, and in what ways your website is failing. Often it is really hard to acquire traffic. These are visitors who, one way or another, have decided to come to your website. If we can help them complete their tasks, we should consider that our civic duty and do whatever it takes to help.

Bounce rate is your best friend, and first step, in understanding whether you are getting qualified traffic to your website. Often it is a more insightful measure than simply computing conversion rate.

Wednesday through Friday: Referrers—Sources and Search Key Phrases

One of the great joys of the Web, compared to other channels, is that on the Web we can start to scratch the surface of understanding customer intent. Among other things, we can attempt to understand why our visitors come to our website. If we knew where our visitors were coming from, we could know a bit more about them and maybe, just maybe, try to create content or experiences that might be relevant to them and help them accomplish their tasks.

Two excellent sources for referring information are the referring websites (URLs) and the key phrases for visitors referred by search engines. Both of these metrics and reports are rich with intent inference. They can tell us where our visitors are coming from, what they might be looking for, whether we are getting traffic from the right sources, and more. As you slice and dice the data, you also can identify how your various traffic streams are performing and where opportunities for improvement might lie.

Why Should You Care?

Aggregated data from our web analytics tools is rarely useful in driving actionable insights. Visitors come to any website to accomplish a myriad of goals (regardless of why a website exists—for example, when was the last time you purchased on Amazon.com?).

Figure 6.10 shows a typical version of a referring domain report and the kind of information you can glean from it. You can view this report either by domain or, as recommended for your biggest referrers, by specific URLs (pages) on your referrer's websites that are sending you traffic.

Referring Domain	%
Direct access or bookmark	41.41%
http://www.google.com	13.13%
http://analytics.blogspot.com	6.06%
http://www.kaushik.net	3.03%
http://www.google.co.uk	3.03%
http://www.marketingpilgrim.com	2.02%
http://images.google.com	2.02%
http://minethatdata.blogspot.com	2.02%
http://blog.acpl.lib.in.us	2.02%
http://www.saschameinrath.com	1.01%
Subtotal	75.75%
Total	100.00%

Figure 6.10 Referring domains report

Figure 6.11 shows a typical version of a search key phrases report. You also have the ability to drill down and understand which specific keywords are driving traffic from which search engine (Figure 6.12).

Search Phrases	%
avinash	2.02%
usability lab creating	1.01%
how to compute conversion rates	1.01%
how to	1.01%
company decision making steps	1.01%
zaaz benefits	1.01%
seven steps	1.01%
design power presentation graphs	1.01%
statistically significant	1.01%
steps to analyze a decision	1.01%
Subtotal	11.11%
Total	100.00%

Figure 6.11 Search key phrases report

All visitors	Total	Google	MSN	Yahoo!	Ask Jeeves	My Web Search	AOL
Total	9090	7384	1279	332	34	16	16
profile tax software	584	455	97	25	1	1	5
profile	430	350	74	5	0	0	1
profile tax	351	272	36	41	2	0	0

Figure 6.12 Search key phrases by search engine report

By allowing us to understand drivers of traffic to our websites, these reports will help us optimize our acquisition strategies and create more-personalized experiences (even if it is repeating the search key phrase on the landing pages). They also can act as triggers for A/B or multivariate tests ("You came from there, and I know something about there, so I am going to put you in test version B and try to see whether I can improve conversion rate"). Finally, these reports drive analysis that is perhaps one of the easiest to do and yet perhaps the mostly quickly actionable.

What Should You Care About?

These reports will have a goldmine of information for you, if you look carefully and embrace a few fundamental facts.

You won't know all of your referrers. Web decision makers assume that we will always know every website that is sending us traffic. In reality, anywhere from 40 to 60 percent of your referrers will be null (or empty or unknown, or Direct Access or Bookmarks, depending on the tool that you use). In Figure 6.10 the number is 41.41 percent (normal).

The normal explanation of this behavior is that the visitors bookmarked the website or typed the URL directly into the browsers. But this is not all of the explanation. You can have null or blank referring URLs in your logs due to the following:

- The visitor has weird browser settings (some browsers will not pass the referrer cleanly).
- Often permanent redirects (301) are not used, and any traffic coming via redirects can appear as null because the referrer is not passed. (For example, if you redirect traffic from yourcompanyname.com to www.yourcompanyname.com, and this is not a permanent redirect, all the traffic is null.)
- Traffic comes from various email direct-marketing campaigns, and the referrer might not be passed correctly from the email programs to your website.
- Your visitor's browser may have hypersecure security settings.

Be aware of these reasons and the fact that a nice chunk of your traffic does not have a referrer. Regardless, you do know the referrers for the rest of your traffic. Understand that and drive action.

Perform deep analysis of your Search Engine referred traffic. According to the latest study by E-consultancy, 80 percent of Internet traffic starts their browsing experience at a search engine (this study was completed in the fourth quarter of 2006). Hence understanding search traffic referred to your website is both an awesome opportunity and a scary customer trend. Search engines have fundamentally changed how customers behave, and it is our turn to ensure that we understand the traffic better so that we can respond to it better. The starting point of all your analysis is understanding which search engines are driving visitors to your website and which key phrases visitors are using. It is normal to find that different key phrases drive more or less traffic from different search engines.

To leapfrog ahead of your competitors, you need to drill down deeper. Figure 6.13 shows one best-practice example of the analysis you can do for traffic by search key phrase from each search engine.

All visitors		Visitors	% Visitors	Total Views	Views Per Visitor	ATOS	Short Visits
Results for: Google	**Total**	9097		16815	1.8	56s	66.5%
profile tax software		524	5.8%	1297	2.4	97s	60.3%
profile		381	4.2%	787	2.0	80s	59.6%
profile tax		317	3.5%	738	2.3	92s	47.9%

Figure 6.13 Search key phrase key metrics analysis

Now you are cooking. The metrics computed are as follows:

Visitors (visits): A count of the number of visits from Google in aggregate and for each key phrase.

% Visitors (visits): A simple percent of the total.

Total page views: The total number of web pages viewed by visitors.

Page views per visit: The total page views divided by total visits. This is a proxy for how "engaging" the website was for traffic from each key phrase.

Average time on site (ATOS): The time spent, on average, for each session.

Short visits (bounce rate): The number of visits that were fewer than five seconds. This is a proxy for "was it quality traffic?"

As you can clearly observe, the kind of rich understanding this can provide is invaluable for one of the most valuable sources of traffic for your website: search engines. You can also add or remove metrics to ensure that data you are getting is most relevant to your website (so you can add conversion rate or revenue, and so forth).

Search engine analysis can help you optimize landing pages for your search traffic. With a solid understanding of performance, you can start to consider landing page optimization. For your highest referring keywords, it might be optimal to create customized landing pages that will "speak" to the visitors and help them complete their tasks. If you already have landing pages, the preceding analysis can help you understand which ones might be in need of love so that they can perform better.

Remember that this metric uses key phrases and not keywords. Some web analytics tools will show a keywords report that aggregates data based on each instance of a keyword. For example, say that these key phrases resulted in one visit each to your website:

- Web analytics

- Web analytics tools
- Web analytics blows
- Analytics amazing

The keywords report would show the following:

- Web: 3
- Analytics: 4
- Tools: 1
- Blows: 1
- Amazing: 1

Of course, as you already guessed, the right report is as follows:

- Web analytics: 1
- Web analytics tools: 1
- Web analytics blows: 1
- Analytics amazing: 1

Tip: This perhaps sounds hard to believe, but please do a quick check that your web analytics vendor is *not* reporting keywords and *is* reporting key phrases. Mercifully, there are only a few vendors that are still reporting keywords.

This is a bit critical because in November 2006 Google reported that for the first time, the number of words in the most used searches totaled three. This was rather surprising to many web practitioners. It indicates that visitors are looking for increasingly specific things and has major implications on our search engine marketing and search engine optimization strategies.

Week 4: Using Website Content Quality and Navigation Reports

The last week of your first month will be focused on gaining knowledge about the wonderful content that you have on your website. You'll gain deep knowledge and face some nonobvious challenges about a set of common web analytics reports that you'll find in the tool that you are using.

You can judge the quality of the content on your website in several ways. Your reports for pages viewed, exit pages, and site overlay (click density) each allow you to focus in a different way and are optimal for a different purpose. In week 4, you'll learn the ins and outs of each of these reports, which will empower you to deploy their analysis for best-fit outcomes.

You'll also learn how to cut through some of the hype that exists behind some of these reports so that you can use your time and precious resources in a valuable manner.

Site overlay is perhaps one of the most exciting reports that you'll use. It also happens to be one of the least appreciated and understood reports. At the end of this week, you'll know exactly how to use this report, which becomes a million times more powerful when you apply segmentation. You can walk in the shoes of your customers—tough work, but very rewarding.

Monday and Tuesday: Top Pages—Most Viewed, Top Entry, Top Exit

Visitors come to websites, and websites have pages, and so pages rule! Mostly true. Since the dawn of the Web, we have been curious about visitors and how long they spend on site and how many pages they read. It was logical that the next thing we would dive into was an understanding of what all these visitors are looking at (or to give it a fancy name: *content consumption*).

There are three main types of page reports that you'll find in most analytics tools: most viewed pages, top entry pages, and top exit pages.

Most Viewed Pages

This metric is also known as most requested URLs, top content, and popular pages. It is a simple count of pages on the website that had the greatest number of visits (visitors), as shown in Figure 6.14.

Page Title	%
Occam s Razor by Avinash Kaushik	22.27%
The Great Web Data Capture Debat...Occam s Razor by Avinash Kaushik	7.58%
2006 May Occam s Razor by Avinash Kaushik	7.10%
Occam s Razor by Avinash Kaushik Web Analytics	5.21%
The Blog Tag Game - Something Ne...Occam s Razor by Avinash Kaushik	4.73%
Seven Steps to Creating a Data D...Occam s Razor by Avinash Kaushik	4.73%
Blogging: How-to s, Technical Ti...Occam s Razor by Avinash Kaushik	2.84%
The Awesome Power of Visualizati...Occam s Razor by Avinash Kaushik	2.36%
About Occam s Razor by Avinash Kaushik	2.36%
2006 August Occam s Razor by Avinash Kaushik	1.89%
Subtotal	61.13%
Total	100.00%

Figure 6.14 Pages with the most visitors (percent distribution)

At a page level, most web analytics packages don't report pages with the greatest number of unique visitors, they report on pages with greatest number of Visits (or Visitors, which is the same thing). It is important to be aware of this (and although it is asked for often, it is of little value when you imagine what you are actually trying to analyze: content consumption).

Why Should You Care?

The most viewed pages on your website are a great indicator of why people are coming to your website and what are they looking for. This report is always chock full of surprises (which you should look for), because there is always such a mismatch between what website owners create their sites for and what customers are looking for. These pages also are a great place to start when it comes to focusing your energies, because they own such a disproportionate amount of traffic to your site. They can be great candidates for multivariate testing, for example.

What Should You Care About?

There are two simple considerations that you should make to get optimal insights from this report.

Watch for trends over time instead of focusing on just a point in time. It usually turns out that for sites that don't change all that much, the top viewed pages don't change that often (obviously, this would not be the case for a news website). That should be food for thought for what you should do (focus more or less on these pages?).

Look not just at the raw numbers but at comparisons. The raw numbers may not change that much for your top pages, so compare pages from last week to this week (or yesterday and today, or last month and the current month). Has there been a statistically significant increase in the number of visitors? For example, there could be a page ranked 155 on your site (because of the raw number of page views), but between the two time periods, traffic to that page has increased by 900 percent. This can be a leading indicator of sorts for your website. (Note: this analysis would also apply for top entry pages.)

Top Entry Pages

This simple report shows the top pages that serve as entrance points for visitors to your website. It is also measured in terms of visits (visitors) and not unique visitors. In Figure 6.15, I have enhanced the standard version of the Top Entry Pages report that would usually just show the percentage of visitors who entered at a particular page. The enhancements include the bounce rate and total page views per visit (*depth of visit*, a very valuable metric). The end result is a report that shows the core entry points on your website and how they are performing in providing relevant content and engaging visitors.

Why Should You Care?

Top entry pages are critical in a world that is dominated by search engines. *Search engine optimization* is more than just a buzzword. Most web practitioners have an unhealthy obsession with their home pages (index.html). But visitors from search engines are typically directed deep into the website. As you saw in Figure 6.15, for this website the home page accounts for only 31 percent of the entry visits. The rest of the traffic goes deep into the website.

Custom - www.kaushik.net/avinash

Reporting Period: **2006-12-01 - 2006-12-31** (PST)

Entry Page URL	%	Bounce rate	Page views per visit
http://www.kaushik.net/avinash/	30.70%	71.42%	1.68
http://www.kaushik.net/avinash/2...web-logs-or-javascript-tags.html	12.28%	100.00%	1.00
http://www.kaushik.net/avinash/2...ven-decision-making-culture.html	7.01%	87.50%	1.12
http://www.kaushik.net/avinash/2...hing-new-something-personal.html	5.26%	50.00%	2.00
http://www.kaushik.net/avinash/2...tion-2-death-and-taxes-2007.html	4.38%	80.00%	1.40
http://www.kaushik.net/avinash/2...-and-best-wordpress-plugins.html	4.38%	100.00%	1.00
http://www.kaushik.net/avinash/2...minutes-with-mike-moran-ibm.html	3.50%	50.00%	2.50
http://www.kaushik.net/avinash/2...ications-should-be-free-not.html	3.50%	75.00%	1.25
http://www.kaushik.net/avinash/2...ersion-rate-opportunity-pie.html	2.63%	66.66%	1.33
http://www.kaushik.net/avinash/2...o-measure-success-of-a-blog.html	1.75%	50.00%	1.50
Subtotal	**75.43%**	**76.74%**	**1.48**
Total	**100.00%**	**71.05%**	**1.85**

Figure 6.15 Top entry pages (percent distribution combined with bounce rates and page views per visit)

What Should You Care About?

Are you treating your top 10 entry pages as just as important as your home page? Do this promptly because they are setting your website's first impression.

Because your home page is no longer the "home page," the top entry pages should be leveraged to run your most prominent promotions (merchandising or otherwise). It is quite common that the big "news" of the website is on the home page, but 70 percent of visitors don't even see the home page.

Turbocharge your report by combining the distribution of visitors with bounce rate and page views per visit. These two metrics can be leading indicators of how well each page is performing in terms of getting people to at least engage with the site (bounce rate) and how well each page is doing in terms of driving a deeper visit (page views per visit). The combination of these three metrics can be extremely insightful (as should be apparent even with the simplistic example in Figure 6.15).

Top Exit Pages

Top exit pages is another of the most common reports you'll see. Quite simply, it takes the last page viewed from each visitor session and computes the most common set of last viewed pages. Figure 6.16 illustrates a standard report that shows the pages with most exits on the website. It is quite typical to have the home page have the highest exit rate, even if that doesn't seem obvious.

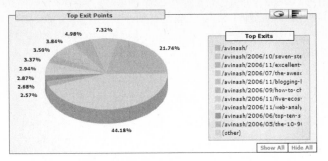

Figure 6.16 Top exit pages (percent distribution)

On paper, this metric is supposed to show "leakage" of your website—the pages where people exit from after they start their session. Remember, this is different from bounce rate, although practitioners often confuse it as *bounce rate for a page*. The Top Exit Pages report should illustrate pages that you should "fix" to prevent this leakage.

Why Should You Care?

For the most part, you should not care about this metric. For most websites, it is a hyped-up metric that tells you little while, on paper, claiming to tell you a lot. This is especially true if the report is at an aggregated level (as in Figure 6.16, which shows top exit pages for all visitors of the website). Frequently you will notice that the busiest pages on the website are also the ones that show up as the top exit pages; in and of itself this fact does not tell you anything.

It seems obvious that if you knew where people were exiting from on your website, you could simply fix that "page" and all would be kosher. In reality, visitors come to your website for a whole bunch of purposes and it is often okay that your top exit page on the website is the page that shows your best-selling product (it will be that page) because a big chunk of visitors want to read about the product and buy it in a retail store.

Another factor going against making this a valuable report is that the conversion rate for most websites (e-commerce or otherwise) is around 2 percent. That means approximately 98 percent of the traffic will exit at places you don't want them to exit (examples of good places to exit are the checkout page, lead submission page, and support FAQ page). When such a huge amount of traffic is exiting (leaking) from your website, and most likely from your most viewed pages, it is extremely difficult from the raw exit rates on those pages to parse out success or failure.

If 50 percent of people who see your Product Details page exit, what percent of that is good (those who read reviews and will buy someplace else such as a retail store), and what percent is bad (those who came to buy, but you upset them with tiny size-six font on that page)? How do you know from simply the exit rate number? It is often, but not always, a futile exercise (see exceptions in the following section), and you are better off using other mechanisms (for example, surveys or usability studies) to figure out why people exit your site at different locations.

What Should You Care About?

Segmenting this report for various traffic streams, campaigns, or customer types can redeem it a little bit and highlight trends that might yield some insights. The only exceptions to this rule are structured experiences that are of a *closed* nature—for example, the cart and checkout experience. You add to a cart, you click Start Check-out, you fill out your address and credit card information, you click Submit, and you see the Thank You page.

In this structured experience, it can be insightful to measure which page is the top exit page, why that page might be causing leakage, and how to fix it (multivariate testing to the rescue!).

Wednesday: Top Destinations (Exit Links)

On the Web, the referring information about the click goes to the target page or website, and not the source. So if www.kaushik.net/avinash has a link to www.webanalytics-demystified.com and someone clicks on that link, the information about that click goes to webanalyticsdemystified.

Because every website (source) has links to other websites (destination), it was a bummer during the early days when the source could not capture this information. To overcome this challenge, websites usually implemented redirects that would capture the click before it exited to a destination. This was valuable because now you knew exactly what destination links were doing to your traffic, and you had the data without having to go to the destination website owner to get the data.

In the last few years, newer web analytics vendors have implemented features in their data capture mechanisms that capture the exit to a destination and, mercifully, you don't have to maintain a painful redirecting mechanism on your website.

Now you have the wonderful ability to quantify the value of your website to other websites, as shown in Figure 6.17. (I might stress that you can do this without adding any extra work onto your IT department). So although exits are undesirable, as discussed in the previous section, these are the good exits because you are causing them to happen by providing these links to your website.

Top Destinations

All visitors

	Total	Oct	Nov	Dec
http://weblogs.hitwise.com	205	184	13	8
http://img88.imageshack.us/img88/6466/thebudgetgraphcom3000hi5.jpg	132	62	39	31
http://analytics.blogspot.com	112	92	13	7
http://feeds.feedburner.com/OccamsRazorByAvinash	110	38	41	31
http://www.webmetricsguru.com	85	52	20	13
http://lunametrics.blogspot.com	83	62	12	9
http://www.omniture.com/blog	77	61	10	6
http://www.deviantart.com/view/9410862	70	36	20	14
http://www.e-consultancy.com/news-blog/topic_13/web-measurement-and-analytics.html	70	59	8	3

Figure 6.17 Top Destinations report (quarterly trend)

Why Should You Care?

If you have an ecosystem of websites (e-commerce, support, corporate, lead generation, and so forth), a Top Destinations report is a godsend for you. Most web analytics vendors will treat these as individual websites, hence separate data, but now you have an ability on each website to know its impact on the ecosystem.

Wouldn't you love to know how many sales and leads your corporate site is generating, without having to ask your e-commerce and lead generation website owners?

Wouldn't you love to segment your core metrics to show people who leave your website to go to one of your partner websites?

Wouldn't you love to understand customer intent a bit better by seeing where different traffic streams exit to? See Figure 6.18.

Top Destinations

All visitors

http://weblogs.hitwise.com	0.7%	205
http://img88.imageshack.us/img88/6466/thebudgetgraphcom3000hi5.jpg	0.4%	132
http://analytics.blogspot.com	0.4%	112
http://feeds.feedburner.com/OccamsRazorByAvinash	0.4%	110
http://www.webmetricsguru.com	0.3%	85
http://lunametrics.blogspot.com	0.3%	83
http://www.omniture.com/blog	0.3%	77
http://www.deviantart.com/view/9410862	0.2%	70
http://www.e-consultancy.com/news-blog/topic_13/web-measurement-and-analytics.html	0.2%	70

Search Engines

http://img88.imageshack.us/img88/6466/thebudgetgraphcom3000hi5.jpg	0.3%	34
http://www.webmetricsguru.com	0.3%	29
http://weblogs.hitwise.com	0.2%	25
http://www.deviantart.com/view/9410862	0.2%	22
http://analytics.blogspot.com	0.2%	22
http://fusion.google.com/add?feadurl=http://feeds.feedburner.com/OccamsRazorByAvinash	0.2%	17
http://feeds.feedburner.com/OccamsRazorByAvinash	0.2%	17
http://www.conversionrater.com	0.2%	17
http://www.intuit.com/about_intuit/careers/why.jhtml	0.1%	14

Figure 6.18 Top Destinations report (two important segments: All Visitors and Traffic from Search Engines)

Notice that the traffic from search engines exits to different links (destinations off your website) as compared to all visitors. This provides great insight into the intent of search engine traffic vs. all other traffic to the website.

What Should You Care About?

With just a few small things you can make the most of this report.

Check to make sure that your vendor supports exit tracking. With some vendors, you have to request this feature to be turned on (sometimes at an extra cost), and with other vendors you might have to ask your IT team for special encoding in the exit links.

If your website is natively using a lot of JavaScript, ensure that you test the JavaScript code from your vendor, which contains exit tracking, very carefully in your QA or development environment. Exit-tracking code from some vendors can cause conflicts with your website code.

If you are sending traffic to partner sites, consider asking them for a referring fee or at least reciprocal links. Send them your data and ask for stuff!

Segmenting data for visitors exiting to other websites can be very insightful. See Figure 6.19 for one such example (the third set of metrics for people exiting from the website and going to `hitwise.com`). This is valuable data, especially if you have lots of links on your website to other websites and it is actionable.

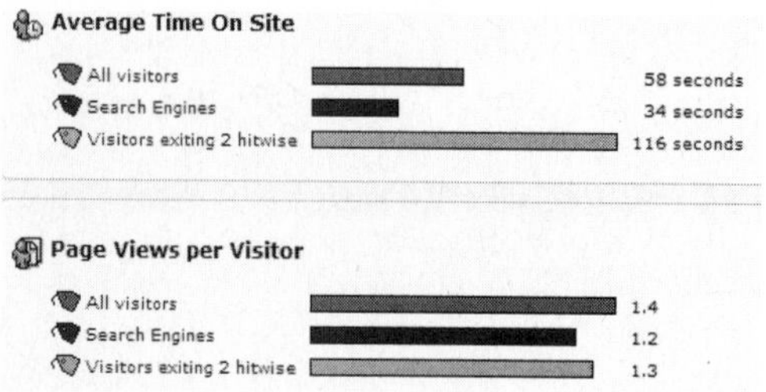

Figure 6.19 Top Destinations report (all visitors, search engine traffic, and those who exit from the site to Hitwise—an exit link on the site)

Thursday and Friday: Site Overlay (Click Density Analysis)

Last but not least, my absolute favorite report—site overlay. I love this one and I am not averse to admitting it.

The site overlay report, also known as click density analysis, quite literally shows where the customers are clicking on your web pages by overlaying the clicks on top of your web pages. See Figure 6.20.

As you'll notice in Figure 6.20, every link on this web page is marked with a little image that tells you which links are being clicked on the page. (The percentage is computed by dividing the total number of clicks by the total number of page views.) Not only can you see click-throughs on each link that goes deeper into the site, but also the number of clicks that are exiting off the website (the clicks that have a red arrow next to them). This allows you to understand the holistic picture of customer behavior on individual web pages.

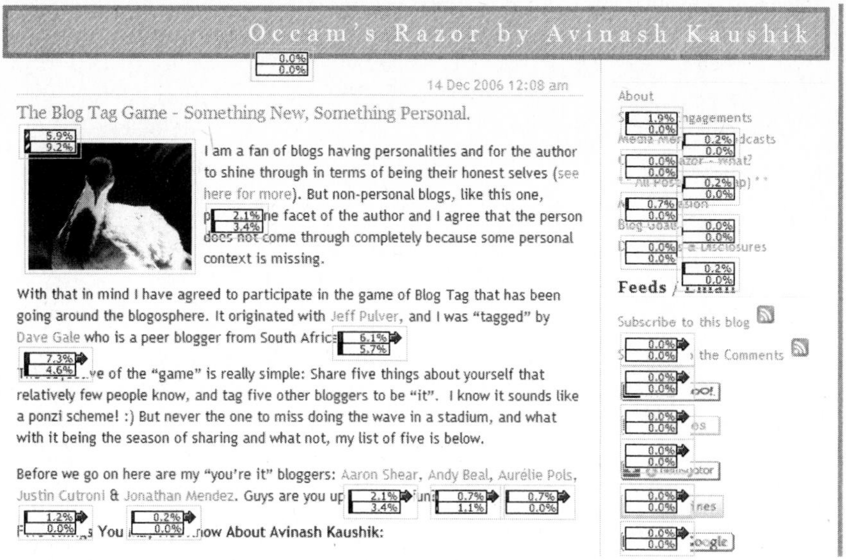

Figure 6.20 Site overlay report (also known as click density analysis or navigation report)

You can easily see, in a way that is impossible in an Excel spreadsheet or table, what customers are interested in on your website and what they don't care about. The report also can indicate site elements that might not be standing out and "visible" to the website customers as much as the site owner would like them to. In the preceding example, the section on the bottom right is getting very few clicks from the website visitors, as evidenced by the 0.0% clicks on the very links that are a core measure of success for the site owner.

Why Should You Care?

The site overlay report is perhaps one of the more significant reports that you'll find in your web analytics tools. There are several reasons for this:

- Clickstream analysis suffers from one big problem: it is just a whole bunch of numbers, URLs, page titles, and graphs. It desensitizes the customer experience. We are so caught up in our world of tables and reports that we almost forget that we are analyzing customer behavior (for us, it is just sessions and cookie values). Click density analysis is a great way to walk in the customer's shoes—for us to enter at our website's top entry pages and then follow along with the customer clicks.

- This might sound a bit unbelievable, but it is amazing how many among us don't even look at our site every day. This is a great way to stay in touch with our websites, and not get caught up too much in publishing reports. This is more effective than you might imagine.

- Every marketer or business decision maker now has an easy way to understand web analytics—not in terms of complicated nine-page reports that are in Excel in six-point font—by simply surfing the website, they can get a great understanding of how their pages are performing. They can not only look at the clicks but in some tools they can also get a better understanding of how the links are performing in terms of business goals (in the following image, G1/Clicks indicates a "conversion" to goal 1, for example).

What Should You Care About?

As discussed above, the site overlay report can be immensely powerful and be a source of important insights. To help maximize the return on your investment, here are a few things you should care about.

Segmentation is key to understanding behavior. If your web analytics tool can show click density for only one segment of traffic, it will be multiple times less effective (simply because on your popular pages, there will be so many types of visitors trying to do so many things).

In Figure 6.20, for example, you'll notice that the distribution of clicks is different for each group of links. The first number (5.9 percent on the title link) indicates clicks for all visitors, and the second number (9.2 percent) indicates only the segment of visitors who come from search engines.

By observing browsing behavior of various segments, you can begin to understand what the different, valuable segments of your customers want (this is called *intent inference*). You can then start to create personalized experiences or think of creative ways of addressing their needs (and of course, in turn, meet your business objectives).

Click density (site overlay) is not very valuable without context. A page analysis report for each web page (Figure 6.21) provides key context and is a life-saving companion to the click density analysis report. Page analysis helps you understand page performance a thousand times better by showing you key performance indicators for the page: visitors who see the page, average time at the page, average time *to* the page, percent entries, percent exits, and—super valuable for SEO—key phrases that drive traffic to this page.

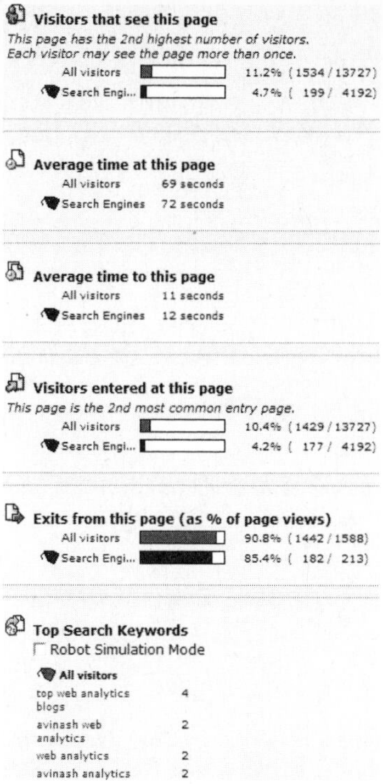

Visitors that see this page
This page has the 2nd highest number of visitors.
Each visitor may see the page more than once.

All visitors		11.2% (1534 / 13727)
Search Engi...		4.7% (199 / 4192)

Average time at this page

All visitors	69 seconds
Search Engines	72 seconds

Average time to this page

All visitors	11 seconds
Search Engines	12 seconds

Visitors entered at this page
This page is the 2nd most common entry page.

All visitors		10.4% (1429 / 13727)
Search Engi...		4.2% (177 / 4192)

Exits from this page (as % of page views)

All visitors		90.8% (1442 / 1588)
Search Engi...		85.4% (182 / 213)

Top Search Keywords
☐ Robot Simulation Mode

All visitors

top web analytics blogs	4
avinash web analytics	2
web analytics	2
avinash analytics	2

Figure 6.21 Page analysis report for the website home page (insightful page KPIs that provide key context)

Just with this simple report, you can understand the value of the home page (just 11 percent see the home page!), how long it takes visitors to find the page (average time to this page), website exits from this page, and finally, whether your page is optimized for search engines and bringing you the right traffic.

To truly extract value from the click density analysis (site overlay), you need all of this context. Otherwise, you have no idea why the page is performing so badly (or well, as the case may be). Again, to stress the importance of segmentation, you obtain insights into not only all visitors, but also your segmented search engine traffic. How cool is that!

If your tool does not provide these KPIs, ask your vendor to enhance the tool. The good news is, many vendors already do this.

Some tools can also provide a great visual summary of customer behavior and clicks on the page, such as the one represented in Figure 6.22.

This closes the "analysis loop" for your top pages by clearly showing how visitors get to this page and where they go next. For example, looking at the left column quickly shows which acquisition strategies are working (if you spent all your money on MSN Search Campaigns, they are not working since they don't show up here). This type of analysis also highlights sources of traffic that are valuable yet were not on your radar (in this report, that would be Wikipedia, which is a surprisingly high driver of traffic).

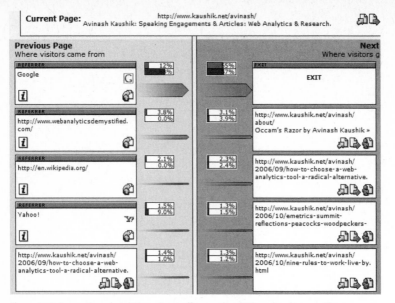

Current Page: http://www.kaushik.net/avinash/
Avinash Kaushik: Speaking Engagements & Articles: Web Analytics & Research.

Previous Page
Where visitors came from

Next
Where visitors g

REFERRER
Google — 12% / 5%

5.5% / 7% — EXIT

REFERRER
http://www.webanalyticsdemystified.com/ — 3.8% / 0.0%

3.1% / 3.9% — http://www.kaushik.net/avinash/about/ Occam's Razor by Avinash Kaushik »

REFERRER
http://en.wikipedia.org/ — 2.1% / 0.0%

2.3% / 2.4% — http://www.kaushik.net/avinash/2006/09/how-to-choose-a-web-analytics-tool-a-radical-alternative.

REFERRER
Yahoo! — 1.5% / 9.0%

1.3% / 1.5% — http://www.kaushik.net/avinash/2006/10/emetrics-summit-reflections-peacocks-woodpeckers-

http://www.kaushik.net/avinash/2006/09/how-to-choose-a-web-analytics-tool-a-radical-alternative. — 1.4% / 1.0%

1.3% / 1.2% — http://www.kaushik.net/avinash/2006/10/nine-rules-to-work-live-by.html

Figure 6.22 Page path analysis (Where does traffic come from? Where does it go next?)

Hopefully by now it is obvious that the click density analysis report is rather deceptive. It is not as straightforward as it looks. Yes, it is easy to find and the clicks are easy to read, but in order for you to find actionable insights, a lot more work is required.

You will discover that your decision makers love the click density analysis for the first couple of weeks. Then they get frustrated because when they make changes to the page, *"My conversion rate did not go up!"*

Educating the decision makers on how to segment is critical, and how to look at clicks in the context of page KPIs and page path analysis is also important. It takes time, so be patient.

Your web analytics tool should be able to provide you with not just the percentages of clicks for each link, but also the raw numbers. You will need the raw numbers more than you think. All of the reports in this chapter, including site overlay, can become exponentially more powerful when coupled with the power of segmentation. You have seen segmentation applied in Figures 6.20, 6.21, and 6.22. I will touch on segmentation throughout this book and you'll learn advanced tips and tricks about segmentation. But even if you have read this far and plan to go no further, you can increase the chances of gleaning insights from even the most basic reports and metrics by simply segmenting them. Give it a try.

Month 2: Jump-Start Your Web Data Analysis

With the basics under your belt, you will spend your second month setting up the foundational elements of your very own web analytics program, customized by business need. I hope there has been enough excitement generated up to this point that you can't wait to get started.

There are many types of businesses on the Web, and each has its own set of challenges and opportunities. In this chapter, you will take a look at three types of websites and identify how to jump-start the web analysis programs with a distinct and unique approach. You'll be able to start quickly but measure real and tangible metrics that will immediately put you ahead of the curve in terms of extracting value.

Prerequisites and Framing

In earlier chapters, you spent time understanding the landscape of web analytics and looked at how the Trinity mindset is critical for gaining actionable insights. You also explored the specific data types that support the Trinity model: behavioral analysis, user research, competitive analysis, and desired outcomes.

In Chapter 6, "Month 1: Diving Deep into Core Web Analytics Concepts," you walked through some of the core web analytics concepts, metrics, and reports. You learned ways to ensure that you have dotted your *i*'s and crossed your *t*'s. In addition, you learned how to look differently at the metrics and reports that have been in front of you all this time (but not told you much).

I recommend rereading the preceding chapters to ensure that the concepts, frameworks, and recommendations are clear and that you'll be able drive action at an optimal pace.

It is assumed for the purposes of this chapter that you have access to the following:

- A website (its purpose does not matter).
- A web analytics tool (name, brand, and price does not matter).
- A basic survey on your site or some other way to collect customer feedback (something basic is fine—see Chapter 3, "Overview of Qualitative Analysis," for your options).

No matter what type of site you're working on, you'll first have to know what reports to create. That will be your first week's activity. After that, I've segmented the second and third weeks' activities according to the type of site you're analyzing. Week 4, regardless of site type, will be spent on reflection and wrap-up. It is assumed that your workload allows you to address one major site type (support, e-commerce, blogs) per month. If they're all on your to-do list at the same time, you're probably going to need more than a month even though some of the techniques (and the reports!) are similar across site types. It gets fun from this chapter on. I hope you enjoy the ride.

Week 1: Creating Foundational Reports

It can feel overwhelming to pop open a web analytics tool and try to find useful information. It is easy for any of us to feel a tad bit lost, if not completely frustrated. Part of the problem is that we go in expecting *answers* when the tools are there simply to provide *data*. But a large part of the problem is that even the simplest tools provide lots and lots of reports.

If you are a small-business owner who is very much a one- or two-person operation, the problem is compounded because you have so many things you're trying to juggle and usually don't have the luxury of having even a part-time dedicated resource available to help sift through the data. But the road is not much easier for massive-sized businesses either. Each faces the unique challenge of how to get going in the most optimal manner.

Getting Started with Web Analytics

It might seem obvious, but starting correctly is critical. There are two important facets of getting started: first, you need to choose the right tool (and you don't even have to spend a lot!), and second, you need to focus on desired outcomes and not on what reports you can extract from the tool. Both of these seemingly obvious items can make or break your effort (even before you crack open a single report).

Choosing the Right Tool

It is important to stress that you don't have to buy expensive software to start your web analytics efforts (see Chapter 5, "Web Analytics Fundamentals"). With the complexity of high-end packages, it pays to learn first by using one of the free packages.

If you have access to your server web logs, the ClickTracks Appetizer product is a great fit (and it's free). It is available at http://snipurl.com/ctappetizer.

If you do not have access to your web log files, as is often the case for many businesses, the free Google Analytics tool is great. It is available at http://snipurl.com/googlea. Google Analytics uses JavaScript tags, which means that you only need access to your web pages to implement the tool.

You can have access to either tool in just a few minutes from either website. Pick the tool that works best for you.

Your website technology provider probably provides one of the many bundled tools free already. These can often be one of the older-generation tools and usually not the easiest to use. I recommend that you go with ClickTracks Appetizer or Google Analytics. Both tools are quite fresh and very much at the cutting edge.

The overall goal will be to implement the free tool on your website, dive into data, learn through grunt work, and move up the food chain to the expensive packages if the initial tools are limiting or as your sophistication grows.

Start with Desired Outcomes, Not Reports

It is so easy to implement the tool and start looking at the data. But my recommendation is to hold your horses just a little bit and first figure out why your website exists (this advice is, of course, not unique to a particular type of business). What are the goals of your website? What are your desired outcomes?

After you have determined your goals, you should initially focus on reports that will help you understand the website behavior tied to those goals. This will result in a great deal of focus on what you'll be looking at and also improve the chances that you'll be able to affect your bottom line.

The wonderful thing, though, is that even the smallest website operation can gain amazingly powerful benefits from web analytics. In fact, I would go so far as to say that on the Web, where even three-year-olds now buy cars on eBay (http://snipurl.com/threeyearold), there is a real competitive advantage to be gained by any business owner who is able to leverage even the simplest of web analytics reports.

Monday: Top Referring URLs and Top Key Phrases

The first thing you are probably most curious about is, *Where are my visitors coming from?* It is a common first question I hear from many website owners. The very next question is something like, *Is Google sending me traffic?* Of course, that is a reflection of Google's world domination as the starting point of the Internet for almost everyone who surfs. We will spend our first day of working on foundational reports by focusing on two reports that hold the keys to understanding where visitors to your website come from and what search key words or phrases they use to find your website. Exciting stuff!

Top Referring URLs

Your goal here is to understand where you are getting traffic from. Most businesses will create their web presence and undertake some outreach activities to drive traffic, but many will hope that the mere presence of the website will bring traffic. This report will help you understand where traffic is coming from (Figure 7.1).

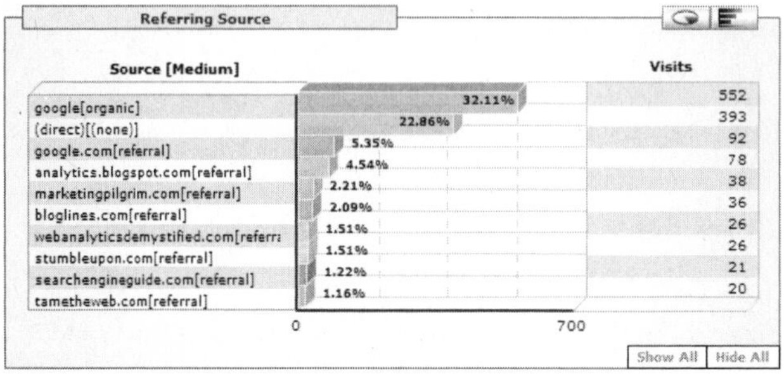

Figure 7.1 Referring URLs from Google Analytics

As one outreach effort, many small and medium businesses (SMBs) create partnerships with other SMBs or associations as a primary way of generating traffic. As you look at the referring URLs, do you see any that are interesting or surprising? Do you have marketing relationships with them? If not, should you? It is effective to understand where people come from, and from that understanding to learn what kinds of traffic are you getting.

If you want to understand the value of each website sending you traffic, a simple drill-down will help. In Google Analytics, simply configure your goal page (this could be a lead, a Contact Me form, or a Thank You page), you should be able to do this in any web analytics tool you are using. It is easy to report on performance of each traffic source (Figure 7.2).

	Source [Medium]	Visits	P/Visit	G1/Visit
1.	google[organic]	552	1.42	0.72%
2.	(direct)[(none)]	393	1.78	2.80%
3.	google.com[referral]	92	1.37	1.09%
4.	analytics.blogspot.com[referra	78	1.78	3.85%
5.	marketingpilgrim.com[referral	38	1.42	0.00%
6.	bloglines.com[referral]	36	1.33	0.00%
7.	webanalyticsdemystified.com	26	2.35	0.00%
8.	stumbleupon.com[referral]	26	1.77	0.00%
9.	searchengineguide.com[refer	21	4.10	0.00%
10.	tametheweb.com[referral]	20	1.10	0.00%
	Totals:	1,719	1.63	1.28%

Figure 7.2 Performance against goals for traffic from each referring source

As you run this report over time, it will help you weed out some of your weaker-performing partners and invest in those that do better. If there is a source that you think should work better, go back to the source website and ensure that your messages and calls to action are accurate.

You have looked at only one report so far, and you are already taking action. This stuff is not complicated!

Top Key Phrases from Search Engines

If not initially, then surely after a little while you will notice your number one referrer of traffic will probably be a search engine. If its stock price is anything to go by, it is probably Google, though it could also be Yahoo! or MSN. The second report you should look at is the top keywords or key phrases that are being searched in search engines that are sending traffic to your website (Figure 7.3).

Search engines are very much the kings of the world, and for business large and small they can have game-changing impact. This might be more true for SMBs because they have small advertising budgets and have to leverage the power of search engines to get traffic to their sites.

Search Keywords

	Total	Google	Yahoo!	Lycos	MSN	AltaVista	Ask
Total	9365	6422	1064	752	570	523	17
persimmon	782	782	0	0	0	0	0
fresh fruits	721	161	0	281	0	261	10
durian	630	630	0	0	0	0	0
fresh fruit	547	127	0	224	0	184	6
pomegranate	492	492	0	0	0	0	0
fruits loom	329	134	142	0	53	0	0
organic fruits	324	167	82	0	75	0	0
star fruits	313	313	0	0	0	0	0
fruits	275	204	0	71	0	0	0
airfreight pineapple shipping	272	168	38	0	66	0	0
organic fruit	272	147	57	0	68	0	0
fruit loom	239	101	90	0	48	0	0
star fruit	230	230	0	0	0	0	0
pineapple shipping	198	44	154	0	0	0	0

Figure 7.3 Keywords driving traffic from each search engine

By looking at the keywords, you can start to infer the intent of your customers. Reading search key phrases can be like reading the minds of your visitors. For example, perhaps you never realized the full potential of selling organic fruits, but because it is one of your top 10 terms, it could be a leading indicator of interest.

If the key phrases that define your business don't show up in the report, you have a valuable opportunity to do some basic search engine optimization (see Chapter 8, "Month 3: Search Analytics—Internal Search, SEO, and PPC" for specific activities you can undertake). Search engines are important to your success, and this report and any effort you put into improving it can pay off handsomely.

Tuesday: Site Content Popularity and Home Page Visits

After you know where people come from, the next logical questions are, *What pages are they visiting?* and *How well is my home page working?* This makes sense; you have all this great content on your website, and so it is important to figure out what people are reading, what is working for you, and what is not. The reason to highlight the home page is different from what you might imagine. It's not that it is any more important than other pages. Read on for the rationale.

Site Content Popularity

Regardless of their size, if websites don't change daily, most site visitors usually consume just 20 percent of the site content. It is extremely important to know which 20 percent. In my experience, we are always surprised by what content is being consumed by our customers. Start with the most popular pages viewed on the site (Figure 7.4).

This list offers plenty of surprises. Sometimes it validates that visitors are doing the "right" things, but more often it shows that visitors are doing all these other things on your site that you didn't anticipate—and that's great food for thought. You have the ability to turn these surprises to your advantage. You can use this information to determine what you should promote on your website that will appeal to your visitors. You can also do little things that can have a big impact, such as running your most compelling promotions on your top 10 most popular pages to ensure that a maximum number of site visitors see them.

	Page Titles	▼ Uniq. Views	Pageviews	Avg Time	% Exit
1.	Occam's Razor by Avinash Ka	2,772	3,543	00:02:43	52.98%
2.	Seven Steps to Creating a Da	705	798	00:04:32	72.31%
3.	Excellent Analytics Tip #8: Me;	582	694	00:05:49	60.23%
4.	How to Choose a Web Analyti	362	467	00:03:05	61.24%
5.	The Awesome Power of Data	360	601	00:01:43	52.41%
6.	Blogging: How-to's, Technical	345	428	00:04:30	68.22%
7.	Five "Ecosystem" Challenges	345	479	00:03:16	51.98%
8.	Web Analysis: In-house or Ou	301	353	00:02:59	60.62%
9.	Top Ten: Signs You Are A Gre	273	363	00:03:03	61.71%
10.	Lab Usability Testing: What, V	265	311	00:02:55	55.95%
	Totals:	11,713	14,624	00:03:00	56.67%

Figure 7.4 Popular site content (top pages viewed)

Percentage of Visitors Who Visit the Home Page

About 90 percent of website owners are way too enamored by their website's home page and spend too much time perfecting it. In reality, about half or less of the site's traffic sees the home page. Do you know what this number is for your website?

Understanding the key home page statistics will help you understand how valuable the home page is. Figure 7.5 shows that only about 28 percent of the traffic sees the home page of this website. However, these statistics can also help provide better awareness of other opportunities—for example, almost 55 percent of the site traffic simply exits from the home page—not a good thing.

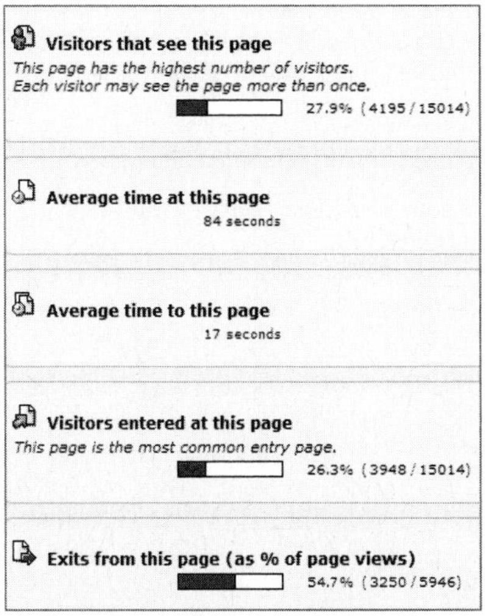

Visitors that see this page
This page has the highest number of visitors.
Each visitor may see the page more than once.
27.9% (4195 / 15014)

Average time at this page
84 seconds

Average time to this page
17 seconds

Visitors entered at this page
This page is the most common entry page.
26.3% (3948 / 15014)

Exits from this page (as % of page views)
54.7% (3250 / 5946)

Figure 7.5 Key home page statistics

You will be able to assign resources optimally and focus on other pages on your website. And now that you have such a great understanding of how to analyze your home page, you can move on to repeat the same analysis on pages you saw in your list of most popular pages viewed.

Wednesday and Thursday: Click Density, or Site Overlay

The click density, or site overlay, report displays your actual pages—just as they look to users—with a click-level indicator next to each link. As you can see in Figure 7.6, the report shows the number of people who click on each link.

Main catalog	This week Bob recommends :				
19%	Banana	Durian	Kiwi Fruit	Mango	Pomegranate
	4.9%	9.9%	18%	19%	24%

Figure 7.6 Click density, or site overlay, report

The site overlay report is great at revealing how your real customers are experiencing your website. There is nothing simpler for any website owner to start with. Web analytics comes to life as you can "see" the clicks and relate to visitors in a new and more profound way.

If you see interesting click density behavior, you can use that as an inspiration to optimize the website through simple experiments with layout, content, and navigation. For example, if you notice that no one is clicking on the blinking text link on the left of the page, maybe it is time that you tried a link that did not blink and had a different call to action. This would be easy to do, and the next day you could go back and see the results of your change.

Note: Whether you are a one-person shop or a multimillion-dollar operation, please ensure that you have a solid understanding of this report and that you publicize it in your organization. It is hard to understand most web analytics, but even a layperson can understand a web page overlaid with where visitors click. It can be a great communication tool and a change agent. But it is important that you first understand exactly what the report is showing and then be able to communicate it effectively (so that when people look at the report, they know exactly what it is showing and what it is not).

Friday: Site Bounce Rate

The bounce rate report reveals the number of visitors who stayed just a few seconds (or in the case of some tools, only saw one page on your website), as you can see in Figure 7.7. These are the people who came to your site but didn't engage, for whatever reason. Different web analytics tools define bounce rates differently, but usually it is visitors who stayed on the website for only five or ten seconds.

	Top Entrances		Entrances	Bounces	Bounce Rate
⊗	1.	/avinash/	2,165	1,353	62.49%
⊗	2.	/avinash/2006/10/seven-steps-to-creating-a-data-driven-decis	634	497	78.39%
⊗	3.	/avinash/2006/11/excellent-analytics-tip-8-measure-the-real-c	401	279	69.58%
⊗	4.	/avinash/2006/07/the-awesome-power-of-data-visualization.h	347	151	43.52%
⊗	5.	/avinash/2006/09/how-to-choose-a-web-analytics-tool-a-radic	284	179	63.03%
⊗	6.	/avinash/2006/11/blogging-how-tos-technical-tips-and-best-w	277	225	81.23%
⊗	7.	/avinash/2006/11/web-analysis-inhouse-or-outsourced-or-so	224	167	74.55%
⊗	8.	/avinash/2006/11/five-ecosystem-challenges-for-web-analytic	217	135	62.21%
⊗	9.	/avinash/2006/06/top-ten-signs-you-are-a-great-analyst.html	212	125	58.96%
⊗	10.	/avinash/2006/05/the-10-90-rule-for-magnificient-web-analytic	210	150	71.43%
		Totals:	8,287	5,679	68.53%

Figure 7.7 Website and page bounce rates

The exact number of seconds that represents a failure varies site by site (and even page by page within a site). Especially for any website owner who has precious few resources to spare, each visitor is valuable and it is hypercritical to know what this number is. After you become a bit more advanced, you can segment for bounce rate by campaigns, referring URLs, top pages on site with high bounce rate, and so forth, to know how valuable traffic is arriving at your site.

You can combine the referring URLs reports with high bounce rates reports to see which sites are referring useful traffic to your site (Figure 7.8). Are you being linked to in a way that doesn't accurately reflect your site? Why are visitors from this referring URL so disappointed when they land on your page? All of these are opportunities for optimization.

Top Referrers

All visitors			Short visit		
Google	55.7%	6422	Google	67.1%	345
www.persimmonnews.com	13.0%	1500	Yahoo!	9.1%	47
Yahoo!	9.2%	1064	www.persimmonnews.com	7.0%	36
Lycos	6.5%	752	www.figleaf.com	5.4%	28
www.figleaf.com	5.1%	582	Lycos	3.7%	19
MSN	4.9%	570	MSN	2.9%	15
AltaVista	4.5%	523	AltaVista	1.6%	8
www.fruitsuggestions.com	0.3%	35	www.fruitsuggestions.com	1.4%	7
www.fruitsuggestions.com	0.2%	24	www.search.com	0.4%	2
Ask	0.1%	17	www.fruitdigest.com	0.4%	2
Other	0.3%	34	Other	1.0%	5
More rows			More rows		

Figure 7.8 Bounced traffic from top website referrers

By creating six extremely simple and easy-to-find reports, you will, in just a couple of weeks, get a solid understanding of the following:

- Where visitors come to your website from
- What search engines and keywords are driving them to your site
- What content (web pages) visitors are interested in

- How valuable your home page is and what you can fix there
- How visitors behave on the top pages of your website, and whether content on these pages is working (especially links)
- Your website's first impression, and where the most valuable traffic to your website comes from

Every one of these reports has an action tied to it, an action that can optimize your website and add to your bottom line.

Notice that measuring the number of visitors, repeat visits, number of pages viewed, or all of those "obvious" metrics are not in this recommended list. These metrics would be little more than distractions to your inital efforts. It is more important to understand some of the deep core things about your website first, and that is what we have covered in week 1. Over time you can get into other reports and dive even deeper into complicated things such as key performance indicators (KPIs) and the like. Initially just focus on the preceding list and you will reap rich dividends.

E-commerce Website Jump-Start Guide

When it comes to businesses on the Web, most of the attention is focused on businesses that run e-commerce websites. Most web analytics, for better or for worse, are focused on e-commerce websites, and you can't throw a stone three feet without hitting conversion rate or another nice e-commerce metric.

The recommendations in this section assume that you are a decent-sized business and have either a part-time dedicated analyst or have hired an outside consultant, even part time, to help measure success. This should give you some sense of scope for applicability of the recommendations and the kind of effort that would be required.

Note: Remember that the jump-start guides in this chapter cover weeks 2 and 3. All site types share the same week 1 steps (which were covered earlier in the chapter) and week 4 steps (which will be covered later).

Week 2: Measuring Business Outcomes

You have taken the time to understand where your website visitors are coming from, what content they are consuming on your website, and how your website is performing in terms of getting the right kind of traffic and initially engaging them.

If you have an e-commerce website, the next task is to understand whether you are making money and whether visitors are converting at a rate that you had expected. Is there positive return on investment (ROI)? You will spend the second week understanding how these two complex elements can best be measured.

Monday through Wednesday: Measure Outcomes

The existence of e-commerce websites is justified for the most part by the ability to generate revenue and sales. So you might as well get into it big time right away.

You'll have to make sure that your web analytics tool's JavaScript tags on your order confirmation pages, and on any other pages that might be relevant, are set up to capture the outcomes data for your website. For example, you'll have an enhanced version of a JavaScript tag on your order confirmation page that will capture the data relating to the orders being placed on your website. Typically this will be the information you need from orders (products, quantity, prices, discounts, and so forth). Alternatively, many businesses also have their own data warehouses or databases with this data properly organized, in which case you don't need to customize your JavaScript tags.

Start by simply helping your business understand what the outcomes are from your website's existence. Keep it really simple (Table 7.1).

▶ **Table 7.1** Core website sales report

Product Category	Revenue	Purchase Units	ASP
Barbie	$345,923	11,550	$30
Bratz	$1,246,676	15,792	$79
Elmo	$372,174	9,316	$40
Thomas the Tank Engine	$105,852	5,158	$21
Winnie the Pooh	$102,871	2,881	$36
Legos	$248,465	8,296	$30
December Sales	**$2,421,961**	**52,993**	**$46**

It is extremely easy for your analysts and key stakeholders to initially understand what is selling on the site. The addition of average selling price (ASP) is key. Marketers want to sell, and ASP is their first hint at how the web is performing vis-à-vis the other channels. It provides them with ideas for promotions and campaigns, as well as a peek into what can be leveraged uniquely on the website.

The next obvious step is to observe trends of revenue metrics over time (Figure 7.9). These trends will highlight seasonality. If you use a stacked bar graph with each segment representing either your website product sales or campaigns, trended graphs can drive key insights and help optimize website sales efforts. For example, notice that different products sell during different time periods (or if you are using campaigns, notice that campaign effectiveness varies and how you can leverage them).

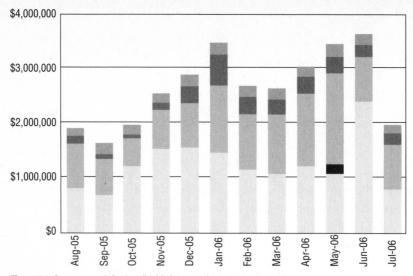

Figure 7.9 Revenue trends by time (highlighting product or campaign mix)

Measuring outcomes is very much an iterative process. It is hard to get it right the first time around; hence we have set aside three days for this. It is important to validate and do a Quality Audit (QA) of the tag to ensure that it is working fine (if you are using JavaScript tags).

After you start collecting the data, it is also important to undertake a reconciliation effort to ensure that the data you have in your web analytics application is accurate. If it is not, establish reasons why it might not be 100 percent accurate (for example, not everyone who comes to your website will have JavaScript turned on, and if your website allows purchases without needing JavaScript, your web analytics application will not have any data for these orders).

If you are not using JavaScript tags and are using alternative means (for example, web logs) to collect data, you will have to expend additional effort to capture and analyze outcomes data. Web logs will not capture the order data by default, so you will have to work with your IT team to find solutions.

Thursday and Friday: Measure Conversion Rate

Finally, our all-time favorite metric: conversion rate. *Conversion rate* is defined simply as being equal to the total number of outcomes (orders, leads, and so forth) divided by the total number of unique visitors.

Table 7.2 shows the conversion rate for a website. Notice that it does not show conversion rate in a silo. It shows conversion rate in context. It shows total visits to highlight a potential increase or decrease of repeat visitor trends (at least to give a hint of it). It shows revenue because at the end of the day, that is what your business decision makers will connect to. Another great benefit of this is that they won't be misled by just looking at conversion rate—notice conversion rate actually went up in April, as did visitors and orders, yet, sadly, revenue went down. It is often a mistake to show conversion rate all by itself. As you do your analysis, it is important to look at metrics and trends and highlight them so that the right questions can be asked for deeper analysis.

▶ **Table 7.2** Monthly conversion rate trends (with key context)

Month	Visits (Visitors)	Unique Visitors	Outcome (Orders)	Revenue	Conversion Rate
Mar 09	580,105	456,831	2,654	$723,801	0.58%
Apr 09	1,048,995	861,480	5,132	$700,701	0.60%
May 09	729,588	599,539	3,128	$761,169	0.52%
Jun 09	549,753	427,071	4,849	$803,321	1.14%

To make your conversion rate reporting more actionable, it is important to segment (Table 7.3).

▶ **Table 7.3** Segmented conversation rate trends

Month	Email Campaigns	SEM / PPC	Ambient Traffic	Overall
Feb 02	7.75%	0.00%	0.45%	0.50%
Mar 02	6.79%	0.74%	0.44%	0.51%
Apr 02	14.87%	0.72%	0.48%	0.61%
May 02	11.30%	0.89%	0.66%	1.00%
Jun 02	22.21%	1.39%	1.00%	1.83%
Jul 02	13.64%	1.07%	0.98%	1.38%
Aug 02	12.57%	1.20%	0.97%	1.63%

You can segment in a number of different ways. Start by identifying your acquisition strategies (what you are doing to generate traffic) and segment by the top two or three (just to keep things simple initially).

Ambient traffic is perhaps the most important segment; it is composed of visitors who just show up at your website (via search engines or word of mouth, for example). For any good website, the ambient traffic will be one of the largest buckets. These visitors convert at lower rates usually, but there are lots of visitors in that bucket—and remember, they are free (you spend money on campaigns; you don't on these nice folks). Hence it is always important to highlight conversion rate for the ambient traffic.

Week 3: Indexing Performance and Measuring Merchandizing Effectiveness and Customer Satisfaction

Measuring performance simply in terms of monetary outcomes or conversion rate is hardly the whole measure of success. That comes from indexing the performance against the goals that you might have for your website. Additionally, you'll have a team of marketers (okay, maybe you have just one part-time person!) who will be working hard to improve the effectiveness of your website by doing some merchandizing or creating demos. As you can imagine, it is extremely important to measure how well those efforts are performing.

In this week, you will spend two days focusing exclusively on measuring something that is not normally an area of focus on your e-commerce website (and answering the question of whether you are solving only for yourself or also for your customers).

Monday: Index Performance to Goals

One of the core reasons that decision makers have a hard time taking actions based on all the data we pump out is that we don't give them enough context. One of the most basic things that you can do on an e-commerce website is to measure against goals.

The challenge here is that you may not have any goals. Perhaps you are a new business and have not yet had the time to gel your web strategy, and consequently you don't have goals. Or perhaps you sit in a large business where the Web is not considered consequential and so you have no web-specific goals. If you are in the former category, wait a few months, look at the trends, and create your own goals (say an increase of 3 percent for Revenue or Conversion or your most important KPI from month to month). If you are in the latter category, absolutely hound your business decision makers, your financial analysts, and your marketers to create goals for your core metrics and then measure your performance. I cannot stress how critical this is.

Figure 7.10 shows trends for revenue over a period of time as indexed against the goal or forecast for revenue that was created, hopefully, at the start of the year. If goals were not included on this graph, you couldn't recognize how awesome January was for the business (what did they do there?). You might also not realize that although for the first half of the year performance was better than expected, that is not the case starting at the middle of the year. Although performance is keeping up with the expected seasonal trend, for some reason the business is doing worse, and drastic action is needed. (Otherwise, they might do really badly for the rest of the year when they are expecting holiday sales.)

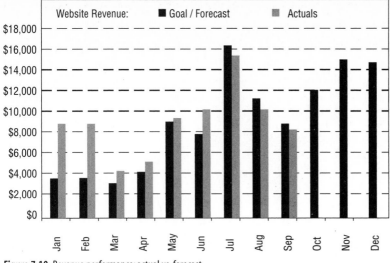

Figure 7.10 Revenue performance: actual vs. forecast

The goals you will create for your metrics will depend on your unique business needs. It is recommended that you have goals for at least these three items:

- Monthly (weekly) revenue
- Unique visitors for your top three acquisition strategies
- Conversion rate for your top three acquisition strategies

Keeping it simple will help focus your analytical efforts tremendously. Now index your performance against the goals and look for surprises in your analysis during the year.

Tuesday and Wednesday: Measure Effectiveness of Onsite Efforts

Every business wants to sell the proverbial fries with the burger. A good example is Amazon.com's approach at including clever suggestions such as "people who bought this also bought that" or "you might also consider buying these other things with your new hair gel."

Your business probably has dedicated efforts to do more than sell your core products or improve conversion rates. You probably have tools that highlight opportunities to sell more (demos and comparison charts), or you undertake interesting merchandising efforts to cross-sell and up-sell to your website visitors. The core differentiator here is that these are efforts in addition to what is happening externally to the website, and these are efforts that are happening within your websites to get your customers to buy more (think of this as you helping them help themselves—maybe this sounds less crass).

It is important on your website to measure effectiveness of these factors. How is your website being more or less effective over time at selling incremental products and ancillary services after the customer is on your site to buy your core products? This is just a random example. You'll have such efforts of your own that are unique to your business.

In Figure 7.11, you'll see the overall merchandising effectiveness of a website that is selling bed and bath products online. You'll notice that they do a pretty good job of selling fries with the burger. But over time, their effectiveness is on a decline. This would be a great time to correlate these trends with the efforts that have gone into improving website effectiveness (it is quite possible that conversion rate is up, but merchandising effectiveness has suffered). From the trends, marketers can also obtain insights into consumer preferences—for example, towels seem to be up, while no one seems to want bed sheets.

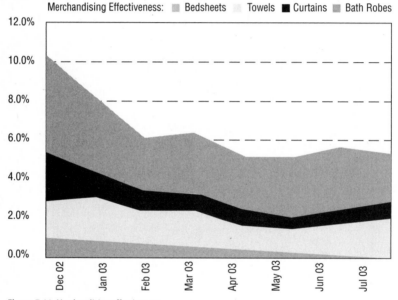

Figure 7.11 Merchandising effectiveness

Your business is unique, and you are going to find your own ways in which the website is trying to be effective at doing its job.

Thursday and Friday: Measure Customer Satisfaction

The last recommendation is inspired by the experience element of the Trinity strategy. The goal is to measure how customers feel about their experiences on our websites and what would they want us to know or fix about those experiences.

Most e-commerce websites convert at a pretty tiny rate (in the 2 percent range). This means that there is a lot of potential for improving the websites to increase conversion, but it also means that there are lots of people coming to our website who are simply not engaging (because they don't want to buy, they did not like something, they ended up there by mistake, they could not find the tools and information they were looking for, or the prices were wrong on your site).

Measuring customer satisfaction on an e-commerce website helps us by providing the qualitative data that we need to make our websites better. Conversion rate and clickstream data can be extremely limiting at highlighting huge opportunities for improvement.

Pairing up customer satisfaction questions with open-ended questions can elevate the understanding to a much higher plane. The open-ended questions that you could ask are as follows:

- If you were here to buy today and did not, please explain why.

- How can we improve our website experience to make it more effective for you?

- If you were not able to complete your task, what were you trying to do?

E-commerce sites exist to sell, but they also exist to help customers do what they are there to do. If you do not have an effective and continuous listening methodology implemented on your website, you'll be limited in your ability to find effective actionable insights.

The preceding recommendations can be a bit complex if you don't have the right set of tools and either internal or external analytics help (from an analyst or a consultant). But every e-commerce website business that would like to have deep insights from the data about the effectiveness and efficiency of their website needs to be able to execute all six of the recommendations outlined earlier in this chapter. So if you don't have the ability to measure all of them, don't give up. Do what you can. Give a copy of this book to your management team and in exchange hopefully you'll get the funding you need to implement the right tools on your website.

Support Website Jump-Start Guide

There is an insightful theory that of all the touch points a business has with its customers, just a small number are moments of truth—essentially interactions that make or break the relationship (and in turn any future profits, customer loyalty, and so forth).

For example, the moment of truth for a credit card company may occur when you call to report your card lost. You are desperate and probably freaked out about charges someone could be making, and when you press 4 (or whatever), the first question out of the operator's mouth is, "What is your credit card number?" Or something equally silly. You just pressed the option to report a lost credit card, and they should know better. They probably just lost a customer, and they definitely lost any good will and positive word of mouth that they had with you thus far.

Moments of truth can happen at any touch point that a customer has with a business. For most online businesses a—if not *the*—critical moment of truth occurs when a customer has a problem and comes to the company website for help. What you do from then on determines any future relationship you might have with the customer.

There is so much information about web analytics all around us and it all seems to revolve around conversion rate or, these days, around search engine marketing (especially pay per click). There are books, blogs, white papers, and conferences. Yet you can't escape from all this detail about money making or getting people to submit leads or to walk down a certain path on your website.

So how should we measure success of a support website in delivering an optimal experience to customers in that moment of truth? Online support is a unique challenge because success is harder to measure; success is not quite as simple as a page view or a Submit Order button.

Week 2: Walking in the Customer's Shoes and Measuring Offline Impact

The first steps of your journey into the complex world of measuring success of your online support website will start with attempting to gain an understanding of how visitors to your website are finding the information that will help resolve their problems. (You'll see right away that we are honing our strategy on taking the customer's perspective rather than measuring standard company-centric KPIs.)

The next step will be to use the web analytics tool, specifically the site overlay report, to analyze the click pattern on the top FAQ pages (with solutions to customer problems) to understand whether they are performing effectively. Finally, we will start measuring the effectiveness of your online presence on your offline presence (your call center, for example).

Note: It is rarely necessary to measure visitors to a support website, at least as any sort of primary objective. Support sites are not in the "demand generation" business, so why should visitor counts be any part of success measurement? In most cases, you don't care how many visitors come to your website. What you care about is how many of those you helped, and for how many of them you delivered a positive moment-of-truth experience. You have to get this in your gut and ensure that everyone around you gets it as well.

Note: We throw an expensive web analytics tool on a support website and we run the standard reports, but most standard analytics reports are quite suboptimal for a support website. For example, a standard approach to measuring success on a support site is to count how many people viewed the pages with support answers (FAQs). Is that really a measure of success, that someone could wade through the site to find an answer page? How do we know it was a success?

Monday and Tuesday: Identify Top Methods of Finding Information

Most support website owners toil away in vain spending time with path analysis, which yields little in terms of insights. Most support sites sit on top of complex knowledge base systems. If you have bad navigation, or "ultra cool" navigation, path analysis is instantly suboptimal because of your influence on the "path" that a visitor can take.

What you really need to analyze on the support website is which options your visitors are using: internal search engine, top FAQ pages, product downloads, links from forums, and so forth (Figure 7.12).

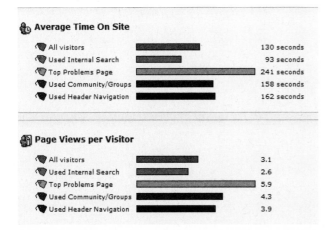

Figure 7.12 Top methods or tools used to find answers

This is important because, as is usual on support websites, if most of your support content can be found only by using your internal search engine, and only 10 percent of the site traffic is using that search engine, it is guaranteed that your customers will be deeply unhappy.

As outlined in Figure 7.13, you can also begin to look at the effectiveness of each tool by simply observing the time that each group of visitors spends on the site. The starting assumption is that more time = not so great. However, please don't jump to conclusions too fast.

Number of Visitors

All visitors	206899
Used Internal Search	5421
Top Problems Page	16542
Used Community/Groups	4297
Used Header Navigation	64916

Average Time On Site

All visitors	130 seconds
Used Internal Search	93 seconds
Top Problems Page	241 seconds
Used Community/Groups	158 seconds
Used Header Navigation	162 seconds

Page Views per Visitor

All visitors	3.1
Used Internal Search	2.6
Top Problems Page	5.9
Used Community/Groups	4.3
Used Header Navigation	3.9

Figure 7.13 Potential effectiveness of top methods or tools used to find answers

For example, it is a tad bit ironic that for the preceding website, the easiest method for finding answers is to use the simple page that has quick links to the top customer problems, Figure 7.12 (Top Problems Page). However, this page causes visitors to spend the most amount of time on the website when the intent was for visitors to use this page to quickly find the answer they want. Top Problems pages exist on all support websites. Does yours have this unintended consequence as well?

Your company's analytics tool might have other strategies that you can use to identify top methods that customers are using to find critical content on your website.

If your analysis indicates that the methods or tools that your customers are using for self-help on your website are not optimal, it is time to start major testing and experimentation to help them help themselves.

The goal here is simple: You have the answers; they need the answers. Help them find the answers fast. Period.

Wednesday and Thursday: Perform Click Density Analysis of Top FAQs

You probably know the top problems that your company's products or services are having. You would know this either from your internal sources or from viewing the top solutions to your product problems on your website (your web analytics package to the rescue).

Use your site overlay report (Figure 7.14) to perform click density analysis on just the top 10 or 20 of those pages. Then identify whether people are taking the action on that solutions page that you expect them to take.

Note: Look only at the top 10 or 20 pages, both to avoid paralysis by analysis and because on most support websites (given the nature of the business), bugs tend to be concentrated, so just a few pages will get 90 percent of the traffic. Check your own statistics by using your web analytics tool and pick the right number for you.

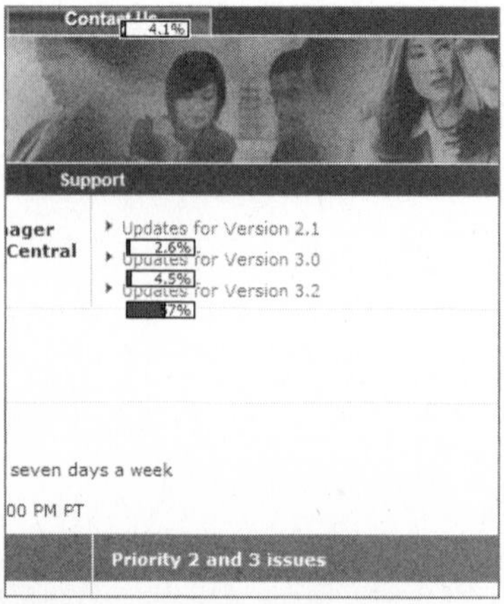

Figure 7.14 Click density analysis (site overlay) for top pages

For example, to fix a problem, you want your visitors to download a patch. Are they doing that? If there are links on that page that take them to different solutions, are the customers able to find those links and are they clicking on them? What is the percent of clicks on links below the fold (and are any of those links important)?

If we find that customers are not doing what we expect them to do on the solutions page, it is time to rethink the content or layout to make it more useful. By using click density analysis on just a small number of pages, you can have an effect on a disproportionate number of your site visitors.

Friday: Determine What Percent of Site Visitors Call the Support Phone Number

The most common reason that visitors come to a support site is to find a phone number they can call in order to get help quickly. This behavior has been reinforced over time because most websites are not great at helping customers, so they simply want to call. But one of the most effective ways to measure your website's success is to measure whether the site is solving problems so well that customers don't have to call you on the phone.

Put a unique 800 (toll free) phone number on your support website and count the number of phone calls to that distinct phone number. It is important to measure that call volume over time. If you are really driving improvements to the website experience, the number of phone calls should go down in proportion to website traffic. (This is one rationale for measuring traffic to a support website!)

Also measure successful resolutions in the phone channel for the callers who came from the website, along with the traditional phone channel metric of time to resolution. The hypothesis is that even if the website was not able to eliminate the call, perhaps it was good enough to provide the customers with the basic information that would make for a shorter phone call (and, in turn, some cost savings to your company).

If you can't use unique phone numbers, you can try something clever in your web analytics tool (if it allows advanced segmentation). You can determine the portion of site visitors who view a FAQ page and then go to the contact page (the one with the phone number), and the portion who do not go to the contact page (the assumption being that they were able to find an answer). Figure 7.15 shows an example.

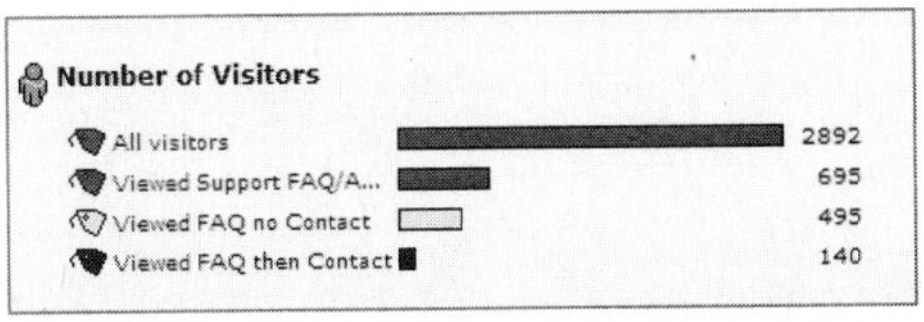

Number of Visitors

All visitors	2892
Viewed Support FAQ/A...	695
Viewed FAQ no Contact	495
Viewed FAQ then Contact	140

Figure 7.15 Using web analytics to measure estimated call avoidance (solving problems on the website so customers don't call)

Note: The numbers in Figure 7.15 are rough approximations. It is possible that the third group (495) did not go to the contact page because they were too frustrated. But if you observe trends in the report over time, it is a great proxy for your site effectiveness in improving self-help (and in turn reducing phone calls).

Week 3: Measuring Success by Using VOC or Customer Ratings (at a Site and Page Level)

Now that you have gotten into some of the traditional and obvious metrics that web analytics helps measure on support websites, you are going to spend a week measuring the not-always-obvious metrics that are usually not associated with web analytics. Still, they are absolutely critical when it comes to measuring the success of a support website.

It is critically important that any web analytics program (and mindset) be expanded to measure these qualitative metrics because clickstream analysis (traditional web analytics) will fall well short of measuring true success of your website from the customers' perspective. Pages viewed can't be interpreted as true success.

Monday through Wednesday: Measure Problem Resolution, Timeliness, and Likelihood to Recommend

Most web analytics packages are quite limited in their ability to provide insights on support websites—simply because they are measuring clicks and are not really good at measuring the heart and brain behind the clicks. As you can imagine, those two items, especially in this case, are of extreme importance.

To measure real success of your website, you should implement a continuous measurement system that is effective at measuring the customers' perception of problem resolution (the stress is on customer perception and not your perception).

You could do lab usability studies or follow-me-homes, for example. But perhaps the most cost-effective and scalable option is to implement relevant surveys on your website. See Chapter 3 for more details.

Here are three amazingly powerful metrics that you should measure:

Problem resolution rate: What percent of survey respondents were able to resolve the problem they had?

Timeliness: What percent were satisfied with the time it took them to resolve their problem?

Likelihood to recommend: What percent are so satisfied that they are likely to recommend your support website to others?

These three metrics measure the core essence of whether you are delivering against the customer expectations for a moment of truth. Figure 7.16 shows these metrics as measured by a continuous survey implemented on three different support websites (as measured against an external benchmark, the last bar in each metric, to better gauge performance). The scores are out of a possible 100 percent. These three questions are almost always paired up with one or two open-ended questions, where customers can type in open text to help us get more context about where to focus our energies.

Online Support Success Metrics

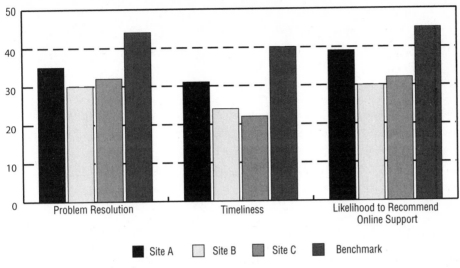

Figure 7.16 Customer-rated metrics

You will be humbled by the first results, but the insights you gain and the changes that result that will have a positive impact on customer experience.

Thursday and Friday: Conduct Page-Level Surveys

It is fairly obvious that like no other website, a support website exists to solve the customers' problems. It does not exist for the company and it does not have to be pretty. It simply has to solve the customers' problems, if they can be solved on the Web, as quickly and effectively as it can. With that in mind, the final recommendation for measuring a support site is to use a page-level survey (see Chapter 3 for details).

Many types of websites use page-level surveys, but they are most useful on support websites (on most others, site-level surveys are prerequisites). I am sure you have seen them on various websites. They are links on the page that read, for example, "Rate this page" or "Please give feedback on this page" or "Page Suggestions" or "Was this article helpful?"

This is a short survey enabling visitors to rate the clarity, usefulness, and ease of finding individual answers. The survey is initiated by the visitor by clicking a link and includes an open-text field for customers to give feedback on why the answer was helpful and how it can be improved. These surveys are simple by design and are easy to implement even in-house at your company (bribe your friendly IT guys).

Page-level surveys are not about the website's design and ease of use or the visitor's overall feeling. They are for feedback that will help you improve individual answers.

Also, it is important to know that page-level surveys are *opt-in*, that is, customers take action to initiate the surveys and therefore they will have low response rates. They will also be skewed a tad bit toward collecting negative responses. This is perfectly okay and reasonable given the context in which you are asking for feedback.

The most important part is the open-text response, which can help you improve the individual answers and to have an upward trend over time for your Clarity, Usefulness, and Ease of Finding metric ratings. For more details on crafting an optimal surveying strategy, please refer to Chapter 3.

Note: Doing analytics on a support website is extremely difficult because you are dealing with irrationality. People are stressed, our websites are not optimal, and there is no patience in getting answers. Standard analytics tools can only go so far. It is recommend that 70 percent of your analysis should be qualitative (from asking questions such as, If you were not able to solve your problem on our site, what was your problem? or How can we improve this support answer?) and 30 percent should be clickstream (quantitative).

Blog Measurement Jump-Start Guide

Because of the sheer diversity of blogs and relative youth of the medium, there is a lack of standardized approaches toward measuring their success. This diversity makes things a bit more complex because blogs exist for so many purposes.

Week 2: Overcoming Complexity to Measure the Fundamentals (by Using New Metrics)

At the moment, there aren't even real analytics tools available to measure this unique medium, where the concept of a page does not make a lot of sense (in most blogs, eight or ten of the most recent posts are on the home page, so which one was "read"?). Even the concept of a website might not make sense because almost all blogs support Really Simple Syndication (RSS) feeds, and frequent readers don't even have to visit the website. They can simply use their favorite feed reader to consume the posts.

Monday: Understand Blog Measurement Complexity and Challenges

To make sense of all this, we have some rather suboptimal options available to us (for now):

- Tools from standard web analytics vendors (ClickTracks, IndexTools, WebTrends, or your friendly neighborhood vendor)
- External blog ranking services such as Technorati (and even Alexa Internet)
- Statistics relating to our RSS feeds from services such as FeedBurner (of course RSS stats don't have any relationship to web analytics stats—for example, are *subscribers* equivalent to *visitors*?)

- Data that our web analytics tools cannot measure but we have some other ways of measuring (such as number of posts, comments, and so forth)

Because we don't have a lot of innovative products to measure blog success, we must use our ingenuity to make sense of it all. The wonderful thing is that even without metrics or tools, fundamental business questions exist (yes even for a blog!):

- What have you actually contributed to your blog or from your blogging efforts?

- Is anyone consuming your blog's great content?

- Are people engaging in the conversation (remember, this is the most social of social mediums)?

- Are you having an effect socially, personally, or in business? Are you standing out among the 70 million–plus blogs on this planet?

- What is the cost of having a blog?

- What are you or your company getting in return for this investment?

As you notice, our critical few "existential" questions (always a best practice) cover all elements of the Trinity mindset: experience, behavior, and outcomes, and as for any website, we want to measure return on our investment.

For the purpose of illustrating key metrics, I am going to use the data of my blog, Occam's Razor (http://www.kaushik.net/avinash).

Tuesday: Measure Frequency and Raw Author Contribution

Blogs exist to have conversations that are topical, relevant, and happening all the time. In measuring *raw contribution*, you are attempting to benchmark your performance. To measure that you will have to use various key statistics for the blog such as number of posts, the life of the blog, number of comments, number of words in each post, etc. Figure 7.17 shows these important statistics for my blog, Occam's Razor.

- Users: **1**
- Categories: **15**
- Posts: **67**
- Comments: **815**
- Pages: **8**
- Words In Post: **113,744**
- Words In Comments: **90,502**
- Words In Pages: **5,701**

Figure 7.17 Critical blog statistics

The formulas we will use to measure the recommended metrics are:

- Frequency = number of posts / time (number of months)

- Raw author contribution = number of words in post / number of posts

For Occam's Razor, the frequency is 9.6 and raw author contribution is 1,698. Generally, bloggers are expected to have a significantly higher frequency, and a lower contribution is acceptable. For your blog, you'll find your own happy medium (and over time you can benchmark against your competition).

These two metrics are especially relevant for business blogs and allow the business decision makers to judge whether they have a blog (indicated by a high number in both metrics) or simply a website that happens to have the word *blog* in the title or page.

For the best insights, observe trends for both of these metrics over time (up and to the right is a good thing for the graphs in this case!).

Wednesday and Thursday: Measure Unique Blog Readership

Content consumption is an attempt at understanding whether anyone is reading what you are writing and publishing. The challenge on a blog is that the content is on the website and also available via RSS. So how do you know true content consumption—visits, visitors, or subscribers?

I recommend computing a metric called *unique blog readership* (see Table 7.4) as a first attempt at rationalizing the different metrics into a web analytics equivalent. It is derived from two sources: the web analytics tool and the RSS tool (in this case, utilizing FeedBurner).

A Recap of Readership Definitions

The following are the key definitions that we had defined earlier.

Visits: Count of all sessions during a time period (from your web analytics tool).

Unique visitors: Count of all unique cookie_ids during a time period (from your web analytics tool).

Subscribers: Approximate measure of the number of individuals who have opted to receive regular updates of your blog via RSS or email. (It is measured by matching IP address, feed reader combinations, and polling behavior of various feed readers.)

Unique blog readers: Count of unique readers of your blog arrived at by adding the number of unique visitors and the average daily feed subscribers for that month.

Note: Like all other web metrics, unique blog readership is at the mercy of your web analytics cookie deletion issue (remember to use first-party cookies) and the evolving nature of measuring blog subscribers (which will get better over time).

Table 7.4 illustrates the Unique Blog Readers metric. It is the combination metric that will allow you to track your success by measuring the overall readers of your blog.

You want this number to grow from month to month as a measure of success. It is also recommended that for your business, as you ramp up investment, you take the data you have and set goals for the Unique Blog Reader metric.

► Table 7.4 Computing unique blog readers

Time	Visits / Visitors	Unique Visitors	Avg Daily Feed Subscribers	Monthly Unique Blog Readers
Jun 06	4,735	2,000	50	2,050
Jul 06	28,643	19,130	117	19,247
Aug 06	8,633	4,192	241	4,433
Sep 06	6,525	3,162	360	3,522
Oct 06	9.935	5,719	442	6,161
Nov 06	11,090	6,100	539	6,639
Dec 06	12,294	7,282	624	7,906

Friday: Assess Conversation Rate

Blogs by their inherent nature are social, and one core reason for their existence is to engage in a conversation with readers. (Otherwise, you have a website and a web page, not a blog and blog posts.) The conversation could take many forms, but one of the simplest ones is readers having a conversation with you via comments on your blog or via posts on their blogs (and sending you trackbacks). Consider the following equation for conversation rate:

Conversation rate (percent) = (number of comments + trackbacks during a time period) / number of posts during that time period on your blog

Referring back to Table 7.4, the conversation rate for Occam's Razor is approximately 12 over the seven-month period. This is slightly on the high side compared to most blogs. What is important here is that you are engaging your readers in a conversation rather than simply pumping words out and talking all the time (blogs can certainly be used for that, but then you have a website and not a blog).

You will create your own benchmark over time for this metric, and the goal will be for the trend to go up over time.

Week 3: Competitive Benchmarking and Measuring Cost and ROI

In week 2, we spent time understanding the metrics that apply to our blogs. We even created a few new metrics that are relevant and applicable only to blogs. In week 3, we will spend time externally benchmarking success (it is also a way of measuring performance of your blog as compared to your competition) and then we will step into slaying the cost and ROI metrics. Many bloggers will perhaps not consider these metrics because blogs are not typically geared toward making money. But any "website" can be measured in terms of cost and ROI, as can blogs, even if in the end we will not make do-or-die decisions for our blogs based on simply the cost or ROI (unless you are a business and you have to justify your existence, in which case you'll also find help in this section).

Monday: Use External Benchmarking—Technorati Rank

Websites have *page strength*, which to some extent is measured by validating the number of inbound links and the quality of the source sites that link to you. For a blog, the closest equivalent is the Technorati rank.

The Technorati rank is your rank on a list of all the blogs in the world as computed by the list of distinct ("unique") blogs that link to you in a rolling six-month time period.

Hence for example, for Occam's Razor, the rank on Christmas day, 2006, is 3,789: the number of blogs, plus one, that have more than 549 blogs linking to them (Figure 7.18).

> **Occam's Razor by Avinash Kaushik**
> Rank: 3,789 (1,273 links from 549 blogs)
> URL: http://www.kaushik.net/avinash
> Updated: 12 hours ago
> [Search this blog] [Search]

Figure 7.18 Technorati ranking details

The unique thing about Technorati that is sadly missing from web analytics in general, is the pressure to stay relevant. You can't be a one-hit wonder, make a great post, get lots of links, and cruise. You have to be constantly out there and contributing, and people have to recognize your work by linking to it. If you don't do it, the result is that because of the six-month rolling window, your ranking will slip.

The Technorati ranking (or any other external benchmark) is also important because it is an excellent external validation of your progress against your "competition." It is also a great way to measure your success in making a "dent" in a space that has so many voices and to see whether you are making a difference.

Most business blogs want to be blogs but in reality are more talk and less conversation. More than for personal blogs, Technorati rankings (Table 7.5) are a fantastic way for business blogs to measure their success and, in all honesty, to judge whether they are really "getting this blogging thing."

▶ **Table 7.5** Occam's Razor web analytics blog Technorati trend

Rankings	Jun 06	Jul 06	Aug 06	Sep 06	Oct 06	Nov 06	Dec 06
Technorati	61,940	20,198	9,744	8,343	5,509	5,083	3,896
Alexa	258,694	142,544	81,634	72,043	73,250	69,588	57,933

Table 7.5 also shows Alexa ranking. Alexa is the poor man's competitive analysis tool that measures the traffic to your website from people around the world who have installed the Alexa toolbar. It is an imperfect measure but it can be useful for

judging how your blog's traffic looks to an external entity. Alexa rankings are useful only if they are under 100,000. If the rank is over 100,000, then according to the Alexa website the rank is very imprecise, and I would recommend it not be used.

Tuesday and Wednesday: Measure the Cost of Blog Ownership

Like all other mediums, this one has a cost associated with it. In the case of blogs, the cost of the hardware and software typically is not as high as, say, serving up an e-commerce website. Most personal blogs can be hosted at third parties for free or for a small cost (from $5–$20 per month). The costs associated with blogs are a deep investment of time and resources to create, maintain, and publicize the blog. For your business, it is important to compute these costs as best as you can.

If you have a personal blog, the computation is much simpler. For example, it could be as follows:

- Cost of hosting the blog and content serving: $10 per month
- Cost of time invested in the blog: 15 hours per week at $75 per hour = $58,000 per year

For business blogs, this can be even easier to compute by measuring the cost of part-time and full-time resources that have been dedicated to the blogging efforts.

It is also important, if not outright critical over time, for businesses to measure the opportunity cost of investing in a blog. According to Wikipedia, the definition of *opportunity cost* is "the cost of something in terms of an opportunity forgone (and the benefits that could be received from that opportunity), or the most valuable forgone alternative (or highest-valued option forgone)."

It is important to measure opportunity cost in the context of the metrics discussed previously. If your success metrics are not delivering against expectations, what else could you do that would be more valuable to your business with the resources you are pouring into blogging? Few businesses measure opportunity cost. They should, because at the end of the day, they are in service to the shareholders.

Thursday and Friday: Measure Return on Investment

Blogging is for the most part connected to people, and people blog for a number of reasons. It can be for altruistic reasons, it can be for brand building, it can be for ego boosting, it can be simply a creative outlet. For businesses it can be a way of getting closer to their customers, getting direct feedback, creating a unique brand identity, being hip and cool—or some might do it just because the CEO wants it.

This multitude of purposes for blogging makes it a tad bit challenging to measure return on investment (ROI). But it is imperative that if you are seriously into blogging (so, not for personal this-is-my-diary-and-I-am-doing-it-because-it-makes-me-happy reasons—which are absolutely legitimate and justified), it important to have a measure of ROI, no matter how crude. Let's cover a few examples of methods you can use to compute ROI.

There was a interesting piece of research conducted by Tristan Louis (http://snipurl.com/aolweblogs) about the October 2005 acquisition of Weblogs, Inc., a blog network, by AOL. That research provided the first yardstick, inbound links, for measuring the value of a blog. Dane Carlson used that research to create a handy dandy "calculator" (http://snipurl.com/blogworth) that can help you estimate the value of your own blog.

This is far from perfect. But it is a great example of outside-the-box thinking that you can use to create your own models for valuing your blog.

Here is a simple personal ROI computation:

Personal blog ROI = blog worth divided by cost (in seven months)

For Occam's Razor, that works out to the following:

307,674 / 31,500 = 9.8 (a return of $9.80 for every dollar invested)

If you have a personal blog, you can also measure other "softer" items such as the number of job offers you have received, the number of conference invitations, the number of newspaper interviews you have been invited to do, whether you got a book deal out of it, and so forth. Each of those has a value that is personal to you.

For businesses, here are a few best practices you can apply to measuring ROI:

- Measure conversion rates for traffic from your blogs to your e-commerce sites (or that of your partners). Blogs don't exist just to sell, but hey, they improve your presence and that can't hurt sales. If you have advertising on your blog (or merchandize your own products), that makes it even easier. If you collect leads off your blogs, measure and apply the same lead valuation as you do for your website.

- Measure improvements in Customer Satisfaction and Likelihood to Recommend metrics that are tied to your blog. If you are going to actively participate in a social medium, this is absolutely an outcome and it is a quantifiable outcome.

- Measure lowered cost of PR such as press releases, newspaper "buzz," and so forth. Having a blog, and a popular one, means that you now have the ability to put your message out more efficiently and in a more timely fashion. You currently already measure ROI on your company's PR efforts. Apply the same to your business blog.

A personal note: Blogging is about passion. It is almost irrational why people blog and put their hearts and souls into it. I should know; I have exhibited this irrationality just as much as others. I can see my peer bloggers cringing at my attempts to even try to use ROI as a metric because for them, and for me, you blog because you care, because you love—pure and simple. Consider measuring ROI simply as a way to justify your existence (especially in a business environment, where love counts for little and ROI counts for a lot). You should be able to justify the existence of your business blog extremely easily (because cost is so low) even with the most conservative estimates of the preceding business measurement suggestions.

Week 4: Reflections and Wrap-Up

You have spent three intense weeks working through some extremely complex and challenging issues. You have earned a well-deserved break from the intensity. Week 4 is the time to do that. It is also time to consider the following brief action items, a small one on each day, to keep the creative juices flowing (but also to secretly take what you have learned from this book and customize it in some way to your own business).

Monday: You have created about 14 reports that contain approximately 20 metrics or KPIs. Reflect on what you have. Given your knowledge of your business, identify metrics that might be obvious misses.

Tuesday: Take some dedicated time to QA your data collection methodologies and your metrics computations. Most web analytics implementations have errors. Now that you have identified your key reports and metrics, it is time to put solid effort into validating that the data for your key metrics is being collected accurately and that your reports are computing the metrics accurately. If not, work with your vendor and IT department to apply fixes.

Wednesday: Present your initial list of prioritized metrics to your key stakeholders and collect their feedback on the following:

- Obvious wins and causes for celebration
- Areas where you can focus for next-level drill-downs in terms of reporting

Thursday: Partner with your key decision makers (senior management) to get help with two key issues:

- Setting goals for the key metrics you have identified thus far
- Making the business case to implement any new measurement methodologies recommended (for example, simple surveys on your site)

Friday: Take Friday off. You deserve a long weekend to recover!

Note: For information about suggested KPIs and metrics for additional types of businesses, please refer to the "Web Analytics Key Metrics and KPIs" document published by the Web Analytics Association and included in the CD-ROM that accompanies this book. The WAA document, published in 2005, includes metrics for content, lead generation, and customer service websites. It also provides KPIs for key website processes such as reach, acquisition, conversion, and retention.

Month 3: Search Analytics—Internal Search, SEO, and PPC

Up to this point, we have taken a systematic approach toward understanding how to create an analytics program—from learning the metrics fundamentals to creating a comprehensive analytical strategy that supports your business goals. I am sure you can't wait to dive deeper into more data and analytics and simply kick it up a notch. Let's do just that in the upcoming chapters—as chef Emeril Lagasse would say: Bam!

In this chapter, you will mine one of the most extensive sources of actionable insights that you will find in your web analytics data: your search data. I will cover the much-hyped-about world of pay per click (PPC), or search engine marketing (SEM), but at the same time will also shine a big bright floodlight on two other important but underappreciated facets of searches: the internal site search and search engine optimization (SEO). Both hold tremendous promises of long-term success for your website and will pay off big for any investment you put into them.

Week 1: Performing Internal Site Search Analytics

The term *search* is commonly associated with external searches—searches that happen outside your website. Many of you are doing at least a little bit of pay per click (search engine marketing), and some of you are also immersed in the world of search engine optimization (SEO). Both of these efforts will drive traffic to your site from external search engines (Google, Yahoo!, MSN, and so forth), but what can you learn from visitors' search behavior after they are on your site?

An *internal site search* occurs when someone visits your website and uses its Search feature to find information. Surprisingly, very few companies pay any attention to search behavior within their own websites. Even companies that are extremely sophisticated with external search campaigns treat internal site search as a stepchild and miss the opportunity to cull insights from their own website's search analytics.

The ironic fact is that websites have become huge, and as they have become more complex, a steadily increasing number of website visitors are opting to jump to the site Search box to find whatever it is that they are looking for.

Monday: Understand the Value of the Internal Search

A simple Google search for metrics seems to indicate a consensus that at least 10 percent of visitors to any given website are using internal site searches as their primary mode of navigating the website. However, this method of finding information is likely to increase for several reasons. As external search engines continue to gain traction as a method of finding information on the World Wide Web, there is a likelihood that searchers will find information by the same method after they arrive at your site.

In addition to the behavioral correlation between external and internal searches, there are factors at a site level that promote this behavior. First, as websites are becoming increasingly larger and more complex, the task of finding information becomes more efficient just by entering a query in a site's Search box. Just look at Amazon.com's home page and you'll get the point! Second, many websites are not designed to be customer centric, either because they serve "one size fits all" static content or because they have suboptimal design. Some website owners or designers have obviously realized this, and internal search now dominates the core navigational elements of the site, as illustrated by Figure 8.1.

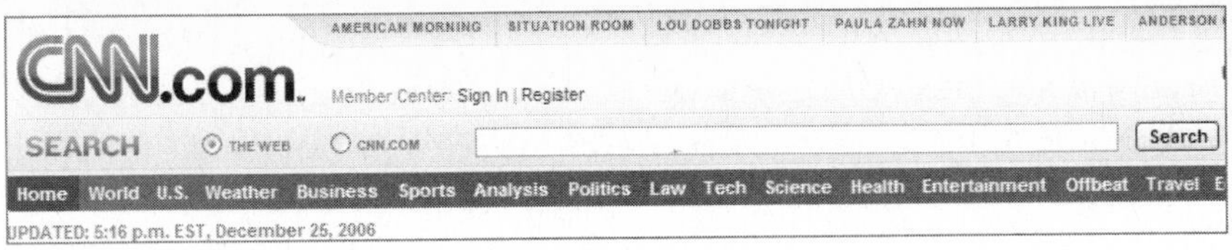

Figure 8.1 Search box dominates CNN.com home page header

Yet internal site search is not optimized on many top websites. This causes customers to simply exit after a quick search (taking their money with them).

There is currently a distinct lack of understanding of the value of the internal search and how it can be used to both improve the customer experience on the site and at the same time help influence website outcomes.

Figure 8.2 shows the results of a search for *desktop software* on H&R Block's website (H&R is the maker of the popular tax software in the United States called Tax-Cut). You'll notice very quickly that seven results came back, and not a single one of the results are for their desktop software product—quite the contrary, the first one is for federal tax forms and the rest lead to the online version of their product, precisely what the customer did not want.

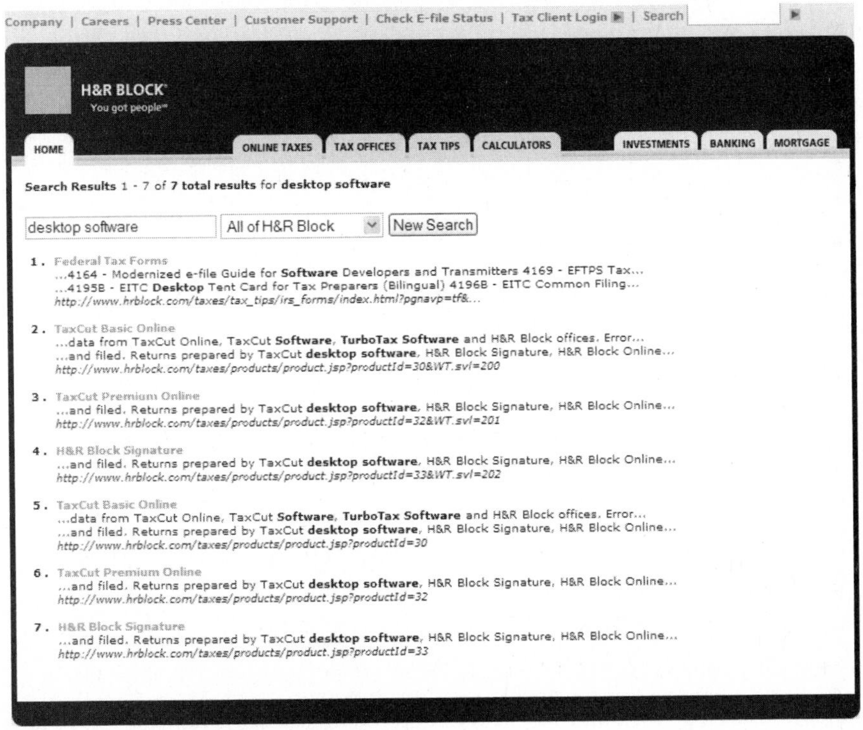

Figure 8.2 Search for *desktop software* on H&R Block's website

As is rather clear from Figure 8.3, H&R Block does sell desktop versions of their software and even offers a download version. Yet its internal search is causing it to lose sales (at between $20 to $60 a pop, imagine what 10 percent of their website traffic not finding the right results is costing H&R Block).

Figure 8.3 H&R Block's desktop software offerings

Common Reasons That Decision Makers Overlook the Internal Site Search

It is quite surprising how decision makers don't ask for internal search analytics reports. Some of the reasons include

- The magnitude of site search usage is not a number that is easily available because many analytics tools don't provide this statistic in a default report. None of the top vendors, at the moment, report internal site search statistics.

- There are all kinds of hairy implementations of internal site search software that compound the ability to integrate reporting. There are too many solution providers and too many customized implementations.

- There is a wrongly held belief that if you optimize for external searches, you are also optimizing for internal searches.

Internal site search is of paramount importance, both to you and to your site's visitors. You'll spend the rest of Monday exploring the reasons that this is true:

External searches have nothing to do with internal searches. Figure 8.4 shows the top external search engine key phrases for the Occam's Razor web analytics blog.

Search Keywords

	Total	Google	Yahoo!	MSN
Total	2698	2557	64	41
occam's razor	65	63	1	1
avinash kaushik	63	62	1	0
avinash	38	34	3	1
90/10 rule	17	14	2	0
kaushik	14	10	0	0
90 10 rule	13	13	0	0
statistically significant	13	13	0	0
web analytics requirements	11	11	0	0
path analysis	10	9	0	1
data visualization	10	10	0	0
measuring conversion	10	10	0	0
multi variant test usability	10	10	0	0
qualitative metrics	10	8	1	1

Figure 8.4 Top external search key phrases

This shows a good amount of traffic from external search engines and some expected and unexpected key phrases. Figure 8.5 illustrates the key phrases that were searched internally on the website during the same time period.

Internal Search Report

This report is currently showing values for the URL parameter

segmentation	0.0%	13
google analytics	0.0%	9
clicktracks	0.0%	9
google	0.0%	9
small business	0.0%	7
web analytics	0.0%	7
omniture	0.0%	7
webtrends	0.0%	6
kpi	0.0%	5
page tagging	0.0%	5

Figure 8.5 Top internal search key phrases

The two sets of keywords have nothing in common because visitor intentions are radically different; you'll notice the same trend on you own website, big or small. The key insight is that most searchers are looking for generic categories in Google or Yahoo! or MSN to locate a relevant site. But after they are on the website, they are looking for something specific.

If you are doing SEO only for external key phrases, you are not solving for visitors on your website. It is likely that when people search on your website, they will get suboptimal search results (see the preceding H&R Block example).

Internal search data can yield an understanding of customer intent and help improve site experience. At least 10 percent of your website visitors are using internal searches to navigate the website. This is a very high number, especially given that most navigational elements on the site such as top navigation, left navigation, links in the body of pages, and so forth, are used by just 2 to 5 percent of the site visitors. You can glean quick and easy insights about customer intent by analysis of data from just this one simple feature of your website. Internal search key phrases are wonderful, absolutely wonderful, ways of understanding visitor intent. You can study them and figure out what your visitors are looking for and how you can help them find it better.

Internal search data can provide great clues about what is "broken" about your site. For example, it provides clues about navigation and links, stuff people can't find easily, or content that is completely missing. A couple of examples:

- If you have a big honking blinking button that reads Subscribe Newsletter and yet that is your top key phrase, you might want to rethink the blinking button.

- If one of the top five key phrases on your internal site search report is Register Product and you don't offer registration, you can see that here is your customer demanding that you do.

In summary, it is hard enough for prospective visitors to find your website. Somehow, if they do manage to find you, measuring and optimizing internal searches is one of the key mechanisms by which you can improve customer satisfaction and improve your conversion rates (if you are an e-commerce website).

Measuring and subsequently optimizing your internal search consists of performing six discrete tasks, detailed in the sections for Tuesday through Friday. Each of these tasks might take a bit longer than just an hour a day, depending on the tools that you have at your disposal.

Tuesday: Spot Internal Search Trends

The most obvious way to use the data from your internal search engine is to glean insights into the use of your website's Search feature and the keywords or phrases that your website visitors are using to find what they are looking for.

Measure Internal Site Search Usage Metrics

This step seems simple enough—use your web analytics tool or the software that came bundled with your internal search engine to measure internal searches (Figure 8.6).

meta	All visitors	Internal Search Users
Wed Nov 1	322	6
Thu Nov 2	363	13
Fri Nov 3	246	12
Sat Nov 4	143	0
Sun Nov 5	160	5
Mon Nov 6	438	21
Tue Nov 7	366	9
Wed Nov 8	412	1
Thu Nov 9	607	7

Figure 8.6 Internal search usage trends

It is usually optimal to have your web analytics tool measure internal searches. That way, you are measuring key metrics by the same methodology. Most bundled reports from internal search tools report *instances* of keyword search and not *visitors* searching. They can be different metrics.

Report on the Top Internal Site Search Key Phrases

At least on a weekly basis, review the top 25 key phrases from your internal search report. (You could look for more; just look for where the numbers fall off a cliff—usually after the top 20–25, or the long tail starts.)

You are looking for interesting and surprising key phrases. Are there key phrases for content that you actually have prominently displayed? Are there key phrases that surprise you—for example, content you don't have?

It is extremely beneficial to look at key phrases that are returning no results on your website (Figure 8.7). This could alert you to spelling mistakes or terms that your users are using that you did not anticipate. For example, perhaps you are selling *window coverings* but people are searching for *curtains* and therefore can't find what they want. Or maybe people are looking for stuff you never anticipated (for information about your competitors, for instance).

Yesterday and today		
Term	**Searches**	**Hits**
blog	10	5
segmentation	4	5
google analytics	2	5
eCPM	1	0
meta tags	1	5
ominture	1	0
omniture	1	5
revenue per page	1	5
webtrends	1	5

Figure 8.7 Internal search key phrase counts and hits
(notice the zeros in the middle)

Wednesday: Analyze Click Density by Using the Site Overlay Report

If your web analytics vendor supports reporting of internal search results via site overlay (Figure 8.8), that can be a great source of actionable insights. Now you can literally see customer clicks (hence reactions) to your top keywords and you can see whether customers think you are serving up relevant results (as opposed to you, the proud site owner, thinking that).

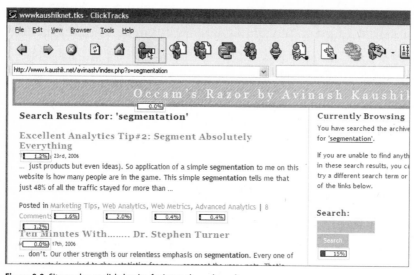

Figure 8.8 Site overlay, or click density, for internal search results

You can also gain other insights from site overlay. For instance, in Figure 8.8, 15 percent of those who saw the search results searched again (sad, because if the results were optimal they would have clicked on a link to an article relevant to what they were looking for and they would not have to search again).

The goal for internal site search results should be to have most of the click density clustered on the top five search results links, and no one should click Next Page (in an age of click happy customers, and relevant results in from search engines like Google, very few people will have the patience to dig deeper to find what they are looking for; if your top five results are not relevant it is more likely that the customers will simply give up and exit).

Thursday: Measure Effectiveness of Actual Search Results

You have figured out how many visitors are using your internal search engine, and you have also learned that keywords are being used to find relevant content. Now it is time to figure out whether the search results that are being returned are any good. From simply measuring, you step into driving change and action.

Measure the Exit Rate from the Search Results Page

You can use your site overlay report to measure the exit rate from your internal search results page (Figure 8.9). This is a leading indicator of search results that are broken. In addition, key phrases that lead to exits are high-priority candidates for a review and update.

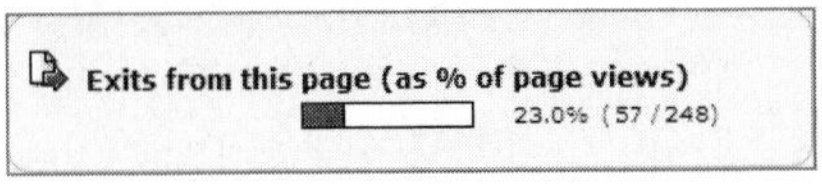

Exits from this page (as % of page views)
23.0% (57 / 248)

Figure 8.9 Website exit rate from search results page

It is optimal to observe trends of this number over time and to have the trend get better (reduce) as you implement improvements.

Measure Effectiveness of Synonyms, or Best Bets

Synonyms, or *best bets*, are links that appear on top of internal search results. These are created by the website owner as a helping hand for visitors.

Best bets (shown as Editor's Choice in Figure 8.10) are created after analyzing what keywords are being used by visitors to the website and analyzing the site overlay report to understand click behavior and whether visitors are clicking on the most relevant links. These best bets provide a way to highlight superior results directly on top rather than relying solely on the mechanisms of your internal search engine.

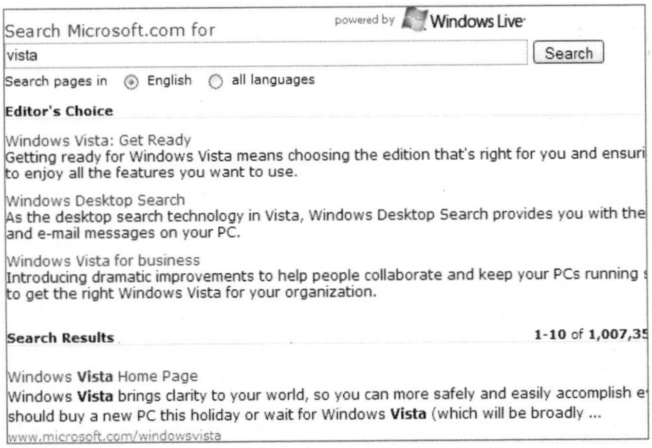

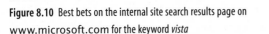

Figure 8.10 Best bets on the internal site search results page on
www.microsoft.com for the keyword *vista*

You can use the site overlay report to analyze the effectiveness of these best bets and to optimize them over time. (Multivariate testing is a great option when it comes to optimizing the layout of the search results page; I will cover this in Chapter 10, "Month 5: Website Experimentation and Testing—Shifting the Power to Customers and Achieving Significant Outcomes.")

Friday: Measure Outcome Metrics for Internal Searches

Because few site visitors will use any other feature to experience your website, it is important to measure outcome metrics for those visitors who use the internal search feature.

You can measure obvious metrics such as conversion rate (if you have an e-commerce website). If your internal search feature is working well, visitors using it will have higher conversion rates. If this is the case, you can use the data to justify more investment into optimal search technology (if you don't have it already).

You should also measure customer satisfaction for the internal site search feature. Are customers happy with it? How would they improve it?

The overall hypothesis is that relevant search results = faster access to relevant data = higher customer satisfaction = higher conversion = more money = higher bonus for you in your annual employee review.

Please realize that simply implementing an expensive search engine tool won't improve your site search. If you have, for example, implemented the spiffy Google Search Appliance (GSA) on your website but your website is suboptimal (because of URL structures, keywords missing from content, missing meta tags and best bets), then all GSA will enable on your website is your customers finding crap much faster than before you implemented the GSA. It is important to do rigorous analysis and fix your website to ensure that your customers are able to find what they want—quickly.

Week 2: Beginning Search Engine Optimization

SEO is hot. The keyword *SEO* returns 110 million results in 0.05 seconds on Google. The key phrase *search engine optimization* does not do that bad either: more than 39 million results in 0.08 seconds.

According to Wikipedia, "Search engine optimization (SEO) as a subset of search engine marketing seeks to improve the number and quality of visitors to a website from "natural' ('organic' or 'algorithmic') search results." Figure 8.11 shows a visual representation of results that fall under the organic or natural results umbrella.

Pay per click (PPC) marketing has garnered most of the search marketing budgets over the last several years because of its perceived ability to "deliver visitors." Hard distribution of spending between PPC and SEO is not readily available, but a quick Google search indicates that the split between budgets is 90 percent PPC and 10 percent SEO. Increasingly though, the realization is dawning upon marketing professionals that while PPC spending can deliver visitors often it comes at great cost and PPC is also suboptimal for building long-term relationships with customers or a sustainable advantage over your competitors. In effect, you are "renting traffic." This, combined with a small upward trend in user wariness with paid campaigns, has put the focus back on SEO.

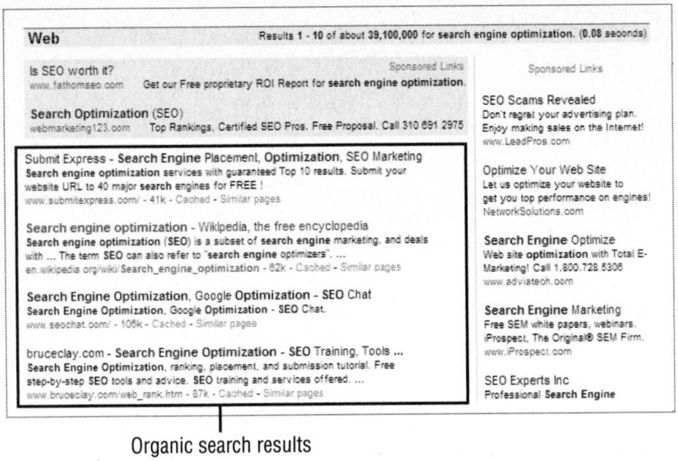

Organic search results

Figure 8.11 Organic search results in Google

It is important to point out that PPC is not going away anytime soon. Although effective SEO strategies will yield long-term results, they also require investments, and it takes longer to yield results. Hence a combination of PPC and SEO will make for an effective search engine marketing (SEM) strategy. Still, there should be little doubt that SEO needs to have a lot more focus and effort in your company (no matter how much of it you have today).

The objective in SEO is to improve the organic listing of a company's website pages for the keywords and key phrases that are most relevant to what the company does (products, services, information, anything). Techniques applied in SEO efforts help improve the page rankings in various search engines. Each search engine has its own unique ranking methodology that is applied to any given website's pages, and when a user searches for a particular keyword or key phrase, the search engine applies that unique algorithm to return the most optimal results.

There is a dearth of any real good off-the-shelf analytics for your SEO efforts. One of the reasons is that most web analytics tools have not yet given any deserved attention to SEO reporting. The other reason is that there is such poor understanding of what SEO is. This lack of understanding means that most marketers and analysts either don't spend enough time analyzing the effectiveness of their SEO efforts, or even if they want to, they don't know where to start.

Because I am very passionate about the amazing value that SEO efforts can bring to any website, I recommend spending one whole week becoming really knowledgeable about what SEO is, and its dos and don'ts. Before you undertake SEO analytics, it is important to understand how search engine optimization works. The goal of week 2 is to help you become that much smarter about what the complex world of

SEO is all about so that you can put together an effective SEO analytics strategy. Perhaps more important, you can have intelligent conversations with the SEO consultants and agencies who promise to optimize your website in 15 hours (!).

As in all emerging fields, there is a lot of FUD (fear, uncertainty, and doubt) around. This section should help elevate your education, and help fight FUD. For an in-depth understanding of SEO, you can use purchase one of the many books available. I recommend *Search Engine Optimization: An Hour a Day*, by Jennifer Grappone and Gradiva Couzin (Sybex, 2006).

The following are some strategies you can use to improve your organic page rankings in the main search engines. Spend each day understanding what each strategy is and documenting how your website is doing for each.

Monday: Understand the Impact of, and Optimize, Links

The cornerstones of any SEO strategy are the links that come from other sites to your site, the links that you have on your site (and where you link to), and how you code the links. The four big buckets in this category are as follows:

Relevant Inbound Links Relevant inbound links are extremely important in computing the ranking of your page by major search engines. You can get free links, you can buy links, or you can exchange links with other websites with relevant content. Remember that it is relevance that is important. For example, if your website trades in exotic pets, a link to your website from Intuit.com might not be quite as valuable.

Authoritative Inbound Links Some links have more power than others, so links from the BBC or major web directories (such as dmoz.org) or .edu domains have greater authority and hence more weight.

Internal Website Links It is optimal to cross-link the pages on your website and to link to relevant content deep within the website. Providing multiple paths into your site improves opportunities for spiders to crawl your website and index all the content because most search spiders will go only three levels deep into a website.

Anchor (Link) Text Links that have relevant text in the anchor (the visible text you see as a clickable link) will be more valuable. For example, if you link to my blog, using *Avinash web analytics blog* as the link text has more influence than *click here*.

Tuesday: Link to Press Releases and Social Sites

Over the course of 2006, both press releases and social networking sites have gained importance as tools to improve your organic search results. Hence it is critical to your SEO efforts that adequate oversight is put on your efforts in these areas:

Press Releases These might wane over time, but for now press releases on your website and on the other core agencies such as Business Wire, PRWeb, and PR Newswire are helpful for your SEO efforts. Optimizing your press releases to link back to your site and correctly using your most important, and relevant, keywords can be a great way to improve the rankings of your relevant pages.

Social Networking Sites These, on the other hand, are increasing their influence and becoming more important for SEO efforts. Links to your website from relevant social sites are highly valuable. Examples include MySpace.com, del.icio.us, and authority blogs (those with greater than 500 unique inbound blog links in the last six months, as reported by Technorati).

Wednesday and Thursday: Optimize Web Page Tags and Content

Search engines are fairly "dumb." They are little machines running around trying to make sense of what your website is all about, and the result of that analysis dictates which keywords trigger your site to show up. You can make this complex effort easier for a search engine robot by providing it with hints as to what you are all about. This is where meta tags, page titles, page content formatting, and the words on the page itself come into play. In the end, the game is all about the search engines understanding your site well enough to deem its content to be relevant when someone searches for keywords and phrases related to your site.

You'll spend these two days understanding the importance of tags and content, and auditing and documenting how your website is doing (are you missing tags, do you have page titles and descriptions, is your content formatted correctly, and so forth). Here are a list of variables that are, or were, important for SEO effectiveness:

Website Meta Tags, Meta Keywords, Description The search engines have gotten smart to the fact that many sites simply stuff their meta tags with keywords and descriptions regardless of relevance to the content on the page. Therefore, these options have lost their weight in the page-ranking algorithms. Sure you should have these on your pages; just don't expect magical results after you are finished putting meta tags on all your pages. You'll have to do more.

HTML Page Title The page title remains very valuable to search engines trying to get an understanding of what the page is about. Page titles carry important weight in helping compute your page relevance. I advise you to use the most relevant page descriptor in the page title. Also, do check that all your pages have page titles.

Text and Image Formatting (Text Types and Alt Tags) In the body of the page itself, we use various text types (H1 headings, HTML tags, bold text, and so forth) that continue to remain important and are ranked higher than normal text on a page. It is important to make judicious use of heading tags and bold text when using your most relevant keywords and content descriptors on your pages.

For images on your website, use alt tags (please!) because they help search engines determine the content of an image, and of course it helps with 504 disability access compliance.

Page Content It goes without saying that the copy on each page is important. Search engines simply grab all the content on a page and then use pattern matching and scoring attributes to apply ratings. They look for what content is on the page and how it is formatted (see the preceding discussion of text and image formatting).

Friday: Provide Guidance for Search Robots

This is another facet of making things easier for a search engine. Rather than it trying to figure out your complex website structure and how it should organize the data, you can be proactive and tell the engine where all your content is and how to crawl your website.

Sitemaps are one of the cheapest strategies to help improve the ability of spiders to crawl and index your websites. Now you can make your life easier by using services such as XML Sitemaps, which will build your sitemap for you and even upload it into a search engine (if the search engine allows it) to assist the spider in indexing your site. Visit http://snipurl.com/xmlmaps for one such service. Oh, and don't forget to add a link to the sitemap page from every web page on your site.

Simple SEO Don'ts

The following are some don'ts when performing SEO:

- Don't try black-hat tactics. Getting banned is unpleasant (and it lasts a long time). Black-hat tactics are deeply frowned upon by the search engines and are *illegal* ways to game the system to your advantage.

- Don't have your most valuable content on secure (HTTPS) pages; spiders don't typically index those. The information about your products and services, for example, should probably not be on HTTPS pages.

- Don't do other obviously wrong things such as keyword stuffing, using hidden texts, or using misleading 302 temporary redirects.

- Make judicious use, only where absolutely necessary, of JavaScript wrappers around links (pop-ups, and so forth) because spiders don't execute JavaScript. There are sites using JavaScript even to link to other pages on the site. This might prove to be a barrier for the search spiders, and they won't be able to index your important content.

All of the preceding strategies take time and effort to accomplish from your end. It will take time to clean up your site and get your IT team to do all they have to do and your marketers to update the content, and so forth. An additional challenge is that it takes several weeks or months for the search engines to then spider your website and those of your partners, and to update their rankings and relevance metrics for your pages, and then for you to show up higher in relevant organic search results listings. As you can imagine, this means that more than anything else, SEO analytics is a game that requires a lot of patience. It takes time for you to detect a signal.

Week 3: Measuring SEO Efforts

Measuring the effectiveness of SEO efforts is part science, part art, and part a "faith-based initiative." There are a number of specific reports and metrics you can track, and those are outlined in this section. But there are also efforts you will put into improving your branding and into ensuring that you improve your brand via search engine opti-mization. These are tough if not impossible to measure, and you will have to categorize these under "faith based initiatives."

It is also important to realize that in some sense you are always in a bit of an uphill struggle with search engines because they are constantly changing their algorithms. Your competition is changing all the time, and your website and those of your partners are also evolving. All this means that it is important to pick your critical few metrics and keep a close tab on them when measuring progress. Use the best practices and reports discussed in this section to audit your consultants and their reporting. But add in a dash of faith as well because there are, and will be, things well beyond your control.

You'll spend week 3 diving deep into metrics and KPIs and reports that you can use to measure results of your SEO efforts.

Monday: Check How Well Your Site Is Indexed

You have two options for this. First, you can do a simple *site:www.domain.com* search in Google to get an understanding of how well your site is indexed (Figure 8.12).

Figure 8.12 Google indexed results for site:www.wiley.com

As you can see in the figure, there are 148,000 pages indexed in Google for www.wiley.com. If you are Wiley, you know how many pages you have, so it is easy to see how well your site is indexed.

Now compute your inclusion ratio:

Inclusion ratio = number of pages indexed / number of pages on your website

Second, you can run a robot report to check how frequently your website is being visited by the search engine robots and how deep they get. Figure 8.13 illustrates how you can quickly understand site indexing by the main search engines (by looking at the number of pages visited) and also how deep into the site spiders are crawling (by looking at the individual page names). This report is generated from your website's web log files; the JavaScript-based data collected by most web analytics tools won't have robot visits data.

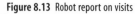

Figure 8.13 Robot report on visits

If you use both approaches, you will be able to measure over time whether your efforts to get all your content indexed and organized are yielding results.

Tuesday: Track Inbound Links and Top Keywords

Because links from other websites carry a huge weight in improving the ranking of your pages, on Tuesday you are going to spend time understanding who is linking to you and whether valuable websites are linking to you. You will also learn how to check your ranking for the top keywords for your business in order to determine your performance today and then to track improvement over time.

Track Inbound Links

You have two options for tracking inbound links:

- Use the *link:www.domain.com* search in Google to track the number of inbound links to your website (Figure 8.14).

- Use an excellent tool at Marketleap.Com (http://snipurl.com/linkpop) to check your link popularity (Figure 8.15).

Figure 8.14 Inbound links to www.wiley.com

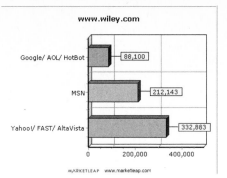

www.wiley.com

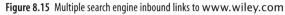

Figure 8.15 Multiple search engine inbound links to www.wiley.com

It is pretty obvious from Figure 8.15 that different search engines exhibit different types of behavior. Therefore, it is important to check your inbound links in other engines beyond Google.

Inbound links have a lot of value in the rankings of your website pages and content. You can use both methods to measure progress over time from your SEO efforts.

Track Your Ranking for Your Top Keywords

By how hopefully you have identified a core set of the top 10 or 20 keywords on which you want to focus the most, at least initially, to keep things manageable. Be a bit wary of fly-by-night SEO consultants who will promise great ranks for three- or four-word key phrases that might not be relevant to your business. Improving your rankings for keywords and phrases more relevant to your business will add long-term value (and obviously have optimal ROI).

You should run a report that shows your ranking for search results for those pages.

Figure 8.16, generated by using Marketleap (http://snipurl.com/linkpop), shows the results across multiple search engines for the keyword *taxes* for www.hrblock.com. It shows great news: they show up on page 1 for this hyperimportant keyword for them.

⊙ LINK POPULARITY CHECK	⊙ SEARCH ENGINE SATURATION	⊙ KEYWORD VERIFICATION

Report Generated on Tuesday, December 26, 2006 at 11:40 AM (MST)   **Report ID # 1837771**

Site to verify: www.hrblock.com
Keyword/Phrase: taxes

Engine	Placed	Page	URL Found
AOL	Yes	1	www.HRBlock.com
Google/ AOL/ HotBot	Yes	1	www.HRBlock.com
Lycos Pro	Yes	1	www.HRBlock.com
MSN	Yes	1	www.hrblock.com
Netscape	Yes	1	www.hrblock.com
Yahoo!/ FAST/ AltaVista	Yes	1	www.hrblock.com

6 Placed within the first 3 pages, out of 6 engines and directories.   0 Not placed within the first 3 pages.

Figure 8.16 Ranking on search engine results pages for top keywords

You can also use other tools to generate the same data. Some web analytics tools now come bundled with the ability to check rankings for your keywords. For example, Figure 8.17 is from my web analytics blog's keyword ranking using ClickTracks.

Keyword Ranking	Google	Yahoo!
avinash	1	3
avinash kaushik	1	1
occam's razor	6	14
90/10 rule	1	3
kaushik	4	1
top 10 key metrics web analytics	1	6
data driven decision making	19	-
razor thought google	2	6
death and taxes poster	7	6
top ranked blogs	7	2
competitive intelligence analyst	8	-
qualitative metrics	2	1
path analysis	13	-
90 10 rule	1	3
statistically significant	11	-

Figure 8.17 Automated keyword ranking report from ClickTracks

At a glance, I can see that the overall ranking for keywords is good, and I can see some nice surprises as well (high ranks for the keywords *90/10 rule*, *top 10 key metrics web analytics*, *competitive intelligence analyst*, *qualitative metrics*, and so forth). Over time you can measure progress. For example, four months ago for the keyword *avinash*, the blog did not even show up in the top 50. Now it is ranked number one. This is a great outcome for SEO efforts.

You can do exactly the same kinds of analysis and measure the impact of your own SEO efforts. There's no need to guess or buy into hypotheticals—you can measure it. By using the strategies discussed here, you can get a micro-level measure of the progress you are making for your most important keywords as well as be explicitly aware of areas of opportunity.

Wednesday: Split Organic Referrals from PPC

Track organic search referrals to your website over time. This one's simple, and you should be able to use your standard web analytics tool to track this. Your PPC campaigns probably come with a specific ID. Just filter that out to get your organic traffic (Figure 8.18).

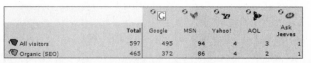

	Total	Google	MSN	Yahoo!	AOL	Ask Jeeves
All visitors	597	495	94	4	3	1
Organic (SEO)	465	372	86	4	2	1

Figure 8.18 Organic traffic tracking across search engines

But you don't have to stop there. You can go a step deeper and track the quality of your organic traffic (Figure 8.19).

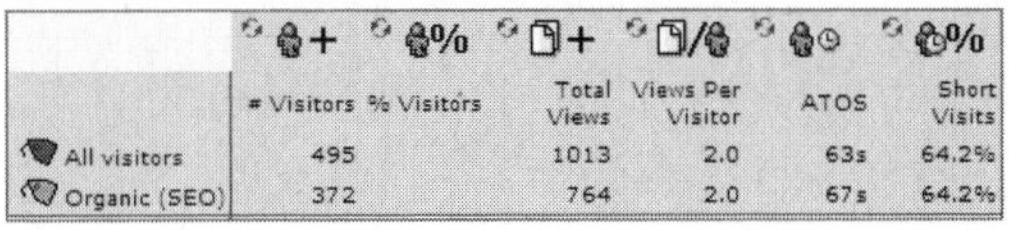

	# Visitors	% Visitors	Total Views	Views Per Visitor	ATOS	Short Visits
All visitors	495		1013	2.0	63s	64.2%
Organic (SEO)	372		764	2.0	67s	64.2%

Figure 8.19 Organic traffic quality (average time on site, page views per visitor, short visits)

You should also be able to run the report in Figure 8.19 for individual keywords (especially your top keywords) and keep track of the trend over time to determine the following:

- Are you getting more organic traffic?
- Is it good quality traffic that is engaging with your website?

You can define what the most important measure of quality is for your company. I suggest average time on site (ATOS) and short visits (bounce rate). ATOS indicates that you are receiving traffic that is engaging with your website, and short visits indicates that it is the right traffic in the first place. (If 64 percent of the people are bouncing, the traffic you are receiving contains lots of perhaps incorrect visitors, but at least the correct portion stays for 67 seconds, which is a bit longer than average (for all visitors) for the site in Figure 8.19.)

Note: It is important to point out that search engines change their behavior all the time, and it is critical to check how your web analytics tool defines *organic traffic* (what parameters or logic it is using). It has been found more than once that a web analytics tool was identifying organic traffic completely incorrectly, but it was not discovered for a few months, causing lost sales. Check the logic that your vendor is using and validate that it makes sense for your favorite search engines (just do a search on Google for your keyword, click through the organic results, and look at the URL and the URL parameters).

NOTE

Different search engines behave differently. It is important to run the preceding reports to create a customized SEO strategy for the couple of search engines that might be most important to you. You might be surprised at which search engines send you quality traffic for your specific business.

Thursday: Measure the Value of Organic Referrals

Track conversion rates and outcome metrics over time. There is perhaps little to be said here because this is so obvious. Yet it needs to be said because most companies are so fascinated with PPC that they usually track those to infinity, but they ignore SEO outcomes tracking.

For your website, track key metrics just for organic traffic. Make it a best practice to show results next to that of PPC campaigns. This will help you understand the value of the organic traffic. If you are computing cost per acquisition (CPA), you'll have an interesting contract with PPC (costs for each click, remember) and SEO (which is free—okay, so it is not free; put in an estimate for your SEO efforts).

Measuring conversion rate helps you show the bottom-line impact of your SEO investments. It is much easier, and prevalent, to show conversion and revenue for PPC but just as important to show that for SEO. Don't forget to show the long-term impact of SEO.

Friday: Measure Optimization for Top Pages

In SEO, we are optimizing pages, content on pages, and inbound links to improve the ranking of our pages for top keywords and in turn to get more relevant visitors. Hence it is important to measure page-level metrics. Two important ones are the keywords that are driving organic traffic to your top pages, and the bounce rate for organic traffic to those pages.

For your top 20 pages (or for your most important pages), tracking the keywords that are driving organic traffic to those pages and tracking whether those are the right keywords will help you measure the results of your efforts in updating meta tags, page titles, and content and in getting pages indexed and more.

Figure 8.20 shows the number of visitors who came to this page, the home page, by using various keywords. This clearly illustrates that some of the keywords that should drive traffic to this home page (such as *web analytics* or *web analytics blog*) are not, even though website meta tags and the page HTML tags and content have been optimized for those key phrases. Clearly it is time to try other things.

Top Search Keywords
☐ Robot Simulation Mode

All visitors

avinash	69
avinash kaushik	55
occam's razor	51
kaushik	15
occams razor	7
More rows	

Organic

avinash kaushik	55
avinash kaushik's	2
"avinash kaushik"	2
avinash kaushik's blog.	1
occam's razor avinash kaushik's	1
More rows	

Figure 8.20 Top organic keywords driving traffic to the home page

Measuring the bounce rate for organic traffic to those same top pages can be a leading indicator that although you are getting traffic, it is not the right traffic. Bounce rate can also indicate that your page content or design is not effectively communicating the connection between the keyword and your page to visitors arriving from search engines (or worse, you are optimized for the wrong key phrases). Figure 8.21 shows the page exit rates for all visitors to a website and for the segment of visitors who come as a result of clicking on an organic search results link.

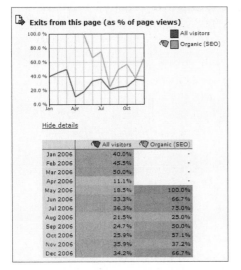

Figure 8.21 Page Exit Rate for All Visitors and Organic
Search Results Traffic

The trends in Figure 8.21 are interesting, as always. Initially, the home page of this important website was not indexed at all, and it received no traffic from search engines. Then it started getting traffic, but the wrong kind (as you can see by the 100 percent exit rate for organic traffic in May 2006). Then it got better over time, but the exit rate recently started to climb again. There is so much meat here to bite into and take action on (especially combined with the preceding recommendation about determining which keywords drive traffic to each page and contribute to the high exit rate).

Note: SEO is not just a story of the site. It is mostly the story of a collection of individual pages. To ensure that your story is being presented correctly by the search engines, it's critical to perform page-level SEO analytics for your highest trafficked and most important website pages (they might not be the most trafficked).

NOTE

Perhaps it is obvious from this section that I love SEO, and I don't use the word lightly in the book. SEO is the right long-term thing to do for any business. With a small amount of sustained investment, the benefits far outstrip any other website acquisition strategy that you might execute. It is not just about trying to get a higher Google page rank, which is a suboptimal measure of overall SEO effectiveness (even if your SEO consultant says differently). SEO is a result of doing many small and some big things right that will pay off huge for you over time.

Week 4: Analyzing Pay per Click Effectiveness

If SEO is hot, PPC is hotter still. When marketers get together at parties, it is embarrassing for one to admit that he does not have a PPC campaign running that very moment, and God forbid if he doesn't do PPC at all. Oh the shame of it! Although this observation is in jest, it is true that there is a lot of hype around PPC. Marketers just jump in, because it is so easy to do either by themselves or by sending money to an agency. It is also easy to show results because if you bid enough on your keywords, someone will click on the link and show up on the site.

Note: Sometimes PPC is wrongly referred to as SEM, or search engine marketing, which really is the combination of SEO and PPC.

But the days of measuring click-through rates (CTRs) as success metrics are slowly reaching their end. With all the hype and publicity, there is also increased accountability on marketers to measure success in a much more nuanced manner and tie it directly to the bottom line.

Let's take a step back and understand what pay per click marketing is. Figure 8.22 shows the PPC results as they appear on most search results pages. The PPC results appear on the top and to the right of the organic search results in almost all the search engines. The position of each PPC ad is determined by the amount that each advertiser bids in a dynamic marketplace (for example, AdWords, Yahoo! Search Marketing, or Microsoft adCenter).

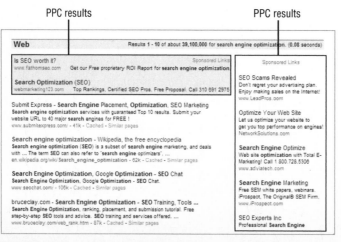

Figure 8.22 PPC (pay per click) search results in Google

Monday: Understand PPC Basics

A lot has been written about PPC analytics, and so this section focuses on just the key essentials. Later in the book I will cover advanced concepts about optimizing your PPC campaigns.

One of the biggest challenges of measuring end-to-end success for PPC campaigns is that for the most part, your keyword generation, keyword optimization, and keyword bidding strategy (and hence data) is outside "the system," at least the system that you have access to: your web analytics tool.

There are a number of tools now in the market that have built-in data access to the search engine APIs that allow them to automatically download at least some core data from the search engines. These include campaign attributes, impressions, clicks, and cost per click at a minimum.

For most interesting types of analysis, you will have to take extra steps to integrate PPC data into your web analytics tools. This starts with your ability to identify PPC campaigns (either by using a URL parameter or, if your tool allows, via the direct search engine API access and downloading your PPC data).

It is important to know that you will have to take proactive steps and work with the folks running your campaigns (sometimes internal company employees, but more often external agencies) to bring your PPC data into your web analytics tools. For example, you don't want to be stuck in a relationship with an agency that will not give you access to the logins and passwords to your AdWords account, which will allow you to download your data into your web analytics tools. I realize it sounds hard to believe that your own PPC or SEM agency would not let you access your own data, but it happens more than you might like to think.

For all your PPC campaigns, you should expect to report on the metrics that you'll work with Tuesday through Friday. Each of these metrics are available in a slightly unique way from each search engine program (Google, Yahoo!, MSN) and it is well worth the effort to investigate how you can get this data and then to standardize the measurement in your own reports.

Tuesday: Measure Search Engine Bid-Related Metrics

The very first day's work will focus on measuring the core metrics related to your keywords bidding. Data for these metrics will typically be at your search engines and either you or, if you are using one, your agency will have access to this data. Your task will be to standardize the definitions for these metrics in your company (and your agency) and work to create the reports that incorporate these metrics for your pay per click campaigns.

Start at the highest level, for your overall campaigns program, and then drill down to keyword groups and then down to each keyword level to optimally analyze the performance of your program and make changes to your bidding models as necessary.

Here are the most important search engine bid related metrics and their standard definitions:

Page inventory: The number of available page slots for ads

Impressions: The number of times the ad has been shown to a search engine visitor

Average position: The average rank at which the PPC ad was shown (usually a number between 1 and 8)

CPM: Cost per thousand (1,000 impressions)

Clicks: Total clicks (they are not unique and don't equal visits)

CTR: Click-through rate (clicks / impressions)

CPC: Cost per click

Campaign Cost: CPC × clicks

Wednesday: Define Critical Bottom-Line-Impacting Metrics

Wednesday's activities will focus on measuring the key performance indicators that highlight the impact on the bottom line of the company. It is surprising that the success of most pay per click campaigns is still judged by the amount of traffic that they drive to the website. You have learned that that is just a part of the story, because it could all be the wrong type of traffic.

Increasingly, companies and agencies are putting more and more emphasis on measuring ROI and hard-dollar returns for their investment. The metrics that you will define and measure today will help your company obtain a much richer insight into different facets of outcomes so that you can in turn optimize your keywords and bids for those keywords to gain the maximum benefit. These metrics are as follows:

Outcomes (acquisition): Total outcomes for each campaign or effort. Outcomes can be orders, leads, page views, or anything defined as a goal for the campaign.

Conversion Rate: Outcomes / clicks (notice the difference between this and the definition in your web analytics tools, where the denominator is either visits or unique visitors).

Revenue (Sales): Total revenue from the campaign. Raw dollars.

CPO: Cost per order (outcome) = campaign cost / total outcomes

CPA: Cost per acquisition = campaign cost / total outcomes

AOV: Average order value = revenue / outcomes

ASP: Average selling price (usually for individual products or services, accounts for any discounts given).

ROAS: Return on advertising spending = revenue / campaign costs

Thursday: Measure Unique Visitors

You get bonus points for measuring not just click-throughs and visits, but also unique visitors. If you are integrating your web analytics data with your PPC data in your web analytics tool, you can also measure the following delightful metrics (your agency's JavaScript tags won't report this data, but they will be able to report the metrics identified on Tuesday and Wednesday):

Unique visitors: Number of unique visitors generated by each campaign

Cost per unique visitor: Campaign cost / number of unique visitors

Most PPC analytics is fairly "desensitized" because it measures only clicks and visits. The reason unique visitors and cost per unique visitor are important is that they help us measure people, as close as we can, by using the Unique Visitor metric from our web analytics tool. This also helps us understand our customers' repeat visit behavior and what could be motivating that, which leads to possible insights that feed into further site experience optimization.

Can't-Live-without-'Em PPC Metrics

The world of PPC analytics can be difficult to optimize based on so many variables (and remember, you don't even have access to all the variables that go into optimizing keyword bidding!). You should be aware of and internalize all of them, but if push comes to shove, at a minimum insist on measuring the following:

- Impressions
- Click-through rate
- Conversion rate
- Cost per acquisition
- Return on advertising spending

These critical few were tough for me to choose but should give you the most rounded picture of your PPC campaigns.

Friday: Learn PPC Reporting Best Practices

Pay per click campaigns seem deceptively simple to do and even easier to measure success for. This is very far from the truth. Here are some best practices (learned from painful real-life experiences) that should help you avoid some of the problems and help you move to positive ROI faster by driving the right actions:

- Measure at an aggregated level, but only to compare to all other campaign strategies. At the most aggregated level, data is not very helpful or actionable.

- Results for each search engine will be quite different for a number of reasons. Any segmentation strategies you have should start at a search engine level and then go down from there, like this:

  Campaigns > Categories > Offers > Creatives

  becomes

  Search engine > Campaigns > Categories > Offers > Creatives

  Google seems to be the sole focus for most pay per click campaigns. As you report your data, look for meaningful trends and patterns in the "smaller" search engines, which can present great monetization or arbitrage opportunities.

- Over time, develop a deep understanding of what pages and campaigns work to drive which kinds of outcomes.

- If you have a massive number of campaigns, often it can be hard to separate signals from all the noise, especially at a conversion rate level. Consider having a column in your reports that automatically computes statistical significance. Shoot for greater than 95 percent confidence in the significance and you'll be able to much more easily pick up the signals that you should use to drive actions.

- If you are outsourcing your campaigns, ask your agency to present analysis and not data. In that scenario, clearly these experts are better qualified to provide you with analysis. If your current contract does not state it explicitly, it is a great idea to ask the agency to provide analysis including a performance summary, trends, areas for improvement, and recommended actions.

Trust me—it is a lot of fun to do PPC campaign analysis. If you are a numbers geek, PPC can give you such a high from so many variables and so much math, and you can find actionable insights and truly add to your company bottom-line results (be they revenue related or cost savings related).

Month 4: Measuring Email and Multichannel Marketing

Companies expend a large amount of effort in acquiring customers both online and offline. As a percentage of total marketing budgets, spending for online marketing is dwarfed by the spending for offline campaigns for most Fortune 500 companies. The balance is slowly shifting in the favor of online marketing (even if it has a long way to go). One catalyst in this shift is the options for measuring online campaigns' ROI; offline campaign ROI measurement is largely still a faith-based initiative.

This chapter covers the staple of all companies: how to do robust email analytics, and the biggest wish-list item of all marketers, how to measure the effects of their marketing spending from a multichannel perspective. Each provides its own set of challenges and opportunities, and effective analytics for either can be a game-changing proposition for any company.

Week 1: Email Marketing Fundamentals and a Bit More

Emails are both a thorn in our sides (@%$*!*^# spam!) and a blessing in terms of having changed our lives when it comes to communications (though some of us still miss writing letters and sending them via snail mail). Today almost everyone you know probably has an email address and they probably use it as a, if not the, primary medium of communication. What this has meant to marketers over the last 10 to 15 years is that email has also become a linchpin of their marketing campaign's portfolio. In fact, if you are a typical person in the United States, you likely receive 15 marketing emails (aka "spam") for every valid email that you receive.

Email marketing in current times resembles a cat-and-mouse game: legitimate marketers are trying to become increasingly sophisticated at finding the right customers to send email to, and at the same time software advances and email spammers are locked in a tussle to see who wins. Increasingly powerful junk filters, which have a high false-positive rate, are on the rise; they are on email servers, in Yahoo! Mail and Microsoft Outlook, and on Exchange servers. Still, for most companies email continues to be an effective way of communicating with prospective and current customers.

Monday: Understand Email Marketing Fundamentals

Numerous studies from sources such as Forrester Research, Gartner, eMarketer, and the Direct Marketing Association (well you would expect it from them!) consistently publish metrics indicating that email remains one of the most effective channels when it comes to marketing and ROI. Even with low email open and response rates, the even lower cost of contact helps in making this channel so effective.

Email communications are used by businesses for several purposes:

- Acquisition (finding new customers)
- Increased sell-through (mining existing customers for repeat sales)
- Retention (keeping the customers you have via special programs, email value-added messages, and special offers)
- Standard communications (order status, for example)

Before you start your analytics, it is important to understand, at least at a high level, that there are several important steps to the process of executing email campaigns:

1. Define business objectives and how email fits into them.
2. Identify core criteria for email campaigns (what, why, how, when, and so forth).
3. Create and execute campaigns (mine your email list, scrub it for do-not-contacts, create the right text or other type of offering, and send it to your email vendor).
4. Analyze your campaigns.

Email analytics can focus on both ends of this process: defining objectives and criteria as well as campaign analysis.

For the first part, there are advanced and sophisticated data mining techniques that are available, and applied, to the customer data that your company has in order to find the right customer to communicate with at the right time. The principle of garbage in, garbage out also applies here. If the results of your mining efforts are suboptimal, then even the right creative or the best offer for your customer will provide the outcome your company is looking for. There are sophisticated tools and techniques that are dedicated to improving your hit rate, for the right customer at the right time.

For the second part, there are analytics that are applied after the emails are fired off. Email is an extremely cost-effective medium, and the power of optimal analytics enables you to improve the effectiveness of your company's campaigns, and in turn, ROI. Perhaps more important, you can improve the experience of your company's customers, who may be sick of you sending a new offer on a washing machine, for example, when they bought one from you a week ago.

Tuesday and Wednesday: Measure Basic Response Metrics

Response metrics cover the initial part of the customer experience—from when the email is sent to when the customer might come to the website. These metrics will hopefully lead to a win-win outcome for the customer and the marketing company.

For optimal analysis of your email campaigns, you'll be reporting these important pieces of data:

Emails sent: The number of emails that were sent.

Emails bounced: The number of emails that were simply bounced back (because of a bad email address, network problems, or other issues).

Emails opened: The number of emails that were opened by recipients.

Unsubscribe: The number of email addresses that were unsubscribed by recipients.

Clicks: The number of clicks that were generated after emails were opened. Think of these as being roughly equivalent to the web analytics Visits metric.

By using the preceding data, you can create a nice little funnel that helps you visualize response effectiveness. Usually, you will also compute the following KPIs:

Delivery rates: (Number of emails sent – number of emails bounced) / number of emails sent

Unsubscribe rate: Number of unsubscribe requests / number of emails delivered

Open rate: Number of emails opened / number of emails delivered

Response rate (click-to-open rate—CTOR): Number of clicks / number of emails opened

Measuring the response rate (CTOR) helps you determine list quality and also the effectiveness of your offer or message.

One interesting thing to get used to when performing email analytics is that the numbers tend to be really small. This is because you'll send a hundred thousand emails, but probably only ten thousand might get opened. Then you'll segment those numbers further, and it can make the percentages look really small.

It also goes without saying that you are not measuring the preceding metrics at the most aggregated level. To find real insights, you'll report the data and do subsequent analysis by customer segments: offers you send out, timing of the emails, geographic locations, years of relationships with your company, the last visit to your website, and on and on and on. Real actionable insights will come from these segmentation efforts and rarely from the aggregated data.

Thursday and Friday: Measure Outcome Metrics

You'll finish the week by focusing on measuring the effectiveness of your email campaigns in delivering for your company's bottom line. (At the end of the day, it doesn't matter how many visitors you drove to the site. What matters is how many of those visits lead to outcomes, revenue or otherwise, for your company.) For each campaign, you will report on standardized metrics that you are already used to in your traditional web analytics world. The data that is used for this analysis is fairly standard:

Outcomes (orders or leads): Number of outcomes generated by the campaign

Revenue metrics: Money, quantity, products, and so forth

The KPIs you'll measure for outcomes are as follows:

Email conversion rates: Outcomes / number of emails delivered

Revenue & Average order size: For each campaign

Revenue per email delivered: Total order value / number of emails delivered

It is important to consider more than just the conversion rate because each segment of customers that you are targeting will have only a finite ability to be mined and drive conversions. Metrics such as revenue per email delivered also can help identify non-campaign-related attributes that might be causing your conversion rates to be lower than you would want them to be.

One best-practice tip when it comes to measuring outcomes is to create goals up front for your campaigns. This seems rather obvious, but it is rarely done in most businesses. Asking for a goal is a great way to insert some discipline into the process, and of course it is a great way to measure success and identify gaps in outcomes. Even if your conversion rate is 3 percent (pretty good for certain types of email campaigns), knowing that your goal was 4 percent provides a different yardstick for declaring success.

Week 2: Email Marketing—Advanced Tracking

During week 2, you'll learn how to step beyond performing the standard activities effectively and deal with some of the advanced tracking. You will also learn how to avoid some of the common pitfalls that can stymie your progress. You will close out week 2 with the critical task of integrating standard email analytics with your standard web analytics tool. This combination can help you reap rich rewards by providing a holistic view of your email campaigns in the context of other campaigns as well as providing a raft of metrics from your web analytics tool to meet your unique needs.

Monday and Tuesday: Measure Website Effectiveness

It takes so much to get people to your website that I recommend that you use your web analytics tool to measure your website's effectiveness at delivering increased response rates (in conjunction with email offers of course). I have set aside two days for this task because it seems obvious and simple, but it is not. There are complexities involved in measuring the recommended metrics that require careful thought along with a review of your website and analytics environment.

The metrics you should measure are as follows:

Website conversion rate: Outcomes / number of campaign unique visitors

Campaign site bounce rate: Number of campaign visitors who left in fewer than 10 seconds / number of campaign visitors

Visits to purchase: Number of visits by a unique email campaign respondent to purchase

Additionally, you should measure location effectiveness. You can also use your friendly web analytics tool to measure effectiveness of campaign landing pages. For example, does it matter whether you direct traffic to custom email landing pages instead of just sending visitors to the normal website home page and product pages?

As is obvious in Table 9.1, different campaigns perform differently when visitors go to either a landing page or a home page or you are doing split testing (the first couple in the table, ID 1 & ID 2, for example). You can use standard web analytics to measure effectiveness of these strategies.

▶ **Table 9.1** Landing page effectiveness for email campaigns

Email Campaign ID	Conversion Rates		Notes
	Home/Product Pages	**Custom Landing Pages**	
Campaign 1	35.0%	28.2%	Test, one way
Campaign 2	22.6%	4.9%	Test, the other way
Campaign 3		4.2%	Hmmm
Campaign 4	1.9%		Nice
Campaign 5	1.7%	2.4%	Interesting
Campaign 6	30.2%		What!!!

The awesome part is that based on your analysis, you'll identify campaigns that don't need custom landing pages or offers, which can mean that marketers can set up their campaigns quickly and efficiently and save your company money to boot.

The goal in measuring these metrics is to simply measure how effective your website is at converting visitors after they land from email campaigns.

Wednesday: Avoid Email Analytics Pitfalls

There are some common pitfalls that can easily be avoided when dealing with data from your email campaigns. For some reason, not enough analysts are aware of these important pitfalls, and as a result the analysis presented could be quite suboptimal. As you do your analysis, please take time to understand the effects that each of these three items has on your email campaigns:

- Increasingly, all the bounced emails are not reported accurately. Email might be blocked from being delivered to your intended recipient but not bounce back. Email can be held in spam queues and just sit there or be deleted directly there. This can negatively influence your delivery rates and other basic metrics.

- Open rates can be measured, usually, for HTML emails by embedding web beacons in the email. If the email client does not support HTML, you won't know whether the email was opened. The Preview function in Outlook also does not download images and therefore does not send the web beacon response. Both of these issues mean that your open rate could be greatly different from what you are reporting.

- Treat data about unsubscribe requests with a great deal of attention. There are stringent laws and penalties for contacting someone who has unsubscribed to your email communications. But additional analysis of the reasons behind unsubscribing can help your marketers evaluate the messaging and offers if certain types of offers lead to a large number of unsubscribes.

Along with presenting your analysis to your stakeholders, take time to educate them about the preceding points and how they might affect your metrics. Then they can appropriately adjust their confidence in the metrics and adapt their decisions. For example, you can observe trends of your metrics over time and research any benchmark numbers for how many people use non-HTML email clients and then adjust your Open Rate numbers accordingly so as not to drastically underestimate the metric for your company. And remember, as always, that if you track trends in the metrics over time, the effect of some of these pitfalls is lessened.

Thursday and Friday: Integrate Your Email Campaign with Your Web Analytics Tools

One of the biggest challenges in terms of doing email analytics is that data for email campaigns is still in an external silo, usually with your email service provider, and not in your web analytics tool. While at the moment web analytics tools simply can't give the kind of insights that email service provider tools can, you should still make some effort to integrate your email campaigns and your web analytics tools.

This will help you become more knowledgeable and gain a great strategic advantage. The main reason for this is that most companies that do email campaigns measure only basic response metrics and outcome metrics, but not website effectiveness. You can easily imagine how your website could be the sole cause of reduced conversion rates and revenue if it is not delivering the experience that the customer was promised in the email (content, promotions, products, and so forth).

Ensuring that your web analytics tools are integrated with your email marketing campaigns (via some simple URL parameters, say ecampaign_ids) will help you measure website effectiveness and fill a large gap that exists today in the data that both marketers and email services providers have.

I recommend spending two days on this task because you will have to partner with your IT team, your web analytics team, your email service provider, and your business stakeholders to ensure that the right integration elements are built into the right systems and processes. You will also have to integrate the numbers that you'll get from your email service provider systems and your own system. It is okay for them to be different (they are captured quite differently), but spending time understanding the gap will ensure that you are able to present the rationale to your business stakeholders. Finally, you will have to spend time educating your stakeholders on the advanced analytics possibilities from this integration because most will be used to only the basic metrics. Often you'll discover that the challenge of doing analysis is much smaller than changing minds and exposing them to new and advanced possibilities. That's okay—it's a good fight, so stick with it.

Weeks 3 and 4: Multichannel Marketing, Tracking, and Analysis

Multichannel analytics is more than a buzzword, at its simplest it is the art and science of measuring the impact of marketing efforts on multiple sales / customer contact channels. It is of vital importance, and increasingly so with every passing day. However, anyone who says that they have a handle on multichannel analytics is probably not stating the complete truth. Multichannel analytics remains a challenge and an enigma. Any success that people have had measuring it is either a one-shot deal and not repeatable or it is not scalable. It will take some time for the dust to settle.

Often people make it seem that if only you would part with a bunch of your money, you could have a perfect and quick answer to your multichannel efforts. Reality is different because of the multitude of customer touch points (which are often unreachable or unmeasurable), and the deeply limited and isolated existence of tools and data.

So you've paid for this book and all you get in return is a bucket of cold water. My apologies for that, but it is rather important that we cut the rosiness out of this picture. Only then can we settle down and do the best we can to measure what little we can in terms of the influence of offline channels on the online channel and vice versa.

Week 3: Understanding Multichannel Marketing, and Tracking Offline-to-Online Campaigns

There is no denying that being able to measure multichannel impacts of marketing efforts is the holy grail of analytics—not only because it is so hard to do, but also because increasingly people behave in a multichannel world and if you can effectively and efficiently analyze your efforts, you have a sustainable competitive advantage.

During week 3, you will spend time understanding the amazing evolution that has been happening around us in terms of customer behavior. The lines between customers' offline and online behavior are blurring, forcing companies to provide *nonline marketing*. It is critical to understand this shift because it will form the foundation of your analytical measurement plan. In the second part of the week, you will dip your toes into multichannel marketing and start with tracking the influence of offline campaigns on online experiences.

Monday and Tuesday: Ponder Offline, Online, and Nonline Marketing

It used to be simple. You had stores. Marketers did marketing. You went to stores and bought something. Then came catalogs: you could simply pick up the phone and order, and the white elephant you wanted was delivered to your door. Then came the early Web. The experience was not drastically different, except that you did not have to hold on the phone for an hour and you could shop anytime you wanted. You still got your white elephant, but perhaps you found it faster and were able to purchase it a bit cheaper. We now live in a world where technology and communication options have drastically improved. It is no longer possible to know what types of marketing are driving particular kinds of customer behavior and, more important, where. Let's step back and understand the multichannel world.

Figure 9.1 is a simple representation of customer behavior on two different channels. The physical acts are different, but it is essentially the same process of moving from research to selection to qualification to purchase. We have always spent our marketing dollars thinking that Figure 9.1 is exactly how customers behave. With increasing frequency, the reality is different.

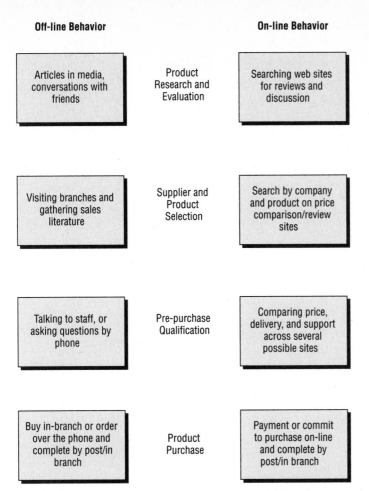

Off-line Behavior		On-line Behavior
Articles in media, conversations with friends	Product Research and Evaluation	Searching web sites for reviews and discussion
Visiting branches and gathering sales literature	Supplier and Product Selection	Search by company and product on price comparison/review sites
Talking to staff, or asking questions by phone	Pre-purchase Qualification	Comparing price, delivery, and support across several possible sites
Buy in-branch or order over the phone and complete by post/in branch	Product Purchase	Payment or commit to purchase on-line and complete by post/in branch

Figure 9.1 Online and offline customer behavior. (Diagram copyright David Huges, www.nonlinemarketing.com)

What your customers are actually doing is moving at their own pace and preference between stages of the purchase process and, critically, between channels. Notice the three hypothetical scenarios shown in Figure 9.2. The first customer researches online, checks out the selection offline, qualifies what product to buy offline, but ends up buying on the website. The second customer starts offline researching in magazines or with friends, does research in stores and continues research online to compare products, goes back to the store to make a final decision, and buys on the website. The final customer does research and compares products and prices online but buys by calling the company phone channel.

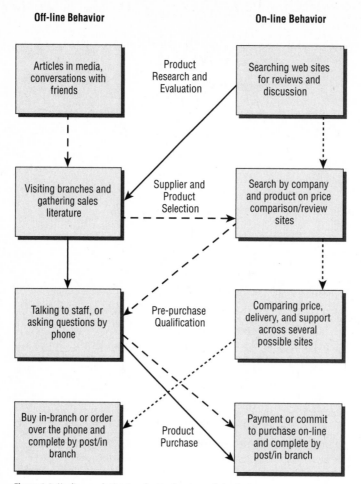

It's Non-Line Marketing...

Off-line Behavior   **On-line Behavior**

Articles in media, conversations with friends

Product Research and Evaluation

Searching web sites for reviews and discussion

Visiting branches and gathering sales literature

Supplier and Product Selection

Search by company and product on price comparison/review sites

Talking to staff, or asking questions by phone

Pre-purchase Qualification

Comparing price, delivery, and support across several possible sites

Buy in-branch or order over the phone and complete by post/in branch

Product Purchase

Payment or commit to purchase on-line and complete by post/in branch

Figure 9.2 Nonline marketing to reflect real customer behavior.

David Hughes of Non-Line Marketing in the United Kingdom (www .nonlinemarketing.com) calls this the *nonline world phenomenon*. His advice is that we in marketing should also evolve from being just online or just offline and become nonline. The challenge then is how to measure nonline (multichannel) customer behavior. In a nutshell, if I might simplify a bit, it is a challenge of data collection.

As your customers flirt with different channels while they go about their research and shopping, how do you collect the basic data to know enough about what is going on at each touch point in order to stitch together a cohesive story about campaign performance? Usually, after you have the data from different touch points, you have the ability to run your standard metrics and KPIs as you normally do, with the only change being that your multiple channels become just different slices of segmentation in your data analysis.

The problem with multichannel analytics is not reporting. The problem is obtaining data to analyze.

For the rest of the week, you'll learn about three primary customer "movement" opportunities and how you can collect data optimally in each case.

Wednesday through Friday: Track Offline-to-Online Behavior and Campaigns

You'll spend the rest of the week on the tracking possibilities for customers starting on the offline channel and moving to the online. You'll learn what you need to do, specifically, to capture data that will allow you to effectively track customer behavior and the success of marketing programs.

Here are the most common offline-to-online movement channels and how to collect data for end-to-end analysis of each:

Newspapers, Magazines, Television The most common method for tracking customers in this case is to use vanity URLs and redeemable coupons:

Redirects (Vanity URLs) These are in newspaper or magazine ads—for example, www.buyquickbooks.com. They also appear at the end of television ads—for example, "Go to www.dell.com/tv for this deal." Both of these redirects have specific tracking codes tied to the original ad that are captured when customers are redirected from dell.com/tv to http://www.dell.com/content/topics/segtopic .aspx/tv?c=us&cs=19&l=en&s=dhs&keycode=6Vc94&DGVCode=TV. Notice the URL parameters. This makes it really easy to track conversion rate or ad response rate.

Redeemable Coupons You can include special coupon codes or special configuration codes in your offline ads that customers can type in when they get to your site, allowing you to track your success metrics.

Figure 9.3 shows how Dell has implemented this tracking. You can take an E-value code that is printed on your personal catalog or in the newspaper or magazine ad and type it into a box on their website. You get the advertised deal, and Dell can collect the offline-to-online data.

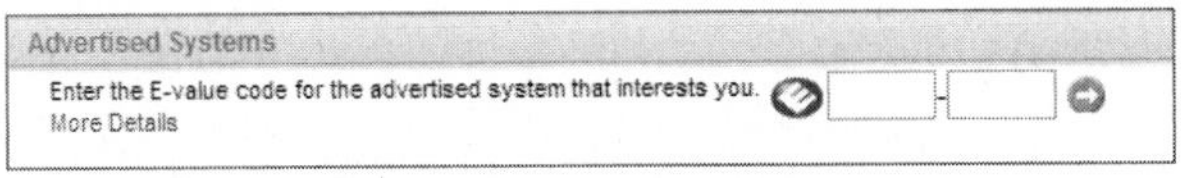

Figure 9.3 Nonline marketing to reflect real customer behavior

Direct Marketing (DM) Campaigns Most DM campaigns that are sent out as letters have been focused on driving customers to the company phone channel or to retail stores. Increasingly, companies are giving customers the option to use either the phone channel or the web channel. For the web portion of the traffic, you can use the following:

Redirects Unique redirects tied to an individual campaign or group of campaigns can make it easy for the customer to get to the website—for example, www.buyquickbooks.com/65 (in the back end, this redirect is coded to pass a unique parameter).

Shared Tracking Codes Because the customer has the opportunity to go to the phone or the web channel, using the same tracking codes for both is usually an awesome strategy—for example, www.buyquickbooks.com/65 and the unique 800 number 800-944-3165 (which translates into offer 65). The reason to do this is that when you pull the data from your phone and web channels, you will have really good insights into how the same campaigns perform in terms of driving people to the website or the phone channel and which works better at converting them.

Company Call Centers (Phone Channel) This is happening with increasing frequency. You call a company and they give you information and try to sell to you, but if it does not work, they still direct you to the site, for a trial or in case you want to convert later. If this pertains to you, here is what you can do:

Email Links If you email customers links to the site after the call or send them a trial link, embed a tracking code in the link.

Redirect If the customer does not give you an email address, give them a vanity URL (redirect) they can remember such as www.buyquickbooks.com/$100off or www.20offquickbooks.com or www.buyquickbooks.com/call. Adding a small discount will ensure that the customer does not forget the vanity URL.

Retail Stores Maybe your company is like OfficeMax or Best Buy or Petco and you want to measure the effect of your offline stores on your online websites. Here are some options:

Online Redeemable Coupons Offer coupons in stores that customers can redeem online. (I am sure you are seeing a trend in this chapter about willingness to give money in exchange for data. Not everyone's cup of tea, but often it is a cheap price to pay for the insights you'll get.)

Online Website Surveys We will cover this in week 4; you could survey customers on your websites and inquire about their offline shopping experience.

Primary Market Research This is an excellent option for big companies. Simply partner with a market research agency and conduct primary market research about the shopping and buying habits of your customers. You will get real-world insights from your customers about the relative value and merits of your online and offline channels.

Week 4: Tracking and Analyzing Multichannel Marketing

Having covered the effects of your offline marketing campaigns on your online marketing campaigns, in the last week of the month you will kick into high gear by understanding what it takes to measure the influence of online campaigns on offline outcomes. This is one of the most underappreciated elements of online campaigns by marketers. You will close the week with some innovative suggestions on leveraging the online channel to measure the effects of your multichannel campaigns on your multichannel outcomes.

Monday and Tuesday: Track Online to Offline Behavior and Campaigns

You'll spend the first two days of this week addressing customers who start at the online channel and move offline to conclude their transactions.

As you can imagine, this is much harder to do or to control in terms of outcomes, because the choice to make the leap from online to offline is largely with the customer and not the company. This is more the case here than in the offline-to-online marketing, where you can still influence the customer.

Here are the most common online-to-offline movement channels and how to collect data for end-to-end analysis of each:

Online to Retail Stores There are products and services that simply can't be purchased online or are better purchased offline. In this case, you have several tracking options:

Printable Coupons Many web businesses allow their customers to print unique one-time-use coupons (one time to avoid abuse) that can be redeemed at the store. Because the coupon is unique, it is easy to track. You can track not only its redemption, but also how many were printed and by whom, how many were from Google search traffic, what keyword was used to find it, for which location, and more. An online printed coupon comes with a whole host of tracking built in because of the beauty of the Web.

Primary Market Research If you have a large business, primary market research is a great option for understanding the multichannel impact.

Postpurchase Online Surveys You may have noticed that when you buy anything from Circuit City stores, your receipt includes an invitation to fill out an online survey (and a chance to enter a $50 sweepstakes prize). These surveys are a great way to understand the motivation behind the decision to buy in the store and the effects of the online presence on that offline purchase.

Store Locator Tracking Perhaps you offer your online visitors the option to search for a local store and to check whether the product is in stock at a local store for pickup. You can use this to get a decent idea of the impact on the retail stores. With companies such as Channel Intelligence, you also have the option of integrating the store data for multiple retail stores into your website. As visitors search through and locate your partner stores, those clicks can be tracked and reported. This is not perfect data, but you have some idea of the number of people coming to your site looking to buy at a retail store, the visitors' ZIP codes, and which retail stores they prefer to buy from.

Online to Phone Channel This is also a common strategy for businesses that want to give their customers choices as to where to buy or sell expensive products that need heavy pre-sales. Your two choices:

Unique 800 (toll free) Phone Numbers This is the best trick in the book, and cheap. Simply use an 800 number on your website that is unique to the site. This is not perfect, but a great way to track calls, conversions, and revenue. Of course, this works just as well for tracking the calls from your website to your support call center. This option is becoming quite sophisticated. For a small price, you can integrate third-party options that will provide a unique 800 phone number on every pay per click landing page. They can even provide a unique phone number for your top keywords and allow you to have amazing sophistication in tracking the offline impact of your online search engine marketing (SEM) campaigns. Imagine the ROI that those campaigns will show if you do this—very nice.

Unique Promotion Codes This option is really simple: give your customers web-exclusive promotion codes that they can redeem when they call your company's phone channel. Here's a spiffy tip: rather than giving the promotion code, just randomly you can have your website visitors fill out a profile (or lead form) with qualifying questions—and then if they qualify, give them a promotion code. Now the spiffy part is that you can dump this lead into your CRM system and surprise the customer by knowing something about them already.

Wednesday: Track Online-to-Online Behavior and Campaigns

Many web businesses will give their customers a choice of buying from their own site or from a partner website. In those cases, visitors are buying from the "channel" and not "direct," which qualifies these sales for multichannel tracking. You can do a couple of things to aid tracking:

Top Destinations Most web analytics tools now come with a report on top destinations (also called *exit links*). This allows you to track the traffic that you are sending to other online properties. This is a great, free resource for you to track your referrals to other online properties (yours or those of your partners).

Affiliates Tracking Many big and medium sized companies ignore this option. Affiliate tracking is a science now, and rather than having to beg your online partners to give you data, you should simply sign up for their affiliate marketing programs. Amazon.com is a great example. They won't give you data, but if you use their affiliate program to send you clicks, they will automatically provide you with visitor counts, orders, revenue, and more. Other websites do the same.

Thursday and Friday: Track Online-for-Multichannel Behavior and Campaigns

This is not really multichannel, but your own website is a great source of collecting data that will help you understand your holistic multichannel impact. You can use a couple of methodologies in the silo that is your website (and the silo that is your click-stream or qualitative data) to gauge how good a job your website is doing at providing your multichannel nonline marketing needs.

Surveys You can deploy surveys (please see Chapter 3 for best practices) on your website to help you understand customers' channel preferences and whether your website is having a true multichannel impact. Figure 9.4 illustrates an example of measuring the purchase preference by channel for four websites of your company.

Website Visitors: Channel Preference for Purchases

☐ Online ◼ Retail Stores ◼ Phone (Call Center) ☐ Other

Figure 9.4 Measuring customer channel preference for purchases

If Figure 9.4 reflected the websites of a retailer such as OfficeMax, it would be interesting (and highly actionable) to note that a majority of website visitors prefer to buy online and therefore all the website content written to help visitors buy offline needs to evolve.

If these were the websites of Amazon.com, it would be interesting that such a large chunk of website visitors prefer to buy at a retail store (about 35 percent of ac.com). This might suggest looking for ways to create partnerships with the retail stores to benefit from this wonderful traffic. It would also suggest that maybe Amazon.com should open kiosks in the huge number of malls in the United States to sell products in stores (exactly as Dell has done in the last year—they now have Build Your Own PC kiosks in malls across the United States to complement their "direct" phone and web channels).

MCVIs If you are a true multichannel business, you also have the ability to compute the influence of your online channel on your offline channels. ForeSee Results provides a service that allows its clients to compute the multichannel value index (MCVI). This index helps measure the *"likelihood that your customers will purchase your products and services from any available channel after their online experience."* It is a great proxy for the revenue impact of your website via offline channels. You have the ability to measure this not only at a point in time, but also over time if your website is adding more or less value to your offline channels.

Figure 9.5 shows the MCVI for top online retailers as measured during Spring 2006 and the holiday season 2005. The data was collected from approximately 10 thousand online panelists who visited these websites. The data clearly illustrates which sites have moved in the right direction and which have regressed. When you pair this data with your web analytics data (visitors, conversion, revenue, and so forth), you can quickly see how easy it is to paint a complete story about the value of your website. If you are Sony Style, would it have mattered if your revenues were up 150 percent online during the same time your MCVI dropped so dramatically? Yes, if there was a deliberate strategy to shift Sony sales online at the expense of other channels (which is the case for many websites, and that strategic shift will differ from one website to another).

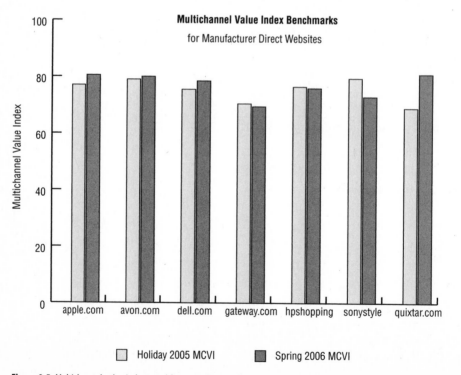

Figure 9.5 Multichannel value index trend for top online retailers

Promotion Code Redemption We have discussed the possibilities of using tracking codes and promotion codes in the offline channels as you drive traffic to your website. You can now leverage your web analytics tool (or your Microsoft Access database or Excel spreadsheet) to compute traffic that you are getting from your offline channels. You can compute conversion rates and revenue, and if you have a Trinity-based platform for analytics, you can also compute customer satisfaction or create optimal customer experiences on your website for traffic from these other channels.

As we close this chapter, it is important to stress again that the challenge with multichannel analytics is not a challenge of reporting. It is a challenge of collecting data and being able to tie the disparate pieces together. Figure 9.6 shows the complete picture of all the different channels, the traffic flowing back and forth (as a result of your nonline marketing efforts), and the various data collection options at your disposal.

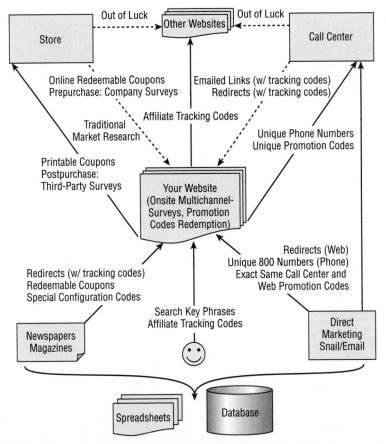

Figure 9.6 Multichannel value index trend for top online retailers

If you use any of the preceding recommendations to capture the data, it will in all probability end up in a database somewhere or in your analyst's Access database or even a nice Excel spreadsheet.

At the moment, in spite of the promises, there are not really lots of off-the-shelf options for integrating all these disparate pieces of data (though for some of the preceding suggestions, your web analytics tool will do fine). The fact that you don't have a globally accepted platform to do multichannel analytics should not stop you. It is complex but certainly within the realm of possibility should your business identify multichannel marketing analytics as a key priority. If you can collect the data, even the Access database or Excel spreadsheet will get you actionable insights. Take that and run with it.

Month 5: Website Experimentation and Testing—Shifting the Power to Customers and Achieving Significant Outcomes

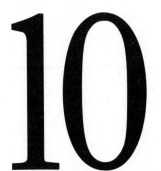

We have discussed the limitations of understanding customer intent simply from their clicks and the sheer diversity of reasons why customers come to our websites.

The practical manifestations of these two problems is that it is significantly more difficult to find actionable insights and it is even harder to find actionable insights that affect your bottom line. (The bottom line is not just revenue; it can be improved customer satisfaction, lowered customer service costs, or simply an inferred benefit to your company brand.)

The essence of customer centricity is to focus on helping your customers solve their problems (instead of focusing on solving the company's problems: revenue). It is also about being much more adept at *listening* to our customers and crafting optimal website experiences that help customers solve their problems. A fantastic method of accomplishing this is to do experimentation and testing.

In this chapter, you will learn why testing is important. You will also learn about the methodologies at your disposal and how to create a great testing program. Now with the free Google Web Optimizer tool you should be able to sign up and quickly implement the lessons that you will learn in this chapter.

Weeks 1 and 2: Why Test and What Are Your Options?

I love experimentation and testing. No caveats, no ifs, no buts. I love experimentation and testing. There is simply nothing better when it comes to getting your questions answered on the battlefield rather than by watching passively from the sidelines and analyzing just the clickstream data.

In the first two weeks, you are going to step back and understand the value of having an effective testing strategy. Then you'll dive deeper into understanding your options when it comes to executing the tests. You will also learn the pros and cons of each methodology, which will enable you to choose the right weapon from your quiver.

Week 1: Preparations and A/B Testing

Most websites don't test. Many people feel that testing is too complex, or perhaps management does not know quite enough about the possibilities and so hasn't made the leap. Simply put, having a robust testing platform means having an opportunity to judge the success of your site at a fraction of the cost and in much less time than you thought possible—with a higher likelihood of success to boot. For most websites, visitors interacting with their online presence vastly outstrips any other interaction medium.

Monday: Understand the Case for Testing

As the Web continues to evolve, there are some interesting and dynamic trends at play that cause a unique problem. The trends fall into two categories: company issues (employees, organizational structures, mindset sophistication) and customer issues (having too many choices, being click happy, having increasing time pressures result in impatience, being here today—gone tomorrow). As a result, it is much harder to know how to create optimal experiences. Here are some of the more obvious challenges that we all face:

Customers rarely give us solutions to implement. Most customers expect suboptimal experiences. When given a chance, these customers will share everything that does not work for them. Still, they will rarely give us solutions to implement. For example, a customer might say, "I can't find the product comparison chart" instead of saying, "Your left navigation structure is missing and the buttons called Comparison Chart are too small and hidden." You can see how this can be a huge challenge.

Even the most phenomenal site experience is stale tomorrow. You could have the perfect site, but because of the way the Web works, your destiny is in the hands of others. Unless you are one of the top-tier websites, you don't have the opportunity to "teach" customers what to expect from a website. For instance, Microsoft and Yahoo! all go Ajax or do flyouts a certain way, or Amazon.com eliminates the header altogether. The Web is constantly evolving. We have not even gotten to Web 2.0 and there is buzz about Web 3.0, while you and I of course are still at Web 1.0. Barely. Unless you have the ability to try new things easily and for lower costs, you are not going to be able to keep pace with your customer expectations and help them with their needs and wants.

Company employees usually don't know what customers want. When it comes to web design in most companies, circumstances, and debates, the HiPPO stands for: Highest Paid Person's Opinion. Company employees, especially the HiPPOs, think their experiences represent those of the customers. Our VP hates our site, and we change it. In reality, company employees are too close to the company and its products and services and know too much about them. In fact, in my experience, 80 percent of the time company employees (yes that includes you, Mr. Spiffy Designer, and you, Mr. Flavor of the Month Agency Guy) are wrong about what customers want. The only way to know that you are solving problems for customers is to have mechanisms enabling you to listen to the customers and have them tell you what they like (and no, it is not always Ajax or Flash).

Imagine trying to do testing in the real world for the perfect song for your 30-second $1.5-million Super Bowl commercial. What are the chances that you (or three guys in your agency) will get it right? Now imagine creating a virtual jukebox on your website and providing a customized playlist of songs for your website visitors. You pick the most popular song from the playlists after 15 days. What are the chances that you have a hit on your hand? Really high.

For your company, compute how much you spend on price sensitivity testing or doing in-store promotions or creating bundles or coming up with the perfect color pallet for the box in which your gizmo will be sold or creating the right checkout or determining the features you should implement in your new competitor killer or validating whether there is a market for the new crazy idea or—the list goes on.

Tuesday: Learn to Be Wrong

Perhaps the linchpin in your business case should be that a solid experimentation and testing platform will prove you wrong. It will prove you wrong quickly and repeatedly (80 percent of the time, from my experience). This could not be more wonderful. Think about it. Wouldn't you give your left arm for the ability to rapidly put your ideas out there and get the people who will ultimately make the decision on your fate tell you what they think of your ideas?

It will be a strategic advantage for your company to have the ability to find out quickly what works and does not work and iterate through that with real customer feedback.

Experimentation and testing in the long run will replace most traditional ways of collecting qualitative data on our site experiences, such as lab usability study. Usability (in a lab or in a home or done remotely) can often result in less-than-ideal websites because it is still, at the end of the day, the opinion of eight or ten people about your website, and sadly that does not quite capture the complexity of why the website exists and all the conflicting purposes for which your customers visit. We discussed in Chapter 3, "Overview of Qualitative Analysis," how the Hawthorne effect also negatively affects the results of a usability study.

For example, if our customers like to surf our websites in their pajamas, wouldn't it be great if we could do usability studies on them when they are in their underwear? With an effective testing program, you can absolutely do that. You will lose some of the richness of the visual in-person feedback, but you will gain massive scale and eliminate the negative effects of the Hawthorne effect.

It is important to realize that experimentation might sound big and complex, but it is not. We are lucky to live at time when there are a number of options available that allow us to get as deep and as broad as we want to, and the cost is not prohibitive either. (And the cost is going down with each passing day—for example, Google's Website Optimizer product is free.)

Wednesday: Gain an Overview of the Methodologies

Experimentation is not new as a business concept. Marketers have been doing testing offline for ages. Different advertisements are routinely tested in various television markets to see which one performs better. Companies such as Procter & Gamble have honed testing into an art form before bringing new products to market. Direct marketers are perhaps the direct predecessors to what is happening on the Web since these DMers have been doing fabulous multivariate testing with various promotions, offers, creatives, layouts, content, and everything else. It is just that DMers were doing it with catalogs or snail mail.

While the world will continue to evolve, at the moment there are three primary methodologies that fill the need for experimentation and testing on the Web: A/B testing, multivariate testing, and experience testing. Of these three, two are most used: A/B and multivariate. Of these, perhaps the most excitement is currently on multivariate testing. You'll spend the rest of this week and all of week 2 learning about the strengths of each.

Thursday and Friday: Understand A/B Testing

This might seem to be an all-encompassing category that represents all kinds of testing. But under the A/B (or A/B/C or A/B/A) testing methodology, you will test more than one version of a complete web page.

Each version of the web page in an A/B test is uniquely created and stands alone. Figure 10.1 illustrates a simple A/B/C test, where three versions of the home page are being tested to see which one performs better against key goals. Version A is usually the control, and the test versions are B and C, each of which has a few variables that are changed against the control and against each other.

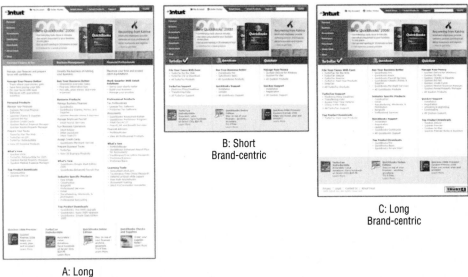

A: Long
Control

B: Short
Brand-centric

C: Long
Brand-centric

Figure 10.1 Example of a home page A/B/C test

You can simply have your designers or developers create versions of the page, and depending on the complexity of your web platform, you can put the pages up and measure. Most website platforms will allow you to serve up a different version of the page to the website visitors and have rules associated with that (show A to 50 percent of visitors, B to 25 percent, and C to 25 percent). Even if you have a static platform, you should be able to send the page to a random set of website visitors.

Pros of Doing A/B Testing

- It is perhaps the cheapest way of doing testing, because you will use your existing resources, tools, and processes.

- If you don't do any testing, this is a great way to just get going and energize your organization and really have some fun.

- My tip: The first few times you do this, have company team members place bets (where legal) and pick a winner. You'll be surprised at the effects on social behavior and at which version wins.

Cons of Doing A/B Testing

- It is difficult to control all the external factors (campaigns, search traffic, press releases, seasonality) and so you won't be 100 percent confident of the results (put 70 percent confidence in the results and make decisions).

- It limits the kinds of things you can test: just big simple stuff.

- The number of variables you can test at a time is also limited. To test many variables, you would need to create tens of versions of the page. Even then, it is difficult to apply the mathematics to determine what the statistically significant outcome is with all the variables you can have.

Bottom Line on A/B testing

A/B testing is the first tentative dipping of the toe into the world of testing. It is extremely simple to create and implement (the hurdle, as always, is finding good ideas to test). If for any reason your platform does not allow you to test in parallel, you should put up versions of the page serially (one on each day, or one each week). The purists will gawk at this, but just go ahead and do it. Try to control for external factors if you can—but if you can't, you will still learn something and get your organization moving in the right direction from a mindset perspective. A/B testing is still useful for huge changes—for example, when you don't want to simply monkey around with a current page, but simply slash and burn it and start all over again. That's A/B testing.

Week 2: Moving Beyond A/B Testing

A/B testing gets our feet wet and gets us going in the world of testing. But if your website is huge or if you want to try lots of tests at the same time or you want to test more than one variable at the same time, you will find it difficult to do that with simple A/B testing. This is because of the complexity in processes, the hurdles you'll have to overcome in getting enough resources, and the time it will take you to test all your ideas (essentially serially). If you find yourself in this bind, it's time to move beyond A/B testing.

Monday: Obtain an Overview of Multivariate Testing

Multivariate testing is currently the cool kid on the block, with lots of hype and lots of buzz. In the preceding A/B test, you had to create three pages. Now imagine modularizing your page (breaking it up into chunks) so you still have just have one page but can change dynamically which modules show up on the page, where they show up, and to which traffic. Then imagine being able to put that into a complex mathematical engine that will tell you not only which version of the page worked but correlations as well.

Figure 10.2 shows how this test might look and work. You can take a standard home page and break it into its logical elements (some vendors call these *zones*). The page in the figure has four elements (you can have as many as you want). By using multivariate testing, you can test different content in each element but, more important, you can test more than one piece of content in each element. How cool is that!

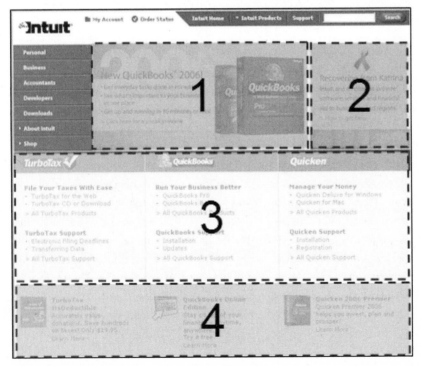

Figure 10.2 Multivariate testing

So, for example, you could have three pieces of content or creatives in each of the four elements (Figure 10.3), in this case you can experiment with three different pieces of content in element #1 in Figure 10.2.

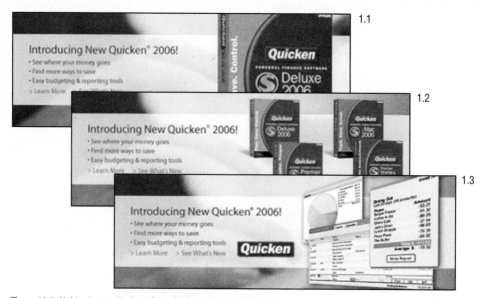

Figure 10.3 Multivariate testing benefit: multiple versions per element

Real multivariate tests inherently change multiple things all at the same time. This is the core differentiator between them and A/B tests.

In our example in Figure 10.2, if you were changing three alternatives in each of the four elements, you would have 81 possible combinations. Using off-the-shelf multivariate testing (MVT) vendor solutions, you don't have to create 81 pages. Instead, the testing platform will take care of creating the combinations. Furthermore, you don't even have to test all the different permutations and combinations; you can apply the Taguchi method, which in the preceding case could test as few as eight versions (also called *recipes*) and yet compute the results as if you had tested all 81.

At the end of the test you can obtain data that will show you the statistical significance of the test results. Figure 10.4 shows the results of varying three different alternatives for a example web page: Subheading, Hero shot (main image on the page), and having a Buy Now button or not. These results indicate that while two of the changes proved to be promising, that third element was actually detrimental. All of the complex math is applied for you already and results presented in a very visually easy to understand manner.

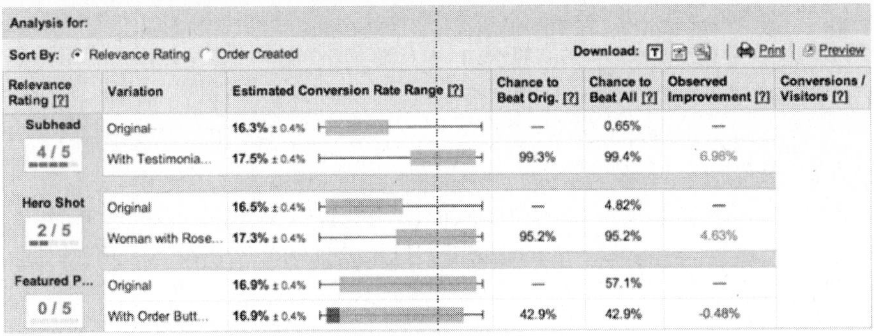

Analysis for:								
Sort By: ⦿ Relevance Rating ○ Order Created					Download: T		Print	Preview
Relevance Rating [?]	Variation	Estimated Conversion Rate Range [?]		Chance to Beat Orig. [?]	Chance to Beat All [?]	Observed Improvement [?]	Conversions / Visitors [?]	
Subhead	Original	16.3% ± 0.4%		—	0.65%	—		
4 / 5	With Testimonia...	17.5% ± 0.4%		99.3%	99.4%	6.98%		
Hero Shot	Original	16.5% ± 0.4%		—	4.82%	—		
2 / 5	Woman with Rose...	17.3% ± 0.4%		95.2%	95.2%	4.63%		
Featured P...	Original	16.9% ± 0.4%		—	57.1%	—		
0 / 5	With Order Butt...	16.9% ± 0.4%		42.9%	42.9%	-0.48%		

Figure 10.4 Applying statistical significance to test results

Tuesday: Consider the Pros and Cons of Multivariate Testing

It is important to set aside a day to understand the pros and cons of multivariate testing. Of all the methodologies at your disposal, you can implement this one perhaps the fastest. Although it is extremely cool and beneficial, it also has some important cons to consider—to ensure that you don't exaggerate to your senior management the results you can achieve and that you are optimally deploying your multivariate testing capabilities.

Pros of Doing Multivariate Testing

- Doing multivariate testing turbocharges your ability to do a lot very quickly for a couple of reasons:
  - There are vendors now such as Offermatica, Optimost, and SiteSpect who can help you get going quickly by hosting all the functionality remotely (think ASP model). They will support things such as content hosting, test rules, and attributes along with all the analytics and statistics. If you are just getting started you can use the free Google Website Optimizer, which will give you all the initial functionality that you need, along with powerful reporting.
  - You don't have to rely on your IT/development team. All they have to do is put a few lines of JavaScript on the page and they are done. This is an awesome benefit because most of the time IT and website platform limitations are a huge hurdle. After the JavaScript is on the pages, you can start and stop tests, and control all elements of the test by yourself (or have your smart marketers do the simple ones).

- Multivariate tests are a perfect fit for structured experiences (going from here to there to there and signing out) and also for landing pages. In both cases, there is a clear purpose for which the visitor arrives (invited or uninvited). If the purpose is clear to you, by using multivariate testing you can quickly optimize to the business or customer outcome.

- It can be a continuous learning methodology. After you put the testing tags in your website, you can constantly test and learn and optimize your customer experiences. For example, you can run a test for optimizing a certain element (or elements) of your Product Overview page, and then at the end of the test make the winner the control by pressing just one button and then right away move to test your next idea. This requires little overhead except for your ability to come up with valid testable ideas.

Cons of Doing Multivariate Testing

- The old computer adage applies: be careful of GIGO. You still need a clean pool of good ideas that are sourced from known customer pain points or strategic business objectives. It is just as easy to optimize the suboptimal quickly as well, but that won't yield much business impact.

- Website experiences for most sites are complex, multipage affairs. For an e-commerce website, it is typical for the experience from an entry to a successful purchase to be around 12 to 18 pages, for a support site even more pages (as website visitors thrash around to find what they are looking for). With multivariate testing, you are optimizing only one page, and no matter how optimized, it cannot play an oversized role in the final outcome, just the first step or two.

- There is a tendency with multivariate testing to focus on the home page and assume that all else will be okay. You should be careful to set the right expectations with your decisions makers about the effects on the complete customer experience. (Otherwise, they end up blaming the methodology.)

Bottom Line on Multivariate Testing

You should definitely do multivariate testing. There is no reason not to in the context of vendor options and speed of deployment. There is simply nothing better for page optimization. But be aware of its limitations and, like any product, use it wisely (even if the vendors tell you that they will return multimillion-dollar returns and make you coffee for breakfast as well).

Wednesday: Obtain an Overview of Experience Testing

Experience testing represents the kind of testing where you have the ability to change the entire site experience of the visitor by using the capability of your site platform (for example, ATG or Blue Martini Software). You can not only change things on one page (as with A/B or multivariate testing) or change one element on multiple pages (for example, the left navigation or a piece of text), but rather you can change all things about the entire experience on your website.

Figure 10.5 shows a simplistic process that a visitor might go through on Microsoft's website to buy Microsoft Money. This is the shortest path the visitor could take. Typically, they would view demos or compare it to Quicken or check deep details, and so forth, and then buy. Even this simple process requires multiple pages that try to do different jobs. It would be tough to A/B test or multivariate test to optimize the visitor's experience.

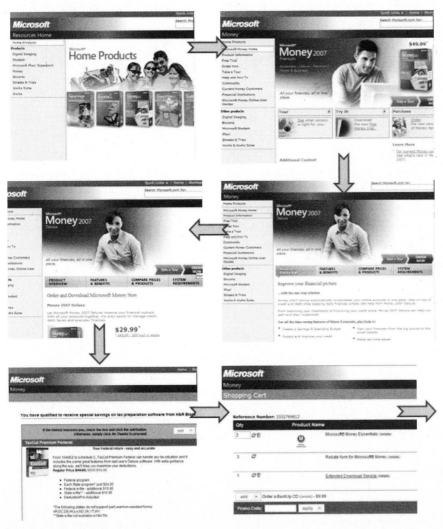

Figure 10.5 Experience testing

If Microsoft's platform would allow it, in an experience test you could try to change and experiment with various experiences on the site. For example, you could create one experience (version A) of the website that segments the site based on Windows and Macintosh versions of products, another experience (version B) that segments the site by current customers and new customers, and another (version C) that presents the site in purple with white font, no left navigation, and smiling babies instead of product box shots. You get the idea.

The difference here when compared to other methodologies is that you are segmenting and changing multipage experiences. You are truly experimenting with different ways of solving your customers' problems by making deep changes, changes that will span multiple pages of the website experience and cover multiple elements of the customer experience (for example, it is not just changing the same promotional/merchandizing slot on all the pages on your website).

By using experience testing, you don't have to create three or four websites. Instead, by using your site platform, you can easily create two or three persistent experiences on your websites and see which one your customers react to best. (Of course, you would use cookies to ensure that no single customer sees more than one version of the site—that would not be a great customer experience!) Because any analytics tools you use collect data for all three, the analysis is the same as you do currently.

Thursday: Consider the Pros and Cons of Experience Testing

What is life without caveats? Today you will spend time understanding the benefits that experience testing will bring to your company and website. You will also spend time learning the costs of doing experience testing. You'll end with how you should sum up experience testing in your mind (and to your boss).

Pros of Doing Experience Testing

- This is Nirvana. You have the ability to test your customers in their native environment (think pajamas) and collect data that is most closely reflective of their true thoughts.

- If your qualitative methods are integrated, you can read their thoughts about each experience.

- You will get five to ten times more powerful results than any other methodology because you overcome some of the limitations of MVT outlined earlier.

- One of the challenges with optimizing and analyzing results is that it is hard to know whether you are optimizing for a local maxima (the "curve" you are on right now) and moving up or you have shifted to a different maxima, hopefully your global maxima (think of this as the "best you can be" curve). By using experience testing, you increase your chances of moving from maximizing your current curve, or local maxima, to a completely different curve that has a higher, global, max and a different slope (Figure 10.6). This can be huge.

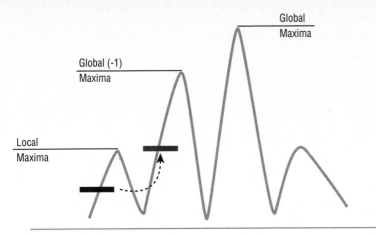

Figure 10.6 Moving from local to global maxima with experience testing

Cons of Doing Experience Testing

- You need to have a website platform that supports experience testing (for example, ATG supports this).
- It takes longer than the other two methodologies to create, execute, and measure results because for the most part you will have to do this yourself. There is no standard off-the-shelf software for experience testing yet.
- It most definitely takes more brain power—big ideas, radical solutions, complex analysis.

Bottom Line on Experience Testing

Experience testing is often aspirational for many companies because it requires a lot more sophistication in terms of people and technology. Increasingly, companies are finding that they have optimized at a page level or at a particular campaign-offer level, but what they need to do is much deeper testing to achieve outsized results that will set them apart from their competition. This should fuel the kind of demand that will see many more vendors enabling experience testing or more website platforms enabling serving of different "scenarios" of their sites. All this gets blurry between testing and content serving and personalization and behavior targeting. It should be fun.

Friday: Reflect

In these two weeks, you have covered an extremely complex topic. Take Friday to reflect on what you have learned thus far and start your own business case, for your own management. Either initiate testing in your company, or (if you already have a program) consider how to take it to the next level.

Identify your current state, your current opportunities, and the questions that your company is unable to answer that would be a perfect fit for being solved by testing.

If you find yourself being swamped by hundreds of pieces of data yet you have no idea what to do with your home page or your PPC landing pages or why no one on your website makes it through the cart, you are perfectly placed to take advantage of testing. Your business case should open with that.

Week 3: What to Test—Specific Options and Ideas

You have drunk the Kool-Aid and you know all there is to know about testing. You have a contract signed with a vendor. You badgered your IT team to place the JavaScript tags or create versions of different pages. Excellent! Now all you need are some ideas to get yourself going. This section will help you with that.

Before I present ideas, it is important to highlight that there is no such thing as two identical web businesses. Every business is unique and has its own ecosystem (people, strategies, emphasis, goals, and so forth). Therefore, it is important to point out that your website needs its own set of ideas to test. What works for everyone else might not work for you. Hopefully, the ideas in this section will still be food for thought.

At the end of each day, make a list of the ideas that are suggested in this section that will work for you. At the end of the week, create a prioritized list of ideas that will form the basis of your execution strategy.

Monday: Test Important Pages and Calls to Action

The first things that are typically considered fodder for testing are the important pages on your website (think of the home page or your comparison chart page, for example) and the calls to action you have for your customers. These are important high-profile testing possibilities that can have an immediate effect on your customers and also help you gain visibility and recognition from your stakeholders.

Test Important Website Pages

One of the easiest gigs to win at in testing is optimizing pages. Identify a few of the most important pages on your website, and find out who owns them and what their purpose is. Then optimize the heck out of them with A/B tests or multivariate tests.

Pages that will fall into this bucket will most obviously be your home page, top entry pages to your website, custom landing pages, and cart and checkout pages.

As you move from home page to entry pages to landing pages, your complexity will reduce. Because the pages are becoming more specific, it will be easier to optimize against a single goal.

The other benefit of starting with important pages is that they usually have great PR associated with them, which can't hurt.

Global elements also are excellent targets. For example, test what kind of headers work on your site (because they persist across pages): branded or soft and fuzzy, bold calls to action or value proposition, tabbed (like Amazon.com's) or no tabs. With one such test, you can touch your entire site and make a persistent impact.

Consider Calls to Action

This one is the next easiest, and you might be surprised how much influence a slightly different call to action can have on your customers. Try to see what works for you.

Think about buttons: Does the Buy Now button work better than Add to Cart? Or do blue buttons work better than green ones? Or should the buttons be below the fold or above? Are text links better than buttons? What else?

Create urgency: This works well for eBay and Overstock.com, for example, which both in their own ways create a (perhaps false?) sense of urgency in the purchase process. Try including messages that create urgency: "Only 5 Barbies left in stock," "Promotion Ends in 15 minutes," "Offer Expires October 16th," "Buy Now and Save." You get the idea.

Trying these will help you understand the mindset of your own customers better and optimize your approach.

Tuesday: Focus on Search Traffic

We usually struggle to identify the intent of our customers. In the case of search traffic, the keyword or key phrase can reveal a lot about a customer's intent. You can run experiments for the search traffic by doing simple things such as repeating the search key phrase on the landing page (be it a custom landing page or just a standard page).

For your most important key phrases, consider creating custom landing pages that reiterate the value that you have to offer tied to the key phrase and a distinct call to action. (This could very well be "Click here to go to the next page." It does not always have to be "Buy now.")

If you don't know what works, the obvious answer is to test. But where it gets more fun is to leverage your existing content and pages with your testing platform. For example, you can use Offermatica to show custom content on the exiting website home page. (*Custom content* can be content tied to your keywords or content from which you have removed some of the ancillary matter to highlight what connects to a user.)

Wednesday: Test Content and Creatives

This is where most people start when it comes to testing, but perhaps it is one of the hardest tests to get right because we think we know what the customers are coming to our website for, but we are usually wrong.

Things you can test in terms of content include the following:

- Quantity of the copy (more words or fewer words)
- Formatting (for example, short or long paragraphs, long pages with anchor tags, or a short page with deep content on different pages)

One of the most radical content tests I have seen simply eliminated all the words on a page, replaced them with one line of text, and measured the effectiveness of this new idea at achieving the key business goal (it worked like a charm). The interesting point here is to think really differently.

Things you can test in terms of creatives include the following:

- People images vs. product box shots
- Lots of white space on the site vs. a heavy image-driven site
- The new completely Flash/Ajax-driven site vs. a Yahoo!-type site circa 1996
- Logs vs. no logos
- Endorsing brands vs. not endorsing them
- Big heroes on the home page or four small ones

On your support websites, you can apply page-level or multivariate testing to rapidly iterate throughout which presentation formats work for the support answers pages or how search engine results should be organized or how to present links to your user forums or blogs.

Thursday: Test Price and Promotions

One of the most underrated uses of testing is for pricing and promotions. Sometimes this is because this type of testing requires integration with the website back end so that offers can be served by your testing platform but they can be accepted and fulfilled by your back end. The other issue is that some testing vendors can't support pan-session controls effectively (so a visitor might come to the site two times in a day and see different prices, which is much worse than you seeing two versions of the home page).

But if that is not a hurdle for you, testing price sensitivity is a fantastic use of a testing platform. You should test which kinds of discounting work: $10 off instantly or a $15 mail-in rebate. Or $10 off or $15 off or $25 off. Or free shipping—having it, not having it, or having it only after a certain order size.

Testing is also a great way to try different product bundles on the site or to rotate through a bunch of promotions or merchandising ideas very efficiently to quickly see which one works for your customers. Test cross-sells and up-sells (not only which cross-sells and up-sells work with which products, but also location on the pages, ordering of the cross-sells, and when to show them—in the cart or product details pages).

You also have the ability to trigger tests based on the source of traffic. One obvious application is to isolate one group of traffic (for example, everyone from your affiliates or from your corporate website or from MSN.com) and test pricing and promotions just on that segment of traffic.

Friday: Test Direct Marketing Campaigns

Due to the advent of HTML-rich email readers, marketers have been able to get a lot savvier about doing more-sophisticated testing via emails as well. They have been able to move beyond simple targeting of various offers to segregated groups of customers with campaigns. Now they are able to dynamically change content in an email itself to test creatives, content, promotions, calls to actions, and more all at the same time.

In addition, you can also test timing via emails (weekends vs. week days, or work hours vs. evenings, for example). With email you know exactly, well almost exactly, who you are sending the email to, and that can provide an additional layer of testing personalization and doing some dynamic messaging to see what produces the desired outcome.

The wonderful thing now with implementing testing on your website is that you don't have to be restricted to just testing in the emails that are sent out. You can now continue the testing and personalization you might have done in your emails through to the website, when the customer clicks on the links in the email and visits the website. This allows you to test even more variables after landing on the websites, or you can test just a couple of things in the email, to keep things simple, and then add the other layers after people click through to your website.

You are not limited to email either. If you do lots of snail mail campaigns, most of the time that traffic will come to your website via redirects or will have to type in a special promotion code. In this case, you also know lots about the customer and their intent. This is a perfect scenario for you to do testing and optimize the customer experience. Remember, testing results in more options as you have more information about the customer.

Even this collection of ideas for your website cannot quite illustrate the possibilities you have with a solid testing strategy to fundamentally improve your website experiences for your customers and add to your bottom line (and one does not have to come at the expense of the other). But perhaps the most promising of all, and most motivating of all, for the employees in your company is that testing promotes *idea democracy*.

In the past, the idea from the person with the biggest title won. Now with testing, it is much cheaper to have a bunch of good ideas and for a very low cost (time and dollars) simply put the ideas out there and let the customers tell us which ones are best. You have the same opportunity as your company founder or head designer or newest expensive cool Marketer/Analyst/MBA to put your crazy thought on the site. How cool is that! Idea democracy.

Week 4: Build a Great Experimentation and Testing Program

The good news is that testing is increasingly being accepted as something any decent web program should constantly be engaged in because it can have truly game-changing influence on a website, its bottom line, and its customers. Additionally, now technology makes it increasingly easy to test your ideas and insights, cheaply and quickly. We are not limited by the long release cycles on our websites or IT or marketing or other such usual hurdles. In the simplest model, a simple JavaScript tag is placed on the site and then using your vendor's system you can run the tests you want and measure success without needing extra work by your developers or IT staff.

Yet in many companies, testing is not quite ingrained in the culture. Other companies are stuck in the very simplistic A/B or bare-bones multivariate tests (which usually don't even leverage the true power of multivariate tests).

Having a contract with a vendor and access to the technology does not a program make. For you to get sustained value from your testing platform, you truly have to create a testing program (people, process, structure, mindset, rewards, and so forth). This is especially true after a few months of testing because over time it becomes harder to show the same 150 percent improvement in conversion rate and all the low hanging fruits have been picked. Creating a program enables your company to get sustained performance from its testing strategy.

You'll spend this week considering recommendations to help you build your own great experimentation and testing program.

Monday: Hypothesize and Set Goals

Today you are going to learn the importance of holding your horses and of doing something extremely obvious: setting goals before you test. Both of these recommendations seem straightforward but they mask their importance pretty effectively. So close your office door and keep a pencil and paper handy for notes.

Get Over Your Own Opinions

It really stinks but this is of paramount importance. If you are running the program, it is important that first you get over yourself. If you are going to convince everyone else that testing and validating opinions should be a way of life, you should first truly drink the Kool-Aid. (In my experience, the more entrenched the opinion in a company, the more likely it is that it is wrong.)

When I go out and talk about testing, I make the case related to entrenched opinions by sharing the most recent three or four times testing has proven me to be disastrously wrong. I share the worst stories, the big losers, like the one in the "Cautionary Tale" sidebar. The points I am making in doing that is that we don't really represent our website customers, it is okay to be wrong, and here is how you can find out quickly.

A Cautionary Tale

When I first saw a demo for a Flash-based shopping cart and checkout process, I was absolutely certain it would be God's gift to our customers. It was simple, it had advanced error handling, it reduced a five-page process into a one-page experience, and it solved some fundamental problems our customers were experiencing during the buying process.

Yet when we tested it live on our website by using an A/B test, the Flash cart initially performed terribly. This was quite a shock. It turns out customers were too used to the more-complicated and "cumbersome" HTML experience and not ready for an optimized cool experience.

I was absolutely wrong about what would have worked, yet without a testing problem we might simply have implemented the Flash-based experience, confident in our opinion that it was a superior option to the HTML experience. This is not uncommon. As company employees, we are simply too close to the company and our products and services. It is hard to take five steps away from that and truly be the customers of our company (and hence represent what they want or need).

Bottom line: You will get a receptive audience and change minds much faster, because you are willing to "open the kimono."

State a Hypothesis, Not a Test Scenario

Most often people will come to you and say, "I want to test different box shots. Can you swap this image with text? We should try different promotions." The golden rule is: Always start with a hypothesis, not test details or a test scenario.

Turn to the person and ask, "What is your hypothesis?" It is amazing how many times people are taken aback by that. Mostly because we as humans don't want to put that much thought into anything.

The magic of this question is that it forces people to take a step back and think. They might come back to you and say, "My hypothesis is that images of people are much more powerful at making a connection than current box shots. Therefore, we will have a higher engagement score (or sales or whatever)" or "My hypothesis is that visitors to the site are more interested in user-generated content than our company propaganda."

Starting with a hypothesis leads to two great outcomes:

- You can now contribute to the creation of the test, rather than just starting with a "I want you to do this."

- Every well-crafted hypothesis contains a clear success measurement (which is how we'll know which test version wins). If you don't see a success measurement in the hypothesis, you don't have a well-thought-out hypothesis.

Set Goals and Metrics Beforehand

Another big mistake that is often made is that even if the success metric is known, we don't bother to set parameters to judge the "victory" by.

Determine the success metrics for the test before you launch and don't forget to create a goal for those metrics.

Imagine that you are launching a test to improve conversion rate. Great. By how much do you think you'll improve the conversion rate? Frequently, that thought has not been put in up front but it is extremely critical for these two reasons:

- It forces you to think, to do some research as to what the current trends in those success metrics are and to go through a goal creation exercise for your test.

- You'll be able to judge whether you should do the test in the first place. You'll be surprised at how many times you'll do the research, and it turns out the effect on the bottom line will be minimal or it will take you nine months to get a solid signal and make a decision. So if testing smiling babies on your home page will improve conversion rate by only 0.001 percent (your projected outcome), maybe that test is not worthwhile and you should think of something more powerful. However, if you do $10 billion in sales on your website, then clearly a 0.001 percent lift will endear you to your company leader or the guy or gal with a bigger title than yours.

Setting goals and metrics from the start will push the thought envelope and at the same time encourage creation of tests that will yield more-powerful customer experience improvements on your site.

Tuesday: Test and Validate for Multiple Goals

This one is important. Almost all testing is single-goal based, especially those from the current swath of multivariate testing companies. Put this JavaScript box on this or that page, put this JavaScript tag on the goal page, crank the lever, sing Happy Birthday, eat cake, and here are the results (and they look good!).

Life and customer experiences are significantly more complex. Visitors come to your website for multiple purposes. If you use the current multivariate or other such testing tools and then work to integrate other tools, that will allow you to measure the impact of your test on all those other purposes.

Perhaps visitors come to your home page to buy, to find jobs, to print product information, to read your founder's bio, or to find your tech support phone number. If you solve only for selling (conversion rate) in your multivariate testing, you might be majorly and negatively affecting your customers who are there for other purposes. Do you know whether that is happening for the tests you are running?

Imagine that roughly 30 percent of the visitors are coming to your website for buying and 70 percent for other purposes. If you don't measure multiple goals, you are optimizing for only the 30 percent and that could have serious impact on a majority of your traffic (and you would not even know—yikes!).

I have stressed the need for integrating various sets of data and tools that you have access to in your implementation of web analytics. For example, integrating outcomes on your website with customer behavior, or clickstream with surveys. This can be a major benefit when it comes to measuring multiple goals.

Consider this simple example of tools integration: You'll get statistical significance and single-goal success from your testing vendor. But with a small amount of effort, and smarts, you can integrate your testing parameters with your survey tool. This will allow you to measure conversion rate and customer satisfaction and get open-ended customer feedback in each test version. Or you can integrate testing parameters with your clickstream tool (from ClickTracks, Omniture, IndexTools, WebTrends, or WebSideStory) which will allow you to measure conversion rate and customer satisfaction and click density and funnel analysis for each test version.

Imagine knowing whether your test improved conversion but also being aware of the collateral impact on other links on your page and other segments of visitors. It can be priceless.

In the first few months, measuring a single goal will work and happiness will prevail. Only by moving to truly multigoal testing, however, will you be able to make optimal decisions, and in turn create a program in your company that will sustain and be a long-term competitive advantage.

Wednesday: Start Simple and Then Scale and Have Fun

Today you will learn about a key paradox of testing: simple or complex. The latter has loads of influence on your customers and bottom line, but the former is the real key to getting your program off to a fantastic start. Also you will learn about the importance of achieving a mindset shift early in the program, by doing things simple and by making it fun, because in the end the mindset shift will help you way more than any big first test would in achieving long-term success.

Accept Simple or "Silly" Initial Tests

Testing programs are run by people who are really smart. Often, though, these people have not truly followed the recommendation to start with a hypothesis. When business users come to them with simple tests, those are scoffed at and scenarios of deeply complex Albert Einstein–type tests are provided. This is the wrong thing to do in early stages of the program.

For the first little while, when your program is in its infancy, your goal should be to win over fans. You want to achieve mindset shifts. The best way to accomplish this is to accept and run the first few simple tests that originated from the minds of your Marketers/Designer/Internal Company decision makers. The wonderful result will be that they will truly get involved in testing because it is their own ideas, and win or lose you have shown them the power of the tool or methodology.

Warning: There is a catch-22 that comes into play with this strategy: you have to do small simple tests to shift mindsets and gain traction, but small tests and small changes will have small results. When testing, if you want to win big, you have to bet big (by making radical changes or trying different or revolutionary ideas). In other words, if you pay peanuts, you'll get monkeys.

Your goal should always be to have the mindset shift proceed toward the direction of doing complicated "big" tests, ones that put a lot bigger things on the line than just playing with the hero image on the home page. In the early stages of your testing program, test the ideas of your users, no matter how small or big, but drive your program to doing more-complex and fundamental tests over time.

Create a Fun Environment

We often forget that this is supposed to be fun. What other situations can you think of where you can "play" with your customers, and they never find out? That is awesome. Testing should be enjoyable and it should stretch our brains.

As mentioned earlier, one simple way to get everyone (IT, marketing, stakeholders, others) involved in the test is to bet on the outcome (only where betting is legal). Everyone loves betting and because these might be their tests, they might like the odds of winning (we don't suffer from a lack of self confidence!). Stay with something small, one dollar for every prediction of the success metric or which version of the test will win.

The impact of this simple recommendation is that throughout the test duration, people will keep checking which version is winning, thus learning complex measurements. After the test winner is declared, you can bet the "losers" will want to pore over every success metric and its definition and computation until they realize that they really did lose, but they just learned so much more than you could have taught them in any other way.

Thursday: Focus on Evangelism and Expertise

The number one recommendation is that you need two key people in any successful program: a testing evangelist and a testing expert.

Most people don't yet get the testing religion. To convert them, you will need an evangelist. Not just someone who "gets it," but someone who through their communication skills, pure love, business understanding, and position can go out there and preach and articulate the value proposition. If this person does not know what *r squared* is, that is okay.

To run your program, you need a testing expert—someone who is steeped in metrics, data, and complex computations. This person has enough business expertise to look at tests, provide good feedback, and even help generate great value-added new ideas (and push back politely on the non-value-added ones over time). This person should meet the *street smart*, *avid explorer*, and *comfortable in quantitative and qualitative worlds* criteria from the great analyst requirements in Chapter 4, "Critical Components of a Successful Web Analytics Strategy?"

This position is important because the testing world is still very young. Increasingly, even if the vendors try to convince you of how great their tool is over their competitors, the biggest challenge we all face is finding great ideas to test and measuring success accurately.

There are many good vendors (I have had a great experience with Offermatica and Google Web Optimizer for multivariate testing). Differences between tools will not be your limitation for quite some time (testing ideas, culture, program sophistication, and implementation will be). So if you like your brother's friend who works at SiteSpect, hire that person. But don't forget your expert.

Friday: Implement the Two Key Ingredients for Every Testing Program

You have learned the importance of having a testing strategy in your company and you have also learned how to go about building a successful analytics program.

Today you will learn the critical importance of implementing two important ingredients that will ensure the long-term success of your testing program. Each ingredient—process and requirements gathering—might take more than a day to implement in your company, depending on your circumstances. It is important nonetheless to understand their importance and ensure that you work toward the goal of implementing both.

Process

Testing is a little bit art, but it is mostly science. For your company to have a sustainable and scalable testing program, it is important to have a well-defined and clear testing process. A good process helps specify the following:

- Steps needed end to end to run a test
- Individual roles that will need to be staffed
- Specific responsibilities for each role in the process
- Clear structure for making decisions

Figure 10.7 illustrates what an end-to-end testing process could be.

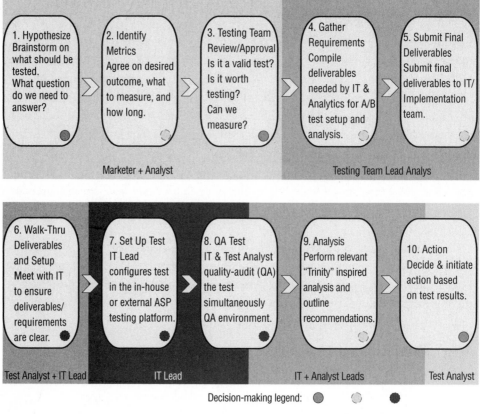

Figure 10.7 Robust testing process: steps, roles, and responsibilities

For your company and its environment, you'll create a process and decision-making structure that is unique to you. Here are important considerations that are optimal to nail down:

- You'll surely notice that although these are "bubbles" on a PowerPoint slide, they are extremely detailed about the steps in the process. I can't stress that enough. Especially if you are looking to scale up the testing environment in your company, it is extremely important to get this part right—as you conduct more tests, you will involve a lot more people and moving parts. If you don't take the time to document the process and help each person understand what needs to happen, you will increase the chances of failure.

- Roles will change depending on what part of the process you are in. Notice that each bubble has a separate but clearly identified decision maker (marketer, analyst, IT lead). Figure 10.7 identifies the best person to pull the trigger to stop the process form moving forward at each step of the process to ensure optimal quality.

- Roles and people in each stage will overlap, and it is important to recognize that. This is a team effort overall, but highlighting the overlap ensures that each person in the team knows exactly where they will be required to contribute, what is happening in that stage, and who the final decision maker is.

> **Note:** The process does not end with launch. This is a common flaw in many processes that I have seen. They either end with launch or they end with analysis. The process in Figure 10.7 explicitly calls for analysis but it also calls for the test analyst to provide recommendations. Then in the last stage it also demands that a business decision be made on the recommendations and that action be taken. It is important to highlight this and to make clear who is responsible for making the decision (the marketer, in this example).

NOTE

Most of us dread the word *process* because it has come to represent pain and very little gain in return. But it does not have to be that way. A well-defined process can be a simple PowerPoint slide that very simply represents a schematic of the process. Even such a simple schematic can make the difference between confusion and missteps to scaling and sanity. You can also choose to start simple and then optimize the process, or add more detail as you learn over time.

Requirements Gathering

More than any other part of Figure 10.7, the one that will make a critical difference is the framework to move from steps 1 through 4. The output of these stages defines everything else that is going to happen in the test cycle.

For your company, you should create a Testing Requirements Document, which will contain these important elements (usually filled out by the marketer or test requestor, with others contributing as needed):

- Hypothesis statement
  - What is the business problem or challenge this is solving for?
  - What is the hypothesis?
- Business case
  - This is a brief statement of why this test should be done. It should include thoughts on the effects expected on the business or website as a result of the preceding problem being solved. This forces the marketer or requestor to think through the test request, and in an environment where there is always more work to be done than resources available to do it, the statement will help in prioritization.
- Test audience
  - Who is going to be in the test? What percent of traffic? What groups of people who come from Google? What behavior on the site will trigger the

test? Clearly articulating the test audience is critical because this will help you evaluate your options about what to test (depending on your definition of who you want to test against). Remember, the more nuanced you become in your understanding of the test audience, the higher likelihood that you will find actionable insights and in turn produce results that affect the bottom line.

- Test details
    - Description and details of each test group (A/B/C, or for MVT the zones and elements).
    - Details on the website pages and content that will be affected.
    - Depth and breadth of the test that might require other integration points (back end or analytics).
    - If available now, links to creatives, content, images, offer details, or anything that will help the analyst evaluate the test request with richer context and figure out all data required to measure success.
- Success measures (done by the analyst and marketer)
    - What are the key metrics that will indicate success?
    - What are the current numbers for those metrics?
    - What are the goals for this test for each metric? By how much should the metrics improve for us to declare victory?
- Outcome actions
    - What changes will be implemented if the test is a success?
    - Who needs to be notified?
    - What might be other next steps based on test findings?

For each test plan, you should have this work happen up front to ensure success. Your requirements document will become the shared vision document that the entire team (which might be composed of people in different geographical areas) can refer to during creation and execution of the test (along with the process document). Everyone stays on the same page, literally, and you have much higher chances of scaling and success.

You'll use your discretion about how deep you want to get for each test. For some, the goal might be to just play for a couple of hours and throw it away. Most, though, will be much more thought out and the effort you put in up front will pay off big during the test. Having a clearly articulated document such as the one I have suggested will help create institutional history that will be extremely valuable in the long run.

Month 6: Three Secrets Behind Making Web Analytics Actionable

There was a wonderful catch phrase in the early '90s: D2I, or data to information. It stressed that data itself was not very valuable unless it was converted into information. It represented the very wise thought that we should not simply stop at the implementation of analytics tools (any analytics tools) but strive to put extra effort into converting that data into information that is useful for decision making.

Since that time, the challenge of converting data has become exponentially more complex because we have so much more data and business online or offline has become a lot more complex as well.

Although we have gotten better over time at trying to capture an increasing amount of data and processing it into information, it has been observed that there is a much greater challenge to deal with: inducing decision makers to take action on the information (insights) being provided from the data.

Week 1: Leveraging Benchmarks and Goals in Driving Action

Moving the mountain of actionability is a complex challenge that encompasses people, mindsets, roles, responsibilities, existing processes, social environments, vested interests, internal politics, and much more. All those variables, which you are already aware of, should give you a glimpse into how hard it is to motivate organizations to take action. On a scale of 1 to 10 (with 10 being the maximum challenge), collecting data is a 3.5, converting data into insights is a 7, and getting your boss and your boss's boss and your boss's boss's boss to take action is an 18.5. That about sums it up.

You will spend the first week underscoring how you can leverage benchmarks and goals to drive action in your organization (this can apply to your web analytics program or any other analytics program).

Monday and Tuesday: Understand the Importance of Benchmarks and Setting Goals

According to Wikipedia, "*Benchmarking* (also *best practice benchmarking* or *process benchmarking*) is a process used in management and particularly strategic management, in which organizations evaluate various aspects of their processes in relation to best practice, usually within their own sector. This then allows organizations to develop plans on how to adopt such best practice, usually with the aim of increasing some aspect of performance."

The power of benchmarking is that it allows you to look at your performance from a different perspective, not your own. You can consider the performance of your metrics within this other context that helps you understand how you are doing and enables you to take actions.

But perhaps the most amazing thing about benchmarking is that suddenly it is not you (or your boss or your tool) making a judgment on the data. You are able to present data in the context of a neutral party, which often is conducive to move decision makers from questioning you or poking holes in your analysis to looking at the data and making decisions (because it is not about the messenger anymore, it is about the message).

One of the primary keys to driving action is context (for example, via use of relevant benchmarks). When you present a table or a graph or a bulleted insight in an email without putting the information in context, it is less likely to induce action. The following is an example of website performance in December 2006:

- Number of visits: 173,539
- Number of unique visitors: 89,559
- Average time on site: 130 seconds
- Page views per visitor: 3.1

These are standard metrics that do tell us something but they don't induce action because the context is missing. What do we compare these numbers to? Are they good or bad? What action can I take?

Consider the golden rule of actionability: Never present metrics without context—some context, any context.

You can simply segment the data at a top-line level to provide that context. Here is how it would look:

- Number of visits:
  - All traffic: 173,539
  - PPC campaigns: 77,140 (44 percent! Really high.)
- Number of unique visitors:
  - All traffic: 89,559
  - PPC campaigns: 39,695 (roughly the same repeat visitors)
- Average time on site:
  - All traffic: 130 seconds
  - PPC campaigns: 180 seconds (nice!)
- Page views per visitor:
  - All traffic: 3.1
  - PPC campaigns: 4.1 (really nice!)

You can see how at the end of this second effort, you would have informed decision makers a bit better with just a little more context.

Another method is to apply trends to the numbers that would give you more context. Here is how that would look:

- Number of visits:
  - All traffic: Nov: 33,360 Dec: 173,539
  - PPC campaigns: Nov: 14,323 Dec: 77,140
- Number of unique visitors:
  - All traffic: Nov: 19,000 Dec: 89,559
  - PPC campaigns: Nov: 8,493 Dec: 39,695

- Average time on site:
  - All traffic: Nov: 131 seconds Dec: 130 seconds
  - PPC campaigns: Nov: 178 seconds Dec: 180 seconds
- Page views per visitor:
  - All traffic: Nov: 3.0 Dec: 3.1
  - PPC campaigns: Nov: 3.9 Dec: 4.1

Notice that with each step, we are getting more context in which we can think. At the end of this little table while you have a lot more data you also have a lot more insights that you can pick out right away and maybe one that you could take action on.

Hopefully, you'll see that providing even a little bit of context helps move us further along the journey of driving action. Two of the most powerful ways to provide context that drive action are benchmarks and goals.

Benchmarking is usually done by using external benchmarks (indicating how others are doing for the same metric), but it does not have to be. You can also use internal benchmarks. What is important is that you use the power of benchmarking to induce action in your companies.

Wednesday: Leverage External Benchmarking

If you can find benchmarks for metrics that you are using in your company, consider that a gift. The reason external benchmarks are so powerful is that you are comparing yourself to others in the industry and usually a mostly neutral authority is presenting the benchmarks (this facet goes over great with senior management). Let's go over some examples of how you can leverage external benchmarks.

An example of a great external benchmark you can use is the American Customer Satisfaction Index (ACSI). The ACSI is sponsored by the University of Michigan and measures most of the US economy. It presents its scores and ratings online at www.theacsi.org for almost all American industries.

Let's say that you, dellcompetitor.net, are a new company in the great PC business and you have been measuring customer satisfaction on your website for some time now and you are really happy with your scores (Figure 11.1).

Should you be happy? Well, you can actually go to www.theacsi.org and get scores for not just Dell but also other major computer makers and judge your own performance against their trends (Figure 11.2).

By comparing your performance against that of a competitor, it quickly becomes apparent that your performance is okay over the last year but there is a wide gap between your performance and that of Dell. If before you were not able to get your company to focus on customers and take action, you can rest assured that your boss will take action now. There is something almost amazing about comparing yourself to your competitors and looking bad and wanting to go out and do something about it. Leverage this wonderful psychological gift.

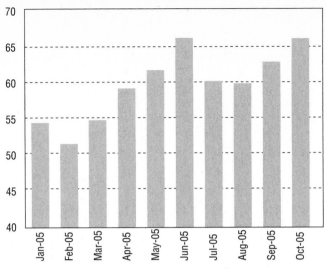

Figure 11.1 Customer satisfaction trend: `dellcompetitor.net`

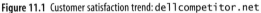

The American Customer Satisfaction Index™

Scores By Company

Dell Inc.

	Base-line	94	95	96	97	98	99	00	01	02	03	04	05	06	Previous Year % Change	First Year % Change
Apple Computer, Inc.	77	N/A	75	76	70	69	72	75	73	73	77	81	81	83	2.5	7.8
Dell Inc.	NM	N/A	NM	NM	72	74	76	80	78	76	78	79	74	78	5.4	8.3
Personal Computers	**78**	**N/A**	**75**	**73**	**70**	**71**	**72**	**74**	**71**	**71**	**72**	**74**	**74**	**77**	**4.1**	**-1.3**
All Others	NM	N/A	70	73	72	69	69	68	67	70	69	71	74	77	4.1	10.0
Hewlett -Packard Company --HP	78	N/A	80	77	75	72	74	74	73	71	70	71	73	75	2.7	-3.8
Gateway, Inc.	NM	N/A	NM	NM	NM	76	76	78	73	72	69	74	72	73	1.4	-3.9
Hewlett -Packard Company --Compaq	78	N/A	77	74	67	72	71	71	69	68	68	69	67	72	7.5	-7.7
International Business Machines Corporation	78	N/A	78	74	71	74	73	75	71	NM	NM	NM	NM	NM	N/A	N/A
Packard Bell NEC, Inc.	NM	N/A	NM	71	66	67	66	NM	NM	NM	NM	NM	NM	NM	N/A	N/A

Figure 11.2 ACSI customer satisfaction trends: personal computers

It is advisable for you to put enough thought into ensuring that your metric can be compared directly against the benchmark (that is, that you are comparing apples to apples). But in general, I am a fan of taking whatever you can get from the outside and getting as close as you can to apple-to-apple measurements. If your methodology is slightly different, you can observe the trends of the numbers over time and benchmark against the trend and not absolute changes. It is certainly not a pure approach, as many in our industry would rightly say, but it can still be incredibly powerful, especially if trended over time, in moving your organization in the right direction to take actions.

Sometimes, though, pure benchmarks such as the ACSI might not be available—for example, in our web analytics (clickstream) space. Each existing web analytics tool measures things differently, and there are so many different types of businesses. We are always struggling with understanding our web analytics metrics performance because usually we are measuring just in our silo. Not having the benefit of an external benchmark means that it is a bit harder to understand performance and drive action.

One excellent option for you is to compare your web analytics metrics against the Fireclick Index (`http://snipurl.com/fireclick`). Fireclick provides web analytics solutions (among other things) and collects data from all its customers. It has created a publicly available index providing benchmarks for key web analytics metrics (Figures 11.3 and 11.4).

Top Line Growth

Business Metrics	This Week	Last Week	% Change
Conversion Rate: Global	2.00%	2.20%	-9% ▼
Conversion Rate: First Time Visitors	2.10%	2.30%	-9% ▼
Conversion Rate: Repeat Visitors	1.90%	2.20%	-14% ▼
Cart Abandonment Rate	69.90%	65.80%	6% ▲

Figure 11.3 Fireclick Index: business metrics

Site Metrics	This Week	Last Week	% Change
Average Session Length (pages)	7.70	7.00	10% ▲
Average Session Duration (min)	3.70	3.50	6% ▲
Average Page Display Time (s)	3.60	3.60	0%
Average Page Read Time (s)	21.30	21.80	-2% ▼
Average Connection Speed (Kbps)	180.50	184.40	-2% ▼

Figure 11.4 Fireclick Index: site metrics

With access to these weekly, monthly, and yearly trends, you can compare your web analytics performance against the benchmark. Your web analytics tool might not be Fireclick and you might measure unique visitors differently. But over time if you hold those two inconsistencies as constant, the trend of deltas between your performance and the Fireclick index can be extremely helpful and actionable.

The Fireclick Index is also available by vertical industries (Figure 11.5), which will get you even closer in terms of your ability to do a Washington-apples-to-Fuji-apples comparison.

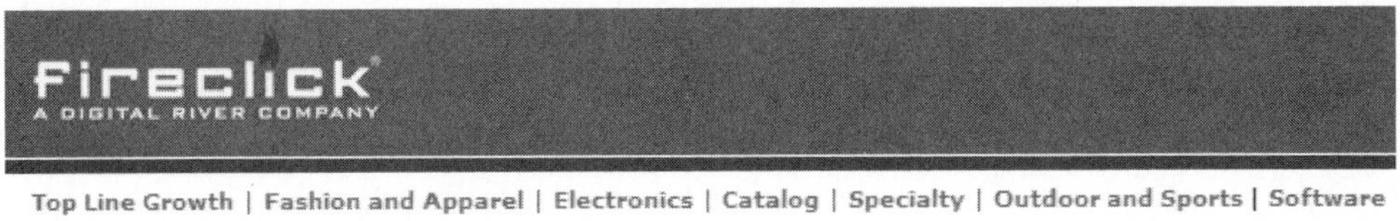

Top Line Growth | Fashion and Apparel | Electronics | Catalog | Specialty | Outdoor and Sports | Software

Figure 11.5 Fireclick Index: industry-specific metrics

To summarize, external benchmarks are perhaps the most powerful out there when it comes to moving from insights to action. They can be a powerful neutral authority in convincing management that the measurement of your website's performance is not based on your own personal opinion but on an external, trusted benchmark.

Thursday: Leverage Internal Benchmarking

If your business is truly unique or you are not able to find any kind of external benchmarks that you can trust, look inward and create benchmarks internally within your company, using your own data. It is surprising that we don't do this more often. Again the goal here is to give more context to the performance of your key metrics in a way that helps you understand the performance better and drives action. Let's look at some methods of benchmarking internally.

Table 11.1 shows how you can easily create an internal benchmark by showing performance for eight days instead of seven.

▶ **Table 11.1** Internal benchmarking: measuring eight days vs. seven

Date	Day of Week	Total Visitors	Unique Visitors	Orders	Units	Units/Order
8/25/04	Wednesday	18,988	17,017	165	199	1.21
8/24/04	Tuesday	19,091	17,148	160	249	1.56
8/23/04	Monday	19,157	17,104	151	183	1.21
8/22/04	Sunday	9,181	8,403	74	113	1.53
8/21/04	Saturday	9,416	8,561	71	83	1.17
8/20/04	Friday	15,605	14,129	128	157	1.23
8/19/04	Thursday	18,246	16,403	140	178	1.27
8/18/04	Wednesday	19,095	17,181	151	170	1.13
Total				1,040	1,332	

Most often we show seven-day trends, but they don't tell the full story. By comparing eight-day trends (Wednesday this week to Wednesday last week, for instance) we are able to have a quick benchmark that tells us how to think about our performance this week. For example it is not just important o know that on Wednesday you achieved higher results than Tuesday, but comparing this Wednesday to the same time period last week provides additional context around seasonality. This simple comparison starts the process of asking the much required "what happened" and "why it happened" discussions.

You can transpose this and imagine its application for 13-month trends so you can compare the same month year over year, or apply the data to the same quarter last year (as is extremely common on Wall Street).

Every web analytics tool out there should make this simple tweak to allow their data to become a smidgen more actionable.

To build on this idea, you can benchmark not only by using time as an element but also by using *contributing segments*, as shown in Figure 11.6.

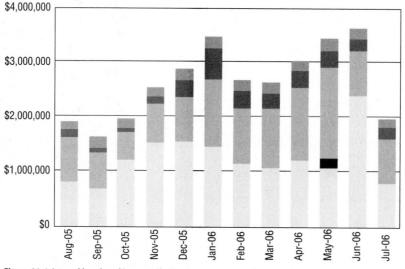

Figure 11.6 Internal benchmarking: contributing segments approach

Figure 11.6 shows the annual trend for revenue. Notice that each bar is segmented (and it does not matter whether the segments are types of products, campaign categories, buckets of customers, or something else). The trend by itself would be quite meaningless. But by using segmented trends, you can create a sense of internal benchmarking and understand over time which segments are performing better or worse (be they products or customers).

If you are lucky enough to work in a company that has many websites, it is even easier to create internal benchmarks. Just use data from your different websites. You can't independently judge the performance of each of your websites, because the data from each is a silo without enough context, but if you pool the data, you can get some nice magic going (Table 11.2).

▶ **Table 11.2** Internal benchmarking: intra-company approach

a) Search engine traffic as a percentage of total site traffic

Search Traffic	Jan 02	Feb 02	Mar 02	Apr 02	May 02	Jun 02	Avg
brand q.com		6.2%	4.8%	4.3%	6.8%	9.0%	5.8%
brand b.com	20.7%	12.1%	13.7%	13.4%	13.8%	14.5%	15.1%
brand a.com	1.9%	0.9%	0.9%	0.8%	1.7%	1.7%	1.3%

b) Google as a percentage of search engine traffic

Google	Jan 02	Feb 02	Mar 02	Apr 02	May 02	Jun 02	Avg
brand q.com		19.0%	25.4%	36.4%	35.5%	23.6%	28.9%
brand b.com	55.6%	57.8%	61.7%	61.3%	66.4%	66.6%	59.3%
brand a.com	11.5%	7.0%	8.4%	8.2%	9.1%	9.7%	9.0%

Suddenly questions become so much easier to answer. For example: Is brand b.com performing well, or is brand a.com? In a data silo, it would be hard for you to judge performance, even if you have trends over time. But now very quickly you can see that brand a.com is in trouble when it comes to search engines. As you compare performance against other internal sites (the second table in Table 11.2), it becomes apparent that the problem for brand a.com is Google (perhaps the Google spider is not indexing the site).

Another good idea for creating internal benchmarks is to use 3-month or 12-month averages on your graphs to create a benchmark against which you can index your performance.

The goal with internal benchmarks is to provide context of any kind from the data we already have. This context can provide insights into the current time period's performance that would allow you to drive action.

Friday: Encourage and Create Goals

Ask anyone whether setting goals is important and you will hear a chorus of "yes, of course!" There is probably not a single reader of this book who would disagree with the importance of setting goals either. Yet if asked for an honest raising of hands from those whose key business metrics have goals, most hands in the room would stay down. We all know that goals are important, yet so few of us actually create them.

If you want to induce action in your organization, you have to have goals. Pure and simple. Goals are critical to decision making for the following reasons:

- They are a great way to focus the organization. They clearly delineate what is important and everyone knows exactly where they are going.

- They promote teamwork and a culture of accountability.

- Goals that have been approved by senior management are great at ensuring that you can find the right funding and staffing to succeed (or at least have a fair shot at asking for resources). With no goals, you don't even know where to start.

- Goals are a tie-breaker for critical forks in the road and even speed up decision making. ("Well, that path does not line up with our goal so we can't go down that one.")

- They provide the perfect way to measure performance (both of the business and of employees at annual review time).

Figure 11.7 shows an example of a trend that we will commonly see reported. It can be conversion rate or it can be one of the many other rates in our portfolio.

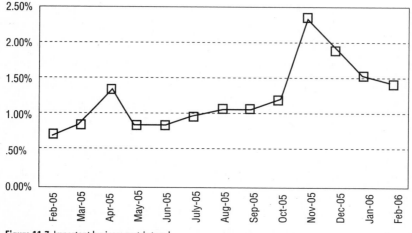

Figure 11.7 Important business metric trend

It looks like you are making great progress on this metric. In general, the trend is up over the last 13 months. But that is a long time, and during that time your business grew and your staff grew. So is this good enough?

Overlaying the goal for this metric over the actual trend transforms its ability to communicate to you and drive action (Figure 11.8). It looks like the goal for the metric was to gradually improve from 1.2 percent to 1.9 percent over 13 months (rather reasonable). For the most part, the actual numbers fell far behind the goals for that time period.

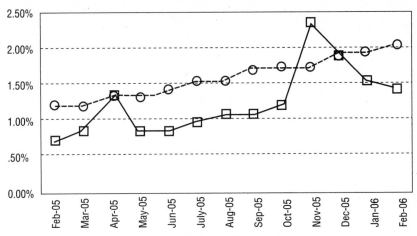

Figure 11.8 Important business metric trend with clearly articulated goal

If you had this graph for the six months (May–Oct) when the trend consistently lagged behind the goals, would you have taken action faster? Perhaps.

Maybe the most important reason to encourage setting goals is that the process will make you think. What do I mean by that?

Let's say that your job is to improve the trend in Figure 11.7 and let's call the metric conversion rate.

The first thing to understand is that conversion rate = orders / unique visitors. So to improve conversion rate, you will have to improve the number of orders you take on the site or you will have to get more unique visitors.

To *increase unique visitors* (hopefully qualified), you might ask these questions:

- Where do our visitors come from?
- Which ones are most qualified? What is our site and segmented bounce rate?
- What is our acquisition strategy for traffic? PPC, SEO, affiliates, direct marketing? What else?
- What is the effectiveness of our acquisition strategy for the last couple of years? What else is new that we can try?
- What are our competitors doing that we can learn from?
- What kinds of skills do we have in our team to support improvements in traffic to our website?

- Can we leverage our ecosystem websites or this new user-generated content (UGC) or blog websites?

  To *increase the orders* on the website, you might ask these questions:

- What is the abandonment rate on our website?

- What are the typical page views per visitor or time on site?

- What is the most influential content on the site? How do we know what convinced people to buy?

- Do we have an effective merchandising strategy? What do people like buying?

- Do we have the budget to offer discounts on the site?

- Do we know why people come to the site? How come less than 2 percent end up buying?

- Why do people bail in the ordering process? Do we have the voice of the customer?

- How is our behavior targeting strategy working? We don't have one, you say? Do we need to? What's the repeat visits rate on our website?

- Can we do experimentation and testing? What are the top pages that we can optimize to improve orders?

- What are sales trends for the same products in stores or on our phone channel?

- What truly innovative things can we do to influence the purchase decision?

Take a pause and imagine this. Simply to improve a seemingly "dumb" metric such as conversion rate, you have to ask all these questions, find all these answers, explore data that you have and lots that you might not have, and put your senior executives on the spot to make some tough calls.

How much harder and time-consuming will it be if you have to do this for your top five key business metrics?

Go into goal setting knowing that it is going to be an incredible amount of work. But in the end you will have all the benefits outlined earlier and you will have a clear shot at a competitive advantage.

One final tip on setting goals specifically for the Web: There is a tendency to set five-year goals for the Web. That is usually suboptimal because we can't even look forward two years—things change so fast. So here is a best practice:

- Have real, concrete six-month goals.

- Have goals, with some stretch built in, 12 months out that you can commit to.

- Set goals for 24 months out if you have to, but be explicit that they are, for the most part, conjecture.

This will ensure that you have goals that are built on a solid foundation and remain relevant as you try to achieve them. It will also mean that they will accomplish their purpose of being a performance indicator and a catalyst for driving action.

Week 2: Creating High Impact Executive Dashboards

We live in a world that is overflowing with data (our world of web analytics especially). The fundamental pace of business is accelerating bit by bit each day, our competition is coming from new areas, and there is a desire to have more accountability from our executives and businesses to deliver results. In such an environment, dashboards empower a rapid understanding of business performance by tracking the critical business data in an easy-to-understand manner. Effective dashboards can be a powerful communication medium and greatly accretive to driving actions.

Yet studies indicate that more than 75 percent of marketers are dissatisfied with their ability to measure the effectiveness of either short-term or long-term performance and have a hard time making data-driven decisions. The core problem behind this dissatisfaction is not that marketers don't have enough data (that is often a minor issue). The core problem is the inability to identify what the most critical metrics are and to communicate performance for those metrics in a way that induces action.

Dashboards can vary by industries, by business functions, by altitude (organization or decision maker level) and by the sophistication of available skills and tools. This section covers the basic, and not so basic, rules that you can follow while creating your own dashboards. These rules will enable you to create effective dashboards that are geared toward driving actions.

Monday: Provide Context—Benchmark, Segment, and Trend

You will spend the first day of this week focused on applying the lessons from the prior week's hard work (hence I have grouped a big bunch of work for you here all in one day!). All three of today's recommendations help in driving action and are critical first things to cover when creating effective dashboards.

Use Benchmarks

Never report a metric all by itself. Rule number one of great dashboards is that there is no metric on a dashboard that exists without context. There are many ways you can show context. You can use benchmarks (internal or external), goals, or even prior performance to give some kind of context. But without context, it is impossible for a metric to provide any value on the dashboard, even if it is the most important metric for your business.

Always Segment

The goal in a dashboard is to communicate not just the performance of one metric but also to improve actionability. Segmentation is a key tactic that makes it easy to understand what might be causing a great performance or a bad one.

Figure 11.9 shows a dashboard element that embodies the first two basic rules (have goals and apply segmentation). The metric, Recommendation Index, has a clear goal that is highlighted prominently. It also shows the performance of four key customer segments for a rapid understanding of where opportunities for focus and improvement lie.

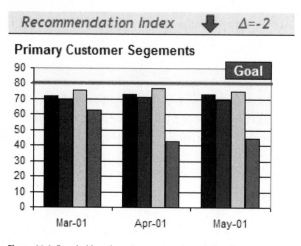

Figure 11.9 Four dashboard metrics segmented, trended, and measured against the goal

Trending Rocks

Absolute a-given-point-in-time numbers segmented against goals are good. If you segment them, they are even better. But if you trend them over time, it can really move your dashboard toward actionability (just as an example, imagine all the seasonality that comes to the fore). In Figure 11.9, in each of the months it is clear that the fourth segment is doing worse when it comes to performance against goals. But it is the trend that highlights that the problem is getting worse over time and perhaps, now, is in desperate need of attention.

In Figure 11.10 you see a simple trend of visitors to the website. It is insightful to see a long-term trend and summarize performance of the site. Figure 11.10 also merges the preceding rule on segmentation. By segmenting this trend for your four big sources of traffic, you can observe that your strategy of investing in email marketing is having its intended effect of increasing traffic (for example, in August).

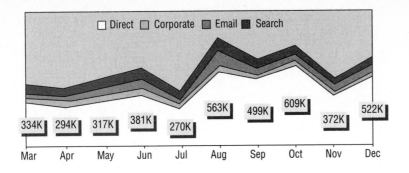

Figure 11.10 Dashboard metrics: segmented trends over time illustrating performance

Trends are a lot more effective than absolute numbers. They provide a big picture and help highlight consistent misses or problems.

Tuesday: Isolate Your Critical Few Metrics

There is such a thing as too many metrics (Figure 11.11).

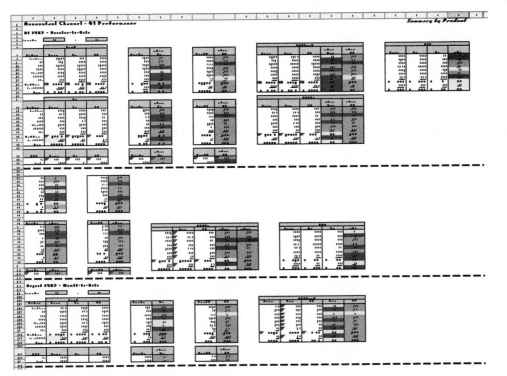

Figure 11.11 Example of a nonactionable dashboard

It should be obvious by looking at this illustration, Figure 11.11, that this is not an effective dashboard. It tracks too many metrics, it attempts to segment some and color-code performance, but in the end it is nearly impossible to distill a cogent understanding of what happened and what action should be taken now.

I advise you to spend lots of time trying to understand exactly what critical few metrics drive the business. As someone inarticulately put it, *"What do we care about if the crap hits the fan?"* What are your bottom-line business critical few? Your answer to that question will make or break your dashboard's ability to empower decision making.

As a general rule of thumb, your dashboard should contain fewer than 10 metrics. Remember that you will need a goal for each of these metrics and you are going to segment most, if not all, of them (and represent the goals and segments on your dashboard). By the time you are finished with that, you might not have space left for anything else.

Wednesday: Don't Stop at Metrics—Include Insights

No dashboard should exist without including a cogent set of insights (in words) that summarize performance and recommend action. Most often dashboards are a collection of numbers and dials and graphs, but they leave it to the awareness and intelligence of the reader to infer what all that data might indicate. Perhaps more sadly, what such insight-free dashboards are missing is the benefit of all the analysis that went into creating them. Even if they are segmented and trended, you have only summary-level data for critical metrics in the dashboard. Having a section for insights allows the intelligence from the analyst to bubble up to the highest level.

Figure 11.12 shows a dashboard from the White House website. Notice that the graphs are quite small, yet sort of legible. Two of the graphs clearly indicate that the data was segmented. Most important, the section in the middle includes a brief written summary of the trends.

You can go one further and ensure that you have a section, way up on top, in the dashboard that shares your insights so that the people looking at the dashboard (the ones with no context of your business) can understand it better. Here are sections you should consider adding to your dashboard:

- Performance summary: What was up, what was down, where is the big gap? This can be just one line.

- Insights summary: What were some of the causes of the hits and misses? What were the underlying shifts in the business? What is the root cause? This can be one or two lines.

- Recommended actions: What should we do next? How do we reverse the decline? What is the new opportunity on the horizon? What's a threat? Based on all the data, what are the top three things to fix? This should be a top-five list.

	Personal Consumption Expenditures	Previous	Current
CHART: Personal Consumption Expenditures	In December 2005, real personal consumption expenditures increased 0.9 percent at a seasonally adjusted monthly rate.	+0.9 November 2005 (% change)	+0.9 December 2005 (% change)
	Provided by Bureau of Economic Analysis as of January 30, 2006.		
CHART: National Expenditures for R&D	National Expenditures for R&D by Performing Sector National Expenditures for R&D Preliminary estimates of R&D expenditures for 2002 indicate a slight increase over 2001.	Previous $274.2 2001 (billions of dollars)	Current $276.4 2002 (preliminary) (billions of dollars)
	Provided by National Science Foundation/SRS as of August 2005.		
CHART: Federal R&D Obligations	Federal Obligations for Research and Development and R&D Plant Federal Obligations for R&D Federal obligations for research and development and R&D plant are expected to increase by an estimated 4.8 percent (to $110.2 billion) in fiscal year 2005.	Previous $106.5 2004 (preliminary) (billions of dollars)	Current $110.2 2005 (preliminary) (billions of dollars)
	Provided by National Science Foundation/SRS as of July 2006.		

Figure 11.12 Example dashboard with trends and insights

Do not create dashboards without insights and recommended actions. These are the only way to push accountability down the chain, to not just send numbers and reports and only send up analysis. It is the only way to ensure that senior leaders will be able to take action sooner and with fewer questions.

Thursday: Limit Your Dashboard to a Single Page

It might not be the most obvious basic rule, but if your dashboard does not fit on one page, you have a report, not a dashboard. Additional layers of this rule are as follows:

- Page Size = A4
- Print margin = minimum of 0.75 inch (all sides)
- Font size = minimum of 10 (for metrics), minimum of 12 (for goals/benchmarks)

That should not leave a lot of room for doubt.

This rule is important because it encourages rigorous thought to be applied in selecting the metric. It should act as a natural barrier to cramming in too much information, make data presentation easier, make the dashboard more understandable (hence more likely to promote action), and make it portable (don't underestimate the power of being able to carry a piece of paper around with 100 percent of your business performance on it).

It might seem like an easy-enough rule to follow, but the fact that this is a task for a whole day should reflect how hard it is to pull this off. Pull out any dashboard that you have handy for your company and try to apply this rule. You'll see instantly how hard this is. But it is also absolutely critical if you are to communicate effectively and drive action.

Friday: Know That Appearance Matters

There is no politically correct way of saying this except that appearance matters. Dashboards must be pretty for them to be used as effective communication vehicles.

Here is the first definition of *pretty* from *Merriam-Webster's Collegiate Dictionary*: artful, clever.

Creating dashboards that are artful and clever enables the information presented to be understood more clearly, which will lead to faster decisions.

A standard dashboard section might look like Figure 11.13. It is fairly clean, it communicates sort of okay, and presents metrics and numbers in an easy-to-understand 2 × 2 matrix. Overall, not bad.

Figure 11.14 shows similar data but in a much different format. You can quickly see how Figure 11.13 might communicate much more effectively than Figure 11.12. There are enhancements, including having the bubble size for each metric communicate importance. It is extremely clear what needs most attention; the numbers are there almost as an afterthought. With Figure 11.13, you have to think a lot less and explain a lot less.

The visual appeal of the dashboard matters a great deal more than we realize. Your call to action is to produce pretty stuff!

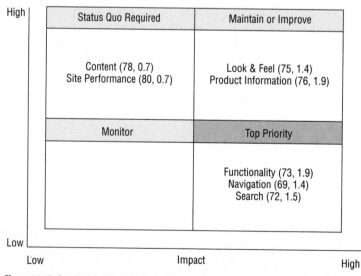

Figure 11.13 Standard dashboard element

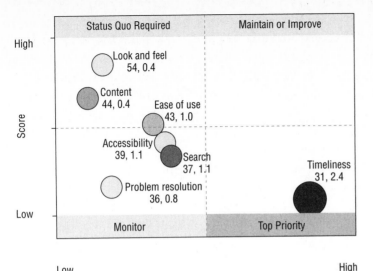

Figure 11.14 "Pretty" dashboard element

Week 3: Using Best Practices for Creating Effective Dashboard Programs

Creating a dashboard that is effective is an important foundational element of inducing action based on your data. The prior section covered specific rules that should be applied in the process of creating a dashboard. This section covers best practices that should be followed if you are to create a successful actionable *program* around dashboards. These best practices are one level above the tactical rules and they are critical in ensuring that your dashboards are actually used and live for a long time rather than being rituals you simply go through every week or month.

Monday: Create Trinity Metrics That Have a Clear Line of Sight

In several places in this book, I have covered the importance of having a Trinity mindset. Applying that mindset is especially critical when it comes to creating actionable dashboards. It does not have to be complicated, but you should deliberately determine whether you have all three elements of the Trinity represented in your dashboard to ensure that you are showing the complete picture.

It is equally important to have a clear line of sight to business goals. Having this line of sight can be the difference between your email about the dashboard being opened and it going directly into the Delete folder after month one.

Apply the Trinity Approach

In web analytics, we typically err toward including lots and lots of clickstream data in our dashboards. They are typically light on outcome metrics (revenue, problem resolution, and so forth) and really light on customer experience metrics.

Senior management often can't connect to the clickstream metrics because the metrics often don't mean much and for your site probably don't change that often either. So the average time on the site probably does not change much at all no matter what you do, and the same thing can be said about page views or others "key" clickstream metrics.

Management can connect to outcomes (especially those that affect the bottom line). Many dashboards are starting to include these. But the ones that management will connect with the most are metrics related to customers, such as improvements in customer satisfaction or task completion rates or percent of people recommending the website. The wonderful thing is that all of these metrics measure strategic elements that will yield results over the long term.

When you create your dashboard, ensure that you are covering all the elements of the Trinity so that your dashboards balance the short-term and the long-term metrics and are able to connect with senior management.

Table 11.3 shows metrics that could bubble up to form a Trinity-inspired dashboard. These metrics also show the value of your website to the company ecosystem very effectively.

▶ **Table 11.3** Trinity-inspired dashboard elements

"Trinity" Element	Metric	Rationale for Inclusion
Behavior	Visits	Shows overall site traffic (online sessions)
	Unique Visitors	Shows unique visitors to the website
	Return Visitors	Helps keep track of visitor retention/engagement
	New Visitors	Tracks the key metric of attracting new prospects to the website
	Avg. Time on Site, Purchasers	Measures how long it takes to complete purchase process online
	Search Traffic (External)	Traffic from search engines
	Internal Search Usage	Shows internal search engine usage
Experience	Customer Satisfaction	Overall customer satisfaction with the site
	Likelihood to Recommend Website	Computes the likelihood that customers recommend our website
	Overall Task Completion	% of website visitors that were able to successfully complete their tasks
Outcomes	Revenue	Most important metric showing finance results
	Visits to Purchase	Related to convince to buy and site efficiency
	AOS	Can identify changes in either customer or available product mix
	Conversion	The critical measurement of how well the website is performing
	Direct Traffic	Measurement of the site efficiency not related to any marketing programs
	Campaign Traffic	Measurement of efficiency of marketing programs
	Checkout Abandonment	Number of visitors who bailed during the checkout process

Maintain a Clear Line of Sight

Often after a quick scan of our dashboard, a reader will not clearly understand a metric's effect on the company's bottom line. The perfect antidote to this is to apply a test that will check how a change in a metric will improve the company's bottom line. What's the line of sight?

It does not matter whether you are running an e-commerce website or a support website. All the metrics on a dashboard should have a clear *line of sight* to the strategic business objectives. This will ensure that the dashboard will be embedded into the way of life of the company.

The ultimate goal for your company, if public, is to deliver shareholder value. Shareholder value is measured by the stock price, your company revenue and earnings, and growth. Your CEO probably has key business objectives for the year that will deliver against all of these shareholder metrics. Here is an exercise that you can do: take each of the critical few metrics from your dashboard (remember, you just have 10) and map them to the CEO's objectives for the year.

If you are able to map page views per visitor all the way up to a CEO objective, you have a clear line of sight. If you can't, it is not a good metric.

Going through the line of sight exercise will help you understand whether you are working on things that are important to the company and whether you'll be able to get the kind of exposure you need to take action if you need to. It also means that if you are able to improve these metrics, you will be a superstar because it will be easy to see how you have added value by improving the CEO's business objectives.

Tuesday: Create Relevant Dashboards

Having made it so far in this chapter, and this week, I am sure you feel that dashboards are these tablets of stone that have to be carefully chiseled with important metrics and then worshiped. Quite the contrary. Most dashboards become irrelevant quickly, especially on the Web, because business does move at the speed of light (whether you are a Fortune 100 company or a small or medium business). Actionable dashboards have structures and processes built in to ensure that they remain timely and relevant, as you'll see here.

Short Lag Time

Dashboard metrics should have a short time lag. You should be able to collect them, process them, and report in the required time frame. You can imagine how reporting for January performance in the first week of March might be rather suboptimal when it comes to taking action. This will certainly mean that you will have to make tough choices in selecting your metrics and even abandon some that might not meet the short time lag rule. You can take those metrics, if they are still critical, and add them to a separate addendum that gets presented every quarter or every two months. This should keep your dashboard clean, focused, and actionable.

The short lag time rule also applies in a slightly different perspective as well. Metrics you choose for your dashboard should be able to provide a performance signal in the measured time period. For example, if a metric changes only every three months, it is perhaps suboptimal for a weekly dashboard. You can, akin to the computational lag time requirement, move it to a different addendum that gets presented less frequently.

Churn

Contrary to popular belief, dashboards are not carved in stone and hence are not permanent affairs. Dashboards, like humans, constantly evolve. That is exactly what your mindset for dashboards should be and it can be incredibly hard because organizations like stability, and senior management often likes predictability when it comes to measuring success. You can keep a few (25 percent) of your metrics stable for a long period of time, but you should plan on the dashboard having some level of *churn* all the time (metrics should be eliminated, almost deliberately, as soon as it is discovered that they are no longer relevant). If you have a dashboard that measures monthly performance, then over the course of a year you should have churned out at least 15 percent of the metrics because as the Web changes, at least a couple of your key metrics will change with it. Generally, you should not be churning more than 25 percent of your metrics in a year; more than that indicates that you didn't do an effective job identifying your key metrics.

Everything evolves. Businesses change, people come and go, high-level priorities evolve, we become smarter (or we become dumber but acquire people who are smarter than us!), our competitors think of new and clever things, and so forth. Why should our dashboards and metrics on dashboards stay the same over the span of a year?

Planning for the evolution and churn is mandatory. Ensuring that evolution is the only way to ensure that your dashboards don't become stale and end up as pieces of paper that don't add any value and consume way too much of your time.

Wednesday: One Metric, One Owner

This is the primary way that you will ensure that action will be taken. Ensure that every metric on the dashboard has a clearly identifiable person who is to be, in an ideal world, held responsible for all facets of delivering on the metric.

In your respective dashboards, and during presentations to senior management and stakeholders, ensure that the name of the owner is prominently displayed and that the team knows who the go-to person is (Table 11.4). Having clear ownership will ensure that your dashboard will continue to have the care and feeding it needs for its sub-element metrics. But it will also ensure that when you are in meetings and your CMO wants the answers, it is clear who will provide leadership when it comes to resolving each metric and taking action.

▶ **Table 11.4** Trinity-inspired dashboard elements—with owners

"Trinity" Element	Metric	Owner	Rationale for Inclusion
Behavior	Visits	Steven	Shows overall site traffic (online sessions)
	Unique Visitors	Steven	Shows unique visitors to the website
	Return Visitors		Helps keep track of visitor retention / engagement
	New Visitors		Tracks the key metric of attracting new prospects to the website
	Avg. Time on Site, Purchasers	Michell	Measures how long it takes to complete purchase process online
	Search Traffic (External)	Kevin	Traffic from search engines
	Internal Search Usage	Kevin	Shows internal search engine usage
Experience	Customer Satisfaction	Owen	Overall customer satisfaction with the site
	Likelihood to Recommend Website	Owen	Computes the likelihood that customers recommend our website
	Overall Task Completion	Owen	
Outcomes	Revenue	Victor	Most important metric showing finance results
	Visits to Purchase	John	Related to convince to buy and site efficiency
	AOS	Dave	Can identify changes in either customer or available product mix
	Conversion	Dave	The critical measurement of how well the website is performing
	Direct Traffic		Measurement of the site efficiency not related to any marketing programs
	Campaign Traffic		Measurement of efficiency of marketing programs
	Checkout Abandonment	Marie	Number of visitors who bailed during the checkout process

Of course, ownership will not be successful without a competent support structure. It is the responsibility of senior management, the CMO in this case, to ensure that the resources are available to the metric owners so that they can deliver what they are being held responsible for.

Thursday: Walk the Talk

This recommendation is geared more toward your most senior management than toward you (well, you too). It is important to walk the talk when it comes to dashboards. They can't be these one-time events that happen every week (and the related emails go directly to the trash box) or happen every month as simply a big gabfest.

Make them a way of life, carry them around, bring them to meetings, stick them to the walls of your cubicles. They should be facilitators of active and everyday decision making (even monthly dashboards). Senior management should show, through walking the talk, that they are using the dashboard to prioritize the work that happens in the team (rather than having a dashboard and yet relying on their gut to drive work). They should use dashboards to measure the personal success of the metric owners. Some facet of their own compensation (even if 2 percent) should be tied to meeting the dashboard metrics.

Walking the talk will promote a culture that gels around a common set of metrics and objectives. And that at the end of the day is priceless.

Friday: Measure the Effectiveness of Your Dashboards

In a book that has stressed customer satisfaction and the voice of the customer, you should have anticipated this recommendation: survey the key stakeholders and consumers of your dashboard.

Ask your stakeholders to rate various facets of the dashboard's effectiveness and its ability to drive action. Ask them how you are doing and how else can you improve, and just for good measure make the survey anonymous (it is amazing what people won't tell you even in the most open and honest company environments, because they are just trying to be nice).

The voice of the customer will be critical to keeping the dashboard meaningful and relevant over a longer period of time and ensuring that it is adding value.

If you collect feedback, it is imperative that you present your findings and also that you incorporate the VOC. This is the only way to reinforce the importance of the VOC to you and also to ensure that you will receive good feedback when you ask for it again. If you ask and you receive, ensure that you give back. It's simple.

Week 4: Applying Six Sigma or Process Excellence to Web Analytics

A common challenge that stymies lots of companies, especially advanced ones, is that although they have clickstream data and advanced web analytics tools, have embraced the Trinity mindset, are into testing and experimentation as well as surveys and usability, they find that for some reason web analytics is not quite as institutionalized as they would like it to be. Somehow even after such an investment in tools and skills, they are still not quite able to induce action. It is all still ad hoc. It is as if a lens or filter needs to be applied that would help bring a sense of focus, consistency, and predictability from which the company can benefit.

Methodologies and approaches inspired from Six Sigma or process excellence can help solve this problem.

Process excellence (PE) is a set of activities designed to create excellent processes. Process excellence includes Six Sigma but it also includes other initiatives as well.

Six Sigma is a business improvement methodology that comes from Motorola and was made truly famous at the General Electric Company (GE). The overall spirit of Six Sigma is to look at the business as a series of processes. The goal is to improve processes by eliminating any "defect" in each of the processes. Quoting from Wikipedia, *"The core of the Six Sigma methodology is a data-driven, systematic approach to problem solving, with a focus on customer impact."*

The common theme between both ideas is to think of business as a collection of processes that should be well defined, measured, optimized, and executed with an eye toward reducing the number of defects in the process to deliver for the end customer.

I believe, along with many others, that what is missing from web analytics thus far is the Six Sigma/PE-inspired mindset that forces us to think of activities we perform in terms of *processes* that need to be defined, documented, measured, and optimized. By learning from Six sigma/PE, we can cross the final hurdle holding us back in delivering sustainable actionability from web analytics for our businesses. To move that final step will require a fundamental mindset shift for companies and their resources and how work is done today. We will move from cowboy land, just a little bit, to living in well-organized suburbs, if not cities. I am sure that prospect is not appealing to some, but it is very much required.

Six Sigma and PE are extremely complex topics and hence I will not go into any great detail for either. This week you will focus on two topics that are inspired by Six Sigma/PE and that will be greatly beneficial for web analytics practitioners. The first topic is the fantastic beauty of thinking about everything we do as part of a process, and the second topic is how we can improve our processes byusing the Six Sigma methodology DMAIC (define, measure, analyze, improve, control).

Monday: Everything's a Process

We don't tend to think of web analytics overall, or the work we do in our day-to-day lives, as a process. But the reality is that every day the web ecosystem in your company is one complicated process that is taking inputs, processing them, and creating outputs. It is perhaps more accurate to say that it is a collection of processes solving for the whole.

Let's consider an example. Figure 11.15 shows a simple example of a web operations process.

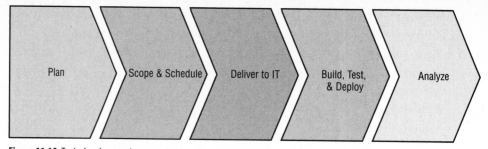

Figure 11.15 Typical web operations process

Each step of the process could be handled by one team or different teams in the company. But each step depends on the prior one for success. Each step in this high level process consists of sublayers of processes that help make it successful. For example, Figure 11.16 shows that the Scope and Schedule step can also be viewed as a process in and of itself.

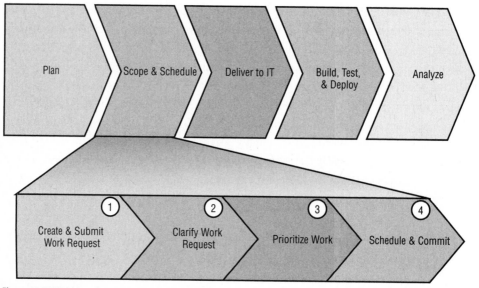

Figure 11.16 Web operations process—step 2 drill-down

You can quickly see how each of the steps in the high-level process will have sublayers. In some cases, each of the sublayers will have their own sub-sublayers that are worth working through and documenting (until a point of diminishing returns, of course).

The exercise of understanding what it takes to execute each step in our day to day delivery of key tasks and taking time to document it with a process excellence mindset is critical to creating a true system that does the following:

• Functions efficiently

- Has the ability to grow and scale
- Provides a shared understanding of what is supposed to happen and when
- Can be measured and optimized

That last one ties back to Six Sigma. For any well-defined process, the goal with Six Sigma is to put critical measures in place for each process, measures that would empower the understanding of "defects" in the process. This would result in decreased variations in the process. Consider Figure 11.17.

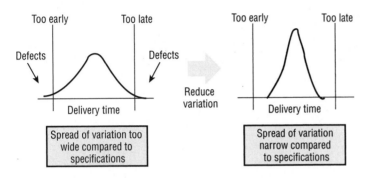

Figure 11.17 Improving the sigma by reducing variations

Let's say that this figure shows a plot of all the times when a daily delivery of a package from your UPS driver occurs (though it could represent your daily website release or report automatically published—or imagine your own situation). The delivery is supposed to happen every day at 9 A.M.

The first graph illustrates a delivery schedule that is widely dispersed with points (defects) that occur far from the mean. The variations from the mean reduce the predictability of the process, increase its complexity, and result in suboptimal customer impact.

Defining the process, understanding the critical customer measures, and optimizing the process steps will result in a graph that looks like the one on the right in Figure 11.17. There are significantly fewer variations from the mean. The net results from reducing variations in a process are as follows:

- Greater predictability in the process
- Lower costs resulting from less rework and waste by reducing inefficiencies, complexity, and errors
- Products and services that perform better and last longer
- Delighted customers (and company employees)

By clearly defining the various processes that make up web analytics, we can understand the process much better, measure it better, and optimize it better over time—everything from website page development, to experimentation and testing, to creation and delivery of dashboards, to daily scheduled reports, to checking for missing tags, and so forth.

Figure 11.18 illustrates a potential process that clearly identifies the big steps to follow for effective merchandising on a typical website.

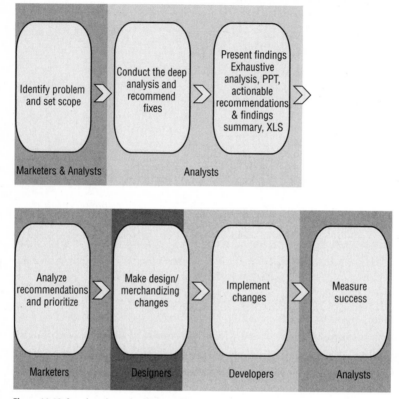

Figure 11.18 Sample web merchandizing and launch process

The process identifies what happens in each step and who is responsible for ownership of that step, and it documents from start to finish the expectations of each step. It is very simple, yet amazingly powerful in providing a solid understanding of what happens and assigning roles and responsibilities. It should be obvious that each step can be measured and optimized for its unique success metrics.

One last example of web processes, Figure 11.19, documents the process, in detail, of moving from requirements gathering to release for an improved customer experience on the websites.

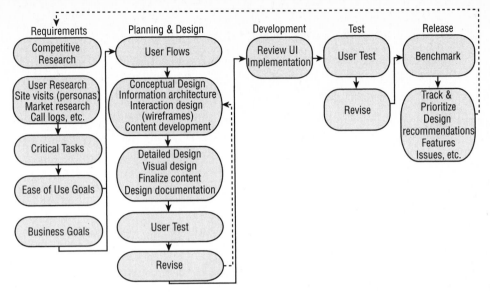

Figure 11.19 Sample customer experience improvement process

Each of the steps in this diagram have associated ownerships, roles, responsibilities, expectations of start-to-finish efforts, success metrics, and all the specific deliverables that need to be completed to move on to the next one. You can easily imagine not just how this would deliver a better end customer experience but how any company can itself ensure that the process can be repeated and performed with the least amount of variation.

Process Creation: Not a Scary, Complex Proposition

There is a common misperception that defining a process takes a lot of time and effort and that all processes need to look like the one shown here.

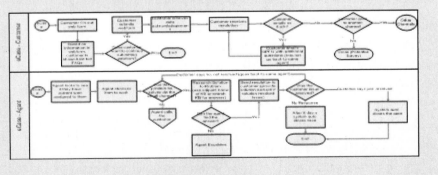

Continues

Process Creation: Not a Scary, Complex Proposition *(Continued)*

You don't have to worry that you have to use a particular software program or create a certain look and feel or format to document a process. It does not have to be painful work. What is important is that you spend time identifying each process in your teams, document by using the formats that you are most comfortable with, identify ownership of each step in the process, and create success metrics to measure its performance over time so that you can optimize it and reduce defects (variations).

The following is a process that uses a completely different presentation layer but accomplishes the same purpose.

Website JavaScript Tagging Process

Provide specific business requirements as to what is expected from the analytical tool. *Owner:* Marketer. *Timeline:* None.

Meet with website development lead to understand site structure, operations, cookie strategy, and so forth. *Owner:* Analyst. *Timeline:* 3 days.

Partner with the vendor to create a customized JavaScript tag for the site to collect the data that is required. The JavaScript tag and instructions are then sent to the website development lead for implementation. *Owner:* Analyst. *Timeline:* 3 days.

Ensure that the tag is implemented exactly as provided and appears on all pages on the site. *Owner:* Dev lead. *Timeline:* 1 day.

Validate that the provided code has been implemented correctly and exactly as provided on the QA website. *Owner:* Analyst. *Timeline:* 1 day.

Validate that some data is flowing through to the application (clicks or page views from the QA site). *Owner:* Analyst. *Timeline:* 2 days.

Provide feedback to the development lead for any fixes (only if required). *Owner:* Analyst. *Timeline:* 1 day.

Development lead makes the corrections (only if required). *Owner:* Dev lead. *Timeline:* 1 day.

Website migrates from QA to production. *Owner:* Dev lead. *Timeline:* 1–10 days.

Three days after launch, analyst validates that data is flowing okay and configures security access for all marketers. *Owner:* Analyst. *Timeline:* 3 days.

Conduct training one week after launch and set up basic reports for marketers. *Owner:* Analyst. *Timeline:* 1–29 days.

It is not important how you document the processes that all combine to deliver to your company's customers. It is important that you go through the exercise to identify the critical processes and document them with an eye toward improving predictability, reducing complexity and inefficiencies, and setting clear goals, roles, and responsibilities to create delight for your company's customers and employees.

Tuesday through Thursday: Apply the DMAIC Process

In the prior section, you learned about the importance of processes and reviewed samples of processes that apply directly to our world of web analytics. Identifying your critical process is necessary for you to move into our second Six Sigma/PE-inspired arena: DMAIC (define, measure, analyze, improve, control), shown in Figure 11.20.

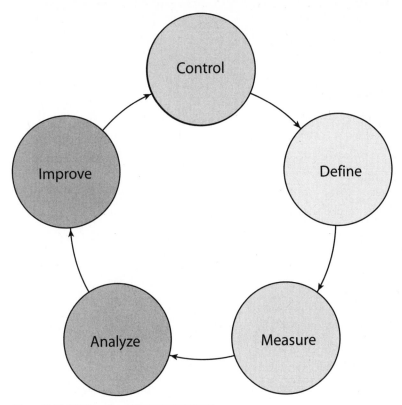

Figure 11.20 DMAIC continuous improvement process

DMAIC is a rigorous process for continuous improvement. DMAIC is relevant and important because it helps us go one step beyond simply identifying a process. It is a closed-loop process that helps eliminate unproductive steps, helps focus on new measurements, and in its essence applies technology for improvement.

It is helpful to think of the DMAIC as a structured problem-solving approach. By applying DMAIC, we can be assured that the processes we have put in place are performing at peak levels and delivering for our customers. For this reason, I believe that DMAIC is particularly relevant and applicable to web analytics. So much of what we do is structured around data and focuses on solving for our customers (internal and external). Applying the rigorous DMAIC approach not only will improve our web analytics supporting processes but can inspire the kind of discipline that is so often missing. It also provides the structure and guidance that we so sorely need (in our approaches, in our reports, in our dashboard, in driving our decision makers to action by providing analysis and insights directly driven by company customers).

DMAIC is a closed-loop process; let's go through each step one at a time.

Define

The goals of the Define phase are to clearly identify and validate the opportunity to improve the process and to articulate this definition in a clear and measurable way. The basic steps of this phase are as follows:

- Define who the customers are and what their requirements are for products and services from the process.
- Use tools such as stakeholder analysis, voice of customer techniques (surveys, and so forth) to identify the critical customers and their Critical to Quality factors (CTQs) that have the greatest effect on quality. It is important to distill down the list of critical few metrics.
- Create a project charter that will contain the problem definition, goal, business case, and high-level project place for the rest of the phases.

At the end of this phase, you have a clear understanding of how to deliver to your customers.

Measure

The goals of this phase are to understand the critical measures of success and to establish a baseline performance by undertaking an extensive (as optimal) data collection and benchmarking effort.

- Develop a data collection plan for each step of the process.
- Collect data from as many sources as possible to determine the metrics that could measure the CTQs.
- Measure the current rate of failures (defects) in the process, with a defect being any output that does not meet customer requirements.
- Identify the inputs into the process that contribute to failures.
- Validate the data collection process to ensure that the data is being collected correctly, and if required, update any data collection process that might be incorrect.

This exercise produces a solid understanding of how the process is performing today, which establishes a baseline measure. Usually at the end of this stage, we have initial identifications of the metrics that we will dive deeper into for the next phase.

Analyze

You should love this phase. Here we dive deep and conduct a root-cause analysis that will help us understand issues that are causing defects in the process. The steps are as follows:

- Develop a hypothesis about causes of defects in the process.

- Analyze the data; perform root-cause analysis on reasons for failures to identify opportunities to improve. The goal is to determine true sources of defects that are leading to customer dissatisfaction.

- Create a specific list of sources of defects in the process.

- Validate the outcomes of the analysis with the stakeholders.

At the end of this phase, you should have a list of improvements to the process, some of which will be quick hits and others that will take much longer and require support of senior management teams.

Improve

All the tough work you have done thus far pays off now. You get to prioritize the specific ideas for defect reduction identified in the prior phase and you get to implement them. Yay!

- Firm up the solutions and assess and address any risk to the process from implementing improvements.

- Identify any new measures that will be required to gauge success in the process from implementing improvements (if things change dramatically).

- Adjust the process to implement the recommended changes and kick off the measurement of the customer CTQs identified in the earlier phases.

- If improvements are not made for any reason, quantify the effects on the business by using data from the Measure and Analyze phases and present this to the key stakeholders.

This is a fun stage because you get to see the fruits of your labor. It is amazing to see process efforts reduced from ten days to three days, or bugs on the live site go down to zero, or reports being published that actually get used and induce action.

Control

This phase helps ensure the long-term successful adoption of the new process improvements. The goal is not to stop until it is clear that improvements have become a way of life.

- Measure postimplementation success of the process improvements and changes.

- Establish ongoing monitoring of the process to ensure that it stays "in control."
- Collect VOC from the key stakeholders and company customers to quantify the impact of the changes from their perspectives.

It is optimal at the end of the Control phase to do a postmortem of the biggest lessons learned and present them to the wider community. This enables you to share the progress made and to identify other areas in the company that could benefit from the knowledge gained from your DMAIC process.

Friday: Reflect on What You've Learned

To repeat just slightly, by using our first inspiration from Six Sigma/PE, you define and identify processes in order to reduce failures and meet customer requirements. Then you can apply our second inspiration to establish what the customer CTQs are and work toward improving existing processes to improve delivery on those CTQs.

Both of these processes—creation and improvement—do not have to be time-consuming or complex. As long as you diligently apply the principles shared in this chapter, you can complete some projects in a few days and realize immediate benefits (for example, how long does it take from the time data is captured to deliver a report to your customers?). Other projects can take much longer (for example, why is it that absolutely no one has made a single decision by using your half-million-dollar investment in web analytics tools?). However, all projects will have commensurate rewards if you persist in documenting the process, identifying your customer CTQs and points of failure (the root causes of defects), and addressing them by making changes (even big ones such as changing your organizational model if that's the root cause!).

My recommendation is to try this on a small scale, as in the examples in the "Everything's a Process" section, and you'll get a feel for how powerful Six Sigma/PE can be in revolutionizing your life.

Month 7: Competitive Intelligence and Web 2.0 Analytics

The Web is evolving so fast that what we had yesterday in terms of data is slightly less relevant today. We just get a handle on static pages, and here come dynamic sites. We get a handle on that, and here comes personalization and targeting. We go at it again and get a handle on that, and here comes social media (blogs, RSS, user-generated content). Then there are rich Internet applications (RIAs) and even more new things.

The challenge is not just keeping up with the breakneck pace of web evolution. It is that what we can measure to make our businesses successful is finite—so lots of change, not enough strategic things to measure. How do you survive?

This chapter covers two topics that will become critical in the near future: competitive intelligence (how to move outside your company data silo) and Web 2.0 analytics (how to measure RIAs and Really Simple Syndication, or RSS, metrics). Your business likely doesn't yet need these difficult and expensive analytics. But when you need to use them, you'll be prepared.

Competitive Intelligence Analytics

In Chapter 2, "Data Collection—Importance and Options," I explained why competitive intelligence is so important and the options available when it comes to accessing competitive data. To briefly recap, doing some level of competitive intelligence analysis is extremely important for the following reasons:

- Currently most reporting that you do probably uses your company data, and that presents a very compartmentalized view of reality. It is important to have the external context within which you can place your performance (even the context of your industry or your competitors).

- This analysis will tease out causality between your own company efforts and results.

- It will help you optimize your acquisition and marketing strategies based on what you can learn from your competitors.

- It will help you develop a competitive advantage.

Chapter 2 also discussed three options at your disposal from a data collection and analysis perspective, some free, some at cost. (Please see Chapter 2 for the benefits and pitfalls of each approach.)

Panel-based measurement: A group of recruits form a panel, their web behavior is monitored, and that data is analyzed.

ISP-based measurement: Data is collected from the various ISPs in the world, and this anonymous data is combined and provided for analysis.

Search engine data: Increasingly search engines such as Google and MSN are providing, for free, access to the massive data that they collect.

Each of these options has something of value that they can offer to help you do competitive analysis. Regardless of your company size or type of business, it is important to emphatically state that you can benefit from doing competitive analysis. If you are a Fortune 1000 company, get access to the paid competitive data providers. If you are a Fortune One Billion company, you can still use some of the free resources.

In the next two weeks, you will dive deep into three specific sets of options that will help you move your competitive intelligence offering from 0 to 900 miles per hour—very fast pace, very practical advice, very fast insights. I promise you, this is a lot of fun, it really is. Put on your Sherlock Holmes hat.

Week 1: Competitive Traffic Reports

The first thing you probably want to know is how many visits you get as compared to your competitor! You have a couple of options for running these reports.

Monday: Share of Visits by Industry Segment

By using tools from companies such as Hitwise (or comScore) for an industry segment (for example, Software—Technology), you have the ability to measure the share of traffic that you are getting and compare that to your competitors' share. It should show you at a quick glance the big boys and girls in your segment whom you are fighting with.

You not only can see how you are performing in terms of your industry segment (Software in Figure 12.1), but you also have the ability to create your own custom competitor set and compare your traffic statistics to those of your competitors.

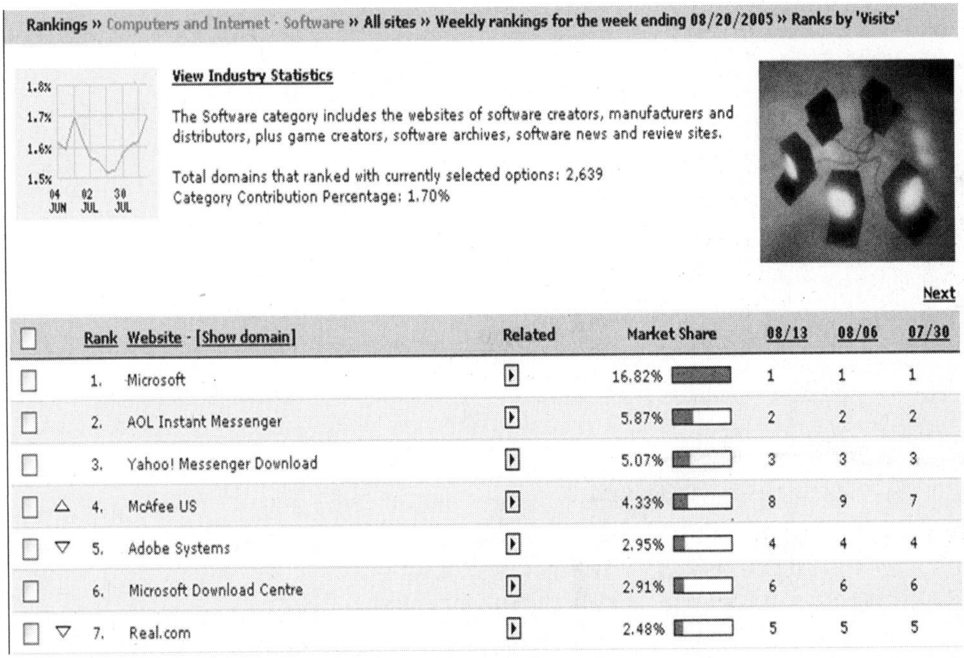

Rankings » Computers and Internet · Software » All sites » Weekly rankings for the week ending 08/20/2005 » Ranks by 'Visits'

View Industry Statistics

The Software category includes the websites of software creators, manufacturers and distributors, plus game creators, software archives, software news and review sites.

Total domains that ranked with currently selected options: 2,639
Category Contribution Percentage: 1.70%

Next

	Rank	Website - [Show domain]	Related	Market Share	08/13	08/06	07/30
☐	1.	Microsoft	▶	16.82%	1	1	1
☐	2.	AOL Instant Messenger	▶	5.87%	2	2	2
☐	3.	Yahoo! Messenger Download	▶	5.07%	3	3	3
☐ △	4.	McAfee US	▶	4.33%	8	9	7
☐ ▽	5.	Adobe Systems	▶	2.95%	4	4	4
☐	6.	Microsoft Download Centre	▶	2.91%	6	6	6
☐ ▽	7.	Real.com	▶	2.48%	5	5	5

Figure 12.1 Market share by industry segment

You can input your core competitors into the tool and measure the share of visits that you have on your own turf (Figure 12.2). This is where you'll see whether you are really dominating or your competitors are kicking your butt. On the other hand, the benefit of Figure 12.1 is that it often highlights your "unknown" competition that has the greatest share in terms of visits. (Because there is only a finite set of visits, if they win too much, you lose, even if you don't directly compete with them.)

	Rank	Website - [Show domain]	Related	Market Share	09/24	09/17	09/10
☐	1.	QuickBooks	▶	52.77%	1	1	1
☐	2.	NetSuite.com	▶	32.56%	2	2	2
☐	3.	Peachtree Software	▶	13.38%	3	3	3
☐	4.	Accpac International	▶	1.29%	4	4	4

Figure 12.2 Market share by custom competitor segment

As always, it is optimal to watch trends over time to get a real good feel for how you are doing (Figure 12.3).

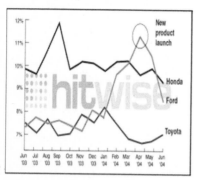

Figure 12.3 Market share trends over time

It is important to measure your share of traffic because over time you'll be able to accurately identify whether the massive traffic increases that you see in your Omniture, WebTrends, WebSideStory, or Coremetrics data are a result of something you have done or general industry trends. Often it can explain increases in traffic on your site when you have not done anything (your competitor is running a massive campaign and you are simply getting a "halo effect" from that, for example).

Tuesday: Upstream and Downstream Traffic against Competition

Referring URLs in your web analytics tool's report give you an idea of which websites are referring traffic to your website. But usually 50 percent of referrers (those who are sending you traffic) are blank. By accessing this data in a competitive intelligence tool, you can get complete access to your referrers. More important—and how cool is this—you can also report on where visitors go next after visiting your website (data you have simply no access to in your clickstream applications unless you link to other sites). Figure 12.4 shows the report for www.peachtree.com and it illustrates, on the left, which websites are sending traffic to www.peachtree.com and, on the right, where visitors from www.peachtree.com go next.

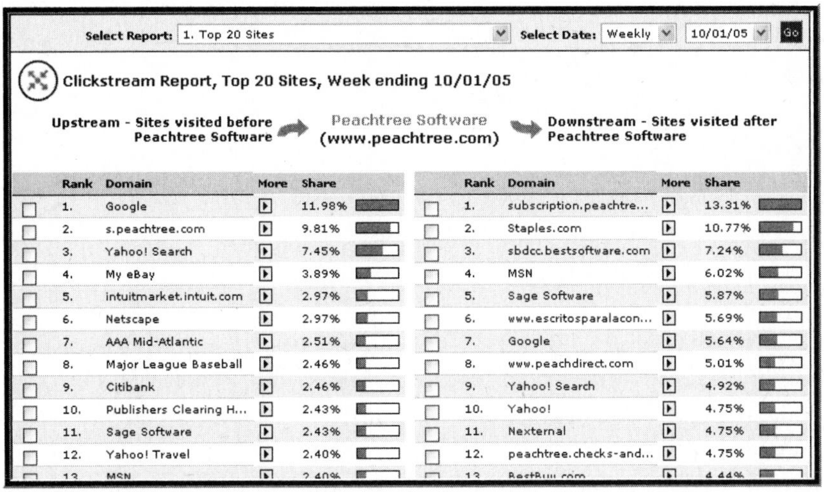

Figure 12.4 Upstream and downstream traffic analysis

This is a great way to peek under the covers and see who is sending traffic to your competitors. You can then compare that to your own strategies and perhaps identify future business partners for yourself. This report also gives you a great feel for *mindset* as you look at where people come from and then what site they go to next. If you have a small cluster of sites that people see before they come to you, you can make an inference about customer intent. For example, in Figure 12.4 it may be great for peachtree.com that such a large percent of traffic goes to subscription next (perhaps that is how Peachtree's owner, Sage Software, makes money) and then on to Staples.com (which is where visitors can buy Peachtree products, maybe because those products are not sold at peachtree.com).

Wednesday and Thursday: Competitor Traffic by Media Mix

Media mix is defined as the core streams of traffic to your site: direct marketing, affiliate, search, and direct/other. This report will show your media mix as compared to your competition, as you can see in Figure 12.5.

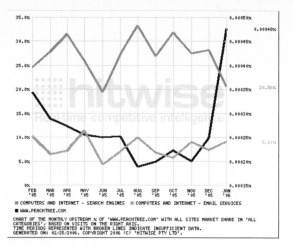

Figure 12.5 Competitor media mix analysis—search engine, email (DM), and direct traffic

This report is insightful because it provides a peek into the acquisition strategy of your competitor, something you would have a hard time getting otherwise. For example, by looking at the media mix report in Figure 12.5, you can summarize the percent of traffic that this website is getting as a result of email campaigns and search engines (including campaigns). You can see exactly when the spending on these campaigns is up (as shown by the graph going up or down) and where you might have opportunities if you wanted to avoid going head-to-head with your main competitor.

Is the media mix for your competitors the same as yours? Very different? Should it be the same? What are their core affiliate sites that are driving traffic to them? Should you go after them as well and have a relationship? Perhaps an alternative affiliate network? How about direct marketing, now that you know how efficiently (or not) they are using email, what should be your strategy?

These are complex questions that you can't even begin to answer with the options you have available through standard web analytics tools. But with competitive intelligence you can start that journey. Even adoption of one strategy based on this data could be worth hundreds of thousands of dollars. So it is complex, and it also costs money to get access to this data, but the payoff could be huge. As always, you have to assess in your own company whether you can take action on this type of data.

Friday: Alexa Daily Reach Reports

Alexa Internet is always greeted with howls of protest, and for some good reasons. Alexa collects data from several million users who have installed the Alexa toolbar in their browsers. It has a bias toward Windows users, who use Internet Explorer. Ratings in Alexa higher than a rank of 100,000 are not reliable. (Please read information at http://snipurl.com/alexaA and http://snipurl.com/alexaB to learn more.)

In spite of that, if you want to see traffic trends as compared to those of your competitors—while holding all the bias as equal for you and your competitors—Alexa can be an acceptable resource. This is true especially if you observe trends over time, as shown in Figure 12.6.

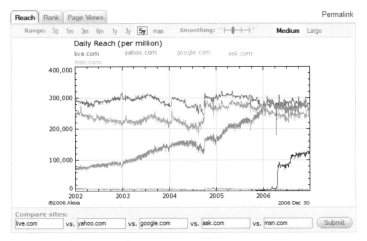

Figure 12.6 Daily Reach analysis from Alexa

This graph is for the major sites in the world. However, you can imagine how you could glean insights about your success as compared to your competitors if you had this type of graph. The growth that Google has shown is impressive, as is that of Windows Live (www.live.com), which came from nowhere and continues to grow (without cannibalizing MSN either).

You can do the preceding type of analysis for smaller sites as well (as long as their individual ranks are under 100,000). Figure 12.7 shows analysis for web analytics bloggers.

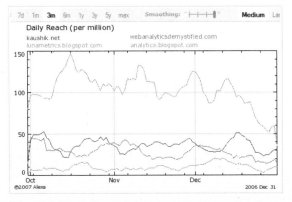

Figure 12.7 Daily Reach analysis, for web analytics bloggers, from Alexa

Figure 12.7 shows a three-month trend for web analytics bloggers. Although their individual web analytics metrics might not be available, you can glean insights from their trends in the context of each other.

It is important to stress that you should not look at the absolute numbers on Alexa. You should look only at trends. Simply ignore the y-axis of that graph. If you want to get a directional read, for free, about the trends of your website and your competitors' websites, this is a good resource.

Tip: Don't look at your site's Alexa ranks (you might not get the right bearing and therefore might misinterpret the data). In addition, remember to compare like-minded sites only (to keep the bias of the data collection methodology as neutral as possible).

Week 2: Search Engine Reports

I have said at various times in this book that search engines are prominent influences of customer behavior. For this reason I have also stressed the importance of doing deep search engine optimization and pay per click analytics (see Chapter 8, "Month 3: Search Analytics—Internal Search, SEO, and PPC"). Those are beneficial and necessary, but for you to get a leg up in this dog-eat-dog search world, you need to get into competitive intelligence!

Monday: Share of Search and Search Keywords

You will start the week by gaining a solid understanding of how you are performing in the highly competitive world of capturing traffic from search engines. You'll also focus on which search keywords are performing well for you and your competitors.

Share of Search Report

If 80 percent of the traffic on the Web starts on a search engine, how much share do you have of that traffic? What about compared to your arch nemesis? The Share of Search report will answer these and other questions. See Figure 12.8.

All the competitors being compared in Figure 12.8 are outperforming their industry average (the lowest line), but two of them are doing amazingly better. If you are not one of them, this report can quickly help you highlight why you might not be getting as much traffic from search engines (something you won't understand from your clickstream data) or that your SEO and PPC efforts are coming to nothing and need to be retooled.

You also have an ability to drill down one more level in this report and compare your share of search engines against your competitors, as shown in Figure 12.9.

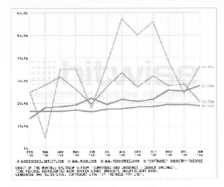

Figure 12.8 Share of Search competitive report

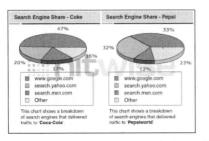

Figure 12.9 Search Engine Share report for Pepsi and Coke

In Figure 12.9, you can see the share of search engine data for Pepsi and Coke. Let's say you work for Pepsi. You can quickly see that you are not performing very well against Coke when it comes to the most dominant search engine in the world (Google). Unless Pepsi deliberately focuses on other search engines (a valid strategy, of course), Pepsi might need to do a quick investigation of whether their site is indexed correctly in Google. (There could be a whole host of other possibilities, but this report will at least highlight an important concern.)

Share of Brand and Category Keywords

Your clickstream analytics can help you highlight what keywords or key phrases are your top 10 or 20. In reality, a whole bunch of traffic for most websites comes from the top 20 or so key phrases. Getting access to competitive intelligence data helps you understand what is your share of clicks is from search engine results—for those keywords when people search at Google or Yahoo! or MSN.

You can start with a look at your branded key terms to understand your share of clicks. It is entirely possible that you dominate those clicks (simply because it is your brand and you are probably optimized for your own brand terms). Sometimes this report can highlight others who might be doing illegal things to steal your traffic from the search engine.

But where this report really comes in handy is when you search for *category key phrases* (phrases that are not tied to your brand—for example, *soft drink*s instead of *Pepsi*). Category key phrases are more important for businesses because they are the source of *prospects*, people who might not yet know your brand and therefore are potentially not your customers. If you are looking to grow your customer base, you really want to focus on category terms. Figure 12.10 shows a category key phrase report.

Websites that received traffic from 'payroll software'
Displaying 1 to 10 of 84 websites. **Click Here** to see more websites.

	Website	Volume	
1.	www.pensoft.com	11.54%	
2.	www.paycycle.com	10.49%	
3.	www.payroll.com	9.44%	
4.	www.officesmallbusinessaccounting.com	7.47%	
5.	www.checkmark.com	5.24%	
6.	www.msn.com	4.45%	
7.	www.taxsites.com	4.19%	
8.	www.redwingsoftware.com	4.19%	
9.	breaktru.com	4.19%	
10.	www.sagespecialized.com	3.15%	

Most Popular search terms containing 'payroll software'
Displaying 1 to 10 of 79 search terms. **Click Here** to see more suggestions.

	Search Term	Volume		Success Rate	
1.	payroll software	28.69%		85.78%	
2.	free payroll software	14.06%		75.12%	

Figure 12.10 Report for share of category key phrase *payroll software*

It is easy to look at Figure 12.10 and understand precisely who is capturing all the prospects looking to buy payroll software for their businesses. If you are 2020software.com, cyma.com, sagemas.com, or realtaxtools.com, you should really be worried that you don't even show up in the top 10 (and your only way to capture traffic is to do PPC campaigns, which are an expensive way to get traffic). If you are paycycle.com, you should be happy because you are doing so well in this competitive intelligence report.

Everyone wants to capture prospects. Simple reports like these can fundamentally change the direction and emphasis of your search marketing efforts, if not your fundamental acquisition strategy. Demand this kind of report from wherever you get your competitive intelligence data.

Tuesday: Search Keyword Funnels and Keyword Forecasts

This day's task is kind of cool. You will learn how to get insight into the shopping / consideration behavior of your customers by getting a peek into their behavior on a search engine and also use data from the search engine (available for free) to understand how the search engine is expecting demand for keywords to change over the coming months.

Search Funnel Report

Microsoft adCenter Labs provides access to this wonderful little report for free (http://snipurl.com/msnfunnel). The search funnel report helps you understand customer intent by reporting what people search for *before* they search for your top key phrases and what they look for *after*. See Figure 12.11.

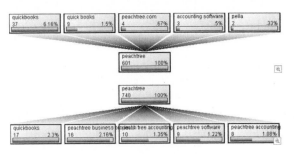

Figure 12.11 Search funnel report for the key phrase *peachtree*

The *pre-funnel* (top portion of the figure) provides insights about what is on people's minds before they think of you. It outlines what your competitors are feeding you as well as what nonbranded key phrases are most relevant. It also includes a couple of surprises—for example, it is hard to discern the relationship between *pella* and *peachtree*, but if you are Peachtree, it might be worth investigating.

Ditto for the *post-funnel* (bottom portion of the figure). Of course, after people search for Peachtree, they want to go back and search for QuickBooks (a direct competitor). But it is surprising that they go back to look for *peachtree business products*, *peach tree accounting*, *peachtree software*, and *peachtree accounting*. If the results of the search for Peachtree (which is a branded term for Sane Solutions and hence easy to "capture") are optimized, the web traffic should be landing on pages that are optimized to give answers related to all four key phrases. The traffic should not have to go back and search for that detail again.

You can gain some very actionable insights from an easy-to-use free tool (even if the data is from searches done only on MSN or Windows Live).

Keyword or Key Phrase Forecast

Your company probably has internal plans for pay per click campaigns around your product launches or selling seasons. What this wonderful free tool, MSN adCenter Keyword Forecast (http://snipurl.com/msnforecast), allows you to do is to get an outsider's opinion of what the next few months look like for your top 10 keywords. The tool will compare your forecast to your competitors as well, as shown in Figure 12.12.

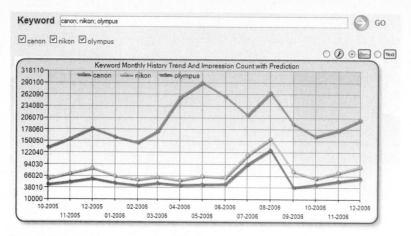

Figure 12.12 Keyword forecast report from MSN adCenter

It is to be expected that during the holiday season, sales of digital cameras will pick up. But the folks running the Nikon and Olympus web strategies don't know that Canon is doing so much better than them, and is predicted to do much better than them even during the holiday season. Could they use this data to adapt their strategies to do much better against Canon? They could come up with a more robust strategy around nonbranded keywords to counter this strong brand keyword trend.

If only for your MSN advertising strategies, you can consider the keyword forecast report as valuable input. You can also determine the size of the opportunity better for your company.

Wednesday: Keyword Expansion Tool

If you remotely touch search marketing and have the tough job of generating an optimal set of keywords to bid on, you realize that the competition is really hard out there, especially for the keywords that you can think of or get from your web analytics application. How do you expand your keyword list to find words or phrases that you don't know? How do you start to look for opportunities for arbitrage (profiting from differences between supply and demand)?

Google has a great free keyword expansion tool (http://snipurl.com/googexpansion) that you can use to quickly expand your keyword list and build up your very own *long tail* (keywords and phrases that are specific and yield few searchers but in total could yield more than your main keywords).

It works quite simply. You go to the website and type in some keywords you are interested in (for the example in Figure 12.13, I used *dell, laptops, dimension,* and *xps*).

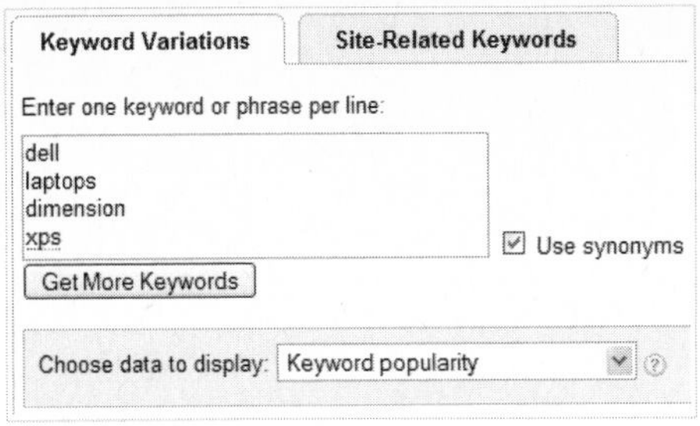

Figure 12.13 Keyword expansion tool from Google

After you click Get More Keywords, the tool provides a list of additional keywords that you could consider bidding on to build a robust portfolio of keywords (182 additional keywords for my four in December 2006). Not too shabby for five seconds of work. Just try it with your top four, five, or fifty keywords, and you'll be surprised. You may also get more praise from executives because you are not just reporting things from your analytics tool.

The tool also has a couple of other great features. Figure 12.14 shows a report from the keyword expansion tool that will tell you how much competitive bidding can be expected for each key phrase and how much *inventory* (search volume) is predicted to be available for each key phrase. This information can go directly into influencing your bidding strategy.

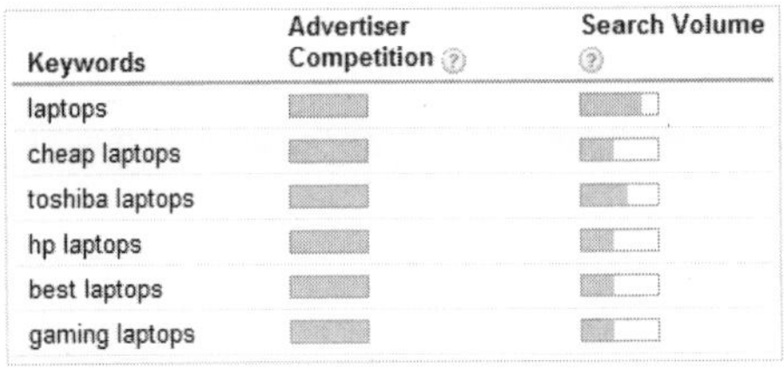

Figure 12.14 Keyword expansion tool competition and volume

Additionally, you can find opportunities for arbitrage where there is not really a lot of competition but lots of searchers (for example, *xps motherboard* in Figure 12.15). There are no hard numbers in either column, but Google has at least gotten you started on a path with some guidance (rather than you going in blind).

It is quite likely that if you are a large spender of PPC dollars, you have an agency that can help you expand your keywords in much more sophisticated ways. They probably can also find arbitrage opportunities with some kind of advanced algorithm. But if you are not a large spender, you can use this tool. Even if you are a large spender's analyst, now you have a smart way to double-check what your agency is doing.

Keywords	Advertiser Competition (?)	Search Volume (?)
centrino laptops		
laptops specs		
laptops prices		
xps motherboard		
laptops ram		
vaio laptops		
laptops price		
xps memory		
xps upgrade		

Figure 12.15 Keyword expansion tool from Google

Thursday and Friday: Demographic and Psychographic Reports

Few website owners have any awareness of the demographic nature of their visitors. Yet knowing whether your visitors are from Mars or Venus could be a major influencing factor in your website design and experience. Access to demographic and psychographic data (customer segments and associated attributes related to personality, values, attitudes, interests, or lifestyles) can also be valuable in helping you find new sources of reaching your targeted segment. It can help you optimize your campaigns and more.

Demographic Prediction

You can use the free demographic prediction tool at MSN adCenter (http://snipurl .com/msndemo) to understand the basic demographic information about your websites (or those of your competitors). See Figure 12.16.

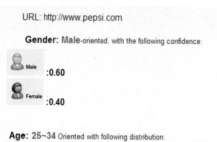

URL: http://www.pepsi.com

Gender: Male-oriented, with the following confidence:

Male :0.60

Female :0.40

Age: 25~34 Oriented with following distribution:

	General Distribution	Predicted Distribution
25~34	27.20%	23.77%
<18	9.80%	20.54%
35~49	23.00%	20.33%
18~24	26.80%	18.88%
50+	13.20%	16.49%

Figure 12.16 Demographic prediction for pepsi.com

The more popular your website, the more likely that the data is accurate. It is sourced from all data that MSN has about its searchers. You can use this data to optimize your website experiences or to validate that your traffic acquisition strategies are working as they were intended to. It can help have some influence on your product marketing, customer experience, and customer retention strategies.

You can also compare your demographic information to your competition's. For example, coca-cola.com (on Dec 31, 2006) had a ratio of 0.24 male and 0.76 female, drastically different from Pepsi. Only someone at Pepsi can decide whether this is good or bad for them (and then figure out how to leverage this newfound information).

Psychographic Reporting

Perhaps the best use of demographic or psychographic data (the latter leverages the standardized Prizm lifestyles data in Hitwise) is to optimize your acquisition strategies and understand the influence of your competitors on the customer segments that you are interested in. Claritas offers Prizm customer segmentation and profiles that identify segments of customers in the United States (by geographic location, for example) and provide insights into their shopping habits, their demographic profiles, and other marketing information.

For example, you can use the tool in Hitwise (Figure 12.17) to run queries against their competitive intelligence data and not only identify the demographic profiles of customers who visit your website, or your competitor's website, but also understand the behavior of these targeted customer segments. Where do "Midlife Success" or "Movers & Shakers" or "Young Digerati" go when they are surfing? What are their preferred websites? You can optimize your campaigns accordingly.

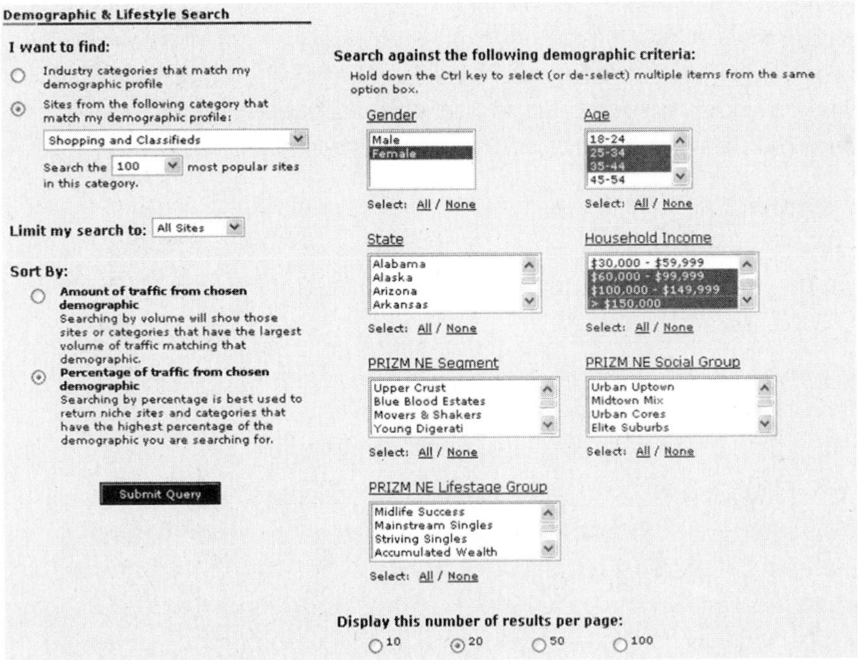

Figure 12.17 Demographic and psychographic analysis in Hitwise

You can also get a lot more sophisticated by targeting people only in certain states, age groups, or household incomes. You can imagine how quickly you can extract maximum ROI from your online campaigns.

Note: To leverage this data, you have to have a good understanding of who your customers are and what customer segments fit with your company's strategic objectives. Not every company has that understanding. But if your company does, you need access to this data!

Competitive intelligence should be the cornerstone of your web analytics strategy if you are to move beyond your own company data silo and derive maximum actionability that adds to your company's bottom line. The current crop of sources (including Hitwise, MSN, Google, and Alexa)—some free and some paid—each have their strengths and weakness (see Chapter 2). But if you familiarize yourself with them and then use the tools, each can help you become a little more knowledgeable and help move your company ahead from a strategic perspective.

Two Competitive Intelligence Pitfalls to Avoid

You've learned why to do competitive intelligence analysis, the specific reports you can use, and the specific actions you can induce as a result of your analysis. Here I want to share two types of analyses that people jump into first when they hear of competitive intelligence. Both are usually misleading, take up a lot of time, and in the end provide few actionable insights.

Conversion Rate

The instant tendency for anyone, especially senior management, is to ask for the competitor's conversion rate and compare it to their own. Usually this is a huge waste of time.

Even companies who are in exactly the same business have radically different business strategies when it comes to the Web. For example, you could be driving all the sales via the web channel to the detriment of other channels while your competitor could have a more holistic web, retail, and phone strategy. So if you compare conversion rates, you are really comparing apples and mosquitoes.

For example, consider Best Buy and Circuit City, two electronics powerhouses. On the surface it might seem like they are in the same business on the Web. But in reality, whether in their retail stores or on their websites, they execute such radically different strategies that even if you knew what their web conversion rates were, it would give you very little insight that you could exploit to your advantage.

It is a classic So What situation (see Chapter 5, "Web Analytics Fundamentals"). Let's say your conversion rate is 90 percent and your competitor's is 9 percent. What would you do? What if it were vice versa? Would you change your fundamental business strategy? Would it really matter?

Two Competitive Intelligence Pitfalls to Avoid *(Continued)*

There is also wide variance in how each competitive intelligence provider measures conversion. Some will simply detect the presence of an HTTPS entry in the visitor session and assume that moving to a secure area of the site is conversion. Others might try to pick up URL stem values that could indicate conversion. Please be cautious of exactly how your competitive conversion numbers are being provided (assuming that you have validated that your business model, business strategy, and site structure is exactly the same as your competitor first).

Measuring simply to know rather than to take action is an expensive distraction that often provides a misleading sense of confidence (or panic, as the case may be).

Pages, or Content, Viewed

This one is tricky. It seems logical that you would want to know the pages that visitors are viewing on your website and on your competitor's website. A common question asked could be, How many visitors are viewing the product detail pages on their site compared to ours? The following discussion outlines some reasons why this could be a suboptimal use of time.

Any data you need for this comparison will need to be deeply customized because, sadly, no two sites follow the same structure for content (and it changes all the time). As an example, here are two pages for the exact same product:

```
http://www.circuitcity.com/ssm/Sony-Cyber-shot-DSC-H2-Digital-Camera/sem/
rpsm/oid/149326/catOid/-13062/rpem/ccd/productDetail.do
http://www.bestbuy.com/site/olspage.jsp?skuId=7698896&type=product&id=
1138084657346
```

In order for your reporting to be accurate, you would have to put in massive effort to ensure that what you are calling Product Page on one site is the same as Product Page on the other site (please see Chapter 6, "Month 1: Diving Deep into Core Web Analytics Concepts"). You can see how this can get expensive and out of hand.

Attributing intent to a page view is quite a stretch. If you see *this* and the purpose of this page is *that*, you must be trying to do *z*. This throws a kink in the content viewed analysis, especially across different websites (and you would have to keep pace with all the changes on sites).

Imagine all the challenges you could have to overcome to measure page views (or content consumed) on a site that is using RIAs and Flash and Ajax, where the total number of page views could be 1 to any current competitive intelligence tool, when in reality the customer could have "viewed" 50 "pages."

This is another example of the So What situation. Apply the "so what" test and only after a satisfactory answer to the test should you plunge into this analysis.

In summary, business models and strategy, acquisition campaigns, site structure/experience, and customer mindsets and intent all influence the success of a competitor. As you do competitive intelligence, attempt to focus on core areas that will help you improve in areas where there is a closer apple-to-apple comparison of the data rather than where your differences could cause you to be misled. The report examples that I have provided are great places to start to look for competitive insights from which you can gain actual competitive advantage. It is great to get into this space now with lots of new companies with new data capture models being formed recently (Compete and Quantcast, to name a couple).

Web 2.0 Analytics

Web 2.0 is a much-brandished buzzword that means almost nothing or almost everything depending on who you talk to. To provide a definition, I'll turn to the wonderful source of wisdom that is Wikipedia (`http://snipurl.com/wiki20`) and the excellent O'Reilly September 2005 article called "What Is Web 2.0" (`http://snipurl.com/oreilly20`):

The phrase *Web 2.0* refers to one or more of the following:

- The transition of websites from isolated information silos to sources of content and functionality, thus becoming computing platforms serving web applications to end users

- A social phenomenon embracing an approach to generating and distributing web content itself, characterized by open communication, decentralization of authority, freedom to share and reuse, and "the market as a conversation"

- More-organized and categorized content, with a far more developed deep-linking web architecture than in the past

- A shift in economic value of the Web, possibly surpassing that of the dot-com boom of the late 1990s

- A marketing term used to differentiate new web-based firms from those of the dot-com boom, which subsequently appeared discredited (because of the bust)

- The resurgence of excitement around the implications of innovative web applications and services that gained a lot of momentum around mid-2005
  In my humble opinion, this perhaps best captures the essence of Web 2.0.

You can imagine how each of the preceding bullets can cause challenges for web analytics practitioners when it comes to measurement and analysis. Our current sets of tools are not very prepared for a world beyond page view website architecture. Increasingly in the Web 2.0 world, it is harder to measure intent, and the click loses its value. One of the emerging trends of Web 2.0 is that increasingly content creators are losing control of their content and the process of creating customer experiences. Increasingly, customers are creating their own customized customer experiences (for the simplest example, think of mash-ups) and customers are being influenced more and more by social media.

Measurement systems for Web 2.0 will continue to emerge and evolve over time. There is not a lot of standardization at the moment, and it is hard to see where all this will end up. For this reason, I will cover two technologies and customer experiences that are very much Web 2.0 and the options that are available to you when it comes to measuring their success: RIAs and RSS. My hope is to share a new way of thinking for the new world and prepare you just a little bit more as it evolves around us.

Week 3: Measuring the Success of Rich Interactive Applications (RIAs)

Web experience for the past 10-odd years has meant HTML and just HTML on a page. There have been incremental improvements; many sites are now dynamic and can react to a trigger (a cookie, parameter, ID, and so forth) to present different content on a page. But essentially it is still a page. We have had Flash for a few years; think of demos or pop-ups displaying software or product features. We have had the ability to rotate the model of the camera 360 degrees before we decide to buy it.

In the last couple of years (primarily since 2005), we have truly stepped into a world where we are moving beyond product demos as "rich" experiences to fully functional desktop-application-type interactivity and experiences in an Internet browser. These RIAs are driven by technologies such as Asynchronous JavaScript and XML (Ajax), Adobe Flash, Adobe Flex, OpenLaszlo, and others.

A couple of famous examples of Ajax-based RIAs are Google Maps and Google Mail (Gmail). Both use Ajax, allowing a web page to be more interactive without having to refresh the page to serve up new content. Your entire experience in Gmail uses one URL (http://mail.google.com/mail). As you reply and delete and forward, the URL never changes. Often the page itself does not reload.

An example of a RIA-driven site is www.miniusa.com. You can go to the site and browse around and you'll experience a rich media experience (in this case driven by Flash) that is like nothing you have seen before. Watch the URL and its changes to see how they are collecting data (or use View Source). You can view a Flex-driven sample website by visiting http://snipurl.com/flexstore. Click on the Products tab and try the experience.

Monday: Understand the Reality of RIAs

RIAs are still very new, as of early 2007, and you might not run into them in the course of your typical web surfing. Yet RIAs hold a lot of promise in terms of benefits to our customers. As always, such interactions come with their own set of challenges, and because we are still at the very early stages, there is the reality of where we are to deal with.

Beyond simply being cool, RIAs provide a number of benefits in terms of improved customer experiences on the Web. They help users find and display content without waiting for pages to refresh (from the server). They are especially beneficial in improving multipage structured processes such as sign-ups for leads, or the cart and checkout process, or booking a hotel by selecting dates and rooms and credit card numbers, all on one page. Figure 12.18 shows a rich interactive experience, purchasing clothing, on gap.com, and more specifically how the site reacts, dynamically, when the add to bag button is clicked before the size of the jacket is chosen.

Figure 12.18 Gap.com RIA experience: error handling

RIA sites have much better error messaging on the page (so you don't have to wait to click Submit to know you are missing a digit on your telephone number, for example). Perhaps one of my personal favorites is the capability to undo your last action. For example, let's say you mistakenly deleted a product from your cart. Now, rather than going back to the product page and finding the item and adding it to the cart, you can simply click the Undo button.

Every web analytics vendor relies on a page and a "page view" to identify a discrete event. As you learned in Chapter 6, the existence of data in the URL or URL parameters identifies an event to the web analytics application. With some vendors, you can also pass a variable via JavaScript to indicate an action ("someone viewed a page in the Products group").

The challenge with RIAs (Ajax or Flex) is that there is no such concept as a page. In Gmail, your URL does not change after you click Reply. For your entire Gmail experience, you'll be on the same URL although you have seen 20 "pages" (a better way to think of this is that you would have initiated 20 *actions* or *events*). If you use

Flash, the browser just sees `something.com/ria.swf` (or similar) and a person could have interacted with 100 "pages." But to the analytics tool, it is just one page view because it needs the URL or a combination of URL and parameters to provide your standardized reports.

The combination of the current architectures of the web analytics tracking tools and the radically different architectures of the new emerging tools such as RIAs makes it difficult to track anything out of the box except that someone loaded the RIA in their browser.

You'll spend Tuesday and Wednesday learning about a couple of ways in which RIA experiences are being tracked. Still, it is extremely important to be aware that today we are at the dinosaur stage of evolution. There are no current standards, just a few vendors reacting to RIAs. At best what we are doing is reacting to the tracking technologies that we know of today.

As RIAs move beyond cool (and I predict that they will—just check out a demo of Adobe Apollo), new technologies will emerge. There will be standards, and it will be easier to implement tracking. We will make it from dinosaurs to humans, but it will take time and it will be radically different from the current "hacks" that are being used to measure RIA success. It is important to bear in mind that what exists today will go away and be replaced with something better.

Tuesday and Wednesday: Learn about Emerging "Standards" for RIA Tracking

Analysts are partnering with business and technical folks to transform thinking from page views to events. There are a few ways to do this. Each RIA is a piece of software with which our users interact, and each button click, choice selection, and mouse movement is a *business event*. Think of the action of Add to Cart or Insert Image (to create a cartoon) or Next or Update. In RIAs, each of these actions is akin to a click and refresh in the HTML world, only in the RIA no refresh is required. As you interact with Google Earth, these events are pan, drill down, move left, and so forth.

The first step in tracking RIAs is to identify why the RIA exists, what customer problems it is trying to solve, and then break down the experience into a series of events. After the business events are identified, there are a couple of different methods used to collect data.

The de facto standard is to extend the current JavaScript tags that you use on your website from your vendor (HBX, WebTrends, ClickTracks, IndexTools). Simply use a customized JavaScript tag and embed that into your business events so that if those events occur, the JavaScript tag will be fired off and a log will store the data.

The downside of using this method is that it relies on the many limitations of page views outlined earlier because essentially you are not capturing events as much as page views. This is suboptimal, but, for example, if you need to know only discrete isolated things, this is fine. If your vendor allows you to pass more discrete variables (for example, the "calls to action" from the RIA), this method can be helpful, especially if your vendor allows you to capture that data and do some custom processing to get the reports out.

Another option is to use custom-defined data collection methods to capture the data. You can leverage your web commerce platform's native ability to capture events (ATG, for example, has this). Simply put, in the RIA experiences you embed the custom code that will capture not just the occurrence of the business event (say, Add to Cart) but also all the context around that event (quantity, product name, type, page, and so forth). Because we are leveraging an existing feature set from your web e-commerce platform, this development is extremely cost-effective and adds only an additional 20 percent to the developer time.

Omniture has recently introduced a solution called ActionSource that provides a customized way to collect the click activity in your RIA. Like the event-logging mechanism, it does not use JavaScript. But unlike the event-logging method, ActionSource provides a standard set of instructions and tools that your Flash developers can incorporate into their development process to collect data, and your team does not have to do any custom in-house development.

Both of these methodologies allow you to collect a lot of data from the RIA but also ensure that you can tie the RIA data to other data sources—for example, your orders data that sits in Oracle or your customer satisfaction survey data.

Thursday and Friday: Learn the Steps for Successful RIA Tracking

We are in the very early phases of moving web experiences from HTML pages to rich interactive experiences. There are few standard tools that offer RIA (Flash, AJAX, others) measurement out of the box, so you will have to improvise a little bit. Regardless of whether your tool supports RIA measurement, you will typically follow these recommended steps:

1. Partner with the business users to identify the core purpose of the RIA. What is the reason for the RIA's existence? What problem are we solving for the customer? What are the "actions" that a customer will typically take? What are the success metrics?

2. After success metrics have been identified, step through the RIA experience with your business and technical counterparts and identify the key customer events that we will need to "tag" in order to capture that event being executed by our web customers.

3. Ask your technical folks to ensure that each identified event is tagged with the right piece of JavaScript tag or web server event-logging technology (for

example, if you are not ATG). Ensure that you are capturing not only the event but also some context, such as session_id, date/timestamp, perhaps that the person was adding Quicken Deluxe to the cart or in Google Earth clicked Pan on the city that they were looking at. It is important to QA this step, both so that all the events are tracked and you are collecting the right data.

4. Develop a simple Perl script, or Extract Transform Load (ETL) program load, to tag data into a simple database. You can use MySQL or Oracle or whatever database that you use in your company. If you already have a data warehouse for your web information, simply load the RIA data into that data warehouse. If you use a tool such as NetTracker, it will parse the logs and provide the data in a database-friendly format.

5. Use straight SQL, or a standard On-Line Analytical Processing (OLAP) tool if one is available, to run queries against the data to compute the success metrics.

If your web analytics vendor will allow you to capture events by passing variables via JavaScript tags, you can also use the functionality they have built into the web analytics reporting tool to measure your success metrics (steps 4 and 5 would be different for you). Unica's NetInsight is one such web analytics tool that has great capabilities built in.

In summary, although RIAs will bring richer desktop-type applications to your website browsers, it is important to realize that all the fluidity in the experience makes tracking harder, especially with current measurement systems. In terms of data collection, there is also a paradigm shift. Currently we launch websites with some standard tags and they collect almost all the data you need to report on. After the fact, you can improve the data collection tag if you want but the tag is pretty much always there. With RIAs you have to put in a lot of effort up front to understand the business purpose and then identify the business events and ensure that they are tagged by developers up front. If that front loading is not done, you have no data. It is as simple as that.

Tip: It is extremely important to test RIAs against currently standard web experiences ("dumb" HTML). In many cases, you will find that simply testing in a lab usability environment will not quite represent how real customers would react. Hence it is important to launch your RIAs in an A/B test environment to validate that indeed it is an improvement as compared to the current experience. It is not uncommon for customers to reject what they are not used to. It does not mean that you fall into despair and do not try; it means that you test and you optimize the experience based on customer feedback. (Chapter 10, "Month 5: Website Experimentation and Testing—Shifting the Power to Customers and Achieving Significant Outcomes," covered experimentation and testing in detail. Please review that chapter for details on how to go about doing this.)

Week 4: Measuring the Success of RSS

From Wikipedia: RSS is a family of web feed formats used to publish frequently updated digital content, such as blogs, news, feeds or podcasts. Users of RSS content use programs called feed "readers" or "aggregators": the user "subscribes" to a feed by supplying to their reader a link to the feed; the reader can then check the user's subscribed feeds to see if any of those feeds have new content since the last time it checked, and if so, retrieve that content and present it to the user.

In other words, RSS is an absolutely wonderful method for your customers to sign up to get the content they are interested in from your website, but have it delivered to them via a method and in a format and at a destination of their choosing.

Monday: Understand the Reality of RSS

RSS is changing the way your customers consume content. Its increased popularity means that web analytics applications, as they exist today in early 2007, are unable to accurately report data for your website.

Here is a quick example. I like keeping up with cricket news and I would typically visit the BBC Sport website and read the news about the Indian cricket team, as shown in Figure 12.19.

Figure 12.19 BBC Sport: Cricket in India

Even with a bookmark to this website, getting there requires a two-step process (one to open the browser and one to access the bookmarks). The team does not play every day, so there may or may not be new content for me. With RSS, consuming content about the Indian cricket team is significantly easier:

1. Go to the Cricket page on news.bbc.co.uk and click the orange RSS icon in the URL window, as shown in Figure 12.20.

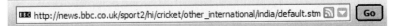

Figure 12.20 BBC Sport: RSS sign-up for cricket in India

2. My feed reader (which happens to be the application Feedreader) automatically opens, asking me to add the XML feed to my subscriptions. See Figure 12.21.

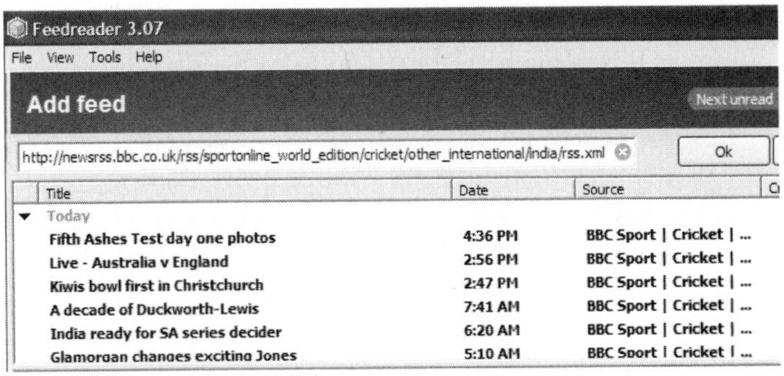

Figure 12.21 BBC Sport: adding the feed for cricket in India

3. Click OK. You are finished.

Now rather than me checking for new stories about my sports team, my Feedreader will automatically check with the BBC Sport website every day. If there is a new story, it will show up in my Feedreader, and I never have to visit the website again. See Figure 12.22.

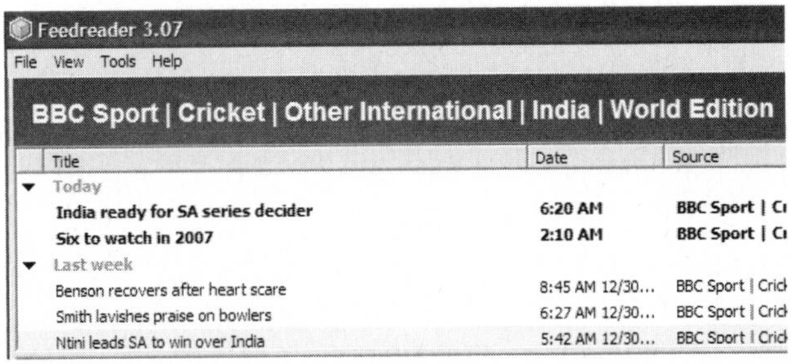

Figure 12.22 Feedreader view of the latest content

Although the preceding example is of a sports fanatic, and most of the buzz around RSS is for blogs, you can imagine how this can apply to your company websites. If you have a content site, this is a no-brainer. You make it easier for customers to get to your content, and you will have more customers. But you can also think of other applications. For example, I have a D-Link router that is not the greatest on the planet. Rather than me proactively checking for the latest updates on the D-Link support websites, it would be great if D-Link offered an RSS feed for the support page. Then, if there were new content, it would show up in my Feedreader and I could download the patch. Figure 12.23 shows the D-link support website and illustrates its lack of support for RSS.

Figure 12.23 D-Link support could provide RSS

The challenge with RSS is that your visitors never visit your website. They are not creating entries into your web log files and they are not executing your JavaScript tags. So your customers are consuming all the content from your website, but your web analytics application data is incomplete because it has no data for these customers.

It is not just that most of the web analytics applications are blind to this data, but also that there are no current standardized ways to track these metrics. You can sign up for RSS using feed readers (as I did in the preceding example) or you can sign up with major services such as Bloglines. My feed reader will say I am one reader, as will Bloglines. The issue is that hundreds of people use Bloglines, but they show up as only one reader in many statistics. Likewise there are many feed readers that each have their own way of behaving, making it hard to have standardized tracking (text readers, such as Feedreader shown in Figure 12.22, strip out all the HTML and present only text). This will obviously change as RSS becomes a much more dominant way of consuming content.

Tuesday: Learn about Emerging "Standards" for RSS Tracking

RSS is still not very integrated into most websites and the analytics tools that are being used by the websites. There is no standard when it comes to tracking RSS. We have a couple of emerging options.

First, you can use standardized feed management services (for example, Feed-Burner). You can outsource your feed management to services such as FeedBurner, which can not only help you manage your feed subscriptions but also provide you with the ability to do various cool things with your feed. Such services will also report the core statistics for your RSS feed, as shown in Figure 12.24.

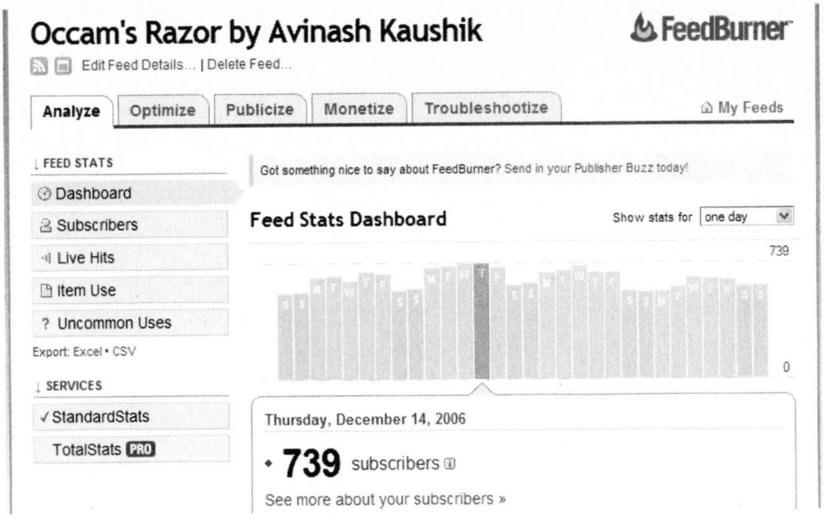

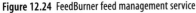

Occam's Razor by Avinash Kaushik

FeedBurner

Edit Feed Details... | Delete Feed...

| **Analyze** | Optimize | Publicize | Monetize | Troubleshootize | My Feeds |

FEED STATS

Dashboard

Subscribers

Live Hits

Item Use

? Uncommon Uses

Export: Excel • CSV

SERVICES

✓ StandardStats

TotalStats **PRO**

Got something nice to say about FeedBurner? Send in your Publisher Buzz today!

Feed Stats Dashboard   Show stats for one day

739

0

Thursday, December 14, 2006

• **739** subscribers

See more about your subscribers »

Figure 12.24 FeedBurner feed management service

Additionally, some vendors, such as Visual Sciences, are integrating feed reporting into their standard web analytics application services. You can add a simple JavaScript tag, and as your feed runs around the world, the data is sent back to your Visual Sciences data collection services and included in your standard web analytics reporting. This will become more common in 2007 and beyond.

Note: The difference between FeedBurner and Visual Sciences is that Visual Sciences will not manage your feeds. For that you can use one of the free services online or implement your own on your website.

NOTE

One of the challenges of this emerging medium is that cookies are not accepted by the feed readers. Some don't accept JavaScript. There are no page views in the traditional sense, and of course no sessions that we are so used to. All this means that it is hard to match existing web analytics metrics in an apple-to-apple comparison. Hence as you had learned in Chapter 7, "Month 2: Jump-Start Your Web Data Analysis," we computed the metric Unique Blog Readers. It is a very different metric from any that are available in current web analytics tools.

You'll spend the rest of the week learning about some of the metrics that are currently de facto standards. You can use these to measure success of your own RSS efforts.

Wednesday: Track Subscribers and Reach

As always, the first thing you want to know is, "Is anyone out there consuming my wonderful content?" Because the standard rules and metrics of the web analytics world don't quite apply to the world of RSS, we will define and measure two new metrics: the loose equivalents of visitors and unique visitors.

Subscribers

For a given time period, this is the number of unique feed readers (online or desktop based) that have requested your feed. It is an approximate measure of the number of individuals who have opted to receive regular updates from your website, as shown in Figure 12.25.

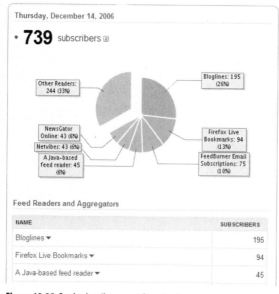

Figure 12.25 Feed subscriber report from FeedBurner

The best way to think of this number is to imagine it as the subscriptions to a magazine or newspaper. This is simply the number of people who are getting your magazine or newspaper. As with magazines, the same person could have a subscription at work and at home, so a small amount of duplication is possible.

With FeedBurner it is also important to remember that this number includes your customers who have signed up to get the feed via email. In Figure 12.25, for my Occam's Razor web analytics blog, it is 10 percent of the subscribers.

Track your subscribers over time. At least in this case, up and to the right is good, as shown in Figure 12.26.

Feed Stats Dashboard   Show stats for [all time ▾]

Figure 12.26 Subscriber metric trend from FeedBurner

Reach

Reach is the total number of subscribers who have viewed the content in a feed during a given time frame. To continue our magazine subscription metaphor, this is the number of people who have opened the newspaper and actually read a story (how wonderful is this—you can't even track that with offline media!).

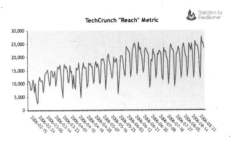

Figure 12.27 Reach metric trend from FeedBurner

The metric Reach is also a directional measure of engagement: of all the people who have signed up for your feed, how many are consuming the content and are hence engaged.

> **Note:** Some applications and practitioners use the term *readers* in place of *reach*. However, I prefer *reach*, which is gaining some traction in the industry.

NOTE

Thursday: Measure Reads and Clicks to Website (Referrals)

Now that you are comfortable with the metrics related to people/customer counts, you can move to the next step of understanding what specific piece of content that you are publishing is being consumed and is causing referrals to your website (where you hopefully have an opportunity to sell products and services or simply engage your RSS subscribers in a deeper way).

Reads (Views)

Reads (Views) computes the number of times each RSS item you have published is read by a subscriber during a given time frame.

In our magazine metaphor, this is a metric that would measure exactly which of the 90 stories in the magazines have been read by your subscriber. (I admit that in the cool world of Web 2.0, this is essentially measuring something equivalent to page view, so the page view is not really dead!)

This is a great way to understand which content is more popular with your subscribers and which is not. You can use this data to prioritize the areas that you can focus on to fuel your subscriber growth.

Clicks to Website

Clicks to Website is a metric that computes which RSS content is driving traffic to your website during a given time period.

In our magazine metaphor, think about being able to measure which scandalous high-profile celebrity story is causing your magazine subscriptions to soar, or more people to sign up for your sister publications.

A number of businesses publish RSS feeds of their content, but often they will have only partial content published in the hope that you'll be tempted by the preview content and click over to the website, where you will promptly empty your wallet to get a paid subscription or make some other purchase (such a "non-social-media" thing to do!). There are other reasons why it might be good for your business to have your subscribers click over to the website. (For instance, subscribers might provide you with leads, sign up for newsletters, or consume non-RSS content on your site.)

Figure 12.28 shows a sample report that illustrates this metric. You can use Clicks to Website to understand customer interests and the kind of content that drives subscribers to your website. You can then optimize your articles or posts around that data.

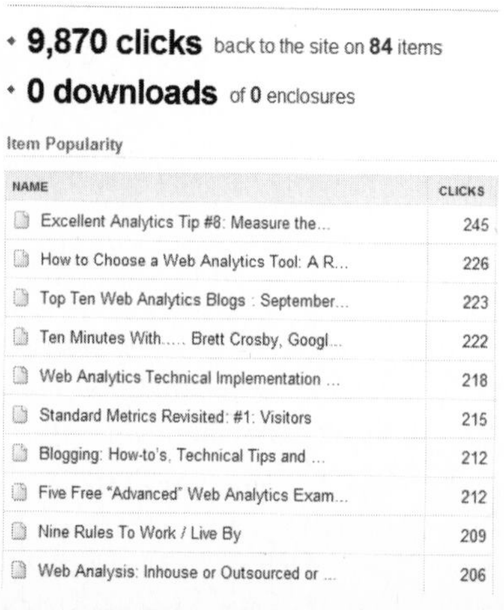

- **9,870 clicks** back to the site on **84** items
- **0 downloads** of **0** enclosures

Item Popularity

NAME	CLICKS
Excellent Analytics Tip #8: Measure the...	245
How to Choose a Web Analytics Tool: A R...	226
Top Ten Web Analytics Blogs : September...	223
Ten Minutes With..... Brett Crosby, Googl...	222
Web Analytics Technical Implementation ...	218
Standard Metrics Revisited: #1: Visitors	215
Blogging: How-to's, Technical Tips and ...	212
Five Free "Advanced" Web Analytics Exam...	212
Nine Rules To Work / Live By	209
Web Analysis: Inhouse or Outsourced or ...	206

Figure 12.28 Clicks to Website metric from FeedBurner

Friday: Analyze Subscriber Location and Feed Reader Type

Through your feed data, you also have an ability to report on two subscriber dimensions that could be useful for analyzing your visitors and improving your RSS feeds: location and feed reader type.

Location

You have an ability to report on the geographic locations of your subscribers, in case your business can optimize the website content or even their marketing campaigns based on this knowledge (see Figure 12.29).

Feed Reader Type

You also have an ability to report on the type of feed reader that your subscribers are using, as shown in Figure 12.29. This data is primarily helpful if you (or your IT folks) are interested in making special customizations to make your published content appear prettier in different feed readers (your subscribers will surely thank you for doing that).

Live Feed Hits

Last 16 minutes (We're live and on the scene!)

25 hits in the last **16 minutes**

All times are translated to your local time zone.

TIME	USER AGENT	COUNTRY
6:40:14 PM (2007-1-1)	Gregarius	United States
6:39:21 PM (2007-1-1)	FeedDemon ▾	Hong Kong
6:39:19 PM (2007-1-1)	Netvibes ▾	France
6:39:10 PM (2007-1-1)	FeedShow ▾	France
6:39:07 PM (2007-1-1)	Lib WWW-Perl package	United States

Figure 12.29 Location and feed reader data for feed subscribers

Armed with this week's information, you can give your RSS analytics a jump start. Wonderful reports and computed metrics that will impress your senior management team are within your reach. Remember that you can use free services such as FeedBurner to fill the gap that surely exists in your web analytics tool at the moment. Now you're all set for at least a decent performance on your entry into the interesting world of Web 2.0.

Month 8 and Beyond: Shattering the Myths of Web Analytics

Like all good existences in the universe, ours has collected its fair share of myths and legends. Some of these myths and legends inspire us and propel us on as we slog day and night through our jobs trying to make sense of terabytes of data at our disposal. Others sadly turn out to be crushingly false when we have little to show for our efforts— all this work and no actionable insights.

This chapter dispels five of the most persistent web analytics myths of our generation and dissects them so you can understand whether there is anything there. If not, we'll explore reasons to move beyond the myths and focus on alternatives in your persistent drive to have analysis be in the service of business goals and actionability.

Path Analysis: What Is It Good For? Absolutely Nothing

Path analysis is the process of determining a sequence of pages visited in a visitor session prior to some desired outcome (a purchase, a sign-up, a visit to a certain part of the site, and so forth). The desired goal is to get a sequence of pages, each of which forms a path, that lead to a desired outcome. Usually these paths are ranked by frequency of visits (or "use"), as shown in Figure 13.1.

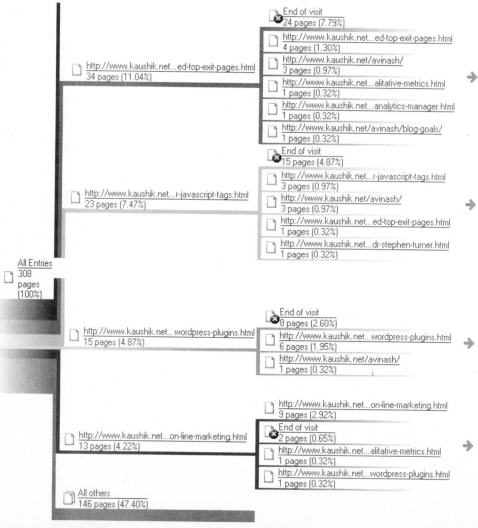

Figure 13.1 Path analysis report

On paper, path analysis seems to make tons of sense. We have websites. These websites have been created for a desired outcome. We have pages that we have created to help the visitors to the website follow a logical path to make it to the outcome. If we can analyze the paths, we can understand where the customers are falling off and hence failing to make it to the outcome we have built our site for. How hard can that be?

We usually strive to do path analysis in a quest to find a magic pill that will tell us exactly what paths our visitors are following on our website. If they follow the path we intended, we celebrate.

If, as it usually turns out, our visitors don't follow the path that *we* want them to follow, then it's back to the drawing board. We either redesign the site structure to get them to follow the path or, worse, conduct hours of "analysis" on what the heck they were thinking when they clicked this button or went to that page (bad customers, bad customers!).

So is path analysis a good use of time? In my humble opinion, the answer is a rather emphatic no, with one exception (which I'll discuss later in this section). Almost always path analysis tends to be a suboptimal use of your time, resources, and money.

Challenges with Path Analysis

Despite being one of the very first things that your boss wants from the web analytics tools (right after visitor counts), path analysis faces a lot of challenges in its ability to deliver any value. Some of the main challenges with path analysis are as follows:

- Imagine a website with five pages. Page 1 is the start, and page 5 is the finish. By simply visualizing it in your mind, you can imagine the number of paths that a visitor could take (see Figure 13.2). Now imagine a website with 100 pages or one with 5,000 pages. The number of possible paths quickly becomes infinity (well, not really, but you get the point). It is difficult to parse any intelligence out of it.

- Most of our tools do a terrible job of representing a common path that might look like this: click forward, click back to home, click forward, reverse to three pages ago, click Buy. Our analytics tools provide path analysis computations that assume a world of linear paths and represent that in their path analysis reports. But it is hard to display these paths (for example, the path in Figure 13.2) in a report, especially in a world of linear path representation. To make matters worse, the path represented by Figure 13.2 is hard to compute. Yet this is exactly how our customers browse our websites.

- On most websites the path with the highest frequency (the most common path) is usually followed by less than 5 percent of visitors, and usually the number is closer to 1 percent. As a responsible analyst, could you make any decision based on what such a small fraction of site traffic is doing?

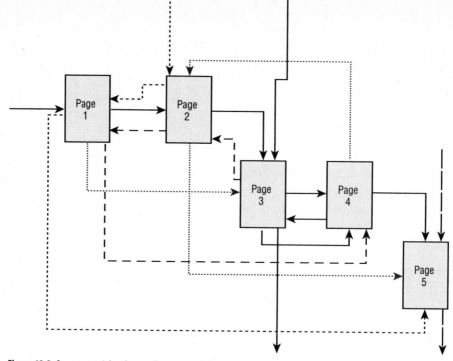

Figure 13.2 Some potential paths on a five-page website

- Even if the most common path is followed by 90 percent of the visitors on your website, the current path analysis has two fatal flaws:

  - It can't indicate which page in a series was the most influential in convincing a customer to deliver the outcome you want, a piece of data that can actually make this actionable.

  - Current tools combine traffic into one bucket, when in reality each segment of traffic behaves differently (say email marketing traffic vs. search vs. bookmarks vs. print ads). With all these customer "intents" mixed in, it is hard to discern which exits from the path were good and which were bad. (There *are* some exits that are good—for example, exits from a page that lists support options or exits from the product overview page by people who were there to just learn about your products. They found it and then they exited. Now how do you separate those people from people who came to that page to buy but could not find the Add to Cart button or comparison chart and then exited?)

All of the preceding points combine to make it difficult to glean insights that we can use to make our websites more endearing to our customers.

An Alternative: The Funnel Report

Rather than slaving away on path analysis, with not much to offer in terms of reward, there are alternative types of analysis available. Perhaps the best one is offered by the unique Funnel report, misnamed because it is not really just a funnel report, in the ClickTracks web analytics application, shown in Figure 13.3. The Funnel report addresses some of the critical flaws that render path analysis reports useless and it also provides some interesting and new pieces of information.

In Figure 13.3, rather than creating a linear view of your website (page 1, then page 2, then page 3…), you can take your entire website and represent it as a few core pieces (related content groups). So, for example, for a 5,000-page e-commerce website, you can have essentially just these five pieces:

- Website entry points (home page, custom landing pages)
- "Convince me to buy" content (comparison charts, product line information, competitive differentiators, demos, external endorsements)
- Deep product information (product details, system requirements, customer ratings, FAQs, parts/components included, images)
- Cart
- Checkout

In Figure 13.3, each group of content will be represented in the Page Group Influence (center) column. Each group can represent either one page or a grouping of many pages (so all product detail pages for all 500 products on your site can be represented by one *block* if that makes sense for you). This provides a very simple high-level view of your site, with each group represented as a stage.

There are two things that the Funnel report empowers you to understand at a very deep actionable level.

First, it gives you an insight into content consumption. It is amazing that we are so absorbed in looking at the tree level in all tools that we really miss the forest. The Funnel report helps you understand content consumption by computing the percent of site traffic that sees any group of content. This leads you to understand what customers are able to find and what they are looking for (there's a subtle difference there).

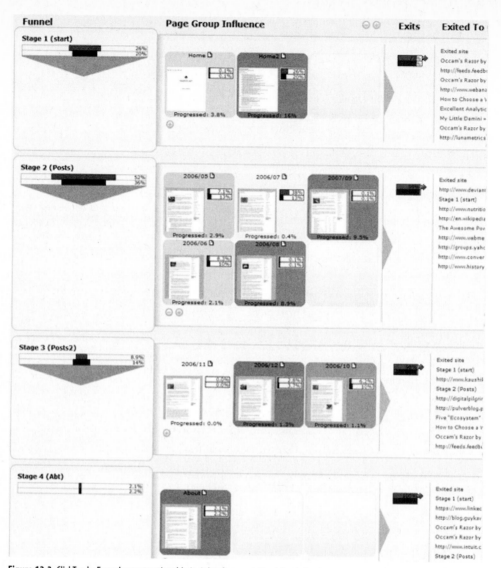

Figure 13.3 ClickTracks Funnel report: actionable insights from website visitor behavior

For example, you can understand that the most valuable content you have created is in stage 3 of Figure 13.3, and yet a tiny fraction, 6.9 percent, of the site visitors are consuming that content. This is scary. It calls for either realigning resources to content that is being consumed more, or if you want people to consume groups of content in stage 3, then maybe you need to redesign the navigation or do search engine optimization or merchandising.

A tool (for example, from WebTrends or IndexTools) also allows you to group large pieces of content on your site to help you understand content consumption. You should absolutely understand this key metric for your websites.

Second, the Funnel report helps you understand page or group influence. This is the money shot. If you structure your website with an outcome at the bottom (for example, an order, lead, or tech support answer), the Funnel report will compute how influential each page on your site is in "influencing" people to move toward the outcome. ClickTracks will analyze all the visitor sessions on your site (and hence the pages viewed) and take the pages that most people see as they move on to the next stage and code it darker in the report (and also report that as a percent).

This is awesome because you can simply look at the darker shaded pages and know, for example, that no one cares about system requirements but rather the page on our "10 year no-questions-asked return policy" is the most important one in convincing people to add to their cart.

At a glance in Figure 13.3, you can identify the content on your website that customers have voted as influential with their clicks (remember, clicks that are tied to an outcome!). With this you address one of the most critical flaws of analysis: even if 90 percent of the people on your site follow the same path and 10 pages to purchase, what content influenced them to buy? Now you can start to answer that question.

In the Funnel report it is irrelevant whether visitors go from A to B to C to D, or from A to D to C to B, or from B to D directly. It does not rely on a "path" existing; it just looks for what visitors see and for the outcome of visitors seeing each piece of content.

Notice the rightmost column in Figure 13.3, Exited To. If your website visitors do not follow the stages that you have constructed in your report, where do they go? This column helps you validate whether you have the right understanding of customer behavior or need to redo your report (and reexamine your understanding of the site). For example, if most visitors go from stage 1 to stage 3, maybe you need to change your report because your customers don't care about stage 2.

Finally, it is also quite easy to view how different customer segments are influenced by different content. Figure 13.3 shows two customer segments, All Visitors (the green bar) and Search Traffic (the blue bar). Each group seems to be interested in different pieces of content. Imagine this type of knowledge turned around so you can understand the unique needs of each customer segment and then apply that to personalization.

I believe that more and more web analytics vendors will offer some way of doing this type of analysis because of the potential for deep insights that it can enable.

Path analysis as it is practiced currently is ultimately like communism (with sincerest apologies to anyone in my audience who might be offended). There are overt/covert intentions to control things, to try to regulate, to say that we know better about you what you want, to push out a certain way of thinking.

The Web, on the other hand, is the ultimate personal medium and one in which we all like different things, we all have specific preferences and opinions and a certain way we want to accomplish something. The beauty of the Web is that all that is possible, and it can be done cheaply with easily accessible technology. So why do typical path analysis and why try to push a certain way of navigation, browsing, or buying? Why not get a deep and rich understanding of our customers and then provide them various different options to browse our website however they want to and get to the end goal the way they want to?

Conversion Rate: An Unworthy Obsession

Wake up any web analyst, or even better a website owner, in the middle of the night and ask what he measures. His first two words will be *conversion rate*. It is also highly likely that when you woke him up he was in a dream/nightmare trying to improve the conversion rate of his website!

Most web analytics practitioners define conversion rate as the percent of site visitors who do something that the company who owns the website wants them to do—submit an order, sign up for an email, send a lead, and so forth. It is also less frequently measured as movement from entry to a particular page or from one page to the next.

Measuring conversion rate is usually the cornerstone, if not the king, queen, and the court jester, of any web analytics program. It is perhaps the very first KPI that is measured by any good analyst, and we can't seem to get enough of it. We report it up and down the chain of command, and it occupies a place of prime importance when we present to senior management.

After all, why would you not? The logic is that if your conversion rate is 2.2 percent (as indicated by a Shop.org study for retail sites in the second quarter of 2006) and if you improve it by 0.01 percent, you will make a million bucks (replace that with a really high number for your company).

This seems simple enough, yet there is perhaps no other metric more detrimental to solving for a holistic customer experience on the website because of the company behavior it drives.

The behavior most observed is that people obsess about conversion rate and spend massive amounts of energy on getting it up a smidgen. Entire site strategies exist simply to move the number up at the cost of caring about anything else.

This is a result of the incessant focus on the company's bottom line (see Chapter 4, "Critical Components of a Successful Strategy") and also because of a lack of understanding of the complexity that drives visitors to a website.

Problems with Conversion Rate

The recommendation here is that you should stop obsessing about conversion rate. Put the overall site conversion rate in an appendix of your weekly or monthly presentations, but that is about it.

There are two core reasons for this recommendation:

- Overall site conversion rate (nonsegmented) for your site is a nice-to-know metric, but it is quite meaningless in terms of its ability to truly **communicate actionable** insights. You have 100 visitors, 2.2 percent of those converted, so where do you start to look for what the heck happened?

- A minority of visitors who come to any website come to buy (a minority usually is defined as less than 50 percent of site traffic). Consider Amazon.com, eBay, Intuit, or the Apple Store—all of which have major e-commerce sites. So if a minority of people visit your website to buy, why should we obsess about conversion rate? Are we not guilty of letting this relentless focus on conversion rate result in sad negligence toward those other website customer segments? See Figure 13.4.

If you solve for conversion rate, are you solving for all your traffic? Are you improving the website experience for all your customers?

The most likely answer to these questions is a big whopping no.

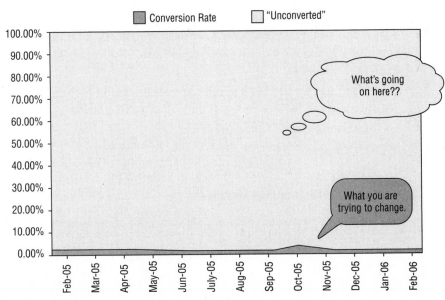

Figure 13.4 Conversion rate in perspective: solving for the few

So what customer segments might you be missing if you focus only on conversion rate?

- Customers who come to your website to *research*. They will never buy from your website. Maybe if you do an awesomely kick-butt job on the website, you might convert them, but it is highly unlikely. An example of this is using Amazon.com to primarily read customer reviews or to watch the new Bill Maher show in the Amazon Fishbowl section (where you'll see ads for Amazon products), or to read specs or print web pages with product information.

- Customers who come to your website to *learn* about your company. They are looking for jobs, press releases, your company founder's bio, details about why you exist, your blog, a way to unsubscribe from your emails, and so forth.

- Customers who come to our websites for *help*. These people are looking for support or for driving directions to your office or they want to send you a nasty email or register their product, for example.

- Customers who come for reasons that we don't know because we simply never bothered to ask (this segment is huge, by the way).

All these segments—and there may be different ones for your website—will never buy from you. All these segments are not static. They change based on market conditions, actions your company takes (for example, campaigns or branding), and stuff your competitors do.

Obsessing about conversion rate means focusing on 20–40 percent of the traffic on your website (the "convertible" minority of the 98 percent marked unconverted in Figure 13.4). It also means potentially implicitly ignoring major chunks of traffic for whom you might not be creating optimal customer experiences (by focusing on improving pages, content, whatever).

Perhaps most important, an obsession about conversion rate means you solve for the short term, the now, and just Submit Order, at the cost of solving for long-term metrics such as customer satisfaction.

So if overall conversion rate is not the optimal answer, what is a compelling alternative?

An Alternative: Task Completion Rate by Primary Purpose

You should consider replacing conversion rate, or complementing it, with *task completion rate by primary purpose,* as shown in Figure 13.5.

Figure out the core reasons for visitors coming to your website by asking them the question, perhaps in a survey, *Why are you visiting the website today?* The answer options will look something like this: to research products/services, to purchase products/services, to look for company information, register the products I have already purchased, look for support, and so forth.

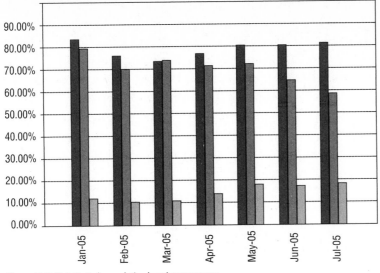

Task Completion by Primary Purpose ■Research ■Purchase □Support

Figure 13.5 Website task completion by primary purpose

Also ask each of those website visitors the question, *Were you able to complete your task today?* The answer to this question will be yes or no.

Do a little cross-tab in Excel (the data will come from a surveying mechanism) that will compute for you why people come to your site, or Primary Purpose, and what their success looks like, or Task Completion Rate. Figure 13.6 shows an example.

▶ **Table 13.1** Critical cross-tab: solving for all customers and for the long term

Primary Purpose	Task Completion Rates Trend							%Traffic for each Purpose
	Jan-05	Feb-05	Mar-05	Apr-05	May-05	Jun-05	Jul-05	
Research	80%	73%	70%	73%	77%	77%	78%	24%
Purchase	76%	67%	70%	68%	69%	62%	56%	19%
Investor Relations	78%	75%	76%	74%	72%	75%	77%	7%
Jobs	42%	45%	35%	47%	26%	40%	38%	12%
Support	11%	9%	10%	13%	17%	16%	17%	38%
Overall	57%	54%	52%	55%	52%	54%	53%	

If you can do this, you suddenly are massively aware of why people come to your website (last column above). You know how many of them are there to buy etc., and you know where your website is failing you.

This wonderful analysis will yield insights that will tell you exactly what you need to do to improve your website experience for all major customer segments, which in turn will improve your website's task completion rate. It is *impossible* that higher conversion rate will not follow.

It is much harder to solve for multiple goals, to move from solving for conversion rate to solving for task completion for your groups by primary purpose. It will be hard to convince key stakeholders around you about the value of measuring task completion rates and to bless the associated projects to improve customer experience.

Be prepared for that and stress that thinking in terms of task completion rate will provide a long-term sustained competitive advantage that would be hard for your competitors to replicate.

In the end, when the dust settles, the objective of a customer-centric web strategy is to create satisfied site visitors no matter why they come to your website and secondarily it is about short-term revenue. The mindset shift required is from thinking of conversion as "the site visitor doing whatever it is that you want them to do" to "the site visitor doing whatever they wanted to do."

I promise there is good karma associated with that latter one.

Perfection: Perfection Is Dead, Long Live Perfection

The ever resourceful Wikipedia defines perfection as *"a state of completeness and flawlessness."*

As analysts, and even as decision makers, we are seeped in metrics and numbers and math and things adding up. We seek confidence in data to make decisions that can make or break our businesses (or our personal lives). More than others, we seek perfection because of our backgrounds in numbers and Excel and, most important, logic. If A plus B divided by C equals five million dollars, then we will take action Q, but only if we have utter confidence in A, B, and C.

To achieve a level of perfection, we spend more money on better tools; we slice, dice, hack, and smack the data until we feel that we understand everything about it; we spend time waiting for more data or different data; we wait for someone else to make the decision or we make no decisions at all; we lose money, time, resources, and value.

It seems to make sense that it is risky to make decisions based on imperfections and that it could be expensive to make decisions when things (numbers, in our case) don't seem to all add up and make perfect sense.

The problem in the real world is that nothing is perfect. It sounds obvious, but it is not quite as obvious. The challenge for web analytics specifically is that we rely on a set of deeply imperfect systems to collect data, process it, and analyze it. These imperfect methodologies include cookies, JavaScript tags, data hopping around the world passing anonymizers and firewalls, pages loading, and web structures staying the same, and so forth.

The result is that often our core human instinct to seek perfection (perfect understanding, predictability in data, stability in numbers) actively hinders our ability to find insights from our data, insights that ultimately might make or break our businesses. This is much more of a challenge for analysts because we are used to things matching up and making sense. In all of our prior experiences (in finance, ERP systems, data warehouses, business intelligence, phone sales etc.), we are used to our ability to count off numbers and apply quality controls and cleansing mechanisms that would make the data perfect (or very close to that). The Web, on the other hand, does not make sense, in more ways than you can imagine.

Perfection on the Web is dead (well, it was never there in the first place). You will have to steel yourself for that realization and adapt your mindset to make decisions and take actions in an imperfect world. It absolutely requires some level of comfort with "faith-based analysis" to ensure that some of the suboptimal outcomes (delays, cost overruns, lack of actions, time wasted) won't happen.

Even if the pursuit of perfection is futile on the Web, it is possible to make massively effective decisions that will change your business and improve customer experience. In this section, I'll provide some examples that illustrate the challenges of perfection.

Perfect Data

Chapter 2, "Data Collection—Importance and Options," covered all the data collection methodologies at our disposal. Every methodology has its problems in terms of its ability to collect data. Furthermore, every web analytics vendor applies their own filters and logic to computing numbers, making it even harder to really know what the number you are looking at means.

As an example, Figure 13.7 clearly states it is showing *unique visitors*, but this vendor is actually showing *visitors*. (The vendor is measuring a count of sessions, which translates into visitors, and not a count of unique persistent cookie IDs, which would translate into unique visitors.)

Perfect data is a myth; it is not possible at the moment on the Web. You can't wait for the numbers to be stabilized before you report them. When you slice and dice the data, they will sometimes show 200 visitors and 0 unique visitors (which is not possible in the real world, as you can imagine, but is possible in web data). If you have a couple of different tools on your website, they won't reconcile no matter how hard you try.

When you analyze and report on data from the Web, assume a comfort level of imperfection and simply move on. Assume that your visitor counts will change from month to month (for the same historical months). Just be okay with it because in reality if you hold the data collection methodologies and the web analytics vendor as a constant, you'll be fine because it is more important to look at trends.

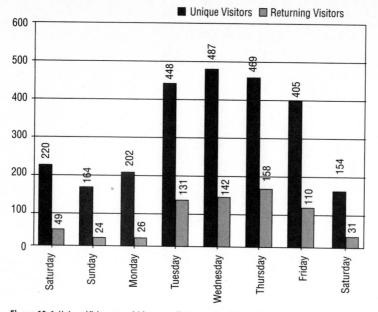

Figure 13.6 Unique Visitors trend (that actually is counting Visitors)

Web at the Speed of Web

You could be a small business or a large business. There is no disputing the fact that the Web, and businesses on the Web, move really fast. Most websites are living, breathing organisms that change often, whether the changes are to web pages, promotions, search rankings, or competitive pressures. The challenge with wanting to make perfect decisions is that in this unique ecosystem, you will probably be late to the market with your insights or potentially react at a speed that will not be optimal for your business. You have to be able to read the tea leaves and apply judgment and make a decision.

For example, say you are running a multivariate test and you learn in four or five days that with 90 percent confidence, two of your eight page variations (often referred to as recipes by some vendors/practitioners) just stink. Kill them and move to the six that show promise. You could wait to get to 95 percent confidence or 99 percent confidence. But by killing the obvious doozies, you will be able to send more traffic to the more promising six recipes and get a winning answer faster.

It is a given that you won't make a decision on the clicks of three visitors, but you have to move even if you have not yet reached 99 percent confidence. This is hard to do for many people because it is not how we are innately wired. Yet there is no other medium where this axiom is more true: Apply judgment, think smart, move fast.

Fractured Multisource Data

One of the biggest reasons why you have to be comfortable living in the world of imperfection is that most of the time you will not have access to all the data. Your banner ad performance data is with DoubleClick, but your pay per click (SEM) campaigns data is with your agencies. You have no idea whether the latest spike was because of television advertising or whether your sales have tanked because all your customers decided to go to retail stores. You also for the most part don't know what your competitors are up to (or for that matter, the search engines).

You have access only to your website clicks data and sometimes to your deep outcomes data (orders, product mix, revenue goals). This means you have access to only a limited set of data and you have to make decisions based on that. Lots of things won't make sense or add up (remember, you don't have access to all the data). You will have to have the ability to make the best of what you have and be comfortable with gaps and holes. Alternatively, you will have to be really good at getting your hands on some of the other data and try your best to merge it or correlate it (you can rest assured that it won't tie) and make decisions.

It takes a special kind of analyst to be comfortable in the world that is painted here. It takes a flexible mindset to leave past experience and move into this new, more complex world. It certainly takes a supportive management team to accept the imperfect world we live in and yet figure out how to thrive in it.

Real-Time Data: It's Not Really Relevant, and It's Expensive to Boot

Every good wish list for a perfect web analytics tool starts with the desire to get real-time data. The thought is that because of the fast pace and ever-changing nature of the Web, getting real-time data is mandatory to being able to take advantage of all that the Web has to offer from its innate ability to cough up so much data.

The real-time data desire seems to be so pervasive that every little and big web analytics vendor prominently advertises how real-time their data is. The first vendor says I can do every five hours, the next guy says I see that and I raise you three hours, and the next gal says you guys are sissies because I can give you real real-time and give you live traffic streams and send that to your BlackBerry mobile devices.

If you're a weatherman, real-time data is relevant and important. But is getting real-time data really relevant for your web business? Do you really need it? And what's the real cost of getting real-time data?

This spoils the surprise, but for a majority of web businesses the answer to the first and second questions is no. Because most of us think it is yes, it makes the answer to the third question a little bit scary (and rather suboptimal for most businesses in terms of detrimental impact).

Results of Getting Real-Time Data

So what is the typical result of getting data near real-time (roughly defined as faster than every couple of hours)? Here are five common outcomes of hyperfocus on real-time data:

Much More Reporting, Much Less Analysis We already live and swim in a world of too much data, so much that we have a hard time finding any actionable insights from what we have even after we hack at it for hours or days. Real-time data usually worsens that by giving you even more data faster, with less time, and you are left to find the proverbial needle in the haystack (a nontrivial task, as you can imagine). Because it is likely that you paid a lot for the spiffy real-time data functionality, there is also loads of pressure to show results from the investment, further fueling the cycle of reporting and data spewing.

Detrimental Impact on Resource Allocation It is a common theme in the industry that we don't apply the 10/90 rule (see Chapter 4). One reason is that it is hard to find the right people with the right skills for the job. But a secondary reason is that in the world of web analytics, we have a lot of complex data that can never reconcile to anything else. Now imagine what happens with real-time data.

Our finite resources now have to make sense of all this, pardon me, mess but with less time on hand and provide insights. Almost always because of real-time data there is a negative impact on the resources and bandwidth allocation because there is organization and management pressure to justify return on investment (remember, real-time data is not free—you pay to have access to data that fast).

Choice of Suboptimal Web Analytics Solutions This one is really common. Web analytics tools are chosen based on complicated all-encompassing RFP processes (see Chapter 5, "Web Analytics Fundamentals," for an alternative, and optimal, way to choose a web analytics tool). Usually the committee that is narrowing from 85 tools to 2 will reject any vendor that is not "real-time." (Remember the mindset—who would not want data in real time? It's like asking someone if they would like a delicious Krispy Kreme doughnut. How do you say no to that?) Most often this means that lots of tools that might have met other important criteria (say, advanced segmentation or integration with other sources) get kicked out. In the end, you might end up choosing a tool that is real-time (and expensive) yet in a few months, when you are more educated in web analytics and reports and what's important and start to dig deeper, you'll find all the limitations that will result in low-quality insights from the tool.

Increased Complexity in Systems and Processes If you have an in-house solution, real-time analysis means having to buy increasingly powerful machines (usually multi-CPU and loads of memory) that can capture data and process it fast enough to make it available in real time for you to use it. Remember that you can't use raw data logs (web logs or JavaScript-tag-based).

Additionally, to pull real-time off, we will also have to implement increasingly complex processes inside and outside the company. In your company, for example, you'll have to implement faster processing schedules and allocate resources (at least 0.25 to 0.5 person) to watch and make sure everything happens as expected and finally implement reports to run, to process all the data to humans.

From an outside perspective, you'll have to put additional processes in place that will pull data from outside sources (say AdWords or affiliates). This adds more steps and complexity into your systems and processes, complexity that is often not considered by marketing folks but inserts a nontrivial cost into the ecosystem.

False Sense of Confidence Sometimes you'll observe a false sense of confidence that all is well with the world because you have real-time data streaming into your BlackBerry. Of course this does not occur in every organization. But it exists more than we might prefer. This false sense of confidence means that we are less likely to look at the real cost and downside of getting the data.

In summary, the impact of real-time data is that you will pay more for your web analytics tools than might be optimal, you'll fuel a culture that will do more reporting than analysis, and you will end up adding complexity to your systems and supporting processes that in turn will add lots of hidden costs.

A Checklist for Real-Time Data Readiness

This obviously does not mean that you should never want real-time data. Here is a simple check-list to use to judge whether your organization is ready for real-time data and to increase the odds that you will get enough bang for the, end-to-end, increased bucks you'll spend:

Statistical Significance Do you get enough visitors to your website that you can make statistically significant decisions by using real-time data? You not only have to get enough overall traffic to the site, but you also have to get enough data in segments if you want to make real-time decisions.

For example, if you want to make real-time decisions about marketing promotions or AdWords campaigns, do you get enough traffic and outcomes (orders/leads) to make a statistically significant decision? If you get 13 visitors and two outcomes from two different campaigns every four hours, you can't make a confident decision comparing that to anything else.

Statistical significance is not just about raw numbers; you don't need a million visitors a day to get significance. But you do need enough visitors exhibiting the right behavior you are looking for and for them to do it often enough every 15 minutes, or every hour, for you to separate valuable signals from all the noise.

Awesome Analytical Capabilities You not only capture data in real time, but you have dedicated analysts who can analyze the data very quickly to find nuggets of valuable insights by looking not just at one piece of data, but data end to end. For example, they would notice not only that you got lots of clicks on this new creative from Google or Yahoo! PPC campaigns, but that this traffic is also placing more orders for the right products than other sources of traffic.

Along with analytical capabilities, you also need people who have optimal business acumen (maybe superoptimal). Numbers by themselves, no matter how fast they come at you and in how much quantity, won't help you make good decisions. For that you need people with good business acumen (people who understand your business really well, have a great grasp of your web ecosystem, and have lots of common sense). As a wise person said, reporting is not analysis!

Diversified and Empowered Decision-Making Structure Does your company have a decision-making structure enabling a front-line analyst to make decisions and authorize or execute changes based on data? Do you require VP approval before web pages go on or off? Do you need a HiPPO to sign off on promotions or campaigns changes?

For action to be taken from real-time data, decisions need to be made fast. Usually it will be your analyst or marketing manager observing these statistically significant differences. In most companies, these people don't have the authority to stop or green-signal anything based on data. That happens via a company labyrinth that needs to be navigated. If that is your company, then would it be worth it to pay all the cost of real-time data?

Awesome Website Operational Execution Capabilities Your company has a web operations team that can execute on a dime. They are able to push out the right creatives, remove nonperforming promotions, change the AdWords strategy, update landing pages, change email blasts that are already in the queue, send different instructions to your ad/search/marketing agencies who can also make changes very quickly. If it takes you two days to execute changes to your website (or campaigns, or agencies), the value of real-time data might be really questionable.

These are four extremely simple rules. If your organization capabilities meet all of the preceding requirements, you are well set to take advantage of getting your data in real time. But if even one of the preceding requirements is not met, perhaps you want real-time data only because you want to know and not because you want to take action. That knowing can be extremely expensive (in terms of people, process, and money), and distracting, if you don't meet the requirements to drive action.

An Exception to the Real-Time Value Rule

Real-time data is perfect in one scenario: an automated system that can make micro decisions based on rules or scenarios that the system can execute against. In this scenario, some (but not all) of the preceding issues become less critical. For example, imagine that you have an automated system that based on your rules can react to website visitors. Your rule could be to show a promotion to everyone who has been on the site for 10 minutes, and the automated reaction could be to compute session length in real time and maintain the capacity to show a pop-up promotion. In this case, data helps technology to react in real time to create unique customer experiences.

The important differentiators in such a scenario are as follows:

- The system reacts and makes decisions, not humans.
- The time to make decisions is eliminated (the system—software or hardware—reacts in real time), not humans.

We will see more and more of these types of approaches in the near future. Because they overcome limitations outlined earlier, they will be successful in capitalizing on real-time data in a way that we have sadly been unable to.

Standard KPIs: Less Relevant Than You Think

The web analytics field is complicated, with lots of data and lots of reports and lots of directions that you can go in. This challenge is compounded by the fact that we have lots of website visitors who come for lots of reasons beyond what the website was intended for (and, to kick us when we are down, usually we don't even have good insights into all the reasons that customers come to our website).

To overcome this challenge, and it really is a challenge, the natural tendency is to go out and find the "standardized" KPIs for web analytics or for your particular type of website (e-commerce, support, lead generation, advocacy, and so forth) and install them as KPIs for your business. You go out and pick choice KPIs from a good book, blog, article, or favorite advisor. You'll discover that the process leads to less success than you would have hoped for. It might take a small amount of time to figure that out, but you will.

In this short section of the book, I want to share a couple of elements that are overlooked when you might choose to adopt externally blessed KPIs (*yes I notice the irony that this book recommends some KPIs as well!*). My recommendation is for you to consider these four elements when making your KPI choice to ensure that you actually derive the anticipated benefits:

Remember, You Are Unique This is not just a self-worth-boosting affirmation. No two websites are alike, even if they do exactly the same thing. No two businesses execute their web strategy exactly the same way (and often they execute their strategies in radically different ways—think of website book selling by Borders, Overstock.com, Amazon.com and Barnes & Noble.com).

Before you copy and paste a formula from a standard recommended KPIs list, you should understand the reason for your website's existence and even more deeply strive to understand what key levers your business is trying to pull in order to be successful on the Web. Only if you believe that the KPI measures the true levers you are pulling should you adopt it, even if it is the sexiest KPI on earth and all your other friends are reporting it.

Question Reality There are loads of KPIs floating around that seem to be fantastic and give deep insights. Reality, on the other hand, is quite different. Be sure to understand, as profoundly as you can, all the core components of the KPI that you are choosing and stress-test the assumptions behind that KPI to ensure the following:

- You understand it really well.
- It is measuring something of value to you.
- You buy into the assumptions that the KPI formula or logic is making.

It is critical, as in the following sidebar example, that you question reality and apply critical thinking to the KPI that you are choosing. This will ensure that if and when you do pour resources into reports and measurements, they will yield actionable insights.

Stress-Testing a Standard KPI: Visitor Engagement Index

Recently I had a conversation with a reader of my blog who asked me to opine on a disagreement that he had with a professor about how to measure the visitor engagement index. He shared that the definition the professor gave was visits divided by unique visitors. He did not think that was right. His perspective was that on sites not using cookies, the denominator should be visits. So what did I think?

I could have responded on the technicality of the definition of the metric (visits/unique visitors). Instead my response was that the visitor engagement index metric was a suboptimal and useless metric because it is reading too much into data, stuff it should not be.

This might be a recommended way (technically feasible and mathematically correct) to measure this KPI, but it is sourced from a world where clickstream is the only choice and there is no other way to measure engagement. There is an implicit assumption in the metric definition that more visits by visitors are good. But as you can imagine, it is just as likely that "unique visitors" are making more "visits" to the website because the website is crap and not helping them find what they want. There is no way to actually discern from existence of multiple sessions from the same visitor that that was a good thing or a bad thing.

There are other, better ways to measure visitor engagement. The preceding is not one of them, even if it is a standard KPI.

Apply the So What Test Chapter 5 covered the three layers of So What testing. It is recommended that you apply this test to every KPI you end up choosing to ensure that it is the right KPI for you and to guarantee that the KPI will return the love that you will pour into its nurturing and growth.

Growth Businesses Have KPI Churn It is important to realize that even if the KPI passes the preceding tests and is useful to you at this time, you should go back and apply the recommendations periodically (especially "Remember, You Are Unique") to ensure that your personal list of standard KPIs is still relevant to your business and is providing the right lessons.

The only constant in business, and life, is change. Over time, the business challenges and strategic objectives evolve. You should expect 20 percent churn in your main KPIs every six months to a year. If they are not changing at least that much, either not a single dimension of your business has changed on the Web in that time (highly unlikely) or your KPIs are stale and have not gone through the preceding recommended exercise.

In summary: No one except you knows what your standard KPIs should be (all blogs and books and experts aside). The best that external inputs can do is start to move you along in your exploration of what is right for you (and it is likely not to be what is right for everyone else). Remember that you are unique, question reality, apply the So What test, and over time keep pace with business strategy evolution and ensure that there is the right churn in your own standard KPIs. That's your simple recipe for awesome success.

Advanced Analytics Concepts— Turbocharge Your Web Analytics

You can be an analytics superstar. Yes, you can. Regardless of how long you have been on the vast web analytics ocean, no matter whether you are on a raft or an ocean liner, in this chapter you will learn simple advanced web analytics methodologies/concepts/tricks that will help you elevate your game and get to your destination faster, cheaper, and more well rested.

I am perhaps stretching this analogy a bit too far, but contained in this chapter are key items that will help you take a fresh look at your data, and allow you to sift through it more intelligently to find insights that you or your key stakeholders can take action on.

Unlock the Power of Statistical Significance

We all wish that our key internal partners and business decision makers would use web analytics data a lot more to make effective decisions (as was discussed briefly in Chapter 13, "Month 8 and Beyond: Shattering the Myths of Web Analytics"). Questions that are foremost in our mind are as follows: How do we make recommendations and decisions with confidence? How can we drive action rather than push data?

The challenge is one of being able to separate the signal from the noise and make it easy to communicate that distinction. One powerful ally that you have in this quest is our good old friend statistics (perhaps an often underappreciated friend).

The concept that we will leverage specifically is called *statistical significance*. From the ever resourceful Wikipedia: "In statistics, a result is called significant if it is unlikely to have occurred by chance. A statistically significant difference simply means there is statistical evidence that there is a difference." Computing statistical significance between two sets of outcomes helps us be confident that we have reliable results and that the difference is important (or so small that it is not important).

Let's explore the practical application of statistical significance by evaluating two real-life scenarios.

In the first scenario, you are in charge of your company's email campaigns. For your most recent campaigns, you send out two offers to potential customers. After you analyze the data, here is how the outcomes look:

Offer 1 responses: 5,300

Orders: 46

Conversion rate: 0.87 percent

Offer 2 responses: 5,200

Orders: 55

Conversion rate: 1.06 percent

Is offer 2 better than offer 1? It does have "better" conversion rate, by 0.19 percent.

Can you decide which one of the two is better with fewer than 60 orders? For offer 2 you received 9 more orders from 100 fewer visitors. That sounds good.

Applying statistics and running these numbers through a simple statistical significance calculator tells us that the results, the two conversion rates, are just 0.995 standard deviations apart and not statistically significant. This would mean that it is quite likely that it is noise causing the difference in conversion rates.

Tip: You can download a statistical significance calculator at `http://www.teasley.net/free_stuff.htm` (or direct URL: `http://www.teasley.net/statcalc.xls`). Moore Wallace online statistical significance calculator: `http://snipurl.com/calc2`. You can also check out these two online calculators to compute statistical significance: Analytical Group significance testing tool: `http://snipurl.com/sigtest`

In the second scenario, you send out two offers to potential customers as a part of your email campaigns. Here is how the outcomes look:

Offer 1 responses: 5,300

Orders: 46

Conversion Rate: 0.87 percent

Offer 2 responses: 5,200

Order: 63

Conversion Rate: 1.21 percent

Running the numbers through our simple statistically significant calculator tell us that the two numbers are 1.74 standard deviations apart and the results rate 95 percent statistically significant.

A 95 percent significance is a strong signal. Based on this, and only a sample of 5,000 and more than 60 responses, we can confidently predict that offer 2 is better than offer 1 when it comes to getting more of our customers to convert.

Is this really hard to do? No! After you have downloaded the spreadsheet (`http://www.teasley.net/statcalc.xls`), all you do is simply punch in your numbers in the highlighted cells and you are on your way (or you can visit one of the websites above and compute the significance). This methodology can be easily applied to all facets of your insights analysis, including the following:

- Search engine marketing campaigns
- Various direct marketing campaigns and offers
- Any kind of percent metric (percent of traffic that reaches a goal from entry point 1 or entry point 2, or the effectiveness of the landing page to convert visitors, for example)
- Differences between results for your A/B or multivariate tests

There are a few powerful, but subtle, benefits to presenting statistical significance rather than simply conversion rate:

- You are taking yourself out of the equation; it is awesome to say, "According to the gods of statistics, here are the results."

- Focusing on the quality of the signal means that we appear smarter than people give us analysts credit for (this might sound trite, but in a world where there is so much data and complexity, the importance of *signal quality* cannot be understated, at least with respect to inspiring confidence in you and your numbers and driving powerful business results).

- You take *thinking* and *questions* out of the equation. Either something is statistically significant and we take action, or we say it is not significant and let's try something else. There is no reporting, just actionable insights.

Tip: As a best practice, aim for 95 percent or higher confidence. That is not always required but it is recommended.

Note: "Statistics are like a bikini. What they reveal is suggestive, but what they conceal is vital." —Aaron Levenstein. Remember that as you dive deeper, wiser words were never uttered about statistics.

Statistical significance is just one small "tool" in the statistics arsenal. It is advisable that you (or at least your analysts) have a well-rounded awareness of the principles of statistics and seek relevant opportunities to apply them in your own analysis. Increasingly this type of awareness is becoming almost mandatory as we aggressively charge into areas such as multivariate testing.

Use the Amazing Power of Segmentation

Throughout this book, you have looked at many examples of segmentation, even if they have not been explicitly called out as such. By now, either through reading this book or through your own experience in analysis, you've probably established that absolute numbers (KPIs) that represent just one data point are rarely useful. For example, what was the conversion number in May? Just by itself, it is not useful.

Having understood that reporting a number just by itself is not useful, we all migrated to measuring trends, which gave a bit more context to our metrics. For example, what is the trend for my conversion rate from January to May (or even better, from May last year to May this year)? The resulting table or graph provides nice context relating to current performance (if we are up or down over a time period or over the same time last year).

But even trends don't give us the entire context we need to find the kinds of insights that we can convert into action. For that we establish a new nirvana rule: Never report a metric (even the most hyped or your favorite KPI) without segmenting it a few levels deep. That is the only way to get deep insights into what that metric is really hiding, valuable information that you can use.

The power of segmenting a metric is that you peek behind the curtain and find out more about the metric. These are just a few of the benefits that you will gain if you become a slave to segmentation:

- It is impossible to segment any metric without putting in the effort to understand what you are reporting and the business value that the metric represents. It is hard work to do this deep dive and gain this understanding, but it is extremely valuable. Besides, what does not kill you makes you stronger.

- Segmenting allows you to quickly hone in on critical pieces of data where you can dive deeper to find the key insights that will induce real and meaningful action.

- Our senior executives and decision makers don't understand all the complexity and magic that is a web experience. Showing them segmented trends is an extremely effective communication tool (and the best part is, you barely have to talk, because the picture will tell the story).

- Segmenting metrics deeper automatically means that your data will become more and more relevant as some of the factors that "dirty" your data become a smaller part of the whole.

Let's explore the power of segmentation by using a simple example, one that perhaps you run into every day in your job.

A typical metric that you surely report on is visitors to your website. This extremely standard metric is shown in Figure 14.1

Figure 14.1 Monthly visitors to your website

We have just established that reporting this metric in isolation is not useful. Your boss asks, "How many visitors did we get this month?" You answer, "1,298." That is not useful information to your boss because he has no idea whether this is good or bad.

Segmenting by Bounce

You could take this one tiny step further. You could measure the number of visitors to your website who did not simply bounce off your website. (*Bounced visitors* are those who stay on your website for five seconds or fewer—or you can use ten seconds—or those who saw only one page, or whatever makes sense for your company.) When you count the numbers that did not bounce, or *stayed in the game* if you will, you get Figure 14.2.

Figure 14.2 Monthly visitors along with those who stayed longer than five seconds (did not *bounce off* right away)

This extremely simple segmentation tells you that just 48 percent of all the traffic stayed for more than five seconds. You never had a chance with the others.

Let's say your traffic this month was up over the last few months. Instead of getting (or taking) credit for that, this simple segmentation will prompt you to dig deeper into what happened. What were the reasons for 52 percent of the traffic leaving so quickly (bouncing)? Were you running the wrong type of campaigns? Are your meta tags wrong and hence the wrong types of visitors suddenly showed up? This segmentation will prompt questions about what the number was for prior months. It will do all of the right things that will gently encourage you to step behind the 1,298 visitor number and truly understand what is going on with your website. It will be work that will be closer to analysis than reporting and will surely yield actionable insights.

But you don't have to stop with simply counting visitors that bounced, or even use that metric. Another way you could segment this traffic is by the hottest thing on earth: search engines.

Segmenting by Search

You have great traffic. The number 1,298 was higher than your expectations, but how many did you get from all search engines, and how many from Google? The theory is if your website is optimized for searches, you should be able to capitalize on that. Take a look at Figure 14.3.

Figure 14.3 Visitor metric segmented for all search engines and those from Google

Figure 14.3 gives you more context for your total traffic, context that was missing from Figure 14.1 that showed all traffic by itself. This segmentation indicates that you getting only 18 percent of your traffic from search engines, and 85 percent of that is from Google. (Critical question: is that good or bad?)

There is a recommendation sitting in there about your search strategy and perhaps diversifying to other search engines. (According to the latest numbers, Google has 47.8 percent of overall search traffic, so you are potentially not well placed at the moment to capitalize on visitors using the other search engines.)

Alternatively, your CEO could ask, "My influence circle is wrong—if search is not hot for us, where are people coming from? And why? Do we need to change anything?" All great questions, as you'll concur.

Combining Search and Bounce

You can go even further and stitch the story together with the bounce segmentation number, as shown in Figure 14.4.

Number of Visitors

All visitors	1298
>= 5 seconds	618
Search Engines	240
Google	203
Google AND > 5 secs	69

Figure 14.4 Key potential visitor segments, identified using ClickTracks

Figure 14.4 might be a home run for you. One picture shows a great story, and all of it in one place. You can see the number of visitors you had in a month, the number who stayed for more than five seconds (hence gave your website a chance), and the number who came from search engines and more specifically from Google. Finally, you can see the quality of traffic that you are getting from Google (as inferred by the amount of traffic from Google that stayed for more than five seconds).

Your story possibly is as follows: "We are getting a good amount of traffic from Google but of that only 34 percent is staying for more than five seconds. Because such an unusually large amount of traffic is from Google, compared to other search engines, the culprit might be our PPC/SEM campaigns contributing to the high bounce rate. In that case, we are much worse off because we are spending money but people are not staying on our site. We need to stop and reevaluate our PPC/SEM spending."

This is not a nice story, but at least one that tells you a lot with just five minutes of work, and you have at least a couple of actions you can recommend right away.

Trending Segmented Data

You can truly turbocharge your segmented analysis by applying a powerful weapon called *trending*. If you were to analyze the preceding segmented data over time, the picture that would emerge is shown in Table 14.1.

▶ Table 14.1 Monthly visitor trends with segmentation for search traffic and those that bounced

	All Visitors	All >5 Secs	%	Total Search Engines	%	Google Only	%	Google > 5 Secs	%
JAN	229	102	45%	23	10%	15	65%	9	60%
FEB	135	68	50%	20	15%	19	95%	5	26%
MAR	175	108	62%	28	16%	23	82%	13	57%
APR	74	37	50%	22	30%	15	68%	3	20%
MAY	137	59	43%	26	19%	24	92%	13	54%
JUN	50	21	42%	7	14%	6	86%	2	33%
JUL	103	59	57%	10	10%	8	80%	3	38%
Overall Benchmark from Trend					50%		15%	81%	44%

It is not pretty, but I am sure even without any context you can look at these numbers and draw out so many nice insights that could lead to actions. The numbers are small in this example, but perhaps you can imagine how this can be helpful when you analyze the massive data from your website.

In Table 14.1, the Overall Benchmark from Trend is a simple average of this year's performance. This gives you a cool way to see how the latest month is doing. In Chapter 11, "Month 6: Three Secrets Behind Making Web Analytics Actionable," we discussed this method of creating internal benchmarks by using data from your own website to get more context on performance. Of course you can make this table even better if you have preset goals and did not have to use this simple benchmark.

Hopefully, you see the power of segmentation demonstrated even by such a simple example. For your website and business, maybe time on site is not important. Maybe it is page views, or conversion rate, or number of leads, or DM campaigns. Maybe you rely on only PPC/SEM. You can segment by referring URLs, or by visitors who see certain types of content or buy certain goods from you, or by visitors who use an internal search engine vs. those who don't, or by organic traffic, or by visits from affiliates, or by visitors who access the site via the home page vs. deeper into the site—the possibilities are endless.

Understand what your business is and your areas of strategic focus, and then segment away. Please take a vow that today is the last time you will send an Excel dump of a Top Pages on Site report to the entire company. Change that report to Top Pages Viewed by All Visitors by Search Traffic and by Top Affiliate Partners (or whatever).

Remember that there is no KPI that can't be made more effective by applying segmentation. Segmentation is what enables you to ask and answer questions about your website, answers that lead to action. Your instinct on seeing a metric should be to desperately want to segment it three levels down at least. There is no way you won't end up an analytics superstar.

Make Your Analysis and Reports "Connectable"

Most web businesses have someone responsible for looking through the standardized reports from the web analytics tool and sending reports out. So reports go out on a set schedule, published either on a website or sent via email as attachments. They are nice and they are numerous, and the person sending the reports then sits back and waits for praise and for the business to take action.

Sadly, action and praise are rare occurrences. What is more common is frustration that no one is using the reports. The analyst might say, "The business just does not get it" or "We have so much awesome data, yet no one is using it" or "What is so hard? I have created the report and sent it to you—why are you not taking action?" I am sure you have your own stories.

The job of a web analyst is a hard one, and even if you overcome the data hurdles, there is still the challenge of convincing people to listen to you and take action based on your analysis and insights.

There are many reasons why companies have loads of data but they don't really use it to take action. One of the core reasons is that non-web-analysts have a hard time connecting with numbers. Analysts swim in `session_ids` and `shopper_ids` and `evar's` and parameters and strings, and often the analysis that comes out of all that excellent work is dry. One of the reasons our decision makers don't jump up and take action is they have a hard time relating to our analysis due to its dryness.

Quite simply this means that we should take as much of the technical, or dry, stuff out of our analysis and recommendations. Try to make it easy to understand from the perspective of non-analysts and business users. We have to speak in the language of non-analysts in order to induce action.

Using Pretty Pictures

Making the reports user-friendly could translate into using "pretty pictures" (slides, graphs, colorful tables, or click density report screen shots). It could also mean using language and terms that hide some of the dryness and make our data easy to understand and to relate to.

For example, rather than showing the most valuable traffic on your website by using a table that indicates Size of Customer Segment, Page Views by Each Segment, and Time Spent by Each Segment, you can create a pretty picture, as shown in Figure 14.5.

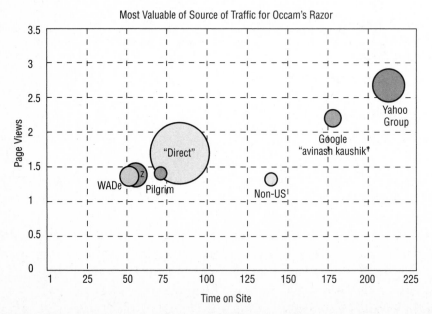

Figure 14.5 Most valuable sources of traffic: intersection of page views and time on site for key customer segments

Figure 14.5 is extremely easy to read. It practically screams out the insights, and anyone can understand it with little explanation. Here is the delightful part: it takes ten minutes to do this in Excel, eight of which are spent collecting the data.

There are even more pretty picture examples that I am positive you have come across (many I am sure you already use).

Using Connectable Language

In this section, you'll learn about a much rarer technique: using language to make data more user-friendly. For purely illustrative purposes, we will use a simple example and a metric called site engagement (see Chapter 13 for details on this metric).

There are many ways to define *site engagement*, but a definition frequently used is the "number of pages viewed" on the website. Most web analytics practitioners publish a report that shows site engagement as well as the number of purchasers on the website. It is an interesting and perhaps even important piece of analysis to do.

To create your report, remember three important reporting rules:

- Absolute numbers are usually suboptimal.
- Trends are magnificent.
- Segmentation is God's gift to analysis.

Now you crank up your favorite analytics tool and produce the report in Table 14.2.

▶ **Table 14.2** Percent of traffic and site engagement

Site Engagement	Month X	Month X+1	Month X+2
Less Than One Page	41.0%	42.8%	43.4%
Three Pages or Less	21.9%	21.9%	21.6%
More than Three Pages & Did Not Meet Goal	28.1%	28.4%	27.3%
Placed an Order (Met Goal)	9.0%	6.8%	7.6%
Placed More Than One Order	0.11%	0.09%	0.10%

This is an insightful report. As you look at it, potential actions jump out at you, the analyst, right away. A business or non-analytical user, on the other hand, might pick up a clue or two but would not get as much out of it as you might want them to. This is mostly because it takes time to digest the material, and it is really hard to connect to the "customer segments" in the first column. It just looks too hard to understand, and so a business user might not make the attempt—one more wonderful report from you not used.

Now let's try to make this connectable. Add a simple sprinkling of the English language, a dash of business understanding, and—abracadabra—the output becomes Table 14.3.

▶ **Table 14.3** Percent of traffic and site engagement: "connectable" version

Website Visitor Segments	Month X	Month X+1	Month X+2
Abandoners	41.0%	42.8%	43.4%
Flirters	21.9%	21.9%	21.6%
Browsers	28.1%	28.4%	27.3%
One-Off-Wonders	9.0%	6.8%	7.6%
Loyalists	0.11%	0.09%	0.10%

Now when our marketers and business decision makers see this data, they are able to internalize it significantly better because it *speaks* to them. They can relate to the English terms much better than the segments as defined by page views. The numbers are the same, but this table will scream out its insights and in turn suggest relevant actions to your decision makers.

In real life when this kind of transformation was applied, here is what happened:

- The users immediately wanted to know the definitions. This meant that they actually bothered to learn what each segment was in a way that did not happen before.

- They looked beyond the site conversion rate (represented by the One-Off-Wonders and Loyalists) and took the next step to truly understand the opportunities that the first three sets of numbers represent (Abandoners, Flirters, and Browsers).

- Because the terms used are reflective of the *persona* way of thinking the terms became ingrained in the company culture (especially marketing). People started taking about Flirters and how to convert them into Browsers and meetings were held to specifically target Browsers and get them to become buyers and special programs were created for Loyalists (because they were so rare).

 Note: Don't underestimate the power of your customer segments becoming a part of decision-making culture; they can be galvanizing for the organization and truly game-changing in driving customer centricity.

- Additional monthly analyses were created for each segment and someone was assigned to "take care of the Browsers and give them some love." (Translation: What action can we take?) This promoted focused attention and accountability.

This is an extremely simple example of making data and analysis more "connectable," but it illustrates the power of stepping beyond your *technical* thinking and into the world of your decision makers. As a result, doing something simple can have a big impact.

Choice of words and careful thinking can enliven the simplest or the most complex report, helping you communicate your message more effectively. In many cases, this can also bring about fundamental change in your organization (translating into more value from your reporting and analysis, and enhancing the ability of your organization to make decisions, which should trickle down to better customer experiences on your websites).

Of course, you don't have to let go of the inner Excel geek in you to accomplish all this. A quick press of a button in Microsoft Excel 2007, and voilà (see Table 14.4):

▶ **Table 14.4** Percent of traffic and site engagement: "connectable" Excel geek version

Website Visitor Segments	Month X	Month X+1	Month X+2
Abandoners	41.0%	42.8%	43.4%
Flirters	21.9%	21.9%	21.6%
Browsers	28.1%	28.4%	27.3%
One-Off-Wonders	9.0%	6.8%	7.6%
Loyalists	0.11%	0.09%	0.10%

Your simple connectable report is now even more connectable and easier to understand. The actual numbers become secondary, and the story comes off clearly even to the mathematically challenged.

> **Note:** The original creative spark for this specific approach came from listening to a presentation by Tim Boughton of Holiday-Rentals.com and the WVR Group at the Emetrics Summit in London in 2006. I've evolved Tim's suggestion a little bit.

NOTE

Use Conversion Rate Best Practices

Chapter 13 discussed the myth of conversion rate and whether it is a worthy obsession. The essential message there was that although we are all extremely focused inward on our companies and we pay loads of attention to conversion rate, that obsession might be causing us to ignore large segments of our customers who visit our websites for purposes other than purchasing. In Chapter 13 it was also suggested that a better metric to obsess about might be *task completion rate by primary purpose*.

All of that is not to say that conversion rate is not an important metric when used with the right level of focus and attention. This section covers the most important basics of conversion rate and lays out eight best practices that you can apply to your conversion rate measurement program to reap maximum benefits in return for your efforts.

A Review of Conversion Rate

Let's review the definition of conversion rate. Conversion rate, in percentage, equals *outcomes* divided by *unique visitors* during a particular *time period*.

Outcomes

From a macro perspective, any reason for which your website exists should highlight the customer outcome. Most frequently this is the total number of orders submitted or total number of leads collected or total number of newsletter/email sign-ups. For non–e-commerce websites, it can be the number of people who completed a task—so for a support site, the number of people who got to a FAQ or an answer or a knowledge base article (this is a really crude measure of success for a support site, but it is something).

Unique Visitors

There is a lot of heat around this topic. Some people are in the Total Visits (Visitors) camp and others are in the Unique Visitors camp. The Total Visits metric counts every session on your website (so if you are the only visitor and you visit the site five times in one week, that equals five total visits and that is what you would use). Unique Visitors counts each unique visitor (so in this same example, this would equal one unique visitor for use in the denominator). It is important to realize, regardless of what camp you find yourself in, that trends are what is important. So if you stick to whatever you prefer, just be consistent over time and you'll be fine (don't feel the need to get "un-brainwashed" from whatever camp you are currently in).

My personal recommendation is to use Unique Visitors. This stems from my view that every session is not an opportunity to get a customer to hit Submit Order. (I do realize this sounds scandalous, more so because like a majority of you I live in the world of e-commerce most of the time.) There is something almost un-customer-centric about treating every visit as an opportunity to sell or convert, when the customer might not be there to be sold.

Shopping and web surfing is a delicate dance of "come to see who we (the company) are, go to another site to read reviews, then come to see our benefits, then ask your spouse whether it is okay for you to buy, and then come purchase." I am probably missing a few other steps in there. Using Unique Visitors is a better read of what is really happening on your website because it accommodates this dance and gives you "credit" for those prior sessions when the dance was on. More important, as a practitioner I feel metric definitions should incorporate on-the-ground reality and using Unique Visitors accommodates that reality.

A Review of Conversion Rate *(Continued)*

Uniqueness is currently measured by setting a persistent cookie (call it `shopper_id` or `unique_cookie_id` or something akin to that) most of the time, and they are a bit unreliable, though not as much as the hoopla that surrounds them would indicate, and hence this is not perfect. But it's still the best we've got.

Most important, remember that consistency and trends are more important than your position in this debate.

Time Period

If you are measuring weekly conversion rate, it is the sum of orders during that week divided by the sum of unique visitors during the same week. Weekly unique visitors is not the sum of unique visitors on each day of the week (i.e., it is not Monday plus Tuesday plus Wednesday plus… so on). That would be imprecise.

Monthly conversion rate is the sum of orders during that month divided by the sum of unique visitors during the entire month. Again, it is not recommended that you sum daily unique visitors for each of the 30 (or 31) days to get a total for the month.

All of this might seem to be too much detail just to get started on the metric, but this detail reflects the importance placed on this metric and how most of the time we don't even agree on its definition or how it should be measured. The detail ensures that your program is off to an awesome start. Work to ensure that the marketers understand how you are measuring conversion rate and work with your vendor to understand exactly how they are reporting each component of the conversion rate calculation to you (if they are not doing it right, ask them to do it right, and be prepared to have a debate).

The following are the eight best practices, starting with the most important, for getting the biggest bang for your proverbial buck from investing in measuring conversion rate.

Forget about Overall Site Conversion Rate

There is no other metric that will tell you less about your website than overall conversion rate (assuming you have more than $5,000 in sales on your website). But overall conversion rate is easy to measure, so if you feel you need to do it, go ahead and get it out of your system.

Trend over Time and Don't Forget Seasonality

Throughout this book, my love for trends and segmentation is pretty obvious. Most definitely determine trends for conversion rate. What is unique about this metric is that more than others it is really affected by seasonality, and so do things like 13-month trends or look at five quarters or eight days. Figure 14.6 shows an example.

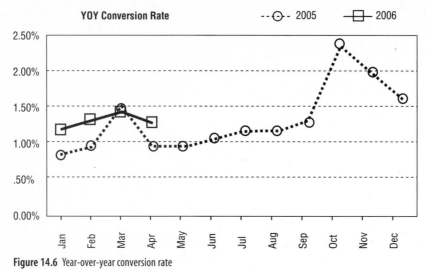

Figure 14.6 Year-over-year conversion rate

In each case, you will have the same period from history to compare. That will give you a lot more context and avoid suboptimal reactions resulting from comparing time periods that have nothing do to with each other (for example, last month compared to this month, unless your "season" is that, which it could be). An incremental benefit of this best practice is that it truly highlights your ROI by resulting in conversations such as, "You have added nine people to your web team over 12 months and the conversion rate has moved from 0.8 percent to 1.1 percent only!" or something akin to that.

Understand Your Website's/Company's Acquisition Strategy

This is not a report. It is a conversation or investigation with your business partners, and it is an extremely important step that any analyst needs to complete. Too often the conversion rate measurement effort starts with what the web analytics tool can provide and reports are emailed out. That is the wrong order.

Instead, figure out what your core business acquisition strategy is and then measure conversion rate to execute elements of that strategy. Is your company heavily into direct marketing (email, snail mail, and so forth)? Are you spending excessively on PPC? Or maybe you are about to plunk down a million dollars on a new affiliate marketing strategy or maybe on SEO. That's what you should be aware of and that's what you should measure.

Do this before you get too deep into conversion rate measurement because it will without a doubt lead to more meaningful analysis from you. Even more important, you will measure what is significant to your company rather than what your friendly neighborhood web analytics tool is throwing at you.

Measure Conversion Rate by the Top Five Referring URLs

This sounds really simple and silly, but there is usually a huge disconnect between what the company strategy is and where the traffic actually comes from.

So, for example, if you are a complex business with many websites, you might not necessarily be measuring conversion rate for your corporate site, which might be sending you tons of traffic. Or from some blog that started to praise you a lot. Or from www.live.com, which has the best indexing of your website content (say even better than Google or Yahoo!). You get the idea. You will always find hidden gems in the referring URLs. Measuring conversion for your top five referring URLs is a great insights-finding insurance policy. You can also provide these websites to your marketers to help influence their customer acquisition strategy. (For example, "We are spending loads of money over there, but look, here is where we should be spending money, on this list of specific websites.")

If you find that this report shows you the same stuff as some of the others detailed in this section, you can stop it. But if you are not doing this, I bet you are missing something really delightful.

Don't Measure Conversion Rate by Page or Link

This is a request you all get, all the time, and often execute on. It goes something like this: "What is the conversion rate for my Product Overview page?" or "What is the conversion rate of the links on the Comparison Chart page?" or "What is the conversion rate of our home page?" Answering these questions is a rather suboptimal exercise.

Most websites are complex multipage and multilink web experiences. Visitors to the website consume different pieces of content from different pages. In such an environment, how could you possibly measure conversion rate by page? Unless your web scenario is extremely simple (for example, two people come to the site, one enters at the home page and the other at the product overview page, and you can get to the checkout directly from both pages), measuring conversion rate of each page is misleading.

In the click density (site overlay) report, some web analytics tools show conversion rate for each link on the page. The hypothesis is that x percent of people who clicked on this link purchased. Unless all these links lead to the checkout, this is a useless piece of information.

In a complex multipage web experience, simply the fact that someone saw a page or clicked on a link will not be enough to attribute any credit to that page or link for "converting" someone. You'll be inferring value from the click and applying your own imposition of it onto the customer. How do you know, from the click, that that link or page was of any value to the customer? Because they clicked it?

Measuring the value of a page to a customer is a worthy cause. To do that, you can measure page influence as described in Chapter 13. That is a far superior way of measuring whether a web page is doing its job (when compared to attempts to measuring that via conversion rates).

Segment like Crazy

Most websites convert in single digits (usually low single digits). With such a small ratio of people converting, the *insights gold* is hidden deep in your site data. It is critical that you segment your data, yes, *like crazy*, to find those insights. This means showing the top five segments of conversion rate (or another number, depending on what's best for your company). We have discussed two already, referring URLs and core acquisition strategies (DM, PPC, SEO, affiliates, and so forth). Table 14.5 shows the conversion rate trends for key business segments for a sample company, notice as there are new strategies more segments show up. We start with just five but we end up with eight and get a better perspective on the whole picture.

▶ Table 14.5 Trended conversion rate segmented for contributing elements

Segmented Conversion Rate	Apr-07	May-07	Jun-07	Jul-07	Aug-07	Sep-07
Direct Traffic	2.2%	1.9%	1.7%	1.6%	1.4%	0.6%
Email Marketing	4.5%	2.4%	1.3%	5.3%	2.8%	4.4%
Newsletters	2.1%	2.9%	0.7%	1.0%	1.4%	1.6%
Search Engine Marketing			3.4%	2.3%	2.8%	0.1%
Corporate Referrals			3.1%	1.9%	1.9%	3.0%
Traffic from Ask.Com						2.0%
Traffic from Occam's Razor	2.3%	2.2%	2.4%	2.0%	2.0%	2.1%
Unknown	0.01%	0.04%	0.03%	0.02%	0.03%	0.09%

That is just a start. You should have indented subsegments for each of the top five—something such as the conversion rate of the top five subsegments for each segment of the conversion report, so you can really show where the desired outcomes are coming from. Translation: For email marketing, you should segment the top five campaigns and then for each of those segment your top five converting offers. Apply the same segmenting to your search campaigns and other categories. This is not too complex for any top website. All this information will fit on one page (and with size 10 font).

Segmentation is not difficult, but if you follow the earlier recommendation to understand your website or company acquisition strategy and then apply segmentation, that will have a powerful effect on your ability to find deep insights from measuring conversion rate.

Always Show Revenue Next to Conversion Rate

This is another extremely simple trick to provide context. We usually create a report that will show various conversion rate buckets (as in Table 14.5). But conversion rate just by itself can be misleading in terms of opportunity for any website. My recommendation is to show the actual revenue number (or leads or newsletter sign-ups or whatever is your conversion) next to the conversion rate percent.

What you will find is that some of your highest conversion rates don't bring in the most revenue. The most revenue could come from the line in your report with the fifth-highest conversion rate (or whatever), as shown in Table 14.6.

▶ **Table 14.6** Conversion rate with its best friend, revenue

Segmented Conversion Rate	Jul-07		Aug-07		Sep-07	
	Conversion	Revenue	Conversion	Revenue	Conversion	Revenue
Direct Traffic	1.6%	$515,067	1.4%	$621,869	0.6%	$565,751
Email Marketing	5.3%	$50,372	2.8%	$190,150	4.4%	$131,939
Newsletters	1.0%	$7,919	1.4%	$780	1.6%	$4,987
Search Engine Marketing	2.3%	$680	2.8%	$1,760	0.1%	$12,547
Corporate Referrals	1.9%	$186,261	1.9%	$200,455	3.0%	$226,341
Traffic from Ask.Com					2.0%	$10,121
Traffic from Occam's Razor	2.0%	$7,597	2.0%	$4,428	2.1%	$6,299
Unknown	0.02%	$67,051	0.03%	$3,232	0.09%	$4,390

In Table 14.6, observe the contrast between the cell gradients (a visual representation of the numbers) for each segment for each month. Ain't that impressive? Can you locate the insights instantly? In two seconds a marketer will know what works and what needs to be done when it comes to acquisition budget allocations.

Typically, people see a high conversion rate and think, "Let's do more of that." But the highest conversion rate could result from you giving deep discounts (which you can't do all the time) or from segments of customers you can't find more of (existing customers). Providing outcome numbers next to the percent gives more meaningful data to your decision makers. Sounds simple, but it is effective.

Measure Conversion Rate with a Goal in Mind

This is not always possible, but it is a highly recommended best practice. Having a goal gives context to your actual number. Asking your business decision makers for a goal forces them to think about where the revenue (or other outcomes) will come from, in turn causing them to really analyze their execution strategies and to plan them ahead of time as much as possible.

Having a goal guides the conversation and analysis and the deep dives that will yield insights. Figure 14.7 illustrates conversion rate in terms of a goal. Asking for a goal will result in you being integrated with the business decision-making process. (The user of the web analytics tools is usually not the one who sets goals, but almost always has great insights into the dynamics of conversion rates and hence how to improve them.)

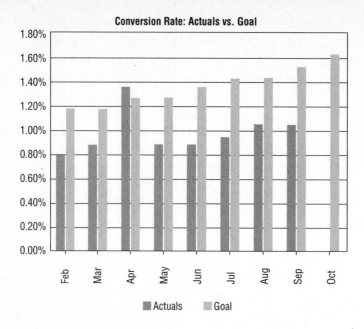

Conversion Rate: Actuals vs. Goal

Figure 14.7 Conversion rate: actuals vs. goal

Like the earlier recommendation to understand the acquisition strategy, this recommendation should result not only in a the report, which is important, but in a social and cultural change in your business. In web analytics, goals are hard to find and yet there is enormous pressure from your business leaders for insights and recommended actions. Ask for a goal, force them to think, and create an environment where you, dear analysts, lay some responsibility for business planning and execution at their door. In the end, you will look like a hero if you help push this change in the typical company culture.

Tip: I do realize the irony that all the recommendations in this section might, just might, end up getting you to obsess about conversion rate more than you should. Pick the right amount of time that you should put into conversion rate. In that time, ensure that you are following the preceding best practices and over time increase the sophistication of the analysis that your business does.

Elevate Your Search Engine Marketing/Pay Per Click Analysis

Search engine marketing (SEM), or pay per click (PPC), is the hottest thing around. Everyone is doing it, and if you are not, you dare not admit it for fear of looking crazy.

There are more agencies and consultants out there than you would care to count, and all of us are trying to work with all of them, trying to do our best to get the highest possible rate of return on our investments.

The other interesting trend, a great juxtapositioning, is that while lots of companies spend money on SEM/PPC, few of them are laughing all the way to the bank as a result. Most are probably not maximizing return on investment (ROI), and a good percent of those are simply pouring money down the drain.

The most common execution strategy for PPC campaigns for mid- to large-sized companies is to partner with an agency that will invest your money and get you a good ROI. One result of this is that it creates a data silo. The agency is good at PPC but they have a tiny view of the website data (just the tag they might have placed on the website to measure the conversion or ROI event). A marketer or web analyst can play a killer role in helping your company truly measure effectiveness of your PPC campaigns. You are unique because you can cut through the crap by using your awesome analysis powers, your access to all the data, and your ability to think beyond base metrics.

This section describes five best practices (presented from easiest to hardest) that you can use to great effect to provide significant insights to your decision makers and a competitive advantage to your company.

Measure Your Bounce Rate (in Aggregate and by Top Key Phrases)

Chapter 6, "Month 1: Diving Deep into Core Web Analytics Concepts," defined a bounced visitor as someone who stays on your website for fewer than 10 seconds. Some folks define this as visitors who stay on the site for one page or less; this is fine as well.

The conversion rate for most sites, according to Shop.org's most recent study, is about 2.2 percent. That is probably close to what your overall conversion rate is as well. We are thrilled when our PPC campaigns have a 3 percent conversion rate and we ask for more money to spend. But because we are paying for this traffic, we should expect much more than just a bit-better-than-normal conversion rate.

Measuring the bounce rate for PPC traffic in aggregate is an eye-opener, as you can see in Figure 14.8. It usually turns out that the bounce rate is really high (60+ percent or often even higher). Decision makers are shocked that 60 percent or 80 percent of the traffic that they are paying for with every single click stays for such a small amount of time (in 10 seconds or fewer, you can't convince anyone of anything).

It gets even more interesting if you measure bounce rate by key phrase. This will very quickly highlight *stinkers*—phrases that drive traffic that stays for five seconds or fewer (or only one page).

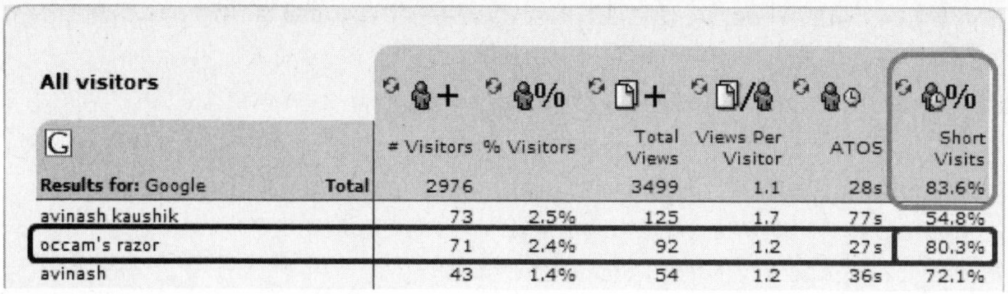

All visitors						
G		# Visitors	% Visitors	Total Views	Views Per Visitor	ATOS	Short Visits
Results for: Google	Total	2976		3499	1.1	28s	83.6%
avinash kaushik		73	2.5%	125	1.7	77s	54.8%
occam's razor		71	2.4%	92	1.2	27s	80.3%
avinash		43	1.4%	54	1.2	36s	72.1%

Figure 14.8 Bounce rate for Google PPC campaigns

The point of the recommendation is to really dig into your traffic. It is possible that the key phrase is the right one, but people are landing on the wrong page or that you are not repeating the value proposition on the landing page, or the offer is missing. After you know there's a problem, you can fix it and set the bar higher for PPC/SEM campaign conversion rates.

It is important to remember that if you are partnering with an external agency to manage your PPC campaigns, they typically don't have bounce-rate data (because they are not collecting all the typical web analytics data). If they don't have it, you are your company's only hope to do this important analysis and feed the results back to your agency.

Audit Your Vendors/Agencies

The de facto standard for PPC campaigns is that agencies are running campaigns by using sophisticated analysis (bidding) and measure success by using third-party JavaScript tags on your website. This is good progress. But there is more, and it involves your help.

There are often problems with third-party cookies. Each agency seems to be using a different kind of data capture and data processing system. They also define the same metrics differently (even metrics such as Repeat Visitors or Visits to Purchase) and they don't do any analysis on site effectiveness because they are, rightly, optimizing your bids.

My recommendation is to request—or force, as the case may be—your agency to add an extra URL parameter at the end of the URL string that is used in campaigns with various search engines. This should be a parameter that your analytics tool (from Omniture, WebTrends, WebSideStory, or IndexTools, for example) will recognize. This parameter can usually be something simple, such as kaushik.net/avinash?source= google-avinash_10_90_rule, that helps delineate the traffic source and key phrase.

Now power up the segmentation in your tool, slice off the PPC traffic, and match up key metrics such as counts of visitors, time on site, bounce rate, and conversion rate by using your own web analytics tool. The goal will be to match up the key metrics that you are getting from your agency or agencies with ones from your web analytics tool.

The numbers will not tie because of the core differences in data collection, but they will typically fall within 10 percent, and in that case you are fine. You will often find that they will be off by 25 or 35 percent. That would be a great time to compare notes with your agency because if they are measuring success 30 percent higher than you, your campaigns likely are not performing as well as you think.

Another benefit is that with the inherent knowledge of your business that your agency does not have, you can truly analyze what this traffic is doing, understand the behavior, and work on site optimization. I have to stress that the agencies are doing the best they can. They are not trying to mess with you. It is simply that there are limits to what they can do, and you need to step up and take responsibility.

You are also not trying to replace the tactical or operational reporting that your agency is doing. Leave that to them because they are probably good at it. What you are trying to do is add value by auditing their metrics and doing a higher-level analysis by merging your PPC data with your web analytics data. This later part is something they can't do.

Measure PPC Campaigns Cannibalization Rate (vs. Organic)

A typical implementation of PPC campaigns is that we start buying our branded key phrases (ones that have an obvious connection to the products and services that our companies offer). The outcome always is that traffic shows up, we pay Google and Yahoo!, there are sales, and success is declared.

But if you have done decent SEO, it is possible that you might still have received traffic from search engines anyway from organic results, especially your well-recognized branded key terms. Do you know how much you are cannibalizing your organic (free) traffic by doing PPC? Translation: Are you paying for traffic that you could be getting for free?

Cannibalization rate is a powerful metric and something you should be watching all the time. Based on the results of that analysis, you should be optimizing your PPC spending. Some good agencies are doing this. Demand it from yours.

Figure 14.9 shows what a typical output of a cannibalization rate measurement looks like. In this case, this website was getting an average of 14 percent traffic from organic search engine referrals. In March they started to do PPC campaigns. You can see the bottom part of each bar reflecting the contribution of PPC campaign traffic.

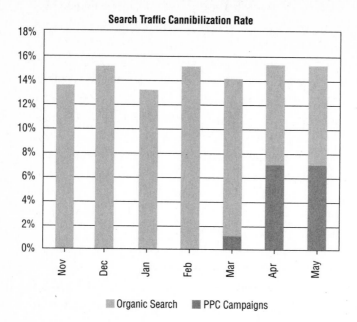

Search Traffic Cannibilization Rate

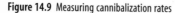

■ Organic Search   ■ PPC Campaigns

Figure 14.9 Measuring cannibalization rates

Two things jump out:

- There seems to have been a marginal increase in the amount of overall traffic coming to the site from search engines (from 14.2 percent before to 14.9 percent after).

- It is obvious that the organic traffic has shrunk as the PPC traffic has increased.

  This company has started to pay for traffic it was previously getting for free.

It is possible that the bidding was on the wrong key words. It is possible that the PPC traffic was landing on suboptimal pages. It is possible that *make up your best possible excuse and insert it here*. What is important to realize is that your agency is probably not measuring organic traffic; they would have shown great success as a result of your PPC campaigns (not their fault for incomplete measurement). But all along your money is being wasted.

Cannibalization is not easy to measure. It requires coordination with your agency or in-house experts and blessing from your management. But one simple option you have is to take some of your most popular branded key phrases, assuming you don't have heavy weekly seasonality factors, and turn off your campaigns for those key phrases for a week. Measure number of visitors, bounce rates, engagement with site, and conversion rates. Turn on the campaigns next week and measure the same metrics again, for the PPC slice. Compare the two sets of numbers and you have a nice idea of how much you are cannibalizing your organic (free) traffic when you spend on PPC. Another option is to go dark on PPC for a few days or weeks and measure the effect.

Both suggestions (going dark on some campaigns, or totally stopping on some days or weeks) are really simple ways to measure cannibalization. I am sure you can think of 10 better ways. What is important is that you measure cannibalization and then make informed choices. Why pay for traffic that you could get for free?

Aggressively Push for Testing and Experimentation

Testing and experimentation is not typically considered in the scope of web analytics, but it should be. Please see Chapter 10, "Month 5: Website Experimentation and Testing—Shifting the Power to Customers and Driving Effective Actions," for more on this simple fact. A key ingredient for running a great test is to isolate either a segment of traffic by source or a segment of traffic by customer intent. Either way, you have an insight into why the visitors might be on your site and in turn you can craft a wonderful, relevant test.

One of the beautiful things about search key phrases is that you can infer customer intent from them. It is likely that 60 percent of your site traffic is labeled No Referrer and you don't know squat about them and you can't give them relevant content. However, with your search traffic you know something of value. The keyword is the key.

Partner with key marketers in your company and implement a testing strategy (multivariate or A/B or whatever you like) that will allow you to try different content, pages, structures, layout, and navigation based on what you understand about the intent of those key phrases. The result will be optimal customer experiences for your PPC/SEM traffic and a huge spike in conversion rate, and whatever you are selling. (And if you set persistent first-party cookies, you can "remember" the PPC-driven traffic. Then, when the customers visit again the next time, you know who they are, which test experience worked for them or did not, and your site can start to have much richer interactions with them.)

Chapter 10 has loads of ideas for you to get started with testing your PPC traffic.

Strive for Multigoal Understanding of Visitors

No website exists for just one purpose, not even the simplest one. Yet almost all PPC campaigns are measured by one outcome, or goal (usually a conversion rate of some kind, a purchase or a lead submission, or a visit to a page with relevant website content). If the traffic comes for a few different purposes, why measure them all by one goal? (To beat a dead horse, this is another reason to do testing.)

For your PPC traffic, set multiple relevant goals. For example, along with conversion rate, you can also measure customer satisfaction and task completion rates by surveying that traffic. This will tell you, for example, "Oh 10 percent are converting, but the others were looking to print pages or the tech support number or came to read reviews and the site failed them." You can then take relevant action to optimize your campaigns.

Or if you have a frequent turnover site, set goals for multiple purchases in each month. That is a great complement to just conversion to first purchase.

Or here is a nice one—if you follow the advice for auditing your vendors and agencies, amass data for x period of time and then compute live time value for PPC campaigns and use that to optimize your bidding as well as set a new bar for success.

Bottom line: If you are measuring *single-goal* success for your campaigns, you can become more sophisticated. You can migrate away from focusing on short-term revenue from a narrow stream of traffic to solving for the long term and all the different streams of traffic that your campaigns are driving to your website.

Measure the Adorable Site Abandonment Rate Metric

How many metrics can you call adorable? For e-commerce websites, site abandonment rate is an adorable metric for these three reasons:

- Money, money, money, baby. There isn't a metric out there that can tell you a lot so quickly, and any improvement you make to it will directly and immediately affect the bottom line.

- It measures the customer interaction in a small number of web pages, probably one for the cart and two to three for the checkout. How many metrics out there can compete with that? A few pages and a controlled environment translates into awesome optimization potential (*yes*, I am harping on testing again).

- Win-win: By the time visitors fall into the purview of this metric, they want to give you cash and you want that cash. How could that not be simply the best thing in the world?

In spite of its absolutely adorable qualities, it is surprising that this metric does not have as much prominence as, say, conversion rate. (On a side note, if people want you to improve conversion rate quickly, the first thing to do is measure your abandonment rates and fix them.) People simply don't seem to walk around with abandonment rates on top of their dashboards, and consultants don't center their pitches on helping improve this metric. My theory explaining why is as follows:

- We don't understand the true power of this metric.

- We don't think we can improve the four or so pages (Add to Cart, Login, Billing Information, Review Order, and Submit) that this metric covers.

- There is some confusion about a standard metric definition.
- Usually this number is really "high" (though each site will have d.
  bers), and we are embarrassed to put it in front of senior manageme
- The cart and checkout are areas fraught with IT issues and hence tight
  both of which can be huge hurdles to getting anything done.
- There is no hype around this metric. (Hopefully, this book will fix that!)
  Let me help you understand the adorable metric a little bit better.

> **Note:** Although it is absolutely possible to apply this metric to a lead capture process, or other website processes, for reasons of absolute clarity and maximum impact the focus here is purely on the metric in the e-commerce world.

We can address one of the problems right off the bat by establishing a standard definition of site abandonment rate:

Site abandonment rate (in percent terms) = 1 − (the total orders placed on the website / the total Add to Cart clicks).

In other words, the site abandonment rate is the number of people who intended to buy, by clicking the Add to Cart button, compared to those who actually made it out at the other end, by clicking Submit Order.

If on your website people purchase multiple items in the same session, trends of this metric will accommodate that behavior just fine. The process that this metric measures on most websites is click, add to cart, click, start checkout, create account (or login), click, provide credit card, click, review order, click, submit order. As a result, at its highest level the metric helps you understand how much money is left on the table by your customers.

The preceding definition is recommended because few people measure the process described here end to end. If they do measure it, it is in silos (cart and checkout) and then the tendency is to solve in those silos. That is a problem because the most effective solutions for improving this metric lie in end-to-end thinking (from that first click in the preceding scenario to that last click, end to end).

There are no published standards for site abandonment rate, but the range that is most bandied about is 50 to 70 percent abandonment. In my personal experience at different companies I have seen it at 25 to 55 percent. That should give you some range and context to benchmark your own site abandonment rate.

Depending on the cost of items you sell on your website, each percentage point of abandonment could represent tens of thousands to millions of dollars per month in revenue—hence my recommendation to have an almost irrational adoration of this metric.

e abandonment rate and know where you fall, it is time to seg-
st-level segmentations are cart abandonment rate and checkout

Using Seg

Afte
ate

ent rate (in percent terms) = 1 − (the total number of people who start
total number of Add to Cart clicks).

words, this is the number of people who were motivated enough by
make an initial commitment to buy from you. They could do this for any
reasons (to save the item for easy access or to check shipping, for example),
esents a deeper, next-level, interest than just browsing.

ually cart abandonment rate should explain most of your site abandonment
—that is, the cart abandonment will be a large part of your overall site abandonment. This is because your relationship with the visitor is fragile until this point. The
visitor has added to the cart, but that is not as big a commitment as starting the checkout process.

Checkout Abandonment Rate

Checkout abandonment rate (in percent terms) = 1 − (the total number of people who
complete checkout / the total number of people who start checkout).

In other words, this is the number of people who decided to bail at the last step
of the complex journey that is the purchasing process.

Ideally, this number should be 0 percent simply because there is no excuse for
your website experience failing to deliver at this most critical of stages. Of course, the
number will never be zero but should be really close to it. After all, can't we all optimize the few pages that lead to a normal checkout and make it a flawless experience?

In the context of your site abandonment rate, the checkout abandonment rate
will usually be a smaller number than cart abandonment, simply because if people
make it this far, they tend to get through, unless there are weird things on your site
such as customers having to get to the Submit Order page just to get the shipping
information. Figure 14.11 shows the trend of cart and checkout abandonment rates
over a period of seven months for a e-commerce website.

So now you know your site abandonment. You have taken time to understand
the distribution of departures between the cart and checkout processes, as shown in
Figure 14.10. And, sadly, it turns out that your site is not performing as well as you
had expected. What could you do next?

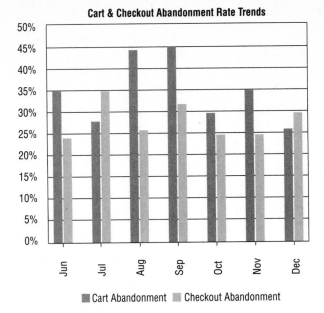

Cart & Checkout Abandonment Rate Trends

■ Cart Abandonment ■ Checkout Abandonment

Figure 14.10 Cart and checkout abandonment rates

Finding Actionable Insights and Taking Action

Some suggestions on moving from simply reporting metrics to finding actionable insights and taking action are as follows:

- Segment the abandonment rates to really understand where your pain points are.

- Do multivariate testing. Both the cart and checkout are absolutely perfect for multivariate testing. They are usually page-level experiences and hence lend themselves well to multivariate testing. Use your favorite vendor tool to first modularize the page and then create variations of content for each module. Let the "recipe creation" process create different versions of the page, go relax for a day (or more depending on how much traffic you get), and identify what page works best for your customers.

- Give this testing process some love and a lot of attention. Remember, there are hundreds of thousands of dollars at stake here.

- If your abandonment rates are really terrible, step back to challenge some fundamental beliefs at your company. You can test these to prove whether they move the right levers for your customers. These would be different for each company, but here are some general guidelines:

- If you have *interruptives* in the process (for example, "Buy this also, please" or 'Upgrade for $5"), try to remove them and see what happens.
- If you don't offer nonmembership (or anonymous) checkout, do so. If you don't offer an option to sign up for an account, offer that option.
- If you have a painful, long checkout data input page, see what happens when you don't insist on asking people to tell you the color of their eyes or some other expendable information.

- Investigate whether there are simple things that people are looking for, information that is only in the cart or checkout process that could "falsely" get people into that process. Two examples:
  - Shipping costs: If people just want to know the shipping cost, make it easier to find than having to go to the Checkout or Add to Cart pages. Not only will this reduce abandonment and give you your real abandonment rate, but it also stinks for your customers that you make this painful.
  - Delivery schedule: How long will it take to get the product? Do you have it in stock? Let's not wait until the end to share this nice information.

- Check that your website is carrying through promotions correctly and reiterates in the cart and checkout process (in bold gigantic letters) the discounts that your customer was promised in the offer or on your affiliate site or your product pages or in your campaigns. It is amazing how many websites don't do this simple thing well.

Bottom line: It is really rare to get a metric that focuses on such a small part of the website experience yet holds so much power to help our customers as well as us. Measuring your site abandonment Rates (and cart and checkout segments) and highlighting them on your dashboards for senior executives will pay huge dividends to your business goals.

Measure Days and Visits to Purchase

There are many good metrics that help us understand customer behavior on our websites—conversion rate, page views per visitor, average time on website, average number of pages to purchase—and you can segment them. But often these standard KPIs leave us hungry and unfulfilled.

Two metrics that don't fall into that category for websites are Days to Purchase and Visits to Purchase. *Average Visits to Purchase* is the average number of sessions from first website interaction to purchase. *Average Days to Purchase* is the average number of days from first website interaction to purchase.

These metrics are not commonly available in a lot of the web analytics tools, but they are in the advanced analytics list because they can provide insights about customer behavior, specifically in the context of an outcome.

> **Note:** For our examples, I am using the term *purchase*, but there is nothing unique about e-commerce. You can use these metrics if your site exists to gather leads or to get people to download PDFs or for tech support. All that is required is a robust understanding at your end of what the "outcome" is on your website. Then you can measure Days and Visits to Outcomes.
>
> NOTE

Most of the current crop of web analytics metrics (KPIs) are very much session based—not all, but most of them. The limitation of session-based metrics is that they presume a "closure" in one session (one visit, if you will). That is usually not the case. Customers visit our website, come back more times, depending on why the website exists, and then maybe close the deal (buy, give a lead, get an answer, send your CEO a nasty email about how dysfunctional your website is).

The two metrics proposed here are true *pan-session* metrics, and because they accommodate for how customers really use most websites, they can be deeply insightful.

These metrics make the following assumptions:

- Your website uses some kind of *sessionization* methodology. For the most part, regardless of whether you use web logs or JavaScript tags to collect data, sessionization happens by using cookies, either via your web analytics tool or your web server platform. Both are fine.

- Your website sets both transient session cookies and persistent, completely anonymous user_id cookies.

- Like anything that relies on cookies, it is optimal to use first-party cookies to improve quality (it won't eliminate errors, just reduce them). If you are not using first-party cookies, it is strongly recommended that you badger your analytics provider to switch you to first-party ASAP. All the big boys and girls support first-party cookies, and there is high ROI from your switch to first-party.

Why should you measure these metrics?

Most often what is lost in all our analysis is the fact that there are many different interactions for someone before they purchase. People come, they see, they come back, they see something else, they go read Amazon.com reviews, they do price comparison, and then for some weird reason, even though you sell at a really high price, they buy from you.

Session-based metrics (for example, all the off-the-shelf path analysis reports you see in your web analytics tools on the market today) don't really illustrate this. As you run your affiliate marketing campaigns, PPC campaigns, or direct marketing efforts, what is the value of the first visit by a customer and should you pay more to get customers into the door because they have longevity?

One final simple reason to measure these KPIs is to get a true understanding of "how long" it takes people to buy from your website (or submit a lead etc.) and whether that behavior is different across different segments of your website customers. If it is, you can exploit this knowledge to optimize your campaigns, promotions, and other efforts to get the best bang for the buck.

How to Measure the KPIs

If your web analytic tool does not allow this kind of sophisticated pan-session analysis, your option might be to extract data out of your web analytics tool and dump it into a database. If you have an existing data warehouse (or your web analytics vendor provides it), you can also use your data warehouse that contains all your aggregated click-stream and outcomes data to do this.

To extract the data yourself, run a SQL query that will do the following:

1. Gather all the sessions for the last x amount of time (six months in our case, hence millions of rows—use Oracle). For each session, the data you will bring in will depend on your website. I recommend all cookie values, campaign values, and pages.

2. Organize the sessions by their persistent user_id cookie value. (Often sites use shopper_id as a persistent cookie. Just ask your web guys what the name of the cookie is. I am sure you have one.)

3. For each "set" from the preceding step, look for the session with presence of your thank_you (purchase) page.

4. Take all the persistent cookie user_ids for all those who purchased in a given month (say July 2006).

5. Look back in the data (six months in the preceding case) to find their first visit.

6. For the Visits to Purchase metric, count *sessions* in the "set" between the first visit and the purchase visit. For the Days to Purchase metric, count *days* in the "set" between the first visit and the purchase visit.

7. Done. Get a glass of champagne—you deserve it.

Finding Actionable Insights and Taking Action

Now you have overall metrics that look something like this (your numbers will look different obviously, but you'll still be surprised). Table 14.17 shows the distribution of the number of days it takes for a purchase to be made on a website from the first visit of a customer to the website.

Days To Purchase	% of Total
0 Days	62%
1-3 Days	9%
4-7 Days	5%
Over 7	24%
Total	100%

Table 14.8 shows the distribution of the number of visits (sessions) that transpire between the first visit by a customer to this website and the visit during which they make a purchase.

► Table 14.8 Visits to purchase

Visits to Purchase	% of Total
1	44.1%
2	24.2%
3	12.5%
4	7.6%
5	3.8%

This in and of itself is really valuable. If this data were real, for your website it would be thrilling to know that a full 81 percent of people convert in three visits (sessions) or fewer and that most of them (62 percent) convert on the same day . If you are the half-empty kind of person, it is rather depressing that you are essentially getting just a couple of shots, in just one single day, to convert someone to a purchaser. The chances someone will buy go down dramatically after day zero (the day of the first visit). You can obviously make the groupings of visits and days that make the most sense for your business.

But perhaps what is supervaluable, especially to your marketers and business decision makers, is to segment this data to get deeper insights into the behavior of your various customer segments (or your campaigns).

You can do the simple one first. Segment by month and get a trend of the data. Are you getting better or worse over time? Is there a seasonality impact of these numbers (so in the dull month of July, do people take their own sweet time but exhibit a different behavior on Valentine's Day)?

But it gets even more thrilling and fun if you segment by your core acquisition strategies (for example, affiliate marketing, "direct" traffic, PPC, SEO, referrers from blogs). You are going to get a real understanding of customer behavior because most likely you'll see something like Table 14.9.

▶ **Table 14.9** Visits to purchase by key acquisition vehicles

Visits to Purchase by "Acquisition Source"	1 Visit Purchases	2 Visit Purchases	Greater than 3 Visits Purchases
Pay Per Click	34%	22%	44%
Direct Traffic	2%	11%	87%
Affiliate Marketing	64%	29%	7%
Overall Website Avg	33%	21%	46%

Even a quick glance at Table 14.9 will communicate that each segment of your customers tends to behave differently when it comes to making purchases on your website. When you report metrics at an aggregated level, it is often hard to know what action to take. In the case of Figure 14.19, that is not even remotely the problem.

As you begin to understand pan-session customer behavior, you are actually getting into things beyond the surface, things that most web analytics tools don't provide. This also means that if you get this far, you will develop an understanding that can be a true competitive advantage for you because this is really hard to do, even for your competitors.

Here are some actions that you can take from the insights that you will glean from measuring Days and Visits to Purchase:

- Optimize spending on key phrases for PPC campaigns, especially as you bid for "category" terms. (When you bid for category terms, you are betting on getting on the radar "early," compared to bidding on brand key phrases. If the number of sessions is small from the preceding analysis, that would be rather depressing, so put less value on category key phrases; this is a completely hypothetical example.)

- Optimize your website content and structure for different segments. Clearly, if I came to you and said you get one session to convince me to buy or I am out, would your website be the same? Probably not. You would throw away all the "extra" content and focus on the most powerful. Alternatively, if the data indicated the purchase behavior was stretched out over days/visits, you could provide more content because visitors seem to want more.

- Optimize interruptives. This is cool, if your web platform allows it. If you know the point of bailing for your customers (say, the third session), you could attempt to offer up a goodie in the next (fourth, in this case) session. Or based on what they have seen so far, show them something more relevant (this is your last chance) or ask for an email address for a future deal.

Of course, other things that make more sense for your unique business will occur to you.

Leverage Statistical Control Limits

To repeat a mantra stated often in this book: Absolute numbers without context are not helpful. Trends are better. But customer interactions on the websites result in outcomes for your company, which yield trends that are rather difficult to decipher and translate into action (see Chapter 11 for more about making your web analytics program actionable).

One factor that is not appreciated enough is that every metric or KPI that you report out of your web analytics tool (or indeed from your ERP or CRM or data warehouse) tends to have a natural *biorhythm*—metrics/KPIs that will fluctuate because of "natural occurrences" that just happen. I call this phenomenon, shown in Figure 14.11, *the biorhythms of KPIs*.

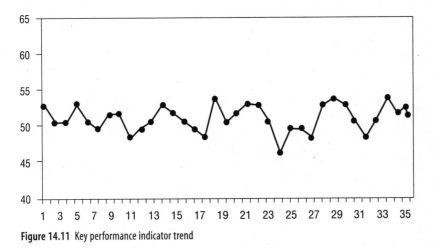

Figure 14.11 Key performance indicator trend

Biorhythms are hard to understand, harder still to predict. Because many of us desire complete understanding of metrics, we spin our cycle like crazy to understand the numbers, to explain them to the management so that they can take some action. Imagine getting a daily or weekly trend that goes up and down, and you have no idea what the heck is causing it, even after you have done your damnedest to isolate all the variables.

These natural biorhythms cause analysts and marketers to do analysis and deep dives where none is necessary. They cause some of us to look "bad" because we can't explain the data. They cause a lack of faith in the ability of data to provide insights.

It does not really matter what KPI is represented in Figure 14.12, and what the x-axis is. As you look at point 7 or 17 or 25, would you know what the trend is telling you? Would you know whether there is a cause for concern or things are okay and you don't need to take any action? Are the high points a cause for celebration?

One wonderful methodology that I have found to be helpful in separating signal from noise is from the world of Six Sigma and process excellence, and it's called *control limits* (and its associated *control charts*). Control charts are really good at applying statistics to assess the nature of variation in any process. Translated into the biorhythm problem, in relevant situations control charts can help trigger deep analysis and action. Control charts were created to improve quality in manufacturing and other similar situations, but they work wonderfully for us in the world of web analytics as well.

There are three core components of a control chart: a line in the center that is the mean of all the data points, an upper control limit (UCL), and a lower control limit (LCL).

Figure 14.12 shows what a trend looks like with control limits overlaid.

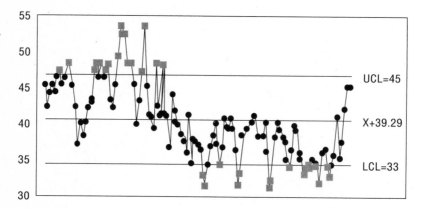

Figure 14.12 KPI trend with control limits illustrating the biorhythm and triggers for deeper analysis

The following details indicate what you are looking at in Figure 14.12:

- X: This green line indicates the *mean*, a statistically calculated number that defines the average amount of variation in your KPI trend. In Figure 14.13, it is 39.29.

- UCL: This *upper control limit* is a statistically calculated number that defines the higher limit of variation in your KPI trend. In the example it is 45.

- LCL: This *lower control limit* is a statistically calculated number that defines the lower limit of variation in your KPI trend. In the example it is 33.

- Black dots: These indicate numbers within the expected variation (natural biorhythm).

- Gray squares: These indicate numbers outside of control limits (called *triggers*).

Figure 14.13 illustrates a natural biorhythm in the KPI trend that is between the two control limits. These are points that show natural variation in the metric and are not triggers for doing anything, even though, as you can clearly see, they vary quite a bit from one data point to the next.

The massively cool thing is that it shows all the points in the trend, think of it as days or weeks or months, when you should have taken action because there was something unusual that occurred. It won't, sadly, tell you what happened, but it will tell you when you should use your precious time to dig deeper. It will provide the triggers. Isn't that awesome? Think of all the time you would have wasted solving the puzzle behind the data points below the mean, which look like "problems."

In a world where we have tons of metrics, where every dashboard has 15 graphs on it, control limits are extremely helpful in leveraging the power of statistics as the first filter indicating when you should dig deeper or look for a cause. If your metrics and trends have variations from day to day and week to week, this is a great way to isolate what is normal and what is abnormal in the trend.

Calculating Control Limits

The general rule of thumb for calculating control limits is as follows:

Average KPI value +/– (3 × standard deviation)

Control limits are calculated three standard deviations above or below the mean of your KPI data values. They are not assigned, but rather calculated based on the natural output of your data. Anything within the control limits should be viewed as expected variation (a natural biorhythm). Anything outside of control limits warrants investigation (triggers). Not only that, but if a series of data points fall outside the control limits, that is a bigger red flag in terms of something highly significant going awry.

Any decent statistical software will automatically calculate control limits and create these graphs for you. Minitab is the one that is used a lot by folks I know (though it is a tad bit expensive). You can also use your standard business intelligence tools to compute control limits, such as those from Brio, Business Objects, Cognos, and MicroStrategy.

You can also always simply jury-rig Microsoft Excel to compute the control limits. You can get started by using the spreadsheet provided on the CD that accompanies this book. This spreadsheet was created by Clint Ivy (http://blog.instantcognition.com). Clint's spreadsheet model illustrates the point by using one standard deviation, but you can easily update it to use three standard deviations.

Note: Control charts scale well. Life would be easy if for every metric you have, there is a clearly established goal that you are shooting for. That goal can tell you how well, or not, you are performing. In reality, it is rare to have goals for the massive deluge of metrics you have to deal with. Limits are versatile enough that you can apply control limits to all your trends.

Practical Considerations in the Use of Control Charts (Limits)

As with all statistics, the more data points you have, the better your control limits will be. It would be hard to create a control chart that makes sense with just five data points (you can create it, but it won't be meaningful).

Control limits work best with metrics or KPIs where it is a bit easy to control for the relevant variables.

For example, it would be less insightful to create control limits for your overall conversion rate if you do direct marketing, email campaigns, search engine marketing (pay per click), and affiliate marketing, and you have loads of people who come directly to your site. There are too many variables that could affect your trend.

But you can easily create control charts for your email campaigns, PPC campaigns, or direct traffic. That would be insightful because you have just one variable (or just a couple) and you will find excellent trigger points for performance, and in turn analysis and in turn action.

You do need to be able to understand a little bit of statistics and have some base knowledge around standard deviations so that you can leverage this optimally but also explain the power of what you are doing to your senior executives.

A Practical Example of Using Control Limits

Figure 14.13 shows a website's conversion rate for direct marketing campaigns.

In Figure 14.13, without the red (UCL) and blue (LCL) lines, it is harder to know each month how the performance of direct marketing campaigns is faring. It is easy to know in January 2005 that performance was terrible. It is much harder to know that between March and July statistically there was nothing much to crab about even though the trend goes up and down.

This last point is important. Anyone can eyeball and take action on a massive swing. What stymies most analysts in separating signal from noise are the nonmassive swings in the data, the biorhythms that *hide* the true triggers.

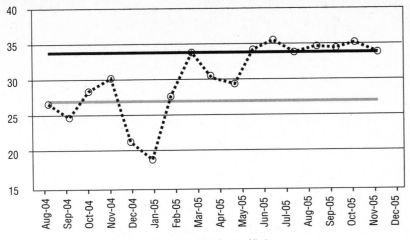

Figure 14.13 Direct marketing conversion rate trend with control limits

Extra-Credit Tips: Dealing with Outliers (If You Want to Kick It Up a Notch)

You can also use a statistical technique called *Winsorization*, which uses percentiles instead of standard deviations and therefore is more resistant to outliers (extreme data points). The basic gist is that you throw out the top and bottom 5th or 10th percentile of your data. Then you calculate your regular descriptive stats based on the remaining data (averages, STD, and so forth) For data sets that have wide fluctuations, this is a simple but practical way to "quiet" things down and focus on the signal while omitting much of the noise. You can find more information at `http://snipurl.com/winsor`.

(Thanks to Dave Morgan of SiteSpect for this tip, `www.sitespect.com`.)

Here's another slight alternative for dealing with outliers. This will give you a more robust calculation for upper and lower control limits by using quartiles:

Q1 = 25th percentile

Q2 = 50th percentile, aka median

Q3 = 75th percentile

LCL: Q1 − (1.5 × IQR)

IQR stands for interquartile range, and IQR = Q3 − Q1

UCL = Q3 + (1.5 × IQR)

For extreme outliers, you can replace the 1.5 IQR mild outlier multiplier with a 3. You can find more information at `http://snipurl.com/outlier`.

(Thanks to Wendi Malley of the WAA Research Committee for this tip.)

Consider using control limits on your KPIs such as cart and checkout abandonment rates. You'll be pleasantly surprised at what you learn (as will your bosses). Abandonment rates are particularly well suited for application of control limits because they are a *structured process*; they are *finite and controlled* and usually tend to have data points that fluctuate within a narrow band. You can see how UCLs and LCLs can be extremely powerful in that case (Figure 14.13 could well be your cart or checkout abandonment rate).

Using control limits is a bit dry and requires some knowledge and patience, but it is so powerful in helping your analysis, specifically when it comes to separating signal from noise.

Remember: Signal > Insights > Action > Happy Customers > Money, Money, Money!

Measure the Real Size of Your Convertible "Opportunity Pie"

All of us want better outcomes from the investments we make in our websites. Outcomes for you could be more orders, more leads, referrals, fewer calls to your phone center, more people clicking on your banner ads—it could be anything. We are hyperfocused on constantly trying to figure out how to improve the outcomes and in turn improve our conversion rate (or revenue or other such outcome-measuring KPIs).

This single-minded focus on solving for the company's bottom line, a worthy cause for sure, does not quite capture the reality that people probably visit your website to solve a multitude of their problems. Not accounting for this delightful oversight means that business decision makers often overestimate what is possible and how many outcomes can be extracted from their websites.

By using the conversion rate metric as a framework, this section will help you understand what the real size of your *opportunity pie* is. In other words, of all the people who visit your website, how many, at first blush, are even *in the game* and provide you an opportunity to convert them (or provide you an opportunity to monetize them in some fashion).

Remember our definition of conversion rate:

Conversion rate (for a given time period) = outcomes / unique visitors

If a website gets 1.075 million visits from 768,000 unique visitors, and that results in 16,500 orders, our standard computation would give the website a nice little conversion rate of 2.1 percent. This is not too bad, considering a Shop.org study of the third quarter of 2006 pegged the industry conversion rate at 2.2 percent.

But if you show that conversion rate to a senior executive, their first thought typically is, "How the heck is it possible that our website is so bad that we can't get more than 2 percent of people to convert?"

The size of the opportunity pie looks huge with this math:

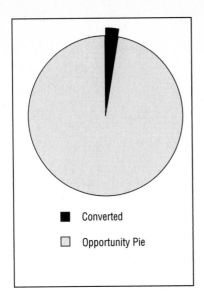

- Unique visitors to the website: 768,000
- Number of outcomes (orders/leads/etc.): 16,500
- Conversion rate: 2.1 percent
- Opportunity pie: 768,000 – 16,500 = 751,500

From there it is just a nanosecond computation that will be given to the person responsible for the website, who may reply, "If you can just get another 1 percent of that 751,500 converted, just a measly 1 percent, that would increase our orders by a humongous 46 percent!" (The math: (751,500 × 0.01) / 16,500)

It seems logical (and reminiscent of many entrepreneurs who head off to China dreaming of massive success by converting just 1 percent of the Chinese population). The problem with the logic is that it presumes that the size of the leftover pie is that big (751,500). The reality is different.

Worry not—there are some simple approaches that you can apply to your data to help you better estimate the real size of your opportunity pie and hence better understand the performance of your websites.

Use Bounce Rate

Bounce rate helps identify the percent of traffic to your website that leaves "instantly." It happens for any number of reasons: wrong clicks in search results, allergic reaction to your website, missing promotion on the page, or any other such thing you can imagine.

By now you're familiar with the concept of bounce rate. A typical bounce rate is around 30 percent (your mileage may vary). Here is the impact on your opportunity pie:

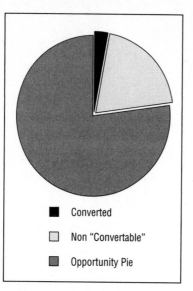

- Converted
- Non "Convertable"
- Opportunity Pie

- Unique visitors to the website: 768,000
- Bounce rate: 20 percent (very conservative)
- Unique visitors "in play": 614,400
- Number of outcomes (orders/leads/etc.): 16,500
- Actual rate of converting visitors: 2.7 percent
- Opportunity pie: 614,000 – 16,500 = 597,900

By using traditional computations, you would have overestimated the size of pie (those folks you could convert) by 153,600! Imagine what that would do to the conversion rate goals set for the website owner. Scary.

Tip: Don't *throw away* the visitors who bounced. Chapter 2, "Data Collection—Importance and Options," discussed why it is important to identify bounce rate and then dive deep into why this traffic is bouncing off your website, perhaps by segmenting it by source, campaigns, or website pages. That remains the recommendation. In this context, and before you execute all those recommendations, measuring your opportunity pie without the bounce rate helps you better understand the size of your opportunity today.

Filter Out Search Bots, Image Requests, 404 Errors, Website-Monitoring Software "Visits"

Many analytics professionals are still using web logs as the source of data for web analytics. (Web logs provide many benefits that are covered in Chapter 2.) A downside of using web logs is that they will natively incorporate visits by search robots (and even if we try to filter these out, it is hard because new ones pop up every other day). This inflates visitor counts, if not filtered. Web logs additionally will also contain "visits" by various site-monitoring software that you might be using. Numbers from web logs will also be inflated by 404s and spurious requests you might have on your website such as DLLs and CSS and on and on, all of which will not allow you to compute bounce rate accurately.

Do your best to filter out all this stuff from your web analytics data source. It is normal for accurate filtering to take out from 10 to 30 percent of your visitor data (this depends on many factors, so your mileage may vary).

Here is the impact on your opportunity pie:

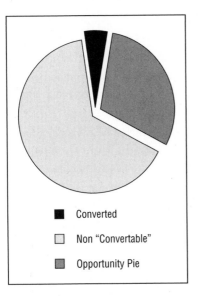

- Unique visitors to the website: 768,000
- Crud filtered out: 25 percent
- Unique visitors "in play": 576,000
- Number of outcomes (orders/leads/etc.): 16,500
- Actual rate of converting visitors: 2.9 percent
- Opportunity pie: 576,000 – 16,500 = 559,500

By using traditional computations, you would have overestimated the size of pie (those folks you could convert) by 192,000!

Crud is not unique to web logs, either. There are plenty of ways in which JavaScript-based data collection methodologies introduce crud into the computations (everything from wrongly coded parameters in the URLs to the web analytics tags not being implemented correctly). Filtering will clean up your data and help you estimate the number of real visitors you have that you can convert—and hence the size of your opportunity.

Use Customer Intent

Imagine walking into a car dealership. You are greeted by a car salesman whose only objective is to do whatever he can to sell you a car today (not even tomorrow, today), mostly because he is paid on commission. The problem is that you are there just to look at the car, maybe take it for a test drive. You have not yet saved up enough to buy a new car. You really don't want to be sold. To the guy in a suit, that does not matter. He is going to *bring it on* rather than focus on what you want (and it is not his fault—incentives drive weird behavior).

Similarly, not every visitor to your website is there to buy, and not every visit is an opportunity to convert. Yet we do path analysis and measure conversion rate the way we do because we behave like that car salesman. (Imagine you went to the car dealership just to get the phone number for their headquarters so you could complain about an issue, and rather than giving it to you right away, the dealership forces you to sit through a 30-minute demonstration of their latest cars!)

This means that measuring the intent of the customers who visit your website is critical to your ability not only to solve for them but also to figure out how many are there to be sold to and how many already own your cars, in fact bought one just yesterday, and are looking for other things when they walk into your dealership (website).

By using market research, website surveys, or other methods, you should attempt to compute why visitors come to your website (I call this *visitor primary purpose*). Then segment out visitors who say they are there to buy and those who are there to research (learn about your products and services). You'll find other segments of people who come to your site looking for support, company information, or jobs, or to register their products, update their contract, or check the status of their orders, among other reasons.

Ideally, you'd be converting 100 percent of purchasers. You'll never hit 100 percent, but work hard to create a frictionless process for them. You should convert a good number of researchers and shoppers; not all want to buy, but they are fair game.

Typically you'll find that around 15 percent of your site traffic is there to buy (purchasers) and around 20 percent is there to do research. This gives you a total of 35 percent (again YMMV, but it is guaranteed that your number is half of what you think it is).

Here is the impact on your opportunity pie:

- Unique visitors to website: 768,000
- Potential visitors who can be converted: 35 percent
- Unique visitors "in play": 268,800
- Number of outcomes (orders/leads/etc.): 16,500
- Actual rate of converting visitors: 6.1 percent
- Opportunity pie: 268,800 − 16,500 = 252,300

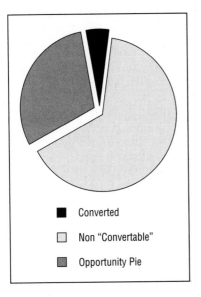

By using traditional computations, you would have overestimated the size of pie (those folks you could convert) by 499,200!

Let me express that another way: when your senior executive asked you to improve conversion rate, you were overestimating the number of visitors you could possibly convert by half a million!

Something that to the CMO looked "so easy" for you to accomplish ("Just convert 1 percent of the unconverted") is nothing short of walking on water for you. I am exaggerating a bit of course, but not by that much.

You can now imagine that the reality of the world is a little bit worse. Some purchasers and researchers will bounce off your site because they landed deep into your site and on the wrong page. You can imagine more scenarios like this. This means the real number of visitors who had the right intent and who stayed long enough to give you a chance to convert them is small.

Now you can easily see why we all work hard on analytics, and marketers work so hard on content and copy and offers, but we can't seem to move the conversion rate by all that much. Lots of initiatives undertaken and projects funded yield frustratingly little in return for all that investment. The reason is that our denominator, unique visitors, is incorrect (in our standard formula, conversion rate equals outcomes divided by unique visitors), so we are grossly overestimating our opportunity pie.

Take Action

Now that you're armed with a wealth of information, what should you do with it?

- Measure conversion rate as everyone else does, just so you have it, and then ignore that number because it will provide little in terms of insights. It can also be downright misleading when it comes to estimating what's possible.

- Compute the size of your real opportunity pie by applying bounce rate, filtering, and customer intent (or add your own recommendations because you'll have unique things that apply to your business).

- Undertake a repetitive education program in your company to educate your decision makers about the size of the real opportunity on your company's website.

- Segment the visitors in the opportunity pie to identify what their true levers are (in getting them to buy). Focus on the why (use surveys, lab usability studies, or experimentation and testing, for example).

When you've done all that, sit back, relax, and enjoy the ride because you have reached the pinnacle of web analysis and helped your company gain a competitive advantage!

The Three Greatest Survey Questions Ever

Chapter 3, "Overview of Qualitative Analysis," discussed all the UCD methods that you can leverage to gain a richer understanding of the *why* behind the *what* (which you understand from quantitative analysis of your clickstream data). One of the continuous measurement methodologies recommended in that chapter is to use surveys. They can be easy to implement, they provide both quantitative and qualitative data that you can analyze, and most important, they deliver the customer's voice directly to you.

Surveys, of course, are just one of the methods at our disposal but their benefits are many and the downside is limited (for additional information, please review Chapter 3 if you have a surveying program in your company). Thanks to their rapid implementation options and customization possibilities, you should seriously consider leveraging surveys for your website (least of all for measuring the real opportunity pie discussed in the preceding section).

If you implement a survey on your website, no matter what methodology you use and how you actually run it, there are three questions that you should absolutely ask in your survey. In fact some of our gurus, such as Jim Sterne, have recommended that the best survey in the world would have only these three questions and nothing else.

What is the purpose of your visit to our website today?

This question can also be framed as "What is the reason for your visit today?" or "What task are you looking to accomplish on our website today?" or "Why are you here today?"

Few website owners have a good understanding of why people visit their websites, and this is one of the best possible ways for you to find out that critical piece of information. The answers that you will read and the distributions among different primary purposes will be eye-opening for you, and they will help explain so much of the "weirdness" you see in your clickstream data (and yes, even your path analysis).

Best practice: Start with a short list of primary purposes for your website. It could include these: research about products or services, purchase products or services, get help/support, apply for a job, check order status, and other. Then provide a space next to the Other option so your visitors can type in why they are on your website. This is a constant source of surprise. People visit our websites for reasons that we would have never imagined. If a purpose keeps getting written in the Other bucket, you can add it to your main primary purpose drop-down list.

Were you able to complete your task today?

If you like conversion rate and revenue, you are going to love this one. This is an extremely simple question that asks survey takers to self-report their own perception of your website's effectiveness in helping them complete their tasks.

By asking this question, we don't have to rely on our hypotheses, such as, "If the visitors saw this page, they might have had their question answered," or "If I am measuring conversion, I can understand how effective my site is," or "Our site is doing great because we just launched a massive quarter-of-a-million-dollar redesign." We have the customer's voice telling us exactly how well the website is performing when it comes to delivering the goods.

Best practice: This is a simple yes or no question. It is optimal to refrain from providing a Maybe option, which some surveys or website owners insist on using. There is no maybe; it is working or it is not. It is also powerful to pair up (slice) the answers to the preceding question with the answers to this one to find the task completion rate by each primary purpose, as shown in the following image.

Continues

The Three Greatest Survey Questions Ever *(Continued)*

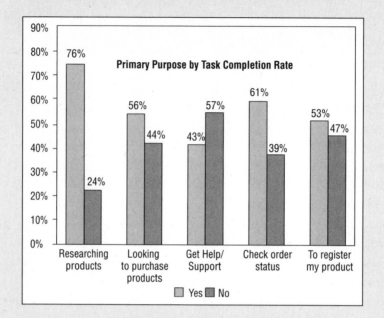

Primary Purpose by Task Completion Rate

Boom! You have a bunch of insights. A quick glance at the pie chart can tell you where you should be investing resources on your website. It can tell you why your conversion rate is 1.2 percent (because 44 percent of people who are on your website to buy could not complete their task). It can also tell you how well your website is performing its ancillary functions (check order status or register products, for example).

Measuring primary purpose by task completion is almost always a game-changing activity (especially trended over time and correlated to your business outcomes).

Now in case you want to know exactly what you need to do to improve the numbers in the graph, you'd ask a third question.

If you were not able to complete your task today, why not?

It can also be framed as "If you were able to not complete your task, please explain," or "Why were you not able to complete your task on our website today?" or simply as "How can we improve our website to ensure you are able to complete your task?"

The answer to this question is open-text VOC, or voice of customer. It is optimal to refrain from making this a drop-down with choices such as improve internal search, update the navigation, and provide more product information. Let the customers talk. Give them a chance to tell you in their own voices the reasons and to provide you with suggestions. It works better than you guessing what the answers might be and suggesting those.

The Three Greatest Survey Questions Ever *(Continued)*

Analysis for this question is done by categorizing the responses into common themes and then rating the percent of times each theme is occurring in the open-ended VOC for those who are not able to complete their task. This is your simple and direct to-do list directly from the horse's mouth, indicating what you should work on to improve your website experience for your customers.

Best practice: Often website owners, marketers, and decision makers expect customers to provide answers in reply to this question. Customers can only verbalize what their problems are; they are not good at verbalizing what the answers should be. Don't be frustrated if you don't get answers such as "Improve the left navigation by using Cascading Style Sheets." Don't expect that, either. It is your job to look through the issues, partner with your designers, researchers, information architects, and web analysts, and come up with ideas to fix the issues that the customers are complaining about. The optimal best practice is to take the best ideas, roll them into an A/B or multivariate test, and let the customers tell you (through their clicks) which fix they like best.

These three simple questions will be the source of a wealth of insights when it comes to helping your deliver on your customer-centric strategy.

Creating a Data-Driven Culture— Practical Steps and Best Practices

This last chapter covers one of the greatest challenges that any successful analytics program has to overcome: creating a deeply entrenched company culture that thrives on making decisions based on data rather than on human feelings.

This is a particularly hard challenge to overcome on the Web because we have so many data sources, each containing fairly complex data. These sources usually do not reconcile with one another, and the data can be ambiguous. Humans are born and bred to expect certainty, and increasingly to expect that certainty quickly without much hard work. We are used to reporting and much less tuned to analysis. Yet it is possible to create a culture that will thrive on data and over time learn new habits. It takes time and patience but it is certainly possible.

In this chapter, you will take a gradual approach by focusing on three core elements: hiring a great web analytics manager , getting expertise from the outside, and following seven steps to creating a data-driven culture in your company.

Key Skills to Look for in a Web Analytics Manager/Leader

It might seem odd that the topic of this journey is the hiring of a manager—not tools, not analysts, not processes, not big sums plunked down on consultants. A *right-fit* manager for your program is the secret ingredient. It might seem that this recommendation is only for Fortune 100 companies, but that is not so. Every program needs this role. To determine when you should hire one, see the next section of this chapter.

The reason for recommending hiring a manager as an initial building block is that so often getting going in the web analytics world by implementing a tool is extremely easy. It is equally easy to get going in the wrong direction—quickly—and then it is really hard to retract and start all over again. The organization and its decision makers will have already made up their minds and opinions will get entrenched. It is not the end of the world, and with enough investment and the right person you can recover, but it is an uphill battle.

The role of a *right-fit* manager is not just to manage a bunch of people for you and to deliver reports. The manager's job is to help you set strategy and make lots of right choices about tools, vendors, resources, and processes. The manager's job is to be an out-and-out evangelist, to use the power of their presence and communication to convert your organization. Their job is to find and nurture the right talent and set them up for success (remember, one person can't do it all). Their job is to be the smiling face that manages to hide the improbable complexity that is web analytics and to inspire the hunt for insights that drive significant actions for your company's customers and bottom line (in that order).

The key to a data-driven culture is a data-driven manager who can be like an evangelistic preacher. Here are seven skills to look for (and please note the skills that you might want to look for that this chapter recommends against).

Deep Passion for the Job

Web analytics can be a tough, sad, and overwhelming business. It is hard to find answers. It is harder still to find insights that will move you beyond the typical *How can we stay afloat for another month?* questions. If you don't absolutely love the job and have a deep-rooted passion for it, it will be really hard for you to survive, even harder to lead a team or fundamental change in organizations.

You have to love the Web. You have to admire its life-changing power, you have to believe that at some level you—yes, you—have the power to change people's lives by killing reports that show, in 8-point font, conversion rate and visitors stats and replacing them with analysis that will fundamentally improve the experiences of your customers and ease their stress. Got passion?

When you interview a manager, look for this raw, almost irrational, passion and realize that this person will need the passion more than you because life in the wonderful world of web analytics is rather tough.

Loves Change, Owns Change

This one exhausts even the very best out there. The Web grows and morphs like an alien being. You just finished adapting to pre-fetching results and here is Google trying to guess searcher intent (and now providing personalized searches, where even your awesome organic listing might not result in you being number one) and then come RIAs and Ajax and then will come something else. Like a tidal wave, change keeps coming.

It takes a special person to build things today with the mandatory mindset that you will throw them away next week or next month. You have to like change, like learning new things, have patience, and have a solid OPML file that proves you are plugged in to the very latest and looking for how to improve what you do every day.

In interviews, ask how many different data collection mechanisms, how many tools, how many research methods they have had direct experience with or been exposed to. Ask for one thing they know of that will mess up the analytics world in the next 180 days. If they have an answer that scares you (because of its effect on your business), you have a winner. Don't let go.

Questions Data to the Point of Being Rude

The core problem with all the tools today is that they efficiently hide insights in massive amounts of data, especially if you use only clickstream. You also get lots of different types of people coming to your website for different purposes, multiple times, using different browsers and locations. We take this really complex behavior and apply simplistic reasoning to it ("*x* percent saw the products page, so that means *z* success for our goal!").

More than analysts, the managers of analysts have to have a deep sense of humility about what is possible. They question the data and analysis, bring a new and different perspective, and can overcome cool recommendations from the latest consultant—all with the simple goal of keeping it real.

In your interview, look for someone with a sense of curiosity and good critical thinking skills.

CDI Baby, CDI (Customer-Driven Innovation)

Great web analytics managers believe that people in the company are usually wrong about what your customers want. In fact, they are unlikely to say, "Omniture is saying *xyz* about the home page behavior, so we need a left navigational control like Amazon.com's because I always use the left nav on Amazon to find what I need." (Replace Omniture with Coremetrics or ClickTracks or WebTrends or another company.)

True innovation and sustainable competitive advantage will come from actions that are customer driven—not always, but most of the time.

What this translates into is a manager who has had exposure to testing, usability studies, surveys, site visits, field studies, market research—or at least a couple of those. What you are looking for is someone who can bring their experience to bear, to find the right ways for you to apply the power of analytics and research to find the right answers for your customers.

In your interview, look for candidates who have more experience than using the latest web analytics or business intelligence tools. Probe deeply about their exposure to and use of user-centric design (UCD) methodologies. Quiz them about three things clickstream applications are terrible about when it comes to representing customer voice, and ask what they would rather use to give that voice, well, a voice.

Not Really Good "Numbers Gods"

This is bound to be controversial because it seems to be the only thing that most companies look for when they hire a web analytics manager: sophistication with numbers, cool Excel spreadsheets, or SAS magic. I find that if your core qualification is that you are a numbers god, you will probably not make a good people manager.

A *numbers god* is defined as someone who chomps down massive spreadsheets for breakfast, lunches on SPSS and SAS, snacks during the day on a couple of complex multivariate statistical regression models, and can't go to bed without a warm glass of mathematical trend correlations.

At some point of sophistication in your web analytics program you do need this person, but not as a manager.

There are a couple of important reasons for this. Numbers gods like to control things (that's what makes them good at being numbers gods). They like perfection and like to nail everything down. They like to predict and anticipate and might have a tough time with ambiguity (which, remember, the web analytics world is all about).

Being great with numbers, the very reason you usually consider someone (*"After all, you are good with numbers, Joey—why don't you lead a team of numbers people?"*), might not make them a good analytics manager.

In the interview, be adequately impressed with the raw finesse that the candidate exhibits with numbers, but filter for people who might just be numbers gods rather than strong leaders who can live with ambiguity (as mysteries rather than puzzles) and motivate people (below them, above them, and around them).

Raw Business Savvy and Acumen

Without this, you can never escape the trap of numbers.

Recently someone shared the result of five days of deep analysis. The core output was correlations between two trends, trying to nail down the ability of one to predict the other. One look at it and it was pretty clear that this person had not asked two basic business questions that would have saved five days of work (and stopped the suboptimal jumping to conclusions that had already happened).

It is not that the person was not smart—he is *numbers brilliant*. It was that he did not have basic business acumen (which I'll define as the ability to step away from the numbers and consider the business interaction that is being analyzed overlaid with business strategy). He never paused to understand the business enough, never exhibited the curiosity to even try.

In your manager, you need someone who is street smart, has business experience, understands business strategy, and can see the forest for the trees. Analytics moves fast; business moves smarter. Your manager will put data in the service of business and not vice versa.

During the interview, I find it optimal to seek out diversity in professional experiences (recently, it was someone who was trained to be a geologist, and before that it was someone who had started their own business and failed to make it work, and before that it was someone who had had tough years during high school and college). Experience beyond just reporting and analysis seems to be a good leading indicator of acumen (though I'll admit that in an interview, business acumen is one of the hardest things to judge).

Impressive People Skills

The number one reason people leave their jobs is not because they don't like their jobs or companies or teams. They leave because they dislike their managers.

Hopefully in this section you have seen a consistent emphasis on non-numbers experience and a stress on customers, analytics in general, and business savvy. But the number one skill you are looking for is the ability to truly lead a team—a team of one or a team of ten, but a team in the truest sense of that word.

Imagine some of the tough situations I've already described. Your manager has to not only deal with all of them but on top of it lead a team of what is sure to be diverse temperamental people and get them to sing in harmony. This can be really hard to do (trust me—I struggle with this).

Find a person with good people skills, a person your numbers gods will respect, a person who can schmooze up to senior management and get your analysts anything they want.

Here's an interviewing tip: Ask the candidate to give you contact information for the last team they lead, the whole team. Then randomly call two or three folks and ask them what they think of your candidate. I promise you that you'll be surprised.

That's it—just seven not-so-simple things to look for.

When and How to Hire Consultants or In-House Experts

There are several models in place across the web analytics ecosystem. Some companies have a completely outsourced model: an external agency or consulting practice manages everything for them. Other companies have everything in-house. Others might have a mix of both. There does not seem to be a single model that is totally dominant.

A mandatory requirement for creating a data-driven culture is to have a decision-making platform (tools, processes, resources) that is intelligent and built deliberately and with forethought to meet the unique needs of each company (yes, you are special, *you really are*). Part of that intelligence is to have a good balance, and the optimal responsibility set, between doing things yourself in-house and getting help from outside consulting companies and agencies. This is both to ensure that you get the right kind of help that you need (depending on the stage you are in) and that you benefit from the experience of others.

The goal for every company should be to have web analytics in-house, led by a team that is empowered to do true analysis by looking at the data end to end and incorporating both the what (quantitative) and the why (qualitative).

Web analytics should be in-house in the long run for these three reasons:

- Any strategic implementation of web analytics has to integrate with other sources of data in the company. It can't exist in a silo. So it needs to pull in core metadata from other parts of the company or outcomes that happen on the phone channel or financial data to measure success, and so forth. Most consultants outside the company won't have access to this data (perhaps they should, but it is really hard).

- Most current consultants, with a few exceptions, will help with clickstream and some outcomes analysis. For web analytics to be truly effective, qualitative analysis (surveys, lab usability tests, site visits, remote testing) needs to be brought under the umbrella in a truly integrated way.

- Contrary to popular belief, decision making is not a structured process. Decisions are made in meetings and in hallway conversations and in 1:1 meetings. In all of those cases, tribal knowledge is critical. *Tribal knowledge* is knowing what is going on in the company. It is knowing what happened last year, it is knowing that something messed up in IT, and it is knowing there is some weird testing going on. This entire critical context is something that, sadly, only people in the company have access to because of their network. And it is often what it takes to bridge the gap between reports and action.

I want to be clear about this main goal because it is something that all should aspire toward. Some of you are already there, though I imagine it is fewer than optimal. For most we are someplace in the journey to that destination and we will need help and guidance along the way.

Figure 15.1 shows a framework to help you think through the stages of the journey.

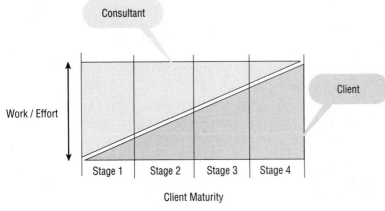

Figure 15.1 Optimal consultant-client relationship framework

Figure 15.1 shows the framework that can be used to identify the optimal relationship structure between an in-house web analytics program and an external consultant or agency. It illustrates the roles and responsibilities between the two in terms of the work that each performs over time as the in-house web analytics program moves from stage to stage of maturity. In this section, you'll learn the details of each stage.

Stage 1: Birth

In stage 1, you have nothing or almost nothing—no web analytics implementation or a really new one. You are just getting started but have some support from management to implement a web analytics program (okay, maybe they just want some data from the website!). Figure 15.2 shows this first stage.

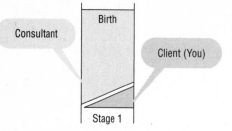

Figure 15.2 Consultant-client responsibilities: stage 1

What Do You Need?

- To implement web analytics tools
- To show promise from data and convert the masses in your company

What Is Your Role?

- Find the most senior person who owns your website and assign that person the accountability for deliverables. If you can't do this, find someone high up who can help you do this. It is critical.

- Don't expect perfection. Don't pick the most expensive tool and don't pay the consultant lots and lots of money up front (you'll do that later).

- Ask to speak to a client that the consultant has recently lost.

What Is the Consultant's Expected Role?

- Talks to the website owner a lot and some data consumers (not all of them just yet, just the ones who are enthusiastic about using data).

- Helps you find and implement the best-fit first tool fast. Notice that I said *first tool*. Chapter 5, "Web Analytics Fundamentals," covered the optimal vendor selection process. Please review that.

- Teaches you not to make the mistakes that all their other clients make (such as measuring hits or top exit pages or daily unique visitors).

- Conducts lots of training sessions and dog and pony shows around your company (this makes you look good and shows promise of what's possible).

What Should You Be Careful About?

Most of what will be done in this stage will be thrown away later, and that is okay. Make sure you set that expectation with your internal company customers and partners. As your first-phase targets, choose people who have data affinity and your friends (so they'll stick with you through the birthing pains). Most definitely don't overstretch and give 500 people login accounts to your new web analytics application. Not just yet.

What Do You Pay Consultants?

You pay your consultants small dollars, for work performed more frequently.

Stage 2: Toddler to Early Teens

You have won over a few converts, the consultants are pumping in reports that people are using, and you are drowning in questions. Some people have started to complain that they don't know what action to take, the VP of marketing is wondering why we keep changing the site even though the analytics tool is not telling you why conversion rate is tanking. Figure 15.3 shows stage 2.

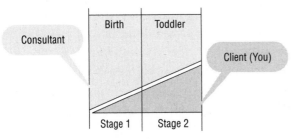

Figure 15.3 Consultant-client responsibilities: stage 2

What Do You Need?

- Consider hiring a web analyst to be the in-house resident expert, someone who'll collect tribal knowledge and be at the beck and call of the VP. If you are a mid- to large-sized company, consider hiring someone who could grow into a manager role (review the skills in previous section). This would really be a key win for your company.

- Create customized dashboards for your business (because you have realized you are unique and standardized KPIs from books don't apply to you).

- You will find lots of data is missing and the tags are not right, so you will need a massive effort to update your tags and collect new data (for example, site structure, site outcome details, new cookies/parameters, campaign metadata, and more).

- For your consultant to kick it up a notch (beyond basic reporting) in terms of the value they deliver to you.

What Is Your Role?

- Help fill the analyst position as soon as you can. (Look for acumen, curiosity, and simple web smarts; look for the top signs in your analyst from Chapter 4, "Critical Components of a Successful Web Analytics Strategy?")

- Have the consultant spend a lot of time on-site talking to the people who run your businesses and to the people who run your websites (IT, for example).

- Find out what the financial goals are for the web business, look for benchmarks, and find out how the success of other channels (retail, phone, and so forth) is being measured. You will need this to show the web success just as your company is used to seeing it from the other channels; I know this sounds odd, but trust me, it works.

What Is the Consultant's Expected Role?

- Really understands your business and your business success criteria and brings their business acumen to the table (as opposed to the tool expertise in stage 1).

- Creates those aforementioned customized dashboards that incorporate core financial or other goals for key metrics to show real success. Metrics on these dashboards will be segmented for the core acquisition strategies for your company (PPC/SEM, direct marketing, affiliate marketing, and so forth) to make the dashboards personal and yours (not from their last client).

- Helps you put standards in place to capture metadata that you need to do optimal analysis (metadata around campaigns, products, website customers, and so forth). The consultant has to help you nail all the data problems (either missing data or bad data) in this stage.

- Teaches you how to do reporting for yourself.

What Should You Be Careful About?

This is a painful stage for you, the website owner and your internal customers. There is more data than you can digest and yet it means little. Be patient; practice Zen. You deliberately want to bring reporting in-house now mostly because it will be cheaper for you to do (and a great way to train your analyst) and you really want to focus the consultant on performing true and powerful analysis (and teaching you that as you move from a toddler to a teen).

What Do You Pay Consultants?

You will pay medium-sized dollars, for work performed less frequently.

Stage 3: The Wild Youth

Web analytics is kicking butt. Dashboards and key metrics rule the roost. Your conversion rate (or problem resolution rate for support sites) has doubled from 1 percent to 2 percent. Your decision makers have realized that path analysis is a waste of time. You now need to kick it up a notch because you have extracted all you can from your web analytics tool. You will hear a lot of questions about why website visitors do what they do and how come Omniture/Coremetrics/WebTrends can't answer the questions (or you have tried to answer the questions with their tools but they are consistently wrong). Figure 15.4 shows stage 3.

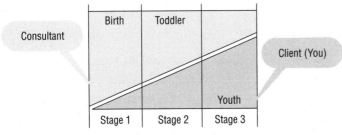

Figure 15.4 Consultant-client responsibilities: stage 3

What Do You Need?

- Experimentation and testing expertise, to realize you are wrong about what your customers want
- To start moving into collecting qualitative data (for example, surveys or usability tests), to realize you are wrong about why your visitors come to your website and what they can and can't accomplish
- Help creating a strategy that would integrate all the new pieces of data you will capture
- More than one consultant

What Is Your Role?

- Expand your team in the company to get other bright people involved in website analysis—product managers (who know the product and their audience really well) and user researchers (who are gods of UCD), for example.
- Find the right consultants. (Your current consultant, whose role will diminish a bit, might be a great reference. Use that person.)
- Identify decision makers who understand customer-centric decision making and cozy up to them (you'll need their sponsorship or air cover or money).

What Is the Consultant's Expected Role?

- Brings tools and expertise to the table for these new things you know nothing about. (This is very much the consultant in the *teach you how to fish* mode, from soup to nuts.)

- Provides knowledge transfer (because soon the general ideas won't bear huge fruits, and you'll have to bring business expertise to the table) and implements best practices.

- Helps you integrate your various data sources so that you can do clickstream analysis for terrible survey responses or figure out the multichannel impact of your experiments or tests.

What Should You Be Careful About?

Start with modest goals and don't underestimate the immense resistance you'll get from your company culture and the HiPPO (highest-paid person's opinion). It is hard for companies to truly have a customer-centric mindset, and at every step you should be prepared to massage egos and reframe things so that they let you bring customer voice to the table and not just kill it because of the HiPPO. Create case studies when you do a great test or find out a huge nugget of information via the research work. Make business users heroes and put the spotlight on them (it will pay you back big).

What Do You Pay Consultants?

You pay big-sized dollars, for work performed a bit initially and then only periodically.

Stage 4: Maturity—You Are 30+

You have truly implemented something akin to the Trinity. You don't have enough people to do the analysis work. You think web pages are lame and you are into Ajax, Flex, and RIAs. Your company wants the web channel to be the essence of its competitive differentiator. (Oh, and your salary is now a million dollars a year because you've helped your company move from stage 1 to 4!) Figure 15.5 shows stage 4.

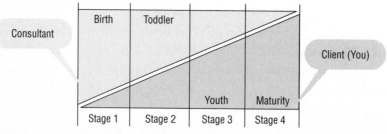

Figure 15.5 Consultant-client responsibilities: stage 4

What Do You Need?

- New and different ways to capture data
- More people
- To create self-sustaining processes that feed active decision making
- Maybe another challenge!

What Is Your Role?

- Be chief cheerleader.
- Find the right talent.
- Find insights from Six Sigma and process excellence (books, maybe).
- Use truly superior consultants who don't do much work except come talk to you and give you ideas.

What Is the Consultant's Expected Role?

- Helps you understand the new technologies you are trying and helps figure out new ways of capturing data.
- Brings truly radical outside perspectives (that a select few consultants in the world have) that will energize you and also help influence strategy (rather than only KPIs or page design).

What Should You Be Careful About?

You are going to be in very rarefied air. Make sure your organization has the appetite for risk and that they back you. You will make more mistakes here (but you will also win big). Be prepared for it and make sure that that is okay. Ensure that you don't go so "process crazy" that people have meetings and do graphs just for the sake of process meetings (this happens all the time). Your job is to motivate your team (analytics/research/web/whatever) and keep the organization on the right track as time and people evolve.

What Do You Pay Consultants?

You pay huge-sized dollars, for work performed infrequently.

In summary, this framework will help identify where you are, what the roles and responsibilities should be in each stage, and what the next stage looks like (and are you ready to move to the next stage).

It's that simple. You now have the secret sauce. Go forth and prosper!

Seven Steps to Creating a Data-Driven Decision-Making Culture

You are almost there. In this section, I'll share my tips and insights that help companies move from just having lots and lots of data to creating cultures where decisions are made not on gut feelings, or by the proverbial seat of the pants, but rather based on data.

The biggest challenge in our current environment is that it is trivial to implement a tool. It takes five minutes. But tools are limiting and can give us only data. What compounds the challenge is that we all have this deep tendency to make decisions based on who we are and our life experiences.

Creating a data-driven culture is perhaps the holiest of the holy grails. Few companies manage to accomplish this. The bigger you are, the harder it is and the more you need to follow the tips in this section and to rely on evangelists and change agents.

Without further ado, here are seven steps to creating a data-driven decision-making culture regardless of your size or location:

1. Go for the bottom line first (outcomes).
2. Remember that reporting is not analysis. Encourage the latter.
3. Depersonalize decision making.
4. Be proactive rather than reactive.
5. Empower your analysts.
6. Solve for the Trinity.
7. Think in terms of process.

Go for the Bottom Line First (Outcomes)

The most common mistake in web analytics is to slap a clickstream tool (from Omniture, WebTrends, Coremetrics, and so forth) on the website and to start sending out reports chock full of clickstream KPIs. This is great for a couple months, but then you lose the audience.

I recommend that you start with measuring outcomes metrics for your website and your core audience (marketers, for example). These are metrics such as revenue, leads, profit margins, improved product mix, and number of new customers. Sit down with your core loyal audience and figure out what motivates them, how their personal salaries or bonuses are paid. Go for those metrics first and not the number of visits each week on your site.

The rationale behind this is that you want to make an almost visceral connection to the consumers of your data, and there is nothing that makes that connection better than what motivates them. The bottom-line metrics can provide the key to making a connection at that level because these metrics likely measure activities that affect not only the company's bottom line but also the data consumers' wallets.

If you can prove to your data customers that you exist to make them personally successful (and not spam them with reports)—by helping them improve revenue, reduce trip costs, or improve customer satisfaction so that they can get a slightly bigger bonus, a slightly bigger pay raise, or simply praise from their bosses—then you have hooked them on data for life and they will be your eternal friends. It can be more addictive than any drug.

Slowly over time you can start to move them from simply focusing on outcomes to analyzing some complex clickstream data and KPIs and from there to using qualitative analysis and testing and competitive analysis and—well, only the sky is the limit.

Remember That Reporting Is Not Analysis, and Encourage the Latter

About 99 percent of web analytics challenges can be summed up by this:

- Data: petabytes
- Reports: terabytes
- Excel: gigabytes
- PowerPoint: megabytes
- Insights: bytes
- One business decision based on actual data: priceless

The point of this equation, especially the first three bullets, is that we spend most of our life doing reporting. The tools don't help; they have 300 canned reports as soon as you open the box, and with not enough features to allow you to do true analysis.

To make matters worse, analysis in our world is hard to do—*data, data everywhere and nary an insight in sight.* Reporting usually means going into your favorite tool and creating a bazillion reports in the hope that a report in there will tell you, or your users, how to spark action. That is rarely the case.

The final compounding factors, the proverbial icing on the cake, is that both reporting and analysis can be time-consuming and all subsuming. They both require huge investments of time, resources, and energies. The million dollar decision that you'll have to make is where to focus the meager resources you have. If at the end of x hours of work your table, graph, or report is not screaming out the action that your business leaders need to take, you are doing reporting and not analysis. You'll have to make an explicit choice as to what you want to spend time on.

My recommendation is that you choose to focus on analysis and not on reporting. This is hard to do because more organizations are structured, culturally, to want reports and not analysis. Measures of success are the number of users with login who have access to your web analytics tool and the number of custom reports that have been published. By automating reporting and creating a smaller footprint of active users, you can slowly migrate from the world of reporting to the world of analysis.

Here are more definitions of reporting and analysis:

Reporting: The art of finding three errors in a thousand rows

Analysis: The art of knowing that three errors in a thousand are irrelevant

What is your choice?

Depersonalize Decision Making

Dinosaurs used to rule the prehistoric word. HiPPOs rule our 21st-century business world. As I said earlier, a HiPPO is the highest-paid person's opinion.

HiPPOs overrule your data. They impose on the business and websites and company customers. They believe that they know best (and sometimes they do). Their mere presence in a meeting prevents ideas from coming up.

The solution to this problem, and "winning" when you go up against a HiPPO, is to depersonalize decision making. Simply don't make it about you or about what you think. Here are some things you can do toward that goal:

- Go outside, get context from other places. Include external or internal benchmarks in your analysis (see Chapter 11, "Month 6: Three Secrets Behind Making Web Analytics Actionable").

- Get competitive data (for example, *"We are at x percent of zz metric, and our competition is at x+9 percent of zz metric"*).

- Be incessantly focused on your company customers and work toward dragging their voice to the table (for example, via experimentation and testing or via open-ended survey questions).

- Create extreme transparency in your metrics, definitions, and computations (use PowerPoint slides and *pretty pictures* that communicate transparency effectively).

The goal is to remove yourself or other entrenched opinions from the table (including the HiPPOs) and let data do the talking—not just any data, but data that is transparent, independent, has external context and, most of all, represents the customer's voice and actions.

In the end they can argue with you, but very few people—those with HiPPOs included—can argue with a customer's voice. The customer, after all, is the queen or king! Your job, through your actions, is to depersonalize decision making.

Be Proactive Rather Than Reactive

Web analytics is often rear-view-mirror analysis. By the time you get the data, even in real time, it is already old. This complicates things quite a bit.

To get ahead, don't wait until someone stops by asking for a report. Get ahead of the game.

Attend strategy and operational meetings. Be aware of upcoming changes to the site or to your campaigns or acquisition options. Before you are asked, have a plan to analyze the impact and proactively present results. You will win kudos and will provide better analysis than what might have been asked for because you were proactive and you were able to apply your own awesome analytical skills.

The goal is to transform the web analytics function from being just a *web analysis* function to being a *web smart* function. This reservoir of data and intelligence determines what decisions should be made to create great customer experiences on your websites (and make money from that).

It is recommended that your web analysts or managers spend 20 percent of their time providing analysis that no one asked for and only they can perform.

To flip the coin, if you are an analyst, and not a report writer, 20 percent of your time should be devoted to poring over data and doing analysis that no one asked for but only you can do because you are the only smart one in the family.

Empower Your Analysts

Almost every company hires an analyst, often a senior analyst, and then quickly proceeds to convert that person into a report writer. *"Here is our Omniture/WebTrends/HBX tool, here is a list of all our internal data consumers, and here are all the reports that they need."* That is a perfect job for a summer intern (they come with the additional benefit of wanting to work really hard for no pay) or even your team administrator.

The job of the management team that wants to see a data-driven culture is to first empower their analysts. This means that management gives the analysts strategic objectives for the website and then gets out of the way. Make sure that the analyst's workload enables them to spend 80 percent of their time doing analysis.

Data-driven cultures rarely exist on the bedrock of reporting. They thrive and prosper on analysis, by one person or by every person in the organization.

You have spent time hiring expensive analysts who are critical thinkers. Why use that investment in suboptimal ways by shackling them with the heavy chains of publishing massive reports in Excel? Set them free, unshackle them, encourage them to take risks and run with the data. In exchange, you will get your data-driven culture.

It is also likely that you will get a highly engaged employee who will be happy, deliver value for what you pay her, and be a potential future leader of your company.

Solve for the Trinity

All the way back in Chapter 1, "Web Analytics—Present and Future," we covered the wonderful concept of Trinity. It states that a robust web analytics program should focus on all three critical elements: experience, behavior, and outcomes. Each element has its unique application and each solves a critical business challenge even as each element *plays ball* with the others, empowering you to make optimal end-to-end decisions.

The lesson from the Trinity is a simple one: doing only clickstream analysis does not create a data-driven culture because clickstream data can't consistently provide deeply effective analysis. Typical business people have a hard time digesting the amazing limits to which we stretch clickstream data. Bring other sources of data that make for richer and full-picture analysis. This will make it much easier to connect with your users and the things that they find valuable and can understand.

Does your web measurement strategy have an ability to answer both the what and the why questions? If you are to create a data-driven culture, it is mandatory that the answer to that question is an emphatic yes.

Here is a top-secret tip: Start with the *how much* (outcomes), evolve to the *what is* (behavior), and then strive for the *why* (experience).

Chapter 1 provides more detail and context on each of these, including strategies you can apply and tools you can use.

Got Process?

Chapter 11 placed great emphasis on applying lessons inspired from the world of Six Sigma or process excellence. The core rationale was that if we think of the work that we do as a *process* that needs to be defined, documented, measured, and optimized, the end result will be a web analytics program that is optimally structured, improves over time, and becomes ingrained in the company as a *way of life*.

Thinking in terms of Process, with a capital *p*, is perhaps the single biggest difference between cultures that achieve the mythical status of being data driven and those who languish. Processes help create frameworks that people can understand, follow and, most important, repeat. Process excellence (Six Sigma) can also help guide you and ensure that you are focusing on the critical few metrics. It can help establish goals and control limits for your metrics so that staying focused and executing your plans becomes that much easier.

Processes don't have to be complex, scary things. The picture shown here (you saw it first in Chapter 11) shows a simple PowerPoint slide that illustrates the exact process for executing an A/B or multivariate test, end to end. It shows who is responsible for each step and what deliverables are expected—very easy to do. The result is that now not just you but everyone knows what to do. Please refer back to Chapter 11 for detailed tips and context on how you can apply process excellence in your company.

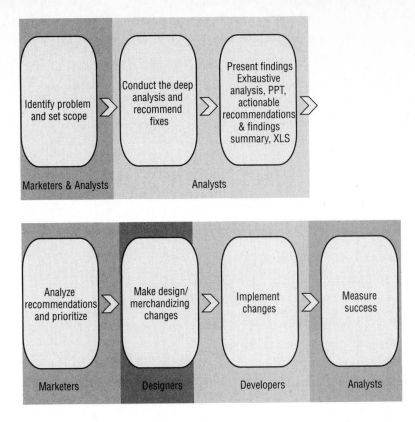

At the end of the day, it is the process that creates culture. Do you have structured processes in your company?

Bonus Tip: Ownership of Web Analytics: Business

I get asked this question all the time: Who should own web analytics? Most companies don't have a single team that owns web analytics end to end. There is a team in IT responsible for the tag, another team in the Project Management Office (PMO) responsible for gathering requirements, yet another team, usually fractured all over or in IT, responsible for creating reports, and someone else responsible for looking at the data and doing something, or usually nothing.

Web analytics should be owned by a business function, optimally the one that owns the web strategy (not the website, the web strategy). This recommendation is based on the fact that web analysis needs to think, imagine, and move at the pace of business. It is a significantly different mindset than that of the technology teams. Each solves for different types of business outcomes.

Continues

For more in-depth recommendations on how to create optimal organizational structures, please review Chapter 4.

In summary, data-driven organizations

- Focus on customer-centric outcomes
- Reward analysis and not the number of emailed reports
- While measuring success against benchmarks
- Which is achieved by empowering your analysts
- Who solve for the Trinity, not just clickstream
- By using a well-defined process
- That is owned and driven by the business function

Good luck and Godspeed!

Index

Note to the Reader: Throughout this index **boldfaced** page numbers indicate primary discussions of a topic. *Italicized* page numbers indicate illustrations.

bottom line first approach for
data-driven culture, **414–415**
Boughton, Tim, 363
bounce rate, **168–170**, *169*
email marketing, 223–224
in opportunity pie, **391–392**, *392*
PPC, **371–372**, *372*
referrers, 148, 169, *169*
segmenting, **355–357**, *356–357*
in SEO, 211
in standard reports, **142–145**, *144*
top entry page combined with, 152
brand/advocacy outcomes data, **40–41**,
41
brand keywords share, **305–306**, *306*
broken sites, clues for, 198
business blogs, 186
costs, 189
rankings, 188
return on investment, **189–191**
business case, 192, 261
business events in RIAs, 317
business leaders, tools for, 108
business outcomes, **170–172**, *172*
business questions method, 76, **79–81**
business savvy and acumen in web
analytics managers, **405**
buttons for calls to action, 251
buzzy metrics, 14

C

caching, 3
calculators
blog value, **190**
statistical significance, 353
calls to action, testing, **251**
cannibalization rate in PPC, **373–375**,
374
capturing data. *See* data collection
Carlson, Dane, 190
cart
abandonment rate, **376–378**, *379*,
390

Flash-based, 255
process analysis, **112**
cases, 93
category keywords reports, **305–306**,
306
CDI (customer-driven innovation), 7,
404
centralization ownership model, **95**
centralized decentralization ownership
model, **96–97**
change, web analytics manager skills for,
403
checkout abandonment rate, **376–378**,
379
actionable insights and actions for,
379–380
control limits for, 390
segmentation, **378**, *379*
chief information officers (CIOs), 93–94
chief marketing officers (CMOs), 94
chief technical officers (CTOs), 93–94
churn
in dashboards, **284**
KPI, 349
CIOs (chief information officers), 93–94
clarity, page-level surveys for, 183–184
click density, 4, *5*, 149–150
analysis, **10–11**
benefits, **168**, *168*
internal searches, **200**, *200*
overview, **156–160**, *157*, *159–160*
click-through rates (CTRs), 214,
216–217
click-to-open rate (CTOR), 221
clicks
email marketing, 221
PPC, 216
clicks to website in RSS, **326**, *326*
clickstream data, 6, 25
customer satisfaction, 177
JavaScript tagging, **30–33**, *31*
packet sniffing, **33–36**, *34*
quality, **108–113**
survey data integration with, **72**

U